Thabo Mbeki's world

Thabo Mbeki's world
The politics and ideology of the South African president

Edited by
SEAN JACOBS and RICHARD CALLAND

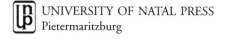
UNIVERSITY OF NATAL PRESS
Pietermaritzburg

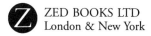
ZED BOOKS LTD
London & New York

Published in 2002 by
University of Natal Press
Private Bag X01
Scottsville 3209
South Africa
E-mail: books@nu.ac.za
Website: www.unpress.co.za

Thabo Mbeki's World: The Politics and Ideology of the South African President was first published outside of Southern Africa by Zed Books Ltd, 7 Cynthia Street, London N1 9JF, UK and Room 400, 175 Fifth Avenue, New York 10010, USA in 2003.

Distributed in the United States exclusively by Palgrave, a division of St Martin's Press, LLC, 175 Fifth Avenue, New York 10010, USA.

© 2002 University of Natal

All rights reserved. No part of this publication may be reproduced or transmitted in any form or by any means, electronic or mechanical, including photocopying, recording or any information storage and retrieval system, without prior permission in writing from University of Natal Press.

ISBN 1-86914-017-6 (University of Natal Press)
ISBN 1-84277-178-7 (Zed Books Ltd Hardcover)
ISBN 1-84277-179-5 (Zed Books Ltd Softcover)

A catalogue record for this book is available from the British Library.
Library of Congress Cataloging-in-Publication Data is available.

Editor: Riaan de Villiers
Cover designer: Sumayya Essack
Typesetter: Patricia Comrie

Printed and bound by Interpak Books, Pietermaritzburg

Sean Jacobs dedicates this book to his parents, Eliza and Paul Jacobs,
as a tribute to their resilience.

Richard Calland dedicates it to his wife, Gaye Davis,
whose love and support has nurtured his own dedication to this
bewildering and bewitching country.

Contents

Acknowledgements		ix
List of contributors		xi
List of abbreviations		xv
Introduction	Thabo Mbeki: Myth and context *Sean Jacobs and Richard Calland*	1

PART ONE: IDEOLOGY

Chapter 1	Cry for the beloved country: The post-apartheid denouement *John S Saul*	27
Chapter 2	Thabo Mbeki and NEPAD: Breaking or shining the chains of global apartheid? *Patrick Bond*	53
Chapter 3	The logic of expediency: Post-apartheid shifts in macroeconomic policy *Hein Marais*	83
Chapter 4	Does the emperor really have no clothes?: Thabo Mbeki and ideology *Sahra Ryklief*	105
Chapter 5	Thabo Mbeki, South Africa, and the idea of an African Renaissance *Peter Vale and Sipho Maseko*	121

PART TWO: POLITICS

Chapter 6	Remaking the presidency: The tension between co-ordination and centralisation *Farouk Chothia and Sean Jacobs*	145
Chapter 7	Thabo Mbeki and the South African Communist Party *Vishwas Satgar*	163
Chapter 8	From 'Madiba magic' to 'Mbeki logic': Mbeki and the ANC's trade union allies *Sakhela Buhlungu*	179
Chapter 9	Down to business, but nothing to show *William Mervin Gumede*	201
Chapter 10	State and civil society in contemporary South Africa: Redefining the rules of the game *Krista Johnson*	221
Chapter 11	Mandela's democracy *Andrew Nash*	243
Conclusion	Thabo Mbeki: Politics and ideology *Richard Calland and Sean Jacobs*	257

Select bibliography 277
Index 285

Acknowledgements

Thabo Mbeki is an enigmatic – and fascinating – politician. Solving the riddles of his leadership must therefore be regarded as an elusive goal; yet it was a challenge we could not resist. Naturally, we were not so foolhardy as to embark on this enterprise alone. Strength in numbers seemed like good sense, so we invited a diverse group of writers to reflect on Thabo Mbeki in a way not attempted before.

We are indebted to our colleagues at the Cape Town-based Political Information and Monitoring Service (PIMS) of the Institute for Democracy in South Africa (IDASA) – Ebrahim Fakir, Judith February, Lynne Abrahams, and Samantha Fleming – whose informal conversations about current political developments in South Africa, often provoked by debate about Mbeki himself, found their way into our writing. Many of the ideas in the introduction and conclusion were tested on them.

PIMS interns Sibulele Gqada, Nyameko Mgoqi, Tanja Timmermans, and Beverley Onwubere undertook many library searches, and made many photocopies. Sibulele, a third-year student in political science and economics at the University of Cape Town, was primarily responsible for compiling the bibliography of pre-1990 references of Mbeki.

A second group of people, in and outside IDASA, also played a role in developing the ideas around this book. They include Ferial Haffajee, Lia Nijzink, Zolile Nqayi, Irvin Kinnes, Elaine Salo, Kerry Cullinan, Siviwe Minyi, Julia Hornberger, Peter Dwyer, Tandeka Nkiwane, Crystal Orderson, Erik Ponder, Jessica Blatt, and Lene Øverland.

Publisher Glenn Cowley of the University of Natal Press stuck with the project from the time Sean went to see him in Pietermaritzburg at the beginning of 2000, and tolerated many deadline shifts. Glenn was bold enough to acknowledge the need for more critical perspectives of South Africa's second democratic president.

The contributors should be commended for producing a set of diverse, individual, and bold essays. Patrick Bond, Hein Marais, Vishwas Satgar, Farouk Chothia, Sakhela Buhlungu, and Sahra Ryklief were with us from the beginning; Sipho Maseko, Peter Vale, William Mervin Gumede, and Krista Johnson joined our enterprise at a later stage.

Sadly, Sipho Maseko died in early 2000. His tragic passing robbed the country of a promising talent and those who knew him of a gracious friend.

We wish to thank Martin Paddio of *Monthly Review Press* in New York City for allowing us to reprint revised versions of two important essays: one by John Saul of Canada, veteran South Africa-watcher and active participant in the struggle against apartheid; and the other by Andrew Nash, a former Cape Town academic now based in New York.

We would also like to thank Riaan de Villiers for his patient and skillful editing of the whole book.

Contributors

PATRICK BOND is a professor at the Graduate School of Public and Development Management of the University of the Witwatersrand. He is the author/co-author of *Unsustainable South Africa: environment, development and social protest* (2002), *Zimbabwe's plunge: exhausted nationalism, neoliberalism and the search for social justice* (2002), *Against global apartheid: South Africa meets the World Bank, IMF and International Finance* (2001), *Cities of gold, townships of coal: essays on South Africa's new urban crisis* (2000), and *Elite transition: from apartheid to neoliberalism in South Africa* (2000). He has authored or edited more than a dozen policy documents for the ANC government, and works closely with social justice activist groups in South Africa and Zimbabwe. He holds a doctorate in economic geography from Johns Hopkins University. He has taught at the Johns Hopkins School of Public Health, York University, and Yokohama National University.

SAKHELA BUHLUNGU is a lecturer in sociology at the University of the Witwatersrand, and deputy director of the Sociology of Work Unit (SWOP). He holds a doctorate from the same university. He previously worked for the Paper, Printing, Wood and Allied Workers' Union, an affiliate of the Congress of South African Trade Unions (COSATU). He also serves on the editorial board of the *South African Labour Bulletin*.

RICHARD CALLAND is head of the Political Information and Monitoring Service (PIMS) at IDASA (the Institute for Democracy in South Africa), and executive chair of the Open Democracy Advice Centre. He studied law at the University of Durham and world politics at the London School of Economics, and then practised as an advocate/barrister at the London Bar until he came to South Africa in 1994. He worked with the ANC in the Western Cape during the 1994 election, and then completed a LLM in comparative constitutional law at the University of Cape Town before joining IDASA in 1995. He has published extensively on constitutional and political issues associated with South Africa's early democratic phase, and co-authored *Real politics: the wicked issues*, published in 2001. He is a political columnist for the *Mail & Guardian*.

FAROUK CHOTHIA is a producer at the BBC's Africa Service in London. He was previously an associate editor of *Business Day* in Johannesburg, and worked for several other South African newspapers, including the *Mail & Guardian*. He also had a previous stint as a radio producer with the BBC World Service in London.

WILLIAM MERVIN GUMEDE is a senior editor of the *Financial Mail*. He recently spent a year as a journalism fellow at Duke University in the United States. He has won several awards for his political and economic reporting, including the Ruth First South African Award for Courageous Journalism (1998), and the Sanlam Excellence in Financial Journalism Merit Award (2001). He is writing a book on the Mbeki presidency.

SEAN JACOBS is completing a doctorate in politics at Birkbeck College, University of London. He previously worked as a senior political researcher at IDASA in Cape Town. Jacobs obtained a master's degree in political science at Northwestern University in Evanston, Illinois, in 1996. He is a former Fulbright Fellow (1996), and a research fellow of the Shorenstein Center on the Press, Politics and Public Policy at Harvard University (1998). He contributed to *Elections '99: South Africa – the campaigns, results and future prospects*, edited by Andrew Reynolds (David Philip and James Currey, 1999).

KRISTA JOHNSON is an assistant professor in international studies at DePaul University in Chicago, Illinois. She holds a doctorate in political science from Northwestern University in Evanston, Illinois. She received a BA in international relations from Johns Hopkins University in 1990, and a diploma in African studies from the University of Cape Town in 1989. In 1998–2000 she spent 20 months in Cape Town doing field work for her dissertation, entitled 'From consensual decision-making to conventional politics: popular participation in contemporary South Africa'.

HEIN MARAIS is a writer, journalist, and researcher. An updated and expanded second edition of his *South Africa: limits to change – the political economy of transition* appeared in late 2000.

The late SIPHO MASEKO was an associate professor in political studies at the University of Stellenbosch. He published in *African Affairs*, and contributed to the volume *The double-edged sword: the struggle for liberation in Namibia* (edited by John Saul and Colin Leys, and published by James Currey). He held a doctorate in political science from the University of the Western Cape.

ANDREW NASH is the editorial director of *Monthly Review Press* in New York. Prior to that he taught philosophy and politics at the universities of Stellenbosch, Cape Town, and the Western Cape. He has published widely on the history of South African political thought. He holds a doctorate from the University of Cape Town.

SAHRA RYKLIEF is the director of the Labour Research Service (LRS), a labour market research institute for South African trade unions. She regularly edits and writes for LRS research publications. She holds a master's degree in political science from the University of Liverpool; previously, she studied at the universities of South Africa and Cape Town. She is a member of the board of Ditikeni Investments, an ethical investment fund for NGOs, as well as the Women on Farms Project, an NGO that organises women in the Boland. She is also an executive member of the International Federation of Workers' Educational Associations (IFWEA), an international association with trade union and NGO affiliates from more than 60 countries.

VISHWAS SATGAR is a policy and political analyst at the Co-operative and Policy Alternative Centre (COPAC), and Gauteng secretary of the South African Communist Party (SACP). He holds a master's degree in labour law, and previously worked for COSATU on labour reform issues. He is currently co-editing a book entitled *New frontiers for socialism in the 21st century – conversations on a global journey*.

JOHN S SAUL is a Canadian academic but is also a veteran of the anti-apartheid movement, principally the Toronto Committee for the Liberation of Southern Africa (TCLSAC), which he co-founded in 1972. He is a professor of social and political science at York University in Toronto, but has also taught at the University of Dar es Salaam in Tanzania, the Eduardo Mondlane University in Mozambique, and, most recently, the University of the Witwatersrand. He is a member of the editorial working group of *Southern Africa Report*, and has authored or edited a dozen books and many articles on Africa. His latest book, *Millennial Africa: capitalism, socialism, democracy*, was published by Africa World Press in 2001.

PETER VALE is senior professor in the school of government and professor of social theory at the University of the Western Cape (UWC). During 1996 he occupied the UNESCO African Chair at the University of Utrecht, The Netherlands. Between 1999 and 2001 he acted as vice-rector for academic affairs at UWC. He has published extensively, both in South Africa and abroad. His book *Security and politics in South Africa: the regional dimension* will be published by Lynne Reinner late in 2002.

Abbreviations

ACT UP	Aids Coalition to Unleash Power
ANC	African National Congress
AU	African Union
AWB	Afrikaner Weerstandsbeweging
AZAPO	Azanian People's Organisation
BEE	Black Economic Empowerment
BEECom	Black Economic Empowerment Commission
CDE	Centre for Development and Enterprise
CHOGM	Commonwealth Head of Governments Meeting
CIA	Central Intelligence Agency
CIU	Co-ordination and Implementation Unit
CODESA	Convention for a Democratic South Africa
COPAC	Co-operative and Policy Alternative Centre
COSATU	Congress of South African Trade Unions
CP	Conservative Party
CPSA	Communist Party of South Africa
CSI	Civil Society Initiative
CSSDCA	Conference on Security, Stability, Development and Co-operation in Africa
DA	Democratic Alliance
DEP	department of economic policy
DP	Democratic Party
EU	European Union
FFC	Financial and Fiscal Commission
FDI	foreign direct investment
FEDUSA	Federation of Unions of South Africa
FGD	Foundation for Global Dialogue

GATT	General Agreement on Tariffs and Trade
GCIS	Government Communications and Information Service
GEAR	Growth, Employment, and Redistribution
GNU	Government of National Unity
HIPC	Highly Indebted Poor Countries
IDASA	Institute for Democracy in South Africa
IDC	Industrial Development Corporation
IFP	Inkatha Freedom Party
ILO	International Labour Organisation
IMF	International Monetary Fund
JSE	Johannesburg Stock Exchange
LRA	Labour Relations Act
MAP	Millennium Africa Recovery Plan
MDM	Mass Democratic Movement
MEC	Mineral-Energy Complex
MERG	Macro Economic Research Group
MK	Umkhonto weSizwe
MP	member of parliament
MPNP	Multiparty Negotiating Process
NAFCOM	National African Federated Chambers of Commerce
NAI	New African Initiative
NAIL	New Africa Investments Limited
NALEDI	National Labour and Economic Development Institute
NAM	Non-Aligned Movement
NEC	national executive committee
NEDLAC	National Economic Development and Labour Council
NEM	Normative Economic Model
NEPAD	New Partnership for Africa's Development
NGO	non-governmental organisation
NIA	National Intelligence Agency
NIC	National Indian Congress
NIS	National Intelligence Service
NP	National Party
NUMSA	National Union of Metalworkers of South Africa
OAU	Organisation of African Unity
ODA	official development assistance
PAC	Pan-Africanist Congress
PCAS	Policy Co-ordination and Advisory Service
PIU	Performance and Innovation Unit
PPPU	Public-Private Partnership Unit

RDP	Reconstruction and Development Programme
SABC	South African Broadcasting Corporation
SACOB	South African Chamber of Business
SACP	South African Communist Party
SACTU	South African Congress of Trade Unions
SADC	South African Development Community
SADTU	South African Democratic Teachers' Union
SAHRC	South African Human Rights Commission
SAMWU	South African Municipal Workers' Union
SANCO	South African National Civic Organisation
SANGOCO	South African Non-Govermental Organisation Coalition
SECC	Soweto Electricity Crisis Committee
SEU	Social Exclusion Unit
SMME	small, medium, and micro enterprise
SOYA	Society of Young Africans
TDI	targeted development investment
TEC	Transitional Executive Council
TNC	transnational corporation
TRC	Truth and Reconciliation Commission
UDF	United Democratic Front
UDM	United Democratic Movement
UNCTAD	United Nations Conference on Trade and Development
UNDP	United Nations Development Programme
WCAR	World Conference Against Racism
WTO	World Trade Organisation

INTRODUCTION

Thabo Mbeki
Myth and context

SEAN JACOBS and RICHARD CALLAND

An impressive mythology – both positive and negative – envelops Thabo Mbeki. Whether this is unwittingly or deliberately cultivated is open to question, but the mystique that surrounds him holds both advantages and disadvantages for the president and his government. Key questions arise: does he have an ideology? If so, what informs it, and how does it translate into practice? Has Mbeki, as president, managed to capture and articulate a clear vision, and a sense of collective values? Does he offer the leadership South Africa needs?

The purpose of this book is to explore Mbeki from an ideological perspective: is there a central strand of thinking that informs his politics and his policy-making? It is also of great interest to examine how Mbeki builds, fortifies, and interacts with his core base and his most important constituencies, especially in and around the African National Congress (ANC)-led ruling alliance. Secondly, we argue that it is important to understand Mbeki in order to grasp how the South African government operates post-1999. Thirdly, we are assuming that Mbeki is likely to remain a key political figure until 2009, by which time the new South Africa's die will largely be cast.

At the time of Mbeki's inauguration in June 1999 – with a two-thirds victory at the polls behind him, and with his own succession to the presidency of the ANC calmly and decisively secured long before – it was impossible to predict that by just mid-2002 there would be such a vociferous debate in the media and in the public arena about his fitness to rule. A quartet of issues had challenged his political leadership and judgement.

First, in late 2000 a major controversy surrounding a vast government arms purchasing deal sorely tested the political management skills of Mbeki and his party, and found them wanting. Several things happened in quick succession: the Special Investigating Unit headed by Judge Willem Heath (a unit which, rightly or wrongly, was widely respected for its prowess in pursuing corruption) was excluded from the investigation into the R30 billion ($3 billion) Strategic Arms Procurement Package. The head of the ANC's membership of the parliamentary public accounts committee, Andrew Feinstein, was removed and replaced with a filibustering party loyalist. The ANC's chief whip, Tony Yengeni, was accused of breaching the code of ethics for parliamentarians by accepting a luxury motor vehicle as a gift from a company involved in the deal, and, in response, failed to either step aside as chief whip or co-operate with the parliamentary ethics committee. He was subsequently charged with several counts of corruption, and will probably stand trial in late 2002.

Second, in a series of events that one senior journalist described as 'too mad to make sense' (McGreal 2001), Mbeki and his backers began to display a palpable paranoia about his ability to stay on as president for a second term. In mid-2001, in what become popularly known as 'The Plot', Mbeki and one of his senior ministers publicly accused three leading anti-apartheid ANC leaders, one of them a member of the ANC's national executive committee (NEC), of wanting to harm the president. It turned out that all three were accused of intending to challenge Mbeki for the leadership of the ANC at its conference in 2002. Following a police investigation, in the course of which none of the three – Cyril Ramaphosa, Tokyo Sexwale, and Mathews Phosa – was actually interviewed, the then minister for safety and security, the late Steve Tshwete, was compelled to apologise to them in public. Apart from what these events said about democracy within the ANC, they also pointed to the ineptitude of the presidency's political management; despite the apparent cynicism of his deliberate blunder in naming the three 'plotters' on national prime-time television news, Tshwete did not resign, nor was he sanctioned by Mbeki. The only sensible conclusion to be drawn from this is that Mbeki approved of Tshwete's action because it served his own political needs, and that Tshwete lied to a parliamentary committee when he told it that he had not discussed the matter with Mbeki before making the original announcement on TV news.

But, however much they reveal about the policy-making and strategising surrounding Mbeki, these events pale into relative insignificance when compared with the two remaining controversies centred on the president. The first – about HIV/AIDS – was largely of his own making, as his romance with so-called 'dissident' theory that questions the link between HIV and AIDS (and, by implication, the utility of anti-retrovirals) deepened throughout

2000. By early 2002 Mbeki and his advisers had allowed his controversial views to dominate his presidency, both at home and abroad. Wherever one travelled, the same – or similar – questions were put: 'Why has he got such funny views on HIV/AIDS?' There has been no easy answer to this question. Mbeki himself has provided no obvious strategic objective other than his desire to insist that poverty is a crucially important factor in the spread of HIV/AIDS. That much is already known, but what Mbeki has been saying goes further: he has also been casting doubt on the (orthodox) theory that HIV causes AIDS. This, in turn, has undermined the policy of his own government's department of health, which is built around orthodox prevention approaches, based in turn on the understanding that HIV is passed on via body fluids.

Despite the fact that HIV is spreading faster in South Africa than anywhere else in the world, the domestic debate on the epidemic has been dominated not by the fight to contain it, but the reasons for Mbeki's apparent rejection of orthodox HIV theory. In March 2002 Tom Masland, southern Africa correspondent of the influential US magazine *Newsweek*, reported that Mbeki was 'feuding with allies, fighting his cabinet, and losing his international friends' over his dissenting views on HIV/AIDS. This, he wrote, justified only one conclusion, namely that Mbeki was 'apartheid's ultimate victim: a bright, cultivated, intellectually curious man turned inward, driven by his unique history into a job for which he is not suited'. The ANC reacted with typical vehemence, accusing *Newsweek* of having joined the 'missiles of attack that have no respect for Africans who think independently' (ANC 2002). However, within weeks, Mbeki's cabinet issued a statement in which it expressly acknowledged the positive role that anti-retrovirals could play in combating the disease, and promised a universal roll-out of nevirapene for HIV-positive mothers 'as soon as possible'.

At the time of writing, this policy shift was still largely untested. When, in May 2002, the Constitutional Court heard an appeal by the government against a High Court ruling requiring it to provide nevirapene immediately to all HIV-positive mothers, the government's counsel was still unable to say when exactly its new policy would be implemented. And, if U-turn it was, Mbeki's own shift in approach had not yet been tested in an interview, either domestically or internationally. When, in early April 2002 – during a visit to South Africa of the Canadian president, Jean Chretien – Mbeki agreed to be interviewed by three Canadian journalists, ostensibly on the subject of the New Partnership for Africa's Development (NEPAD), they subjected him to a barrage of questions about his views on HIV/AIDS, and refused to step off this subject. Whether or not this represented some kind of ephiphanous moment, or was simply the straw that broke the camel's back, is unclear. It does seem, however, that the penny finally dropped for Mbeki: his views on HIV/AIDS was destroying not only his international reputation, but the credibility of the entire NEPAD project. That it should take him so long to reach this understanding is an indictment not just of his advisers' failure to persuade him of the seriousness of the situation, but of his own lack of political wit.

The second challenge that threatened to eclipse Mbeki's presidency was a very different one, that led to questions about his foreign policy-making and his strategic management skills: Zimbabwe. On this issue, Mbeki deserves more sympathy: many commentators failed to understand the nuances of his approach to the growing crisis in Harare provoked by president Robert Mugabe's increasingly eccentric and undemocratic rule. However, Mbeki underestimated the importance of symbolic messages and of publicly restating his own government's commitment to the rule of law. Much of the unease in the febrile international investor community and financial markets at his 'quiet diplomacy' in relation to Mugabe stemmed from a latent anxiety not about Zimbabwe's future, but about South Africa's.

The Mbeki inheritance
No one could have predicted these extraordinary events. How had Mbeki arrived at such a low point, and just halfway into his presidency? A year before Mbeki's election as president of South Africa, Hein Marais (1998) wrote that the mythical stature ascribed to then president Nelson Mandela enabled him to 'float above politics'. This allowed Mandela to be unencumbered either by the *realpolitik* of his party or the attendant need to shore up power bases. Mandela's success lay in his ability – stemming from his iconic stature – to traverse many of the key divides in South Africa and within his own organisation, the ANC: 'modern' and 'traditional', black and white, privilege and deprivation. Marais argued that this was made possible by Mandela's own character and by the assiduously constructed mythology surrounding him. This luxury would not be available to his successor, who would have to wield authority in more conventional ways – by building and fortifying a core base, and constantly cultivating support among interest groups. Marais predicted that, with Mandela's departure, South Africa would pass from the era of the statesman to one of the politician, '. . . from a dependency on the personal charisma of a leader to a reliance on public institutions and democratised political culture' (265). With it, Marais warned, would come 'more intrigue, conflict, uncertainty and, possibly, instability' (265). But this new era also promised 'to render more transparent and [to] clearly delineate tensions that course through society and the ANC' (265).

Elsewhere, the political scientist Tom Lodge (1999) has argued strongly for the need for a comprehensive study of Mbeki because the quality of political leadership matters more in new democracies than in established political systems. Where democracies are young, he writes, institutions are still fluid and more susceptible to being shaped by dominant personalities (110). No comprehensive study of Mbeki's leadership and its implications for South Africa has yet seen the light.[1] This book hopes to help fill the void.

Man of history
Thabo Mbeki is considered to be one of the most important leaders of his generation: in South Africa, where he served as the country's deputy president from 1994 to 1999, and as president since June 1999; as a leading African statesman; and as a spokesperson for the developing world. His words command attention in the economic and political power centres of Washington, London, and Berlin and, whether this is intended or not, have consequences not only for his country but also for his continent. As *The Washington Post* has noted: 'Mbeki's standing at home and abroad is, among other things, important to the United States, which considers him a key political partner in Africa' (12 October 2000).

In an earlier article, *Newsweek*'s Masland and King wrote: 'He [Mbeki] is Washington's favourite African leader – urbane and brainy, the west's best hope for a continent mired in poverty, corruption and disease' (2000).

Mbeki's importance is founded on South Africa's strategic importance on the African continent for the major western powers, in the post-cold war era of complex new challenges: internecine wars, disease, migration and cross-border crime, and, above all, the rapid movement of capital, and concomitant fluctuations in financial markets. To interested individuals outside the continent, from a vantage point that sees Africa as a mere blob on a map shown on television news, and to anyone with a commercial or academic interest in the continent, Mbeki's actions are increasingly important, even crucial. For a largely ignorant, uninformed, and less attentive audience – one that tends to conflate the countries and problems of sub-Saharan Africa – his utterances will gain in importance and weight. For Mbeki is the successor to Mandela, the new bearer of the latter's unrivalled leadership mantle, standing at the forefront of a generation of African leaders shepherding the continent's citizens towards democratic and economic development. Indeed, he has become identified with the rebirth of the continent. As Peter Vale and Sipho Maseko point out (chapter 5), his name has become synonymous with the continent's 'renaissance'.

Like Mandela, Mbeki has accumulated his own mythology – though of a very different, more varied, brand. He has been depicted as a mystical figure, with obscure powers of political manipulation.[2] Separating the mythology from the fact is an important though awkward task. As one writer has observed, Mbeki's leadership is based on respect for the ANC past. Put differently, it rests on respect for what presumably existed under conditions of exile. We have also seen that Mbeki's tendency to cling to the most vegetative patterns of the 'romantic' past has affected, very negatively, his relationship with the media (Mathebe 2001). His biography is therefore important in helping to understand his approach to both ideology and politics.

Thabo Mvuyelwa Mbeki was born on 18 June 1942 in Mbewuleni in the Transkei (then a Xhosa tribal area, and later a 'bantustan', or supposedly 'independent homeland', under the apartheid regime) in what is now Eastern Cape province.[3] His father, Govan, was a prominent figure in the ANC and South African Communist Party (SACP). Mbeki Sr, a contemporary of Mandela, was a teacher, journalist and union organiser, and at one time sat in the Transkei tribal assembly or 'parliament', the *Bunga*, (this at a time when the ANC was advocating a minimal level of co-operation with the colonial state's institutions). The Mbeki family was among the first mission-educated Africans, the beginnings of a rural middle class in the Eastern Cape. Thabo Mbeki's family background has led some to describe him as a member of the 'liberation aristocracy' (along with the Mandela and Sisulu families). His mother, Epainette, is from the Moerane family, which has ties with the Bafokeng royal family. He is one of four children – his brother Zama, a lawyer, was murdered in Lesotho in 1987, probably by agents of the South African government; his youngest brother, Moeletsi, is a journalist and media entrepreneur who worked for the state-run newspaper *Herald* in the initial period of Zimbabwean independence; Linda Mbeki, his sister, is a businesswoman in the small town of Butterworth in the Eastern Cape.

There is some dispute as to when Thabo Mbeki joined the ANC – his father has told journalists he was 'born into the ANC', but he seems to have awakened politically when he began to attend Lovedale College at Alice in the Ciskei as a boarder in 1955. Along with the nearby University of Fort Hare, the college, started by Presbyterian missionaries, was the centre of black intellectual activity and aspirations in southern Africa during the first half of the twentieth century; its alumni include Oliver Tambo, Mandela, Kenneth Kaunda, Robert Mugabe, and even Mangosuthu Buthelezi. Mbeki's contemporaries at Lovedale included Sipho Makana (now ambassador to Russia); Chris Hani (the late former commander of Umkhonto weSizwe, or MK, the ANC's military wing); Winston Njongonkulu Ndungane (the Anglican Archbishop of Cape Town, a vocal opponent of the privatisation of municipal services and an important figurehead of the Jubilee 2000 campaign), and Sam Nolutshungu (late professor of political science at New York's Rochester University, and, before he died, the favourite to become the first black vice-chancellor of the University of the Witwatersrand). In 1956 Mbeki joined the ANC Youth League, but not before flirting briefly with the Trotskyist Unity Movement's Society of Young Africans (SOYA).

In 1960 the ANC was banned. In 1961, his final year of high school, Mbeki was expelled for being one of the leaders of a class boycott against the expulsion of a fellow student. At the time, Mbeki Sr was a fugitive with Mandela. (Two years later, he would be among the 13 Rivonia trialists sentenced to life imprisonment for alleged treason against the state. Thabo would only see his father again in 1989 when the latter was one of a group of octogenarian ANC leaders released from Robben Island.) Epainette had moved her shop to the town of Idutywa, where Thabo joined her to complete his matric by correspondence. The matric done with, he was encouraged by his father to move to Johannesburg, where he launched the African Students Association on the urging of the ANC leadership. He also joined the SACP, and attended a study group led by the leading white communists Bram Fischer (a lawyer later sentenced to life imprisonment for treason, and only released when he was dying of cancer) and Michael Harmel (the SACP's leading ideologue at the time).

Mbeki was sent into exile in November 1962, along with 26 other students. This involved a brief stay in Botswana (where the group was briefly detained by the government), and an air flight to the newly independent Tanganyika (now Tanzania). From there he accompanied Kenneth Kaunda, soon to be Zambia's first post-independence president, to London to stay with Oliver Tambo, Mandela's former law partner who became the effective leader of the ANC after Mandela's imprisonment. Tambo had left South Africa on ANC orders to set up a base for exiled ANC members outside South Africa. Mbeki worked part-time with Tambo, and began studying economics at Sussex University in the coastal town of Brighton.

Mbeki spent six years at Sussex, obtaining a master's degree in economics in 1968 (his thesis: 'Location of industry in Ghana and Nigeria'). On campus his politics often appeared contradictory. He supported the Labour Party, then led by Harold Wilson, and was critical of the New Left revision of Marxism that swept western Europe in the mid- to late 1960s. He remained fiercely loyal to the Soviet Union, which was one of the ANC major sponsors, providing it with financial and educational support, arms, and military training. During those years Mbeki organised protests against apartheid – his greatest achievement was leading a march from Brighton to London to protest against a possible death sentence for his father and the other Rivonia trialists. In 1963 he wanted to join MK, but Tambo vetoed the plan and told him to complete his studies instead.

In 1969 Mbeki was finally sent for a year of military training at the Lenin International School in Moscow. This was routine procedure for up-and-coming ANC leaders. After his time in Moscow, he returned to Britain to a job in the ANC office in the London Borough of Islington, followed by a series of routine ANC desk jobs in Botswana, Swaziland, Nigeria and Lusaka in Zambia, the headquarters of the ANC in exile. It was there that he was first thrust into a leadership position, when he was appointed as assistant secretary of the ANC's revolutionary council. In 1975 he was elected to the NEC. Three years later he became political secretary in the office of the then ANC president, Tambo. Mbeki quickly became Tambo's confidante, speechwriter, and closest adviser. It was during this period that Mbeki also became a leading member of the SACP, the intellectual heart of the ANC alliance. By the late 1980s he had risen to the SACP's central committee.

The late 1980s were Mbeki's heyday. In 1985 he became the ANC's director for information, moving up in 1989 to head the organisation's department of international affairs. In each position he acted as the key ANC figure orchestrating the international anti-apartheid campaign, raising the movement's diplomatic profile and acting as the principal point of contact for foreign governments and international organisations. He was extremely successful in this; indeed, the ANC may even have eclipsed the South African government's department of foreign affairs in the breadth of its foreign contacts. By the end of the decade, economic sanctions began to be widely implemented. Mbeki also became the ANC's chief recipient of a steady stream of delegations from the elite sectors of white South Africa – academics, business people, clerics, students, and representatives of liberal white groupings – who travelled to Lusaka to sound out the ANC's views on a South Africa without apartheid.

Mbeki became known for his sophistication and eloquence. He was referred to as a highly impressive individual by the business people, diplomats, and foreign ministry officials who were in regular contact with him. Media profiles of the period would invariably describe him as pragmatic, rational, scholarly, and, above all, urbane. As James Hamill argues in an essay on Mbeki's rise to the presidency, his soothing diplomatic style undoubtedly played a crucial role in helping to counter the view held by many right-wing political formations in the west that the ANC was, to quote Margaret Thatcher, a 'typical terrorist organisation' (Hamill 1999). And, to western liberals, he presented a reassuringly measured figure.

At some stage in the early 1980s Tambo appointed Mbeki, along with Jacob Zuma (now South Africa's deputy president) and Aziz Pahad (currently deputy minister of foreign affairs) to conduct secret diplomatic talks with representatives of the apartheid regime. This process began in 1987 with a meeting between the ANC and a group of prominent Afrikaners (principally academics). In all, 12 meetings took place between November 1987 and May 1990, mainly at a country house near Bath in Somerset, England. By 1989 Mbeki and his small team were secretly meeting with senior officials of the South African National Intelligence Service (NIS). Despite his public disdain for the ANC's imprisoned and exiled leadership, and a professed disinterest in talks, PW Botha, then state president, was kept closely informed of these meetings. These negotiations ran in parallel with secret talks between Mandela and the then minister of justice, Kobie Coetsee and later a full team of government ministers (the latter talks took place at Victor Verster prison in Paarl in the Western Cape).

Botha deeply mistrusted the ANC's relationship with the SACP, and feared a right-wing backlash if news of the talks got out. This precluded reforms such as unbanning the ANC and starting negotiations over a new constitutional and political order until in late 1989, Botha suffered a stroke and was replaced by his minister of education, FW de Klerk. De Klerk was as conservative as Botha, but, faced with a deteriorating political situation, and an economy in deep recession, he announced on 2 February 1990 that he was legalising the ANC, the SACP, and other liberation movements such as the Pan-Africanist Congress (PAC).

Central to De Klerk's willingness to finally take this dramatic step was the pragmatism and moderation his advisers had found in Mandela and Mbeki. De Klerk understood that both Mandela and Mbeki were playing a crucial role in persuading the mass black constituency to accept the idea of negotiations. He was especially concerned about active political structures in the townships, and the 'young lions' who had led the uprisings of the mid-1980s. Only strong ANC leaders would be able to scale down the expectations of these forces, and bring them around to compromise (Hamill 1999). De Klerk also invited the ANC to start negotiations around a new constitutional order.

In the years that followed, the contest for the position of Mandela's second-in-command and probable successor began in earnest. Between 1990 and 1994, as the ANC adjusted from banned liberation movement to legal political organisation, and began preparing for the first democratic elections, Mbeki played a key role in transforming the party. In 1991 the ANC held its first legal national conference inside South Africa in more than 30 years, in

Durban. The main challenge was to formulate a negotiating position around which the different constituencies in the movement could unite – the returning exiles, the long-term prisoners, and the 'internals' who had led the United Democratic Front (UDF) and its various offshoots. At the same time the ANC faced problems associated with errant populist leaders, and violence among its supporters and those of Dr Buthelezi's Inkatha Freedom Party (IFP).

Mbeki was elected as national chair. However, Cyril Ramaphosa, a former trade unionist, was selected as secretary-general as well as the ANC's chief negotiator at the multiparty constitutional talks, rising to a position that would soon threaten to eclipse Mbeki's. Chris Hani, general secretary of the SACP since 1992, also became a rival, even though no SACP member had ever become president of the ANC.

This may have had something to do with Mbeki allowing his membership in the SACP to lapse during this time. He quietly went about building a support base among the ANC Youth League (with the firebrand Peter Mokaba his most vocal supporter), former exiles (who were entrenching themselves in most of the senior and key ANC leadership positions), and the powerful Women's League (with Winnie Mandela doing much of the campaigning for him).

In 1993 Hani was assassinated outside his home in a Johannesburg suburb by a right-wing Polish immigrant. This left Mbeki in a contest with Ramaphosa to be Mandela's running mate in the 1994 elections.

By the end of that year, the ANC's top brass had begun to see negotiations and a 'historic compromise' as the most favourable political route ahead. Given Mbeki's penchant for negotiations, and his earlier role in diplomatic talks between the ANC and representatives of the apartheid regime, it was ironic that he found himself sidelined by Ramaphosa as the negotiations came to be characterised by intense bargaining.

The question of whom Mandela favoured to be his deputy has been widely debated. It has been said that he was unwilling to impose his choice. According to one view, Mandela was closer to the exiles. In this version, Mbeki was seen to be a 'safer pair of hands', given that he was a confidante of Tambo (whose judgement Mandela trusted) as well as a hard-working person with experience of governmental affairs (he had the highest international profile of the candidates among governments and multinationals). The Mbeki biographer Mark Gevisser (1999) has written that Mandela even consulted senior African leaders such as Kenneth Kaunda and Julius Nyerere, who both favoured Mbeki. They suggested that the latter would keep the movement united in the style of Tambo.

Others have suggested that Mandela favoured Ramaphosa in order to counter claims of ethnic dominance by Nguni-speakers (Xhosa and Zulu) in the ANC's leadership structures – Ramaphosa is a member of the Venda-speaking minority.[4] In his autobiography, Mandela (1995: 709) had expressed a clear fondness for Ramaphosa, whom he described as 'a worthy successor to a long line of notable ANC leaders' (Mbeki hardly got a mention). Whatever the truth about Mandela's wishes, it is now known that subsequent consultations within ANC structures and with its alliance partners (the SACP and the union federation COSATU) pointed towards Mbeki, and he was duly named as the ANC's candidate for the position of deputy president of the country.[5]

On 10 May 1994 Mbeki was sworn in as first deputy president, with FW de Klerk as second deputy president (the interim constitution provided for the post of second deputy president to go to the second largest party). On 7 July 1996 Mandela finally expressed himself on the matter of his successor, telling reporters that Mbeki was 'very talented and very popular, and if the ANC elected him, I would feel that they had made the right choice' (*Houston Chronicle*, 8 July 1996). This was despite the fact that Mandela affirmed that it was not the culture within the ANC for the president to choose his successor. In fact, Mbeki had shared many of the functions all along. He had expanded the deputy presidency, and had long begun to build a power base for when he would take over (see chapter 6). Ramaphosa quit politics.

Since this period, Mbeki's key constituency outside the ANC has been the growing black middle class. He formed a 'consultative council' – dubbed a 'kitchen cabinet' by the media – made up of (only) black politicians, business people, professionals and academics, including the chair of the Independent Electoral Commission, Brigalia Bam; the then chair of the SABC, Paulus Zulu; and the politicians Sydney Mufamadi and Mbhazima Shilowa. Convened by Essop Pahad, Mbeki's leading adviser, the council met monthly at the presidential residence in Pretoria. Mbeki appointed mostly black people, some of them inexperienced, to his expanding deputy president's office in Pretoria. He encouraged black economic aspirations.

Even so, Mbeki recognised the need to sustain a support base where it counts most for the ANC – in the townships, and among the rural poor. His rural development strategy was openly solicitous of many rural chiefs, and plans for 'urban renewal' were released with much fanfare. He actively encouraged rapprochement with Buthelezi and the IFP, to the dismay of militants in the ANC, especially in its KwaZulu-Natal regional branch, which had seen thousands of its members murdered by Inkatha homeland security forces and private militia. Mbeki's old ally Jacob Zuma (then chair of the ANC in KwaZulu-Natal, and currently deputy president in the Mbeki administration since 1999) ably assisted him in this project. At one point, Mbeki's aides were even reported to have suggested an ANC–IFP merger, or offering Buthelezi the second deputy president's post. At the same time, Mbeki began to express openly his dislike of the SACP (as Vishwas Satgar documents in chapter 7) and to alienate the new, younger leadership of COSATU (see chapter 8 by Sakhela Buhlungu).

Mbeki had a tough time with the media, however. Having started out, subsequent to the unbanning of the ANC, as the darling of the media (who made much of his urbanity, elegance, charm, and pragmatism during political negotiations), he later became its whipping boy. Journalists were frustrated. They could fill a notebook during an interview with Mbeki, but at the end find he had said little beyond rhetoric.

In contrast to Mandela, Mbeki has been portrayed in the media as a power-monger, arch-manipulator, and a cunning wooer of factions. As deputy president, he was dogged by this image problem and puzzled by what he viewed as an inaccurate public perception of himself. Much of it is certainly traceable to the adversarial or at best lukewarm relationship with the local media on his part or that of his staff.

This relationship has not improved much since 1994. Mbeki has accused the media of a 'European mindset'. In March 1996 Essop Pahad (then deputy minister in the office of the deputy president) came out against what he termed 'a concerted campaign to damage the image of the deputy president' (*Sunday Times*, 10 March 1996). The ANC denounced a *Mail & Guardian* analysis of a potential Mbeki presidency (24 May 1996) as a 'sinister and unjustified attempt to cast aspersions on his political integrity'. Kader Asmal, then minister of water affairs and forestry, defended Mbeki against the press, contending that '... in the case of the deputy president, reality and perception are too divergent to indicate anything other than a vendetta' (2001). Nor was Mbeki's relationship with the media helped by his insistence on having a regular government slot on the public radio and television broadcaster (the SABC). The media, very protective of their turf, and leery of state interference as well as state propaganda (given the history of apartheid), did not take kindly to the request.

Mbeki enjoyed better coverage in the country's less influential black news media. He was closely linked to the Black Journalists' Forum at whose launch he appeared in January 1997, along with outgoing SABC chief executive Zwelakhe Sisulu. In addition, the then editor-in-chief of *City Press* (the largest circulation black Sunday newspaper), Khulu Sibiya, served on Mbeki's 'consultative council'. (It must be noted that, as Mbeki's views on AIDS became more and more erratic, even the black press deserted him.)

It is clear that his time at Sussex University, his apprenticeship with

Tambo, and his experiences in the exiled ANC were crucial formative elements in Mbeki's life, ideology, and politics.

His election as Mandela's successor may have surprised many outside the ANC, despite his key role in the negotiation politics of the late 1980s and early 1990s. There was quite a concerted campaign to prepare the country for his election. Perhaps one of the keys to understanding Mbeki is that he has, for most of his career, stood in the shadow of greatness – as Tambo's right-hand man, carrying out the tasks that enabled the latter to hold the ANC together while in exile, and then again as deputy to Mandela, when the spotlight bathed the president even though Mbeki, as deputy president, was effectively running the government. Moreover, it must have been hard for Mbeki to see Ramaphosa take the laurels for helping to negotiate the country's new constitution, when it was Mbeki, working behind the scenes, who had persuaded Afrikaner nationalists to come the table in the first place.

It must have been even more difficult to endure the sanctification of FW de Klerk. Although, in 1994, Mbeki became South Africa's first deputy president, even then De Klerk, as second deputy president in the Mandela cabinet, continued to overshadow him. De Klerk was credited, along with Mandela, for negotiating the country's transition. At this time, Mbeki was still a figure in the shadows, at least to those who had not formed part of the ANC in exile, and the media. It was only once Mandela had scaled down his role in government, and once the ANC leadership in late 1996 had endorsed Mbeki as Mandela's successor (and launched a broad-based campaign on his behalf in the media, targeting business and other key sectors), that Mbeki began to attract the attention of the media and the business community. Yet, confronted by increasing media attention, he chose to remain relatively inaccessible, behaving as if he was allergic to the modern fashion of spin-doctoring and public relations (Keeton 2001; Jacobs 1999). This may have compounded his mystique. In the absence of hard facts, fables grow. Popular myth, propagated by the local and international media, suggested that Mbeki's power was all-pervasive; that he had the ability to ruthlessly sideline internal opponents and challenges to his leadership; that his leadership was unpredictable; and that his sensitivity to criticism bordered on paranoia. One could argue that his very inaccessibility lent itself to such myth-making, and that Mbeki did little to refute them. His complicity in the crudely constructed 'Plot' story in 2001 is the most telling recent example of this.

Given Mbeki's place in the global political order, his utterances have sometimes provoked groans of disbelief and protest, even from his closest allies. It became clear to close observers of the presidency over time that his intellectual roaming was something the country could not afford.[6] However, his public statements and pronouncements are not always unreasonable and incoherent – far from it. As Patrick Bond points out (chapter 2), when one scrutinises Mbeki's speeches, it becomes clear that his approach to the global ruling elite is not motivated by personal self-advancement, or even a goal as narrow as increasing more foreign investment to South Africa. Instead, it seems his approach is aimed at engaging the global ruling elite so as to pave the way for a continuation of the South African 'revolution' (Bond 2001) – and for further, wider, grander goals such as an 'African Renaissance'. This is the 'redemptionist' heart of Mbeki, in which he culls beliefs, arguments, and perhaps policies to service greater historical objectives. This may be another key to understanding Mbeki and his philosophy.

Patrick Bond's contribution to this volume was initially entitled: 'Can Thabo Mbeki change the world?' We toyed with the idea of using it as the title for the book, because we believe Mbeki *wants* to change the world. This redemptionism, we conclude, underlies Mbeki's approach to the world. But we agree with Bond (2001): the question is 'not *whether* Mbeki is seeking to "further develop" the South African "revolution" through ever more strategic global insertions, but how he is managing such a challenge; what underlying analysis informs the approach; what strategies and tactics are appropriate; and whether alliances are properly considered'.

How is it that Mbeki – despite his government's formal adoption of a macroeconomic policy friendly to foreign investors, and the apparent acceptance of the global economic system – can complain openly about the unfairness of the international system? For instance, in late 1999, at a gala event celebrating the 'African Renaissance', Mbeki asked profound questions in a brilliant, wide-ranging speech:

> The problem we are facing ... is the reality that many among the developed countries of the North have lost all sense of the noble idea of human solidarity. What seems to predominate is the question, in its narrowest and most naked meaning – what is in it for me! What is in it for me! And all this with absolutely no apology and no sense of shame.

As Bond notes (chapter 2), the scorn with which Mbeki dismisses not only trade *realpolitik* but also the very foundation of Adam Smith's invisible hand as the optimal allocator of resources is noteworthy.

A demanding context
In recognising the wider context in which Mbeki rules, it is important first of

all to acknowledge that South Africa is a country early into its democratic life, with the eyes of the world still upon it, and with international goodwill still in the ascendant. Mbeki's own ascent was overseen by a leader – Mandela – of 'saintly' proportions, an 'iconic mentor', who still hovers paternally in the background, and occasionally ventures into the public domain to 'set the record straight' on ANC policy and principles, even to the extent of openly differing with Mbeki. Mandela has been more direct in his criticism of Mugabe, and, at the international AIDS Conference in Durban in September 2000, he suggested that Mbeki drop the issue of whether HIV caused AIDS, and concentrate instead on bringing curative and preventive measures to bear on the spread of the epidemic. The journalist Tony Karon provided an excellent précis of the challenge facing Mbeki, as seen by western powers, in an essay in *Time* on 24 July 2000: 'Thabo Mbeki has one of the hardest jobs in world politics: following Nelson Mandela as president of South Africa.'

It is crucial to note that South African democracy arrived precisely at the moment when globalisation emerged as the driving force in world politics, with far-reaching consequences for the third world. The South African government under Mbeki is trying to impose change at a time when the nation-state has never been weaker, and within the constraints of this government's self-propelling truism: that it lacks enough 'capacity to deliver'.

Finally, there are the grave socio-economic problems in the country. All the indicators show that the economic inequalities under apartheid have survived, and have worsened in some respects. South Africa is ranked as the third most unequal society in the world, surpassed only by Brazil and Guatemala (COSATU 2001). In 2001 about 45 per cent of South Africans lived in households in which adults earn about R352 (equivalent to US$45) a month. In mainly rural provinces, the figure rises above 50 per cent. Sixty-one per cent of black South Africans are poor, compared to 1 per cent of whites. The largest proportion of people in the top income quintile are white (65 per cent of households) and Indian (45 per cent). Only 17 per cent of coloureds and 10 per cent of Africans earn incomes sufficient to put them in that category. To deal with this inequality while keeping the 'rainbow' intact – which also seems under threat, as race relations are worsening (IDASA 2000) – the government has thus far relied largely on the market. At the core of its policy has been the macroeconomic Growth, Employment, and Redistribution strategy (popularly known by its acronym, GEAR), with its home-grown variant of trickle-down economics and attempts to reduce to the role of the state in the economy and the social arena. This does not seem to be working as advertised, with the benefits of the new order extending to only a small section of the black population along with the bulk of the white population.

Intra-black inequality is now greater than the inequality between whites and blacks. Most working-class black people (the bulk of the black population) are economically worse off than they were a decade ago.

Under Mbeki, thus far submerged contesting interests within the meta-discourse of non-racial unity and reconciliation will become considerably more uncomfortable. Hein Marais has predicted that a more likely outcome is the deployment of increasingly ambiguous variants of African nationalism as stabilising and disciplinary devices to draw the boundaries of permissible dissent – by distinguishing 'legitimate' interests, activities and criticism from 'deviant' or 'destabilising' ones. According to Marais, this shift is already evident in rhetoric about the need to build a 'patriotic' black bourgeoisie.[7] That racism functions as a key dynamic of exploitation is clear to us; that it represents *the* fundamental fault-line separating privilege from deprivation in post-apartheid South Africa is questionable. Such a discourse serves as a screen obscuring the other dynamics which lie at the root of inequality in society, and which animate dissent and resistance. In such a formulation, contradictions of class, gender, and geography disappear into a twilight zone of race and colour (Marais 1998: 266).

The challenge of government

Mbeki's presidency comes at a time of intense demands on South African policy-making and governance. The South African government's mishandling of the HIV/AIDS pandemic and Mbeki's obfuscation on the crisis is testimony to this assertion (Marais 2000). The HIV/AIDS crisis has emerged as the issue on which Mbeki has revealed himself in ways that appal not just foreigners but many South Africans. *The Washington Post* has described his policy response and public pronouncements on HIV/AIDS as a 'series of political missteps, mishaps and misunderstandings' (6 July 2000).

The government is also facing obstacles on the way to effective governance, particularly in the context of a new and complex constitutional order. This includes a glittering array of new rights for citizens, and substantial obligations on the part of the state, especially in terms of its constitutional duty to 'progressively realise' a far-reaching range of socio-economic rights including adequate housing, health care, welfare, and education. In turn, tensions arise between the competing ideals of public sector reform and the reduction of state spending on personnel on the one hand, and the need for service delivery on the other (Naidoo 2000).

When, in March 2001, the editor of the *Mail & Guardian*, Howard Barrell, and one of the paper's columnists, Sipho Seepe, asked Mandela which 'two or three aims you can give us around which to organise our future', he responded as follows:

> The aims around which we should organise for the future cannot be reduced to two or three. Many factors will influence that forward march – things like the health of the nation, education... But to answer your question, what we really require is the growth of our economy. That is the first point. The second is an economy that can provide full employment for everybody, because unemployment is one of our biggest challenges in this country. Then we must build a caring society with law-abiding citizens, a society, which will be able to address the challenges like HIV/AIDS and other terminal diseases, because the situation with regard to health is a very devastating one. And if, therefore I had to give you three issues around which we must organise our future, these are the ones: the growth of the economy, an economy that can provide full employment and a caring society (2–8 March).

Mandela's comments offer a useful basis for framing the key challenges to Mbeki's presidency. This book suggests that his tenure will be judged against the following four challenges.

The first is the legacy of poverty and inequality. Since 1994, there has been no real improvement in this area. Poverty is most acute in rural areas, particularly in those regions that include the former 'bantustans'. The United Nations Development Programme's *South Africa Human Development Report 2000* – which reviews fundamental changes and significant achievements in the political sphere, as well as key indicators of human development and transformation – reflects only marginal improvements in conditions for the poorest.

The second challenge, inextricably linked to the first, remains the tension between the transformation of the country's unequal economic, social, and political institutions on the one hand, and the need for reconciliation between the country's white minority – who until recently enjoyed unrivalled access to the spoils of the country's economy – and the mass of impoverished blacks on the other.

This is related to the third major challenge: forging a united national identity. Research by a policy think-tank, the Institute for Democracy in South Africa, or IDASA (2000), indicates that since 1994 many South Africans throughout the country have a strong sense of South African national identity; however, the pride of white South Africans in national citizenship has declined significantly.

A fourth challenge is to improve the quality of democratic deliberation. Despite the constitution's promise of a 'participatory democracy', political participation remains limited to a new set of policy elites (including multinational corporations, organised civil society, the media, and the domestic private sector). Together they have arrived at a narrow consensus on policy responses to the key challenges outlined above. The more inclusive, democratic, practice of the anti-apartheid struggle, which emphasised self-determination, sovereignty, and the right to (economic) equality of the black majority, has, we believe, been largely eclipsed (see chapter 10 by Krista Johnson).

In order to try to assess Mbeki's performance on these counts, our book is organised into two parts: the first, on Mbeki's economic ideology; the second, on the nature of his relationship with the main political actors and institutions of the contemporary period. Each chapter examines his relationship with particular groups (such as labour) and particular economic forces (such as global capital) while focusing on his broader social, economic, and political vision. The first part deals specifically with Mbeki's – and by extension his administration's – engagement with globalisation, ideology, macroeconomic policy, and foreign policy. The second part focuses on how he builds and maintains his constituencies, or relates to important groupings or interest groups in South Africa. The chapters in this part focus on the SACP, the trade union movement, business (particularly black business), parliament, the cabinet, and civil society.

John Saul's essay, 'Cry for the beloved country: the post-apartheid denouement' (chapter 1), analyses the ANC's journey towards an acceptance of free market capitalism, and records Mbeki's own concern: is it reasonable to assume that modern (global) capitalism will enable South Africa to overcome its grim legacy, and is it therefore reasonable for the South African govern-ment to base its policy-making on such a premise? Saul's passion shows his own sense of betrayal. Like so many, he pinned great hopes on South Africa's new political leadership and its willingness to focus on the 'mounting rage' of the poor, and recognise that neo-liberal capitalism was incapable of delivering what they needed. Socialism or barbarism, Saul concludes, rarely has more meaning than in contemporary South Africa.

Patrick Bond (chapter 2) and Hein Marais (chapter 3) set the scene for the rest of the book. Bond captures Mbeki's dialectic as a leader, and scrutinises some of his most significant blunders as president in the specific, and exacting, context of globalisation. Marais examines Mbeki's macro-economic policy and the role of the ministry of finance as a vital and emphatic area of policy control.

A constant theme throughout the book is that of ambiguity in Mbeki's ideological make-up; however, at least one of the writers does not subscribe to this thesis. In chapter 4, Sahra Ryklief asserts that his ideological orientation is in fact clear. In her view, the 'principle versus pragmatist' argument is a non-debate; applying a class-based analysis, Mbeki is an 'unabashed conservative', she argues, with a fundamentally pro-capitalist approach to economic power. This, she contends, is evident from both his speeches and his history. Importantly, Ryklief adds that a mirage effect is in operation; a conservative with democratic and African nationalist impulses such as his 'will sound and be different from one cast in the mould of Thatcher or Reagan'. She concludes that Mbeki's image as a non-ideological technocrat brilliantly obscures his own political and economic ideology; 'Mbekism is ideologically sound, gaining new converts every day, and intending to go the mile.'

In an essay largely written before Sipho Maseko's tragic recent death, he and his colleague Peter Vale interrogate Mbeki's 'African Renaissance'. They are concerned with interpretations of this idea, and seek to locate these within South Africa's diplomatic practice. Their essay does far more than consider the idea of African Renaissance in the Mbeki era; it includes a substantial review of South Africa's long history of intervention on the African continent. Nonetheless, we make no apologies for its inclusion. Given the emphasis that Mbeki has placed on the idea, no book on Mbeki could be complete without a broader, more critical, focus on the African Renaissance.

The next set of essays relates to the political aspects of Mbeki's administration. Sakhela Buhlungu (chapter 8) adds to the emerging picture with a decisive analysis of Mbeki's relationship with labour, in which he concludes that Mbeki and his advisers have sided with local and international business against the trade union movement, as represented by COSATU. The chapter also establishes a link between 'Mbeki logic' on trade unions and 'ANC logic'. For Buhlungu, Mbeki cannot be understood without understanding the ANC. He quotes the following cutting rhetorical question by a union activist: 'Many workers sing songs about Mandela. Have you ever heard workers singing songs about our new president?'

Vishwas Satgar (chapter 7) examines Mbeki's relationship with the SACP. The influence of the SACP on government policy has declined since 1994, more markedly since 1999, when Mbeki became president. Aside from broader structural factors (the impact of globalisation, the ideological meltdown of communism internationally, and the ascendancy of neo-liberalism), a number of key SACP and trade union members have left their organisations to enter parliament, government, and business. Lacking the resources or personnel to guide or influence policy has limited the influence of the party. It also lacks a dedicated policy unit.[8] On the one hand, this is the result of the declining strength of alliance structures, and the dwindling number of active SACP intellectuals. On the other, parliament and government have access to superior resources to guide policy-making. Government policy-making seems to be controlled by a small group within the ANC (comprising elements in the president's and deputy president's office, cabinet, senior department officials, and party officials) as well as policy advisers predisposed to the World Bank, International Monetary Fund (IMF), multinationals, investors, and the local business community. Furthermore, the alliance has not been working effectively for the past two years (*African Communist* 1997).

Krista Johnson (chapter 10) examines the ways in which the ANC leadership, with Mbeki at its helm, is redefining the rules of the game that regulates relations between the state and society, and the implications of this for participatory democracy and people-driven development. The chapter demonstrates the dominance of the liberal conception of state–society relations in post-apartheid South Africa, but also examines the extent to which the dominant liberal paradigm conforms to the ANC leadership's own perceptions of the relationship between state and society, and rulers and ruled. Mbeki and his followers within the ANC leadership, most of whom are former exiles, and trained in the radical Leninist school of thought that gives primacy to the role of a vanguard party and revolutionary intellectuals, are finding that the reorganisation of state–society relations along conventional liberal lines is quite compatible with their own understanding of the hierarchical relationship between rulers and ruled, and the primacy of leadership over mass action in processes of revolutionary change. Given South Africa's history of mass mobilisation and popular participation during the anti-apartheid struggle, when civil society was politicised from below and focused on not simply opposing the state or seizing state power but redefining the form of the state and its relationship to society, the approach currently promoted by Mbeki and the ANC leadership remains highly contested. Johnson also suggests that, while this perspective is not shared by all within the ANC or tripartite alliance leadership, it is not confined to the elite who have gone into government, as many leaders within civil society share this perspective. By reflecting on the broad underpinnings of the ANC leadership's recasting of state–society relations, and the implications of this for participatory forms of democracy, Johnson contributes not only to continuing debates about the future role of civil society in South Africa, but also those about the role of Mbeki and his advisers in this context.

Farouk Chothia and Sean Jacobs (chapter 6) turn away from dialectical analysis to an examination of how Mbeki operates as president. They note that there is little, if any, academic work on the changing role of the presidency and its position in the post-Mandela power nexus. Existing analyses of the workings of the presidency and how the restructuring of the office under Mbeki has changed the role of its incumbent are largely confined to the mainstream media, as academics have been silent on the subject. They explore the genesis of the restructured presidency, and trace its roots to moves by Mbeki and his closest advisers – when he was still deputy president – to build a power base in and around the office of the president. This chapter suggests that the Mbeki presidency is (and will be) characterised by tensions between a quest for better policy co-ordination to ensure the stated aims of economic growth, job creation, and social development on the one hand, and a tendency to centralise power on the other. Finally, Chothia and Jacobs locate the moves to expand the presidency within a general trend among governments around the world, and particularly point to interesting parallels between the restructuring of Mbeki's office and that of Tony Blair, Labour prime minister of the United Kingdom.

William Gumede (chapter 9) deals with the rapid expansion since 1994 of a new black entrepreneurial class. Evidence of this includes a growing black share of market capitalisation, despite initial setbacks, on the Johannesburg Stock Exchange (JSE). In September 1995 there were 11 black-owned companies listed, worth R4,6 billion. By February 1998 there were 28 companies listed, representing a capitalisation of R66,5 billion – 10 per cent of total shareholdings listed (*The Sunday Independent*, 21 June 1998). In 1996 Africans filled 30 per cent of management posts in the civil service, compared with only 2 per cent in 1994. In the three years between 1994 and 1997 the number of black South Africans earning more than R5 000 a month jumped by 52 per cent, from 310 000 people to 472 000. In his essay, Gumede explores these developments, and describes Mbeki's relationship with the national business community in general and with black business in particular.

At first glance, Andrew Nash's essay on Mandela's model of 'tribal democracy' seems misplaced in this book. However, Nash offers us an instrument for helping to understand Mbeki's apparent contradictions. His analysis of Mandela's approach to 'tribal democracy' extends, we believe, to Mbeki. Nash's exposition of leadership as a building of consensus, and permitting apparently contradictory class interests to be harmonised within a compromise solution, helps to explain both the ANC's approach to governance and Mbeki's thinking itself – an idea we develop further in our conclusion.

Finally, the book includes a useful bibliography, and probably the first comprehensive list – outside of official sources – of references to pre-1990 speeches, writings, media interviews, and documentary film appearances by

Thabo Mbeki. We hope this will help students of Mbeki and his period of government to deepen their understanding of this fascinating and complex politician and leader – the president to whom some of his closest supporters and more influential commentators (*Financial Mail* 2001) refer as the Chief Executive Officer of South Africa Incorporated.

Notes
1. Three other books about Mbeki have appeared thus far. Two – Rantao and Hadland (1999), and Mbeki (1998) – do not greatly illuminate Mbeki's style of leadership. The third – Mathebe (2001) – attempts to examine Mbeki through a more sociological or institutional lens as opposed to what the author describes as a 'behaviouralist' approach.
2. See Davis (1999). More recent examples in the popular press are Myburgh (2001) and Asmal (2001).
3. This biography of Mbeki relies principally on a series of articles by the Mbeki biographer Mark Gevisser that appeared in the *Sunday Times* of Johannesburg in May and June 1999; two essays by the British political scientist James Hamill in *Contemporary Review*; and information gathered by the editors.
4. While it could be argued that ethnic tensions do exist in the ANC, such a charge is not historically true, as ANC leadership structures reflect the potpourri of South African ethnic and racial identities.
5. In a meeting of the remaining ANC 'top five' (outside of Mbeki and Ramaphosa), Mandela had gained the approval of Walter Sisulu (national chair), Thomas Nkobi (treasurer), and Jacob Zuma for his choice of Mbeki. After the elections in 1994, he had also met with representatives of the alliance partners – John Gomomo and Mbhazima Shilowa in the case of COSATU, and Joe Slovo and Charles Nqakula in the case of the SACP – and only Slovo had disagreed (Gevisser 1999).
6. According to a report in the South African political weekly the *Mail & Guardian* (6 October 2000), Mbeki told an ANC parliamentary caucus behind closed doors that the United States and pharmaceutical companies were conspiring to establish a false link between HIV and AIDS in order to boost the sales of anti-retroviral drugs and their profit margins. He urged party officials to brush up on the issue so as to prepare for an intensified campaign by the CIA to undermine his credibility.
7. For an example of the president's own arguments around this theme, see Mbeki (2000).
8. This view is taken from a sympathetic but comprehensive analysis by Adams (1997).

References

Adams, S. 1997. What's left? The Communist Party after apartheid. *Review of African Political Economy*, 72. 237–48.
African Communist. 1997. The functioning of the Alliance. Alliance summit documents. 148, fourth quarter.
African National Congress. 2002. ANC response to Newsweek International article by Tom Masland. 27 February. http://www.anc.org.za/ancdocs/pr/2002/pr0227.html.
Asmal, K. 2001. Sense of loss behind anti-Mbeki tirade: South Africans should take note of the opposition's bitter analysis of an honest leader. *The Sunday Independent*. 8 April.
Bond, P. 2001. Pretoria's perspective on globalisation. *Politikon*, 28 (1). 1 May. 81–94.
Congress of South African Trade Unions. 2001. People's Budget. February. http://www.cosatu.org.za/docs/2001/pbud2001.htm.
Davis, G. 1999. The shaping of governance: the deputy president. Unpublished research report prepared for the Centre for Development and Enterprise.
Financial Mail. 2001. Lead more, manage less: assessing the performance of the CEO of SA Inc. 9 February.
Gevisser, M. 1999. The Thabo Mbeki story: the chief. *Sunday Times*. 20 June.
Hamill, J. 1999. The making of South Africa's new president. *Contemporary Review*, 275 (1605), October. 193–8.
IDASA Public Opinion Service and Michigan State University. 2000. *Public opinion and the consolidation of democracy in southern Africa*. Cape Town: Southern Africa Democracy Barometer. Released on 24 July 2000. http://www.idasa.org.za.
Jacobs, S. 1999. An imperial presidency. *Siyaya*. Autumn. 4–9.
Karon, T. 2000. When the president is a dissident. *Time*. 24 July.
Keeton, C. 2001. A work in progress. *Leadership*. March. 37–41.
Lodge, T. 1999. *South African politics since 1994*. Cape Town: David Philip.
Mandela, N. 1995. *Long walk to freedom: the autobiography of Nelson Mandela*. London: Abacus.
Marais, H. 1998. *South Africa: limits to change – the political economy of transition*. Cape Town and London: University of Cape Town Press and Zed Books.
———. 2000. *To the edge: AIDS review 2000*. Pretoria: University of Pretoria.
Masland, T. 2002. South Africa's lonely rebel. *Newsweek*. 4 March.
Masland, T and King, P. 2000. Flirting with strange ideas. *Newsweek*. 17 April.
Mathebe, L. 2001. *Bound by tradition: the world of Thabo Mbeki*. Pretoria: UNISA Press.
Mbeki, T. 1998. *Africa: the time has come*. Cape Town and Johannesburg: Tafelberg and Mafube.
———. 1999. Speech at the launch of the African Renaissance Institute. Pretoria. 11 October.
———. 2000. Oliver Tambo Lecture to the Second National Institute for Economic Policy (NIEP). Johannesburg. 11 August.
McGreal, C. 2001. Plot thickens in South Africa. *The Guardian*. 2 May.
Myburgh, J. 2001. Mbeki and the 'total formula': the president's leadership style is to surround himself with yes-men and entrench party control at all costs. *The Sunday Independent*. 1 April.

Naidoo, K. 2000. Put heads together for greater good. *IDASA Budget Watch*. October. 5.
Rantao, J and Hadland, A. 1999. *The life and times of Thabo Mbeki*. Johannesburg: Zebra Press.

PART ONE

Ideology

CHAPTER 1

Cry for the beloved country
The post-apartheid denouement

JOHN S SAUL

The dual transition
During the 1990s South Africa traversed from a system of racially driven authoritarian rule to an outcome far more peacefully defined and democratically realised than most observers would have predicted at the end of the previous decade. Given the difficulties of such a transition, the relatively peaceful consolidation of a functioning liberal-democratic system must be regarded as a considerable achievement. Nonetheless, we must also ask ourselves just what the most appropriate criteria for evaluating this dramatic process of change are. One point of reference may be the mid-1980s formulation by Magdoff and Sweezy (1986) which I quoted in the early 1990s in a review of South Africa's then fledgling democratic transition (1991):

> [South Africa's] system of racial segregation and repression is a veritable paradigm of capitalist super-exploitation. It has a white monopoly capitalist ruling class, and an advanced black proletariat. It is so far the only country with a well-developed, modern capitalist structure which is not only 'objectively' ripe for revolution but has actually entered a stage of overt and seemingly irreversible revolutionary struggle.

Magdoff and Sweezy did leave open the possibility of other, less palatable, outcomes, but noted, by way of summarising what was at stake, that 'a victory for counterrevolution – the stabilisation of capitalist relations in South Africa even if in somewhat altered form – would ... be [a] stunning defeat for the world revolution'. Unfortunately, when measured against such a standard, defeat seems to be an appropriate description of what has transpired in South Africa during the past decade. For 'the stabilisation of capitalist relations' is, by any measure, one clear attribute of the country's transition.

Are we setting the bar too high in even thinking of evaluating South Africa's level of accomplishment in terms of Magdoff's and Sweezy's criterion? Not necessarily. After all, South Africa's dramatic transition to a democratic dispensation ('one person, one vote in a united South Africa') has been twinned with a simultaneous transition towards an ever more sweeping neo-liberal socio-economic dispensation that has negated in practice a great deal of the country's democratic advance. But it is also important to reiterate just how much of an advance has in fact been made. In 1991, it did not even seem certain that South Africa would move beyond the system of racial authoritarianism. At that point it was apparent that the passage away from apartheid was fraught with danger; in the early 1990s the country was still a killing-field. And yet, throughout the 1994 election and its aftermath, South Africa was able to realise and stabilise the shift to a constitutionally premised and safely institutionalised democratic order – 'making peace' without suffering the potentially crippling backlash from the right wing, both black and white, that many had predicted, and without suffering the collapse into chaos or dictatorship that some had expected from majority rule. Moreover, this political stability was sustained through the five years of Nelson Mandela's presidency, was reconfirmed by the very mundaneness of the 1999 election, and has been carried unscathed into the Thabo Mbeki presidency. A cause for celebration, surely, on a continent where apparently lesser contradictions have proven to be far more difficult to resolve.

It is true that the door to the transition was opened by some behind the barricades of white power: in the late 1980s it had become evident to dominant business interests and sufficient members of the ruling political elite that a relative stalemate had been reached, and that steps would have to be taken to incorporate the ANC into the circle of legitimate political players. However, the full significance of this development only became apparent in retrospect. What seemed more pressing at the time was the fact that, despite Mandela's release from prison in 1990 and the unbanning of the ANC, then president FW de Klerk and his associates had still not reconciled themselves with the ultimate establishment of an ANC government. Well into the transition (1990–94) they continued to harbour hopes of retaining various elements of the existing racial order in any new constitutional/political dispensation that would eventually emerge from the negotiations. Moreover, De Klerk was almost certainly aware of continuing attempts by the South African military and police to strengthen the hand of Dr Mangosuthu

Buthelezi and his conservative Inkatha Freedom Party (IFP) in the jockeying for political positioning that took place at the time, and actively undermined (both directly and indirectly) the capacity of the ANC to emerge as a hegemonic force in a new South Africa.

Elements further to the right within the white polity also significantly threatened a peaceful transition. The Conservative Party (CP) as well as more overtly fascist organisations such as the Afrikaner Weerstandsbeweging (AWB) (or Afrikaner Resistance Movement), remained players to be reckoned with, committed as they were to turning back the clock to the days of unqualified apartheid. Despite a spate of bombings on the eve of the elections, the white right was therefore largely corralled into the fold of peaceful transition. And even though Buthelezi's own last-minute entry into the election did not create quite as peaceful a process in KwaZulu-Natal, his decision to participate must surely have been produced, at least in part, by the decision of General Constand Viljoen, leader of the Freedom Front, to abandon his own resistance (see Hyslop 1996).

One might argue that the ANC was equally adept at dealing with Buthelezi and Inkatha. The IFP brought to the table a bloody record of harassment of the ANC, often carried out hand in glove with the apartheid state. But it had also developed a significant base among many (although by no means all) Zulu-speakers in the rural areas and squatter settlements of the KwaZulu bantustan, and in workers' hostels, especially on the East Rand. Small wonder that, despite Inkatha's 11th-hour conversion to participation in the 1994 poll, the electoral process in Natal was marked by fraud, violence, and considerable chaos, with 'no-go' areas for one or the other of the chief protagonists in the election, especially in Inkatha-dominated rural Natal, imposing a firm limit on open campaigning, for example. In the end it was not remotely possible to accurately count votes in that province: the result was, quite simply, diplomatically brokered, and in the IFP's favour, this being a choice of tactic made by the national-level ANC in order to draw Buthelezi further into the tent of compromise. This result also meant that the IFP would form the government in the province of KwaZulu-Natal, one of nine such provincial units established within the new federal system affirmed in the constitutional guidelines produced by the interparty negotiations that had preceded the elections.

Here Buthelezi found himself benefiting from a process – that of constitution-making – that he himself had largely chosen to boycott. It was primarily white politicians, denied any more direct guarantees of minority privilege, who successfully held out for a federal division of powers as one means of hamstringing an ANC government that, they feared, might with victory seek to actively use the central government for progressive purposes. Another defence of established socio-economic inequalities was the attempt to bind the ANC to a constitutionally prescribed protection of individual human rights, particularly the right to own property. In addition, the so-called 'sunset clauses' in the interim constitution safeguarded for a period the positions of whites in public employment, the agreement on a 'government of national unity' meant positions for both National Party (NP) and IFP politicians (including both De Klerk and Buthelezi) in the cabinet formed by the ANC after its electoral victory, and an amnesty offered some protection to those who had committed various gross abuses of power in defence of apartheid (even though this was sufficiently qualified to prepare the ground for the subsequent establishment of the Truth and Reconciliation Commission, or TRC).

Of course, these 'constitutional compromises' could be interpreted in other ways. Take the tilt in the constitution towards a preoccupation with human rights. There were those in the camp of national liberation who themselves championed such an emphasis, not in any counterrevolutionary spirit but rather to help guard against the abuse of power by an ANC that – given its own hierarchical, even Stalinist, past – was far from immune to temptations of high-handedness. There were also those who sought to balance the privileging of the right in terms of property by writing into the constitution a much broader range of economic and social rights, designed to validate the continuing claims of the impoverished. Just how such rights (carefully qualified as they were) might be operationalised in a post-apartheid South Africa remained to be seen (not easily, is the simple answer), but that they appeared in the text at all suggests something of the balancing act between a defence of privilege and demands for a redress of historically embedded wrongs that the constitutional moment embodied.

Nor has the limited federalism of the constitution presented any real impediment to the ANC's undertakings. Instead, the provinces have largely become mere instruments in the hands of those who determine national-level budget allocations (and of a depressing brand of infighting in the ANC), rather than vibrant political sites in their own right. It is surely no accident that the ANC did not seem to push particularly hard in either the 1994 or 1999 elections to win the two-thirds majority it would have needed to unilaterally change the terms of the constitution in this or any other sense (although on both occasions it came very close to gaining just such a margin). If the ANC's freedom of action has been constrained in the long term, or a price paid for the kind of negotiated transition the movement did achieve, these penalties have been situated elsewhere than in the constitutional realm.

One obvious instance, many would argue, was the ANC leadership's tacit support for the demobilisation of those popular energies that had played such a crucial role in weakening the apartheid state. To be sure, those energies did find political expression from time to time during the negotiations. Thus the Congress of South African Trade Unions (COSATU), the country's largest trade union and a key ANC ally, effectively manifested its unease at late apartheid policy initiatives by the NP government (and its own absence from the formal negotiations process) with a dramatic two-day general strike against, *inter alia*, a proposed new value-added tax. And negotiators were further reminded of the mass presence beyond the conference halls when, at a crucial moment, the ANC, together with COSATU, employed a series of demonstrations (climaxing in the Boipatong massacre and in Ciskei soldiers firing at a large group of protesters marching on Bisho, capital of the Ciskei bantustan) to reactivate the stalled talks. But, as Jeremy Cronin, an ANC alliance MP and assistant general secretary of the SACP, noted forcefully at the time (1992), there was a tendency to view the latter kind of 'mass action' primarily as a 'tap' to be turned on and off at will by the ANC rather than as a foretaste of continuing popular empowerment. Another ANC activist, Raymond Suttner, had a similar sense of the direction in which things were moving:

> JS [Joe Slovo] is absolutely right to underline the massive victory we have scored at the negotiations. He fails, however, to mention that the past three years have also seen the transformation of our organisations, particularly the ANC. This transformation could have a serious long-term impact. In particular, the negotiations have had a dissolving effect on mass organisation, a tendency for our constituency to become spectators. If we conduct the coming election campaign in a narrow electoralist manner, the dissolution could be deepened. Whatever the victory, we should not underrate the strong sense of demoralisation in our organisations (quoted in SACP 1993).

In fact, elections have fully revealed what little has become of popular mobilisation in South Africa – as has the virtual collapse, since 1994, of the ANC as a mass political organisation (although not as an electoral machine). True, the 1994 poll had the distinction of being a 'freedom election'. By 1999, however, it was difficult to miss the fact that the election had become a mere popularity contest, with the ANC still floating to a considerable degree on its legitimacy among Africans as a successful liberation movement rather than on any record of delivery on popular expectations during its first term in office. Meanwhile, the vote in KwaZulu-Natal continued to be exercised along quasi-ethnic lines (producing, once again, a narrow victory for the IFP), and that in Western Cape along racial ones (producing an NP/Democratic Party (DP) government, with the two parties merged into the Democratic Alliance).¹ Nationally, the DP became the official opposition (albeit with only 11 per cent of the vote compared to the ANC's near two-thirds poll): it did so, significantly, on the basis of a campaign pitched at whites, coloureds and Indians in terms of issues of crime, corruption, and the dangers of the abuse of power inherent in a one-party dominant (also read African-dominant) political system – issues that were tacitly given a racist spin.

Of course, this tendency may also have reflected the fact that there wasn't very much more to campaign about. The DP hewed to a particularly business-friendly, neo-liberal line in respect of socio-economic policy, but even this did not do much to distinguish the party from the ANC itself in policy terms: on many potentially important strategic issues, the space for democratic disagreement and contestation had by now been papered over by a crippling consensus among the main political contenders on the presumed imperatives of economic orthodoxy. Small wonder that some observers have found it difficult to avoid a relatively narrow and unenthusiastic reading of what was substantively being accomplished in South Africa in democratic terms. Thus David Howarth distinguishes the 'democratic transition' South Africa has achieved from the 'democratic transformation' it has not really attempted – using the term 'democratic transition' to refer to 'the process by which negotiating elites manage to oversee the installation of formal liberal-democratic procedures, whereas [democratic transformation] designates the longer-term process of restructuring the underlying social relations of a given society' (1998: 203). Since, in South Africa, these 'underlying social relations' encompass a measure of socio-economic inequality that is virtually unparalleled elsewhere in the world (only Brazil and Guatemala are in the same league on the GINI scale), it is not difficult to see what Howarth is driving at.

Some have viewed the incorporation of Buthelezi into the national fold as one particularly graphic instance of the high price paid for the kind of transition that has occurred. Certainly, this is true if one takes seriously the preoccupations of Mahmood Mamdani who, in recent writing (1996), has suggested that a clear distinction needs to be made between 'citizen' and 'subject' in the theory and practice of democratic struggle in Africa. In particular, he criticises much thinking about democracy for focusing far too exclusively on urban pressures (by self-conscious 'citizens') for change, and overlooking the importance, if genuine democratic transformation is to be realised, of simultaneously helping rural dwellers who are often still trapped as 'subjects' in quasi-traditional structures of authority to liberate themselves.

Does reflection upon Mamdani's model not raise the fear that the ANC, in the name of peace-making, has merely handed over the rural poor (and those who live in the many peri-urban shanty towns around Durban and Pietermaritzburg) of KwaZulu-Natal to the ministrations of the caste of abusive chiefs and warlords who cluster around Buthelezi and his Inkatha structures?

This is, in fact, the argument made by Gerry Maré (1999), the most articulate academic critic of Buthelezi and his Inkatha project; he bemoans the extent to which the unsavoury Buthelezi has apparently forced the ANC to accept him as political player on more or less his own terms. Buthelezi has not been the only, or indeed the central, target of appeasement tactics. Far more important in this respect have been the wielders of corporate power who have lived to tell the tale of the dual transition with increasingly self-satisfied smirks on their faces. For there can be little doubt that, in the end, the relative ease of the political transition was principally guaranteed by the ANC's withdrawal from any form of genuine class struggle in the socio-economic realm, and the abandonment of any economic strategy that might have been expected to directly service the immediate material requirements of the vast mass of desperately impoverished South Africans. This was to occur in a society where, as noted above, the gap between rich and poor has been, and remains, among the widest in the world: a society in which, as one mid-1990s survey demonstrated, 'the poorest 60 per cent of households' share of total expenditure is a mere 14 per cent, while the richest quintile's share is 69 per cent', and where, across the decade of the 1990s, a certain narrowing of the income gap between black and white (as a growing number of blacks have edged themselves into elite circles) has been paralleled by an even greater widening of the gap between rich and poor (Adelzadeh 2000).

Granted, the 'negotiations' in the sphere of economic/class relationships were far less public than the formal meetings of the Convention for a Democratic South Africa (CODESA) and the Kempton Park negotiations. But they were perhaps even more important. As one close observer, Chris Landsberg, wrote in 1994:

> Since 1990, when the democratisation process began, some foreign governments, notably the US and some of its allies – Britain, Germany, Italy and Japan – successfully induced the ANC to move away from its socialist economic policies, including that of nationalisation. Instead, they succeeded in persuading the movement to embrace Western-style free market principles which the ANC increasingly, albeit reluctantly, adopted. It is interesting to note, for example, that Mandela's evolving

position on fiscal responsibility was a direct response to pressures from foreign investors and governments (1994: 290–1).

Moreover, this brand of compromise was merely part of a decade-long process of accommodation, one hailed in retrospect by no less a source than South Africa's corporate think-tank *par excellence*, the Centre for Development and Enterprise (CDE):

> The evolution of the ANC's policy position was ... influenced by foreign perceptions and pressures (from foreign investors, potential investors, the World Bank, IMF and others). Other important policy influences were the Growth for All document of the South African Foundation (representing the country's 50 largest corporations) published in February 1996 (Bernstein 1999: 83).

The result:

> Throughout the 1990s the ANC's economic policies have shown a clear shift towards greater acceptance of the market ... (one sealed) finally in the Growth, Employment and Redistribution (GEAR) proposals of June 1996 (83).

But if 1996 was the crucial year for putting the finishing touches on the ANC's capitulation to neo-liberal orthodoxy, it seems plausible to argue that the die had already been cast during the transition period itself.

Liberating capitalism
As anticipated above, from the mid-1980s the cooler heads in the camp of capital had begun to develop a counterrevolutionary strategy designed to shape the socio-economic transition that would now parallel the political one. The trigger: the near-revolutionary mobilisation of popular forces against the established system that had marked the 1980s. Capitalists, both worldwide and local, now prepared themselves to sever the marriage between the structures of capitalist exploitation on the one hand and racial oppression on the other that had proven to be so profitable to it in the past. Indeed, increased interaction with Mandela in prison and Mbeki and others in exile merely helped to confirm the growing sense that the ANC might be a potential participant in (and even possibly the best guarantor of) a transition that would safeguard the essentials of the established economic system.

The fact that a powerful stratum of Afrikaner capitalists had by now joined the upper echelons of South Africa's business community was also important. This group increasingly became protagonists within the NP of reformist strategies for a deracialisation of capitalism that began to jettison the interests of those Afrikaners – less well-off and most vulnerable to colour-blind competition for jobs and other privileges – who had once formed its chief political base. As O'Meara shows in a magisterial study (1998), the fact that De Klerk held out until quite late in the day for firmer guarantees of continued racially defined privilege proved to be much less important to the outcome of the negotiations than this underlying pull on the part of capital towards granting extensive concessions on the racial-cum-political front. Intriguingly, this pre-emptive strategy was closely tied to another perspective on the crisis which the late apartheid economy was deemed to be confronting, which seemed to further underscore the need for 'reform'.

South African capitalism was increasingly viewed as a prisoner not only of an outmoded (and increasingly politically dangerous) racial ideology, but of an outmoded economic strategy as well: in an ever more neo-liberal age, the racially motivated interventions of the South African state were merely one way in which that state was now regarded as intruding upon the sacrosanct domain of the market, and therefore retarding economic progress. Thus, in its last years, the NP government itself had moved a long way towards embracing neo-liberal orthodoxy, a trend most clearly manifested in the centrality of 'privatisation, trade liberalisation, spending cuts, and strict monetary discipline' to the Normative Economic Model (NEM) that it released in 1993. But, as has already been suggested, the most significant conversion to such orthodoxy was to take place, under intense pressure from the world of capital, within the ANC itself.

There were some countertendencies to this outcome. True, in 1990 many within the ANC were caught flat-footed in the sphere of economic policy, with only some vague if progressive nostrums from the Freedom Charter ('The mineral wealth beneath the soil, the banks and monopoly industry shall be transferred to the ownership of the people as a whole') to fall back upon. Perhaps it was this that allowed Mandela to state militantly immediately after his release from prison in February 1990 that 'the nationalisation of the mines, banks and monopoly industry is the policy of the ANC, and a change or modification of our views in this regard is inconceivable' (Nash 1999: 26) – a position he would distance himself from so quickly and thoroughly that by 1994 he could tell the US Joint Houses of Congress that the free market was a 'magical elixir' that would produce freedom and equality for all.[2] But even if Mandela himself was not to be counted upon in this respect, there was also available a more considered expression within the ANC of a radical sensibility relevant to thinking about the macroeconomic sphere – one grounded, for example, in early position papers developed by its research department.

This sensibility chiefly produced what can perhaps be described as a kind of *dirigiste* neo-Keynesianism, but it nonetheless contained the seeds of a deepening challenge to capital's prerogatives in favour of a prioritisation of popular needs in the sphere of production. Its impact was best exemplified by the prominence at the time in ANC circles of the guidelines to macroeconomic policy entitled 'Growth through redistribution'.

This perspective was also voiced early on by the ANC's new department of economic policy (DEP) – in fact, in its first major policy pronouncement, the 'Discussion document on economic policy' of 1990:

> The engine of growth in the economy of a developing, non-racial and non-sexist South Africa should be the growing satisfaction of the basic needs of the impoverished and deprived majority of our people. We thus call for a programme of Growth through Redistribution in which redistribution acts as a spur to growth and in which the fruits of growth are redistributed to satisfy basic needs (quoted in Marais 1998: 154).

Such emphases were reinforced by the report of the Macro Economic Research Group (MERG) crafted, between 1991 and 1993, by ANC-aligned economists working with progressive counterparts from overseas. And it found significant public expression in claims such as that made in 1992 by the then DEP economist (and present governor of the Reserve Bank), Tito Mboweni:

> The ANC believes that a strategy of 'growth through redistribution' will be the appropriate new path for the South African economy.... In our growth path, accumulation depends on the prior redistribution of resources. Major changes will have to take place in existing power relations as a necessary condition for this new growth path (1992).

For the voices raised against anything like the 'growth through redistribution' model were ferocious, with attack dogs for capital such as the business economist Terence Moll (1991) quickly labelling it 'macroeconomic populism', and 'a dangerous fantasy'. Moreover, a wave of much more capital-friendly proposals (the Mont Fleur scenarios, for example, and the recommendations of both the Nedcor/Old Mutual 'professional economists' panel', entitled 'Prospects for a Successful Transition', and the insurance conglomerate

Sanlam's 'Platform for Investment') soon washed over the macroeconomic debate – even as other global players arranged for key ANC economic advisers and politicians to receive training at business schools and international banks and investment houses in the west, where they were fed a steady diet of neo-liberal economics (Bond 2000).

Ironically, even COSATU, which would eventually become a rather sharper critic of burgeoning neo-liberalism in South Africa, found itself wrong-footed in this early going. Thus its own teams of academic advisers – notably the Economic Trends Group and Industrial Strategy Group – began by advocating various interventionist measures *vis-à-vis* capital, but soon found themselves so taken with models of 'shaped' and 'competitive' advantage and with supply-side and external-market-driven preoccupations that they began to offer advice that fitted quite comfortably with the rising tide of orthodoxy. In the end, the ex-United Democratic Front (UDF) activist Trevor Manuel, who was instrumental in pulling the DEP to the right in the early 1990s, and the former trade union militant Alec Erwin, patron of the COSATU academics, would become, as ministers of finance and of trade and industry respectively, the principal protagonists of the global conformism that came to characterise ANC economic policy at the turn of the century.[3]

One last throw of the dice by the left within the Mass Democratic Movement (MDM) was the document that became, in effect, the ANC's manifesto for the 1994 election campaign: the Reconstruction and Development Programme (RDP). Driven from below to a considerable degree by the trade unions and civic organisations and, many suspect, adopted for opportunistic reasons by the core group of ANC senior leaders, it emphasised the centrality to the planning process of meeting the populace's basic needs, and actively empowering it to drive its own development process. Nonetheless, the central chapters on macroeconomic policy were already markedly compromised in the direction of free market premises, the document as a whole being at best 'less what it is than what it might become' in the context of further class struggles. Unfortunately, it was the rightward pull that proved predominant, reinforced – as Asghar Adelzadeh (1996) has carefully recorded – in a range of government documents, each more neo-liberal in tone and substance than the last, that ranged from the RDP white paper of September 1994 through the draft National growth and development strategy of February 1996 to *Growth, employment and redistribution: a macroeconomic strategy* – the founding document of the GEAR strategy – of June 1996.

And in March 1996 the RDP office, until then strategically located in the president's office as cabinet-level overseer of what was left of a popularly driven development mandate, was closed, its activities folded, ostensibly, into the various line ministries.

For many of the government's most sympathetic critics, it is the extreme, precipitate, and unqualified nature of the ANC government's move towards a neo-liberal strategy that is so surprising. As Adelzadeh (1996) suggests, what has transpired appears to be to a significant extent a self-inflicted wound, an 'adoption of the essential tenets and policy recommendations of the neo-liberal framework advocated by the IMF in its structural adjustment programmes' which is

> all the more remarkable in view of the limited, even negative impact of such programmes, especially in southern Africa, the lack of any leverage that the international financial institutions such as the IMF and World Bank have over South African policy-makers, the lack of any dramatic shifts in economic and political environment to warrant such major shifts in policy orientation, and the lack of a transparent and fully argued justification for the adoption of an entirely different policy framework (67).

What there is, Adelzadeh concludes, is merely 'a lame succumbing to the policy dictates and ideological pressures of the international financial institutions'.[4] Moreover, the pronouncements of these documents have been paralleled by a range of concrete policies that epitomise just such a 'lame succumbing'. Crucial to the constitutional negotiations themselves – alongside the property rights clause – was the agreement to formally guarantee the 'independence' of the Reserve Bank, a reassurance to capital that removed any real leverage (especially in facilitating expansionary policies) over crucial monetary decisions from government hands. Moreover, as a member of the caretaker South African government, the transitional executive council, the ANC spent most of 1993 participating in a range of decisions that firmly cast the die of its future policies once it was in power: inking an extraordinarily market-friendly letter of intent to the IMF in order to guarantee a balance of payments loan, for example, and joining the General Agreement on Tariffs and Trade (GATT). Perhaps the most noteworthy aspect of this latter move was the fact that it set the stage, after 1994, for the ANC government to remove tariffs in key areas much more quickly than even GATT required – with catastrophic effects on many local firms. Moreover, Bond (2000: 200) argues that the same kind of 'moral surrender' to the market was evident in a continuing propensity to cut back corporate taxation, and in decisions such as those 'to repay in full apartheid's $20 billion-plus foreign commercial bank debt, and to phase out exchange controls in the name of attracting new foreign finance'.[5]

These, and a number of other choices made in the early going, were crucial ones, making it cumulatively more difficult for the ANC to opt for the plausible alternative policies that had existed at the outset of the transition. Left critics would argue that many of the ANC's more recent claims of being powerless in the face of the marketplace have a disingenuous ring when measured against the fact that the movement itself had, early in the game, thrown away so many of the instruments that might have been useful in crafting a more assertive strategy towards capital. Instead, and ironically, the ANC has come, full circle, back to the late apartheid government's Normative Economic Model. For the central premise of South Africa's economic policy now could scarcely be clearer: ask not what capital can do for South Africa, but what South Africa can do for capital: an overwhelming preoccupation with foreign investment, an (at best) trickle-down approach to development more broadly conceived, and an attendant encouragement of a culture of stock market speculation (with even trade unions becoming substantial players in the game via their own investment companies) and, for more marginal players, of institutionalised lotteries and other games of chance. All in a context where a sophisticated case can and has been made against the continued prioritising of supply-side economics, and for an approach ('growth through redistribution') that highlights the far more central brake on economic growth that exists on the demand side of the equation.

In the light of such circumstances it is difficult not to feel, with Adelzadeh, that the decision to opt for neo-liberalism was, first and foremost, an ideological one. For, in strictly economic terms, the premises underlying this wholesale capitulation to the market have been desperately shaky. As Colin Leys and I have recently concluded (1999), the likely result is 'relegation to the margins of the global economy, with no visible prospect for continental development along capitalist lines. Africa's development and the dynamics of global capitalism are no longer convergent, if ever they were'. And what of South Africa itself in this regard? In a recent analysis of Africa (1998), the eminent sociologist Manuel Castells states his belief that South Africa has somewhat more room to manoeuvre within global capitalism than other countries on the continent.

He argues this because of the country's size and relatively sophisticated economic structure compared with those of other African countries ('South Africa accounts for 44 per cent of the total GDP of all sub-Saharan Africa, and 52 per cent of its industrial output,' he reminds us). And yet, even Castells must conclude his discussion of South Africa by evoking the possibility of South Africa falling, like 'its ravaged neighbours,' into 'the abyss of social exclusion'. As he writes, 'the real problem for South Africa is how to avoid being pushed aside itself from the harsh competition in the new global economy once its economy is open' (122). Not easily, is the most plausible response, a point reinforced by numbers that do not indicate the dramatic increase in employment forecast by those who launched GEAR, but rather a downward spiral (an estimated loss of at least a half a million jobs between 1994 and 1999). These figures are paralleled by evidence in such spheres as GDP growth, investment, savings, exports, and interest rates that 'virtually all GEAR's targets were missed and missed by a very great deal' (Bond 2000: 193 ff).[6] Indeed, it is difficult to escape the conclusion that, in the words of one analyst, 'GEAR has been associated with massive deindustrialisation and job shedding through reduced tariffs on imports, capital flight as controls over investments are relaxed, attempts to downsize the costs and size of the public sector, and real cuts in education, health, and social welfare spending' (Van der Walt 2000).

Thabo Mbeki and meridianal Thatcherism

Many explanations of the neo-liberal turn the ANC has taken are cast in terms of the structural determinations of its actions defined by economic necessity. For Bernstein (1999) and her big business backers at the CDE, there is no doubt, given the strength of capital and the (benign) workings of the global economy, that 'at the turn of the century, there is not much choice for South Africa . . . There is only one road to follow if we want to . . . put the country on a sustained high growth path'. Evoking the example of 'Britain's Tony Blair [who] has led the Labour Party away from its socialist and union-dominated past . . . [and] is ruthless in ensuring that key members of the cabinet and party "toe the new line"', the CDE suggests that, in South Africa as well, 'a certain degree of toughness is . . . required to impose the new vision on the party and follow through with the chosen policies'. And despite concerns about too slow a pace of privatisation and too little government action to meet the need for greater 'labour flexibility', the CDE survey is nonetheless pleased to cite the fact that 'business leaders who have met Mbeki are positive' and affirm, with minimal qualification, that 'South Africa is fortunate to have a person of Mbeki's quality to lead it into the next century' (Bernstein 1999: 145). The more detailed specification of just how the differing demands of diverse fractions of capital have shaped the policy substance of the transition is more debatable. At the most general level, there is a commonsensical reading that it is the presumed imperatives of retaining as much as possible of the investment funds of large-scale domestic capitalists in the country, and attracting fresh investments from abroad, that determines government thinking. Some observers also emphasise a less South Africacentric logic to the choices made, suggesting the drive of certain key sectors of domestic capital to free themselves of the shackles of their South African siting as sufficient impetus to impose neo-liberal policies on the government. Here the emphasis is on the crucial role of 'the Mineral-Energy Complex' (MEC) that Fine and Rustomjee (1996) have shown as being so central, both historically and contemporaneously, to the South African economy.[7] The increasingly diversified global role of the main components of this MEC (the vast Anglo-American conglomerate in particular), and the extent to which a substantial percentage of the MEC's assets are now held in potentially footloose financial form, provide other strong reasons for it to seek as open an horizon as possible for its movements. Did this factor give an added edge to the pressure on government to relax its controls over the movement of capital, for example, and give its blessing to the decision of numerous key South African companies to relocate their corporate centres offshore?

Critics continue to search for explanations, especially in the light of the fact that the government's choice of strategy has been so unqualified, and its capitulation to the world of market signals and market forces so complete. Not surprisingly, critics have sought additional explanations for the precipitous rush to go much further and faster to the right than even the most informed emphasis on the pressing nature of global constraints seems to warrant. Was the ANC leadership pushed, or did it jump? Is another structural determination not that of the 'imperatives' of class formation, the upper echelons of the ANC having bought quite comfortably into a common class project with the white bourgeoisie, both global and local? Here, it is suggested, the best point of reference for analysing the South African transition might be Frantz Fanon's notion of a false decolonisation: the rising African middle class, both entrepreneurial and political/bureaucratic in provenance, merely sliding comfortably into their political positions as, yes, 'intermediaries' of global Empire and, from these heights, fending off the claims of the poverty-stricken they have left behind.

Such critics find evidence for this interpretation in statements such as that by Mandela who, in as early as 1992 (*The Star*, 15 September) warned a journalistic interlocutor that 'we are sitting on a time bomb . . . their enemy is now you and me, people who drive a car and have a house. It's order, anything that relates to order [that's the target], and it's a very grave situation.' And they will find further confirmation in an editorial in *The Economist* (12 October 1996) which could note – albeit more in glee than in anger – that

For all the fears that resentful ANC socialists would confiscate wealth, the new breed shares the same capitalist aspirations as the old. Though black incomes are barely a sixth of white ones, a black elite is rising on the back of government jobs and the promotion of black business. It is moving into the leafy suburbs, such as Kelvin and Sandton, and adopting the outward symbols of prestige – the BMW, swimming pool, golf handicap and black maid – that so mesmerise status-conscious whites.

One can almost never find examples of prominent ANC personnel who, upon resigning or being removed from public office, announce their return to the ranks of the popular movement: instead, they wind up like the prominent former ANC provincial governors Tokyo Sexwale and Mathews Phosa, who are pursuing the diamond business and casino development in Mozambique respectively. Small wonder that the authors of one careful analysis of the transition (Freund and Padayachee 1998) conjecture that

> on the one hand, the government seems, in a way, very reminiscent of equivalent groupings such as SWAPO in Namibia or ZANU-PF in Zimbabwe, to resemble a club of old party militants who are more concerned to reap the rewards of their own earlier sufferings than to effect major changes in society. On the other hand, with the disappearance of the revolutionary vision which undoubtedly spurred such militants on in the past, what is left is largely a class promotion project, the promotion of a new class of wealthy and powerful African movers and shakers (1179).[8]

Of course, whatever its implications for class formation within the country's black population, one could easily overstate the significance of this trend in broader developmental terms. Structurally, black capitalism has proven to be quite a weak force, especially since the Asian crisis of 1998 and subsequent falling stock prices and rising interest rates that have confounded black capitalists' hopes of repaying the loans with which they initially purchased shares in various enterprises. Also, after an early high-water mark of 9 per cent in 1996, the share of stocks listed on the Johannesburg Stock Exchange held by 'black empowerment enterprises' (often fronts for white enterprises in any case) has declined sharply, with certain enterprises that had been devolved to 'black' ownership even reverting back to their original owners (such as the Afrikaner economic giant Sanlam). In this and other ways, contemporary South African capitalism actually offers little room for the emergence of a vibrant and transformative 'national bourgeoisie', however much ANC statements (and certain of its affirmative action policies) may seek to imply otherwise.

All the more startling, then, is the salience of the discourse that has come to rationalise the role of this ostensibly rising class. In the most general terms, a key trope has been Mbeki's evocation of the 'African Renaissance' to describe the moment, continental and national, that he and his ANC now embrace. His speeches on this theme (notably his 'I am an African' address to the South African constitutional assembly in 1996 and his 'The African Renaissance, South Africa and the world' speech to the United Nations University in Tokyo in 1998; see appendix in Hadland and Rantao 1999) sometimes sound notes of dramatic resonance. Equally often, however, such ideas have come to be attached precisely to the rather narrower definition of 'black empowerment' outlined above, a note struck most dramatically in a speech by Mbeki to a meeting of black managers in late 1999. There the emphasis was on the need to 'strive to create and strengthen a black capitalist class', a 'black bourgeoisie'. Since 'ours is a capitalist society,' Mbeki continued, the 'objective of the deracialisation of the ownership of productive property' is key to 'the struggle against racism in our country'.

There is a problem, however: 'Because we come from the black oppressed, many of us feel embarrassed to state this goal as nakedly as we should'. Indeed, Mbeki added,

> our lives are not made easier by those who, seeking to deny that poverty and wealth in our country continue to carry their racial hues, argue that wealth and income disparities among the black people themselves are as wide as the disparities between black and white. Simply put, the argument is that the rich are rich whether they are black or white. The poor are poor, whether they are black or white.

All of which, Mbeki continued, 'frightens and embarrasses those who are black and might be part of the new rich'.[9] Some hard-boiled analysts of the ANC's history profess no surprise at such an outcome, having interpreted the ANC's entire history as a nationalist movement as the expression, first and foremost, of a narrowly petty bourgeois project. Certainly, the knot of assertive nationalism, middle-class opportunism, liberal-democratic aspirations, and all-too-Stalinoid socialist ideology that have come to define the ANC's politics over time remains to be further untangled. But recall, in this regard, Mbeki's own forceful assertion as early as 1984 that 'the ANC is not a socialist party. It has never pretended to be one, it has never said it was, and it is not trying to be. It will not become one by decree for the purpose of pleasing its "left" critics.' True, he saw fit to add that the ANC represented the 'notion of both an all-class common front and the determined mobilisation of the black proletariat and peasantry,' with this working class to be viewed as 'a conscious vanguard class, capable of advancing and defending its own democratic interests' (quoted in Hadland and Rantao 1999: chapter 7). Nonetheless, despite this latter utterance, Mbeki seems to have had little trouble in adapting comfortably to a bourgeois milieu. Early on in Mbeki's presidency, a columnist in *The Washington Post* (6 June 1999) sought to reassure his readers by quoting the following remark made to him by a prominent London-based investment banker:

> Mbeki holds things close to his chest, and makes decisions in a secretive way. However, he is not a populist, and has been a 'Thatcherite' in his fiscal ideas. His experience in exile introduced him to the financial world – he is unlikely to abandon the close ties to business developed in those years abroad.

And at the public launch of GEAR, Mbeki himself took delight in guying the left by declaiming: 'Just call me a Thatcherite' (quoted in Bond 2000: 83).

The latter moment, in its self-conscious crassness, in its smug ultra-hipness, seems especially revelatory, its very bravado capturing eloquently the prevailing undercurrent of the ANC-dominated transition. To be sure, this was not the undercurrent represented by Mandela's contribution to that transition; Mandela evoked a more traditional ethos in playing his own crucial role during the first five post-apartheid years, muffling societal contradictions (for both good and ill) within a mythos of consensus. But Mandela's was not a politics that the younger generation (with Mbeki at the lead), and epitomised by Mbeki, either could or would choose to play. Their sense of self-importance bore no quasi-traditional markings. It was auto-produced: having pulled off the impossible, the overthrow of apartheid, they are very pleased with themselves indeed. Too smart now to be mere ineffectual lefties, they expected to play the only game in town (capitalism) successfully. It is this kind of coolly self-satisfied, self-righteous, and profoundly ideological thrust on the part of the new ANC elite ('sell-out' is much too crude a term for it) that is the single most depressing attribute of South Africa's transition.

It is worth bearing in mind, of course, that such cadres had seen some kinds of 'socialism' in tatters – in Mozambique and the Soviet Union – and sensed the dangers of the fierce discipline, economic and political, that global actors might inflict upon South Africa if it stepped too far out of line. They also saw some of the weaknesses of the institutions of the state that they had inherited, and the limits these might impose on any attempt to undertake too heroic a collective project. Such considerations (including as well the very pointed sense of just what risky work it would be for them, personally and collectively, to choose to swim against a worldwide tide) may also have helped to counter any misgivings some might have had about the nature of the global capitalist system to which they now pledged their allegiance. For there have been signs of such misgivings. Consider, for example, Mandela's own statement at the 1999 Davos forum that brought together heads of state and multinational corporations to discuss the question: 'Is global capitalism delivering the goods?' According to press reports, Mandela was prepared to ask some questions of his own: 'Is globalisation only to benefit the powerful and the speculators? Does it offer nothing to men, women, and children who are ravaged by poverty?' (Mandela 1999). Or take Mbeki's observation in September 1998 to heads of state of the Non-Aligned Movement that 'the "free market" path of development... has failed to live up to the expectations of the people of the South' (1998a). And what is one to make of his pronouncement soon afterwards (1998b) that South Africans 'must be in the forefront in challenging the notion of "the market" as a modern God, a supernatural phenomenon to whose dictates everything human must bow in a spirit of powerlessness'?

However, despite such radical-sounding pronouncements, such murmurs of dissent about global contradictions more often seem designed to make it that much easier, in terms of local mass consumption, to shuffle off responsibility for any lack of economic progress in South Africa on to rather more shadowy forces deemed to be beyond the ANC's control (see chapter 2 in this volume).

Starting from scratch?
In focusing upon the terms of ANC hegemony, we should avoid any underestimation of the hard edge that Mbeki and his party also maintain in order to lock their project firmly into place – the iron fist beneath the velvet glove of their undoubted legitimacy, as it were. The truth is that many members of that leadership group are people of limited democratic sensibility, who simply do not like to be crossed. Most importantly, Mbeki's own approach to the exercise of power is far less avuncular and 'chiefly' than Mandela's, a style of top-down control and micro management already visible during Mandela's term when the former effectively orchestrated much of the hands-on functioning of the state apparatus. Mbeki's peevishness was also on display during that period. It was he, for example, who seemed principally responsible for the ANC's initial rejection of the TRC's final report, an approach, based on a

demagogic and wilful misrepresentation of that report's mild critique of the ANC's own abuses of power in exile, that undermined much of the positive resonance the report might have been expected to have. As president, Mbeki has further centralised matters in his own hands (see chapter 6 in this volume). The fact that virtually no leading ANC politician would publicly critique his stubborn attempt to contradict progressive consensus on the question of the link between HIV and AIDS may provide some indication of just how far the writ of his authority runs. But his very stubbornness on this issue may also suggest exactly what one would be up against in daring to cross him: in consequence, an air of considerable trepidation scars official circles, with only the occasional bold soul daring to risk career prospects in defence of principle.

Moreover, this distaste for disagreement has proven to be even more pronounced in respect of the policy-making centrepiece of the Mandela/Mbeki presidencies: the commitment to meridianal Thatcherism, epitomised by the adoption of the GEAR strategy. Recall that, from the outset, this document – although never publicly debated, nor even, it would seem, vetted by Mandela himself – was declared 'non-negotiable'. Recall too the tone adopted by both Mandela and Mbeki in defending it. At the 1998 conference of the South African Communist Party (SACP), the ANC's ostensible partner (along with COSATU) in a formally institutionalised political 'alliance,' both men produced paroxysms of rage against any who would have the effrontery to criticise the policy. The language used to whip the ANC's allies into line was harsh, variously described by *Southscan* (10 July 1998) as 'markedly aggressive', a 'scathing... barrage', and a 'public onslaught'. Mbeki accused SACP leaders of 'fake revolutionary posturing', terming them 'charlatans' and 'confidence tricksters' attempting to build their organisation 'on the basis of scavenging on the carcass of a savaged ANC' (see chapter 7 in this volume). As for Mandela, he stated firmly that 'GEAR, as I have said before, is the fundamental policy of the ANC. We will not change it because of your pressure.' And he hinted darkly at the consequences that might well follow from any continued criticism of the strategy.

Although the rhetorical fury unleashed by Mandela and Mbeki at that conference was particularly vitriolic in tone, this kind of attack has been linked to an offensive also directed in recent years at criticisms by the ANC's other major ally, COSATU, and its affiliates. One of the early examples of Mbeki's fury, which has been replayed in speeches to the alliance partners COSATU and the SACP, is a particularly startling address to the congress of the South African Democratic Teachers' Union (SADTU) in late 1998 where he contemptuously characterised the membership as a 'bunch of drunken and ill-disciplined teachers', and lashed out at their union's expressed scepticism about GEAR (see Vally 1998).

Despite Mbeki's apparent unease with COSATU- and SACP-backed protests against the effects of GEAR, the ANC does not seem to have much to fear from the political left. Despite the raw treatment they often receive, the unions have clung to the alliance, once again acting uncritically at election time in June 1999 and November 2000 as a key political tool for mobilising votes for the ANC.

Some labour-linked analysts continue to regard COSATU as a potent player in the transition, able to carve out space within the alliance and within forums such as the tripartite (government-business-labour) National Economic Development and Labour Council (NEDLAC) for forcing a class compromise upon capital that is, at least in some of its particulars, to labour's advantage (Adler and Webster 1999).[10]

They cite, for example, certain progressive aspects of post-apartheid labour legislation in support of their further hopes in this regard, and suggest that, in any case, the world for COSATU outside the alliance with the ANC would be even colder than that which currently seems to exist within it. And it does seem likely that COSATU will accept at least this latter premise for the foreseeable future – despite the pounding it has taken, and despite a certain amount of open debate within the labour movement over the costs and benefits of the alliance.

Inevitably, some will judge that trade union leaders have remained unduly naïve and/or timorous *vis-à-vis* the ANC and the alliance. Their approach has not dictated absolute passivity, however. In May 2001 the trade unions (COSATU, together with its allies in other, smaller, federations) were able to organise a day-long stayaway in protest against joblessness that pulled more than 4 million people away from work and produced demonstrations by hundreds of thousands of workers in major cities – protests that intensified during the latter half of 2001.

Conclusion
Have some within the ANC begun to sense that the Mbeki team's macroeconomic strategy does not and cannot work? If so, perhaps they also suspect that, in the absence of material advance, and with the ruling out of court of a class-based politics, the situation is not likely to stand still. For the fact is that things could quite easily get a great deal worse, when, as a direct reflection of socio-economic polarisation and communal decay, the crime rate continues to rise precipitously (with much of crime being extremely violent), a cruel decline in health standards (most marked in, albeit not exhausted by, the

escalating HIV/AIDS pandemic), and even the danger of increased ethnic and racial polarisation. Under such circumstances the ANC leadership itself (like some latter-day Partido Revolucionario Institucional (PRI), the party which dominated Mexican politics for more than 60 years) may merely fall back on ever more authoritarian and demagogic methods as its preferred means of seeking to contain (rather than resolve) the contradictions that scar the South African social formation. But this also poses the question: are there – whether within the ANC or without, whether building on the old or 'starting from scratch' – the seeds of (in Gindin's term) an 'alternative politics', one that could open up other possibilities for South Africa in the foreseeable future?

Time alone will tell what the Mbeki years will bring. Still, one senses that, for all his cocky self-confidence, Mbeki himself is not always quite certain of how to ride the whirlwind he has helped to create. Despite his apparently unqualified commitment to his chosen role of architect of South Africa's appeasement of capitalism as the presumptive engine of South Africa's economic transformation, one can still find him bobbing and weaving rather uncomfortably – as he did in the run-up to last year's election when he permitted himself some pretty radical-sounding formulations of his own. In one such revealing instance (*Southscan*, 12 June 1998) he not only attacked wealthy whites (afflicted, he said, by 'social amnesia'), but also a 'black elite' that abused 'freedom in the name of entitlement'. This latter group, he charged, 'seeks to hijack the sacrifices which millions of ordinary people made to liberate our country for noble purposes, in order to satisfy a seemingly insatiable and morally unbound greed and personal thirst for wealth and comfort, regardless of the cost to our society'. And he concluded by warning of 'the danger of a mounting rage, to which we must respond seriously'.

An intriguing statement with which to conclude this essay, but perhaps as much for what it says about present-day South African society as for what it tells us about Mbeki himself. Does the slightly desperate tone of such pronouncements suggest, for example, an uneasy sense on the part of the leadership of just how impossible it will be to overcome the grim legacy of racial inequality on a capitalist basis? And perhaps, too, a certain subliminal suspicion that even when local elites do everything possible to conform to global market dictate, the dependent capitalism they seek to facilitate simply cannot be expected to lift off the ground as once it (sometimes) did? Moreover, even if Mbeki and his team can continue, by and large, to dodge these realities, there are others who have begun to recognise that it is precisely in the failure of the promise of neo-liberal deliverance that both the tragedy of South Africa itself and the broader global resonance of the

South African case lies. I have also posed a further question: if the current leadership of the ANC cannot be expected to act upon any such understanding, to respond to the looming South African crisis by focusing 'mounting rage' and potential political volatility into positive and transformative popular energy, then who (if anyone) can? Whatever the answer to this question may be, the stakes are certainly high – for the phrase 'socialism or barbarism' has rarely had more meaning than in contemporary South Africa under Thabo Mbeki.

Notes

1. That alliance has since become undone, resulting in the NP forming an unusual alliance with the ANC.
2. After 1990 Mandela's reversal of ground on the nationalisation question was actually quite rapid, such that by 1994 he could assure readers of the *Sunday Times*: 'In our economic policies . . . there is not a single reference to things like nationalisation, and this is not accidental. There is not a single slogan that will connect us with any Marxist ideology' (quoted in Marais 1998: 146).
3. As Howard Barrell, then a columnist for and now editor of the *Mail & Guardian*, wrote after Mbeki had announced his new cabinet: 'Both [Erwin and Manuel] have won the confidence of the markets, and their presence in their current portfolios is seen as a measure of the government's determination to stick to its current economic course' (*Mail & Guardian*, 18 June 2000).
4. Also see the accounts of the rise and fall of the RDP in Marais (1999) and Bond (2000).
5. See also Marais (1999) and Millward and Pillay (1996).
6. For a further, detailed, critique of GEAR's performance, see Adelzadeh (1999).
7. On this and other related points, also see Bassett (2000).
8. They continue: 'If there was a phrase that captured the imagination of South Africans black and white within a year of the ANC taking power, it was that of "the gravy train".'
9. Closer to the truth, in fact, may be the frank and quite unequivocal statement by a brash emergent African entrepreneur, Tumi Modise, quoted by David Goodman in his strong volume *Fault lines: journeys into the new South Africa* (1999): 'Race is not the issue anymore; it's class.'
10. However, for a convincing response to this kind of argument, see Bassett and Clarke (1999, 2000).

References

Adelzadeh, A. 1996. From the RDP to GEAR: the gradual embracing of neo-liberalism in economic policy. *Transformation*, 31.

———. 1999. The costs of staying the course. *Ngqo!*, 1 (1). June.
———. 2000. Loosening the brakes on economic growth. *Ngqo!*, 1 (2). February.
Adler, G and Webster, E. 999. Toward a class compromise in South Africa's 'double transition': bargained liberalisation and the consolidation of democracy. *Politics and Society*, 27 (3). September.
Bassett, C. 2000. Negotiating South Africa's economic future: COSATU and strategic unionism. Unpublished PhD dissertation. York University. June.
Bassett, C and Clarke, M. 1999. Alliance woes: COSATU pays the price. *Southern Africa Report*, 14 (1).
———. 2000. South Africa: (class compromise) . . . class struggle. *Southern Africa Report*, 15 (2).
Bernstein, A. 1999. *Policy-making in a new democracy: South Africa's challenges for the 21st century*. Johannesburg: Centre for Development and Enterprise.
Bond, P. 2000. *Elite transition: from apartheid to neoliberalism in South Africa*. London: Pluto Press.
Castells, M. 1998. Africa's hope?: the South African connection. In *The Information Age, vol III: end of millennium*. Oxford: Blackwell Publishers.
Cronin, J. 1992. The boat, the tap and the Leipzig way. *African Communist*, 130.
Fine, B and Rustomjee, Z. 1996. *The political economy of South Africa: from minerals-energy complex to industrialisation*. Boulder: Westview Press.
Freund, B and Padayachee, V. 1998. Post-apartheid South Africa: the key patterns emerge. *Economic and Political Weekly*. 16 May.
Goodman, D. 1999. *Fault lines: journeys into the new South Africa*. Berkeley and Los Angeles: University of California Press.
Hadland, A and Rantao, J. 1999. *The life and times of Thabo Mbeki*. Johannesburg: Zebra Press.
Howarth, D. 1998. Paradigms gained? A critique of theories and explanations of democratic transitions in South Africa. In D Howarth and A Norval (eds), *South Africa in transition: new theoretical perspectives*. New York: St Martin's Press.
Hyslop, J. 1996. Why was the white right unable to stop South Africa's democratic transition? In P Alexander et al (eds), *Africa Today*. Canberra: HRC.
Landsberg, C. 1994. Directing from the stalls? The international community and the South African negotiation forum. In S Friedman and D Atkinson (eds), *The small miracle: South Africa's negotiated settlement*. Braamfontein: Ravan Press.
Magdoff, H and Sweezy, P. 1986. The stakes in South Africa. Editorial in special South Africa issue of *Monthly Review*, 37 (6). April.
Mamdani, M. *Citizen and subject: contemporary Africa and the legacy of late colonialism*. Princeton: Princeton University Press.
Mandela, N. 1999. Address to the World Economic Forum, Davos, 29 January. http://www.anc.org.za/ancdocs/history/mandela/1999/nm0129.htm.
Marais, H. 1998. *South Africa: limits to change*. Cape Town and London: University of Cape Town Press and Zed Books.
———. 1999. Topping up the tank: how the ANC has reproduced its power since 1994. *Development Update*, 3 (1). October.
Maré, G. 1999. Makin' nice with Buthelezi. *Southern Africa Report*, 14 (3). May.
Mbeki, T. 1998a. Speech at the opening of the ministerial meeting of the Non-Aligned

Movement (NAM), Durban, 31 August. http://www.anc.org.za/ancdocs/history/mbeki/1998/tm0831.htm.
———. 1998b. Statement at the African Renaissance conference, Johannesburg, 28 September. http://www.anc.org.za/ancdocs/history/mbeki/1998/tm0928.html.
———. 1999. Speech at the annual national conference of the Black Management Forum. Kempton Park, 20 November. http://www.anc.org.za/ancdocs/history/mbeki/1999/tm1120.html.
Mboweni, T. 1992. Growth through redistribution. In G Howe and P le Roux (eds), *Transforming the economy: policy options for South Africa.* Natal: Indicator Project SA, University of Natal Institute for Social Development.
Millward, C and Pillay, V. 1996. The economic battle for South Africa's future. In E Maganya and R Koughton (eds), *Transformation in SA? Policy debates in the 1990s.* Braamfontein: Institute for African Alternatives (IFAA).
Moll, T. 1991. Growth through redistribution: a dangerous fantasy? *The South African Journal of Economics*, 59 (3).
Nash, A. 1999. Mandela's democracy, *Monthly Review*, 50 (4).
O'Meara, D. 1998. *Forty lost years: the apartheid state and the politics of the National Party, 1948–1994.* Johannesburg and Athens, Ohio: Ravan Press and Ohio University Press.
Saul, JS. 1991. South Africa: between 'barbarism' and structural reform. *New Left Review*, 188.
Saul, JS and Leys, C. 1999. Sub-Saharan Africa in global capitalism. *Monthly Review*, 51 (3). July–August. http://www.monthlyreview.org/799saul.htm.
South African Communist Party. 1993. Central Committee discussion of Joe Slovo's presentation. *African Communist*, 135. htpp://www.sacp.org.za.
Vally, S. 1998. Education on trial: the poor speak out. *Southern Africa Report*, 14 (1). December.
Van der Walt, L. 2000. Unpublished communication. July.

CHAPTER 2

Thabo Mbeki and NEPAD
Breaking or shining the chains of global apartheid?

PATRICK BOND

In this chapter I will consider Thabo Mbeki's analysis of globalisation, his demands and strategy for global and continental socio-economic progress, and his preferred international alliances. These topics arise because of his intention, via the New Partnership for Africa's Development (NEPAD) initiative, to establish a 'new framework of interaction with the rest of the world, including the industrialised countries and multilateral organisations' – one that is sufficiently 'radical' to lift African GDP growth to 7 per cent a year (NEPAD 2001: 40, 70).

It will be clear, both from the excerpts from his speeches considered below and from the NEPAD policy document (2001), that Mbeki's approach is consistent with the broader problem of *compradorism*. As he himself has warned,

> Our own intelligentsia faces the challenge, perhaps to overcome the class limitations which [Walter] Rodney speaks of, and ensure that it does not become an obstacle to the further development of our own revolution (2000e).

I will arrive at the pessimistic conclusion that, judging by NEPAD and related international reform efforts, the challenge has already been lost. Mbeki and his main allies have already succumbed to the *class* (not necessarily personalistic) limitations of post-independence African nationalism, namely acting in close collaboration with hostile transnational corporate and multilateral forces whose interests are directly opposed to those of Mbeki's South African and African constituencies.

But Mbeki and his internationally oriented cabinet colleagues – especially the minister of finance, Trevor Manuel, and the minister of trade and industry, Alec Erwin – as well as their staff would no doubt object. They locate their own (national) ambitions as well as the continent's potential transformation not in lucrative personal accomplishments or western-style bourgeois decadence, but rather in the further integration of Africa into a world economy that – they themselves would concede – is itself in need of better regulation and fairer economic rules. The project, therefore, is to reform interstate relations and the embryonic world state system (NEPAD 2001: 28, 40, 52).

But the evidence thus far is that equitable and sustainable growth and Africa's rapid 'integration into the world economy' (52) are mutually exclusive. Although Africa's *share* of world trade declined during the 1980s and 1990s, the *volume* of exports increased, while the *value* of sub-Saharan exports was cut in half relative to the value of imports from the North (Toussaint 2001). In other words, the more Africa engaged in international trade during that period of intense globalisation, the further it slipped backwards. Such marginalisation occurred not because of a lack of integration, but because of too much integration of the wrong sort. For, while it has integrated itself more rapidly into the world economy via 'export-led growth', as demanded by Washington, Africa's ability to grow – either equitably and sustainably, or even inequitably – has actually declined, compared to the period prior to structural adjustment.

Thus, I argue below, the reform strategy will fail, although not because Pretoria has been unable to position its leaders near the helm of global economic management, and not because Mbeki lacks international credibility to implement NEPAD and win vague endorsements from global elites. After all, since 1994, extremely talented politicians and officials from Pretoria have presided over the board of governors of the IMF and World Bank, the Non-Aligned Movement (NAM), the United Nations Conference on Trade and Development (UNCTAD), the Commonwealth, the Organisation of African Unity (OAU), the Southern African Development Community (SADC), the World Commission on Dams, and a host of other important international and continental bodies.

Instead, the failure is already emanating from the very project of global reformism itself, namely its underlying philosophy, incorrect analysis, ineffectual practical strategies, uncreative and inappropriate demands, and counterproductive alliances with global elites rather than with oppressed peoples. For, notwithstanding mixed rhetorical signals, Mbeki and NEPAD effectively exclude (indeed, most often reject) alliances with those international social, labour, and environmental movements that, in their struggles for socio-environmental and economic justice, are the main agents of progressive global change.

South Africa's post-apartheid leadership will not achieve its own limited objectives, much less the more far-reaching transformation required to address the appalling increase in global poverty and inequality, and will, in the process, continue to alienate the political base of the ANC. In concluding that Mbeki cannot establish a new framework of interaction with the rest of the world, but can instead merely front for a slightly modified residual version of 'global apartheid', more hopeful analyses, strategies, demands, and alliances necessarily arise as alternatives.

Analysing the 'globalisation of apartheid'
According to the economists Jonathan Michie and Vishnu Padayachee (1997: 229), 'In the South African context, globalisation has become a synonym for inaction, even paralysis, in domestic economic policy formulation and implementation.' In July 2000 Mbeki told the ANC's national general council that globalisation

> impacts on the sovereignty of small states such as ours... The globalisation of the economy resulting among other things in rapid movements of huge volumes of capital across the globe, objectively also has the effect of limiting the possibility of states to take unilateral decisions (2000c).

He has since proceeded to take this defeatist approach into Africa via NEPAD:

> The poverty and backwardness of Africa stand in stark contrast to the prosperity of the developed world. The continued marginalisation of Africa from the globalisation process and the social exclusion of the vast majority of its peoples constitute a serious threat to global stability... In the absence of fair and just global rules, globalisation has increased the ability of the strong to advance their interests to the detriment of the weak, especially in the areas of trade, finance and technology... Africa's inability to harness the process of globalisation is a result of structural impediments to growth and development in the form of resource outflows and unfavourable terms of trade (NEPAD 2001: 2, 33, 34).

NEPAD dare not admit it, but weak governments have very few threats to make against the strong. The most profound hazards facing western prosperity – most probably associated with American financial and trade deficit crises, Japanese depression, geopolitical tensions, dire environmental damage, and debilitating oil shortages – go unremarked upon in this plan.

In mentioning 'major financial collapse in much of the developing world in the closing years of the last century' (36), NEPAD fails to hint more forcefully that there will be additional crises such as those suffered by East Asia, Russia, Latin America, and South Africa during 1997–99, when currency values fell by a third in most cases and repayment of foreign debts became onerous. The 2000–1 Turkish and Argentine meltdowns suggest that the problem was not limited to the last century, and may be far more persistent if globalisation continues its current trajectory. In Argentina's case, as well as that of Russia in 1998, the only feasible answer was to default on tens of billions of dollars of foreign debt. Here we have the kind of 'threat' that might make sense for NEPAD to foment.[1]

In the same spirit, there are other questions that bear asking. If 'fair and just global rules' are impossible to establish, as they appear to be under prevailing power relations and rising American belligerence, then is it not time to question the imperatives of globalisation? Moreover, if the rules were not fair and just – for example, in the case of the Uruguay Round of the General Agreement on Tariffs and Trade (GATT) of 1993 and subsequent trade agreements, and in relation to international flows of financial capital, including debt repayments under Washington's Highly Indebted Poor Countries (HIPC) initiative – then why did South Africa's post-apartheid rulers join GATT in 1994; sign various free trade agreements with the European Union and United States in 1998–2000; abolish the financial rand, the country's main defence against financial capital, in March 1995; and repeatedly promote the HIPC initiative? Indeed, as Mbeki has learnt since 1994, the systematic lack of fairness displayed towards Africa is also displayed towards South Africa.

South Africa exists within an extremely unfavourable balance of global forces; to point this out had, by the turn of the twenty-first century, become pedestrian. Mbeki forthrightly complains about the unfairness of the international system. For example, in a brilliant, wide-ranging speech delivered to intellectuals gathered at a gala African Renaissance event in late 1999, Mbeki tackled the delays in arriving at a trade agreement with the European Union:

> Stripped of all pretence, what has raised the question whether the agreement can be signed today or not, is the reality that many among the developed countries of the North have lost all sense of the noble

idea of human solidarity. What seems to predominate is the question, in its narrowest and most naked meaning – what is in it for me! – [A]nd all this with absolutely no apology, and no sense of shame (1999).

'What is in it for me!' The scorn with which Mbeki dismisses not only trade *realpolitik* but also the very foundation of Adam Smith's invisible hand as the optimal allocator of resources is noteworthy. He invokes, periodically, deeply ethical contentions, as in this moving address (as head of the NAM) to the Group of 77s South Summit in April 2000 in Havana:

All of us present in this hall represent countries that can pride themselves on the continued existence of a strong spirit of communal, human solidarity among many of our people. The atomisation of the family and the individual, driven by the development and entrenchment of the capitalist system, has not reached the structural permanence it has attained in the developed countries of the North (2000a).

And again, in July 2000, just after Germany had won the right to stage the 2006 soccer World Cup by one vote, he told his party's national general council: 'As the ANC, we therefore understand very well what is meant by what one writer has described as the globalisation of apartheid' (2000c).

It is with such phraseology that Mbeki accomplishes a dual elision: on the one hand, a displacement of the South's problems from the (untouchable) economic to the moral-political terrain, which in turn evokes calls for the reform (not the dismantling) of existing economic systems and institutions; and on the other, as noted earlier, a relentless campaign to persuade his constituents that 'There Is No Alternative' to globalisation. For here, as is evident from Mbeki's address to the national general council, we locate a striking difference in his rhetoric regarding racial apartheid – which the ANC always insisted should be 'abolished' and not reformed – and global apartheid:

Let me now mention that big, and some think ugly, word: globalisation. This is one of the contemporary phenomena we will have to ensure we understand. We will have to understand this, because, whether we like it or not, we are part of the world economy. It would neither be possible nor desirable that we cut ourselves off from that world economy, so that the process of globalisation becomes a matter irrelevant to our country and people.

For Mbeki, the most important practical difference between racial and global apartheid seems to be the contemporary lack of a distinct 'enemy':

> [T]here is nobody in the world who formed a secret committee to conspire to impose globalisation on an unsuspecting humanity. The process of globalisation is an objective outcome of the development of the productive forces that create wealth, including their continuous improvement and expansion through the impact on them of advances in science, technology and engineering (2000c).

Thus, even though – perhaps symptomatically – power relations are skewed, the driving force of globalisation boils down, in Mbeki's neutral story, to little more than technological determinism: 'We readily admit that globalisation is a product of scientific and technological advances, many of which have been market-driven' (NEPAD 2001: 39). Thus the NEPAD document regularly presents technology as the underlying material force (29, 31). This technocentric 'admission' is fundamentally apolitical, and disguises the reality of dramatic changes in class relations, especially the resurgent power of American and European Union capital in relation to working classes there and across the world (as reflected in state–corporate 'partnerships', and the decline of the social wage during the Reagan, Thatcher, and Kohl administrations). Ironically, in October 1998, South Africa's ruling party provided a far more insightful explanation of globalisation – at a time when it needed to engage in left-wing rhetoric in order to pull its political alliance (with COSATU and the SACP) together in preparation for a forthcoming national election:

> The present crisis is, in fact, a global capitalist crisis, rooted in a classical crisis of overaccumulation and declining profitability. Declining profitability has been a general feature of the most developed economies over the last 25 years. It . . . has spurred the last quarter of a century of intensified globalisation (and) resulted in the greatly increased dominance (and exponential growth in the sheer quantity) of speculative finance capital, ranging uncontrolled over the globe in pursuit of higher returns (ANC Alliance 1998).

If this assessment is valid, then, in addition to technological change – which facilitated but did not cause or catalyse globalisation – the more fundamental factors behind globalisation include:

- profound changes in the incentive structure of investments – especially

the decline in manufacturing profits during the late 1960s and, consequently, the geographical search for new markets and cheaper inputs and a switch by many major firms of productive reinvestment into financial assets;
- institutional factors associated with the deregulation, concentration and centralisation of financial sectors, which permitted banks and other financiers to escape national boundaries and search out far-flung borrowers;
- the decaying power of nation states and the increased power of the Bretton Woods institutions and trade agencies; and
- shortened investor time horizons.

All of these factors can, and should be, reversed. None are inevitable. Tellingly, none are even mentioned in NEPAD. South Africa's own experiences also reflect a fatalistic acceptance of Washington's neo-liberal economic dictates, instead of a spirit of self-reliance, empowerment, and struggle against injustice.

Drawing out the strategic implications

This analysis suggests that NEPAD's public reading of globalisation is blinkered and unrealistic. Yet it may well be the case that, firstly, Mbeki privately recognises these contradictions, and, secondly, has privately maintained progressive and humanistic values but, because of the balance of forces, dare not reveal his more fundamental analysis (such as, for example, that which informed the 1998 ANC Alliance discussion document). There may be something to this, but if it was the case, we would expect a more nuanced, sophisticated, and effective strategy. South Africa's own experience is instructive, and again quite depressing, both in relation to lessons learnt and actions taken to combat the excesses of global apartheid.

The mood of liberation in post-apartheid South Africa quickly turned into despair during three periods of powerful international financial discipline, currency crashes, and capital flight in early 1996, mid-1998, and 2000–1 respectively. The primary factors that made South Africa so vulnerable were, firstly, the government's March 1995 decision, taken under intense pressure from local and international financiers, to discard the exchange control mechanisms embodied in the financial rand, and, secondly, the permission granted in 1999–2001 to some of the largest South African corporations to move their financial headquarters from Johannesburg to London. As *Business Day* and the *Mail & Guardian* documented in late 2001, consequent profit and dividend outflows by Anglo American Corporation, De Beers, Old

Mutual, South African Breweries, Didata, and Gencor/Billiton, plus currency speculation by a few institutions facilitated by Deutsche Bank, were mainly behind the currency's crash, over 24 months, from R6 to the US$ to a low of R13,8. Anglo, in particular, did everything possible to externalise assets.[2]

Earlier, the financial rand's liberalisation had the effect of attracting enormous speculative financial inflows, which melted away rapidly in turn as conditions changed and the investor herd turned. All efforts in 1996 to reverse the outflows failed; these included the announcement of the partial privatisation of the state-owned telecommunications utility TELKOM, and the adoption – without consultation, and at the risk of continuing intensive political turmoil among Mbeki's alliance partners – of the misnomered GEAR strategy. From year one it failed to reach any of its targets, except for extremely low annual budget deficits and inflation rates – at least by recent historical standards. Although widely acclaimed by South African capital, GEAR did not change capitalist minds, and net disinvestment continued.

The governor of the Reserve Bank, Tito Mboweni, occasionally lambasted specific New York, London, and Johannesburg banks for their roles in rand speculation, and, in late 2001, tightened currency exchange regulations. Similarly, in his 2001 budget, Manuel temporarily withdrew the 15 per cent international investment allowance that major financial institutions had enjoyed in order to pay for the profit and dividend outflows. In late 2001 he also restricted Investec Bank's international listing so as to minimise profit/dividend outflows. But these actions amounted to shutting the barn door after the horse had bolted. Both kinds of financial liberalisation, on top of GEAR's failures, had done enormous damage; the slight tightening of exchange controls during 2001 was not strong enough to halt the currency rot, nor to reverse the country's seemingly inexorable slide into neo-liberal stagnation.

The country's 'sound' economic fundamentals deteriorated markedly during the late 1990s. Growing foreign imports amplified local deindustrialisation and job losses, while trade with Africa became extremely biased, contributing to geopolitical tensions and a growing stream of economic refugees from neighbouring countries (resulting in growing xenophobia among South African workers). Notwithstanding the battered currency, the consequent rapid rise in exports did not trickle down to the rest of the economy. There was, moreover, a net outflow of international direct investment from South Africa during the first five years of democracy, while the uneven dribs and drabs of incoming foreign investment were largely of the merger/acquisition variety rather than for new fixed investment ('greenfield') projects.

Simultaneously, economic advice poured in from international financial centres, based upon persistent demands not only for macroeconomic policies conducive to South Africa's increased global vulnerability but also for social policies and even political outcomes that weakened the state, the working class, the poor, and the environment. The country's per capita living standards sank to lows last seen during the early 1960s, while the world's worst inequality intensified. By 1998 real interest rates had reached their highest ever levels, and the JSE had crashed further than ever before in its history. And developmental reflections of the alleged 'sound economic fundamentals' during the late 1990s were unprecedented levels of municipal bankruptcies (which forced cuts in water and electricity to the poorest citizens), exacerbated apartheid geographical segregation, and fewer people formally employed in relation to those desiring a job than at any other time in the country's recorded history.

Meanwhile, because Washington's grip on international economic power remained relatively undisturbed during the late 1990s notwithstanding the arc of emerging market crises, other disappointments were still ahead. Massive debt relief promised at the 1999 G-8 meeting in Cologne did not materialise. The guru of 'post-Washington consensus theory' within the World Bank, chief economist Joseph Stiglitz, was fired in late 1999, and was followed out of the Bank's employ by an angry Ravi Kanbur in June 2000 due to the censorious interference of the secretary of the US Treasury, Lawrence Summers, in the drafting of a crucial World Bank poverty report. A 'free trade' deal between Pretoria and the European Union was negotiated and repeatedly renegotiated when southern European countries protested at South African exporters' use of the appellations 'port', 'sherry', 'ouzo', and 'grappa'. Another 'free trade' deal (like Europe's, catalysed and nurtured by lobbyists of large corporations) between Africa and the United States likewise went through numerous palpitations, and eventually included ridiculous riders such as the requirement that clothing exports from Africa to the United States would have to include very high levels of American-sourced textiles. After the débâcle at the World Trade Organisation's (WTO) ministerial summit in Seattle in December 1999, the Doha summit in November 2001 resulted in numerous new liberalisation obligations, with only a minor concession in the form of access to medicines that had already been won in practice by international HIV/AIDS treatment activists.

Mbeki could have learnt from such home-grown and international problems how to implement an Africa-wide plan that also entailed the reform of global economic institutions and processes. His ambitious lobbying schedule of world leaders during 2000–1 suggests that he had all the access he required. However, what he said and wrote during this period confirms that instead of identifying how to uproot the causes of worsening global apartheid, he preferred to work on the symptoms.

When, in May 1999, Mbeki assumed the South African presidency, the world was becoming an increasingly brutal place, as attested to by rising levels of popular protest, both at Northern meetings of the global elites and in numerous Southern settings, from Argentina to Zimbabwe, where structural adjustment had generated intense pain.

Despite this context, Mbeki showed great self-confidence combined with a unique *noblesse oblige*, namely that Pretoria could help bridge the gap between the world's rich and poor. In the wake of defeating apartheid, the ANC – in particular – must dramatically expand its objectives, Mbeki told the Port Elizabeth gathering in July 2000:

> When we decided to address the critical question of the ANC as an agent of change, we sought to examine ourselves as an agent of change to end the apartheid legacy in our own country. We also sought to examine the question of what contribution we could make to the struggle to end apartheid globally (2000c).

His series of trips to the world's political and economic centres during 2000–1 followed his late 1990s 'African Renaissance' branding exercise, which Mbeki endowed with poignant poetics. The contentless form was somewhat remedied in the secretive Millennium Africa Recovery Plan, whose PowerPoint skeleton was unveiled in 2000 to selected elites during Mbeki's meetings with Bill Clinton in May, the Okinawa G-8 meeting in July, the UN Millennium Summit in September, and a subsequent European Union gathering in Portugal. The skeleton was fleshed out in November 2000 with the assistance of several economists, and was immediately ratified by the president of the World Bank, James Wolfensohn, during a special South African visit; this occurred at an 'undisclosed location', due presumably to fears of the disruptive protests that had soured a Johannesburg trip by the new IMF czar, Horst Koehler, a few months earlier.

By this stage, Mbeki had managed to sign on as partners two additional rulers from the crucial north and west of the continent: Abdelaziz Bouteflika of Algeria, and Olusegun Obasanjo of Nigeria. Unfortunately, both continued to face mass protests and widespread civil/military/religious/ethnic bloodshed at home, diminishing their utility as model African leaders. Later, to his credit, Obasanjo led a surprise revolt against Mbeki's capitulation to Northern pressure at the World Conference Against Racism in September 2001, when he helped to generate a split between European Union and African countries over reparations due to the continent for slavery and colonialism. Tellingly, even loose talk of reparations was not found in NEPAD.

But that incident aside, 2001 was a successful year for selling NEPAD. In January, another pro-western ruler with a deplorable recent human rights record, Tanzania's Benjamin Mkapa, joined the New Africa leadership group at the World Economic Forum in Davos, Switzerland. There, Mbeki gave the world's leading capitalists and state elites a briefing that was very poorly attended. A few days later, Mbeki – flanked by Wolfensohn and Koehler – attempted to sell the plan to West Africans in Mali. The meeting of the OAU in Lusaka in July provided the opportunity for a continent-wide leadership endorsement, once Mbeki's plan had been merged with an infrastructure-heavy initiative – the 'Omega Plan' – offered by the neo-liberal Senegalese president, Abdoulaye Wade, to become the New African Initiative. A few days later the Genoa G-8 summit offered soothing encouragement, while 300 000 protesters gathered outside the conference accusing the world's main political leaders of running a destructive, elitist club.

Likewise, Mbeki's visits to Japan and Brussels in October confirmed his elite popularity, perhaps because he made no formal demands for monetary commitments. In the same month the *Financial Times* published enthusiastic endorsements of NEPAD by Johannesburg capital and the multilateral Washington banks: the first written by an heir to the Anglo American/De Beers empire, Jonathan Oppenheimer, and a leading international relations analyst, Greg Mills (2001); and the second by the highest-ranking African officials at the IMF and World Bank, Gondal Gondwe and Callisto Madavo (2001). Finally, NEPAD was publicly launched in Abuja, Nigeria, by several African heads of state on 23 October 2001.

'There are already signs of progress and hope,' NEPAD asserts. 'Democratic regimes that are committed to the protection of human rights, people-centred development and market-oriented economies are on the increase' (2001: 7). The discursive strategy is to convince readers of the (untenable) neo-liberal conflation of free markets and free societies, which typically came unstuck in Africa during the 1990s through what became known as 'IMF riots' during which masses of people took to the streets to protest against neo-liberal conditionalities such as cuts in food and transport subsidies. To this end, NEPAD's core elements include more privatisation, especially of infrastructure (no matter its failure, especially in South Africa); Africa's continued integration into the world economy (despite fast-declining terms of trade); more multiparty elections (typically, though, between variants of neo-liberal parties, as in the United States) as a veil for the lack of thoroughgoing participatory democracy; grand visions of information and communications technology (hopelessly unrealistic, considering the lack of reliable electricity across the continent); and a self-mandate for peace-keeping (which South Africa has subsequently taken for its soldiers stationed in the Democratic Republic of the Congo and Burundi).

NEPAD thus fitted into the globalisers' modified neo-liberal project, by which it was ever more vigorously (and incongruously) asserted that integration into global markets reduces poverty. It is time to turn from Mbeki's analysis and strategic process to the specific content of his vision.

Making demands

In his address in Havana (2000a), Mbeki argued for reforming global apartheid on at least five fronts:

- the alleviation or cancellation of the debt burden of many African countries;
- an effective mechanism to ensure a substantial increase in capital flows to developing economies, as this is a prerequisite for development;
- the reversal of the sharp drop in official development assistance (ODA);
- the opening of the markets of the developed countries to African products, including agricultural products; and
- the transfer of technology.

We will consider these one by one, with the issue of technology transfer exemplified by the crucial challenge of HIV/AIDS treatment.

Debt relief

It can be argued that Mbeki's approach to debt relief has already done incalculable damage, mainly because of his failure to endorse the Jubilee Movement's campaign against 'odious debt', including apartheid debt. Numerous vitriolic debates between civil society and Pretoria have occurred on this issue since 1996, and do not bear repeating in full here. Suffice it to say that, as Jubilee critics argue, had Mbeki and his predecessor, Nelson Mandela, been truly serious about the debt issue, they would not have:

- agreed to repay the apartheid foreign debt to commercial banks when this was last rescheduled in October 1993;
- claimed, repeatedly, that the South African government has no foreign debt (thereby ignoring roughly US$25 billion in parastatal and private

sector debt for which the post-apartheid South African state inherited repayment and guarantor responsibilities);
- negated the possibility of demanding reparations for previous foreign credits to the apartheid regime; and
- repeatedly endorsed the HIPC initiative of the G-8, IMF and World Bank, which has proven to be a distraction from the cause of debt cancellation.[3]

By October 2001 this last point was more widely recognised, so the NEPAD document contains the argument that HIPC 'still leaves many countries within its scope with very high debt burdens . . . In addition, there are countries not included in the HIPC that also require debt relief to release resources for poverty reduction' (NEPAD 2001: 155). (Presumably Nigeria is the main country referred to here, since post-apartheid South Africa has always tried to avoid lowering its credit rating by questioning debt repayments.)

Yet, rather than attempting to challenge the HIPC initiative in a forthright manner, the NEPAD strategy is to:

> support existing poverty reduction initiatives at the multilateral level, such as the Comprehensive Development Framework of the World Bank and the Poverty Reduction Strategy approach linked to the HIPC debt relief initiative. . . . Countries would engage with existing debt relief mechanisms – the HIPC and the Paris Club – before seeking recourse through the New Partnership for Africa's Development (118, 149).

Only later will NEPAD 'establish a forum in which African countries may share experiences and mobilise for the improvement of debt relief strategies' with the aim of ending 'the process of reform and qualification in the HIPC process' (150). The idea of sharing experiences and mobilising to improve 'debt relief strategies' is portentous. But HIPC is already widely derided – especially by the Jubilee South movement – as 'a cruel hoax'. Along with the Comprehensive Development Frameworks and Poverty Reduction Strategy Programmes (formerly Structural Adjustment Programmes) of the World Bank and IMF, HIPC deals are fundamentally committed to maintaining existing power relations and the neo-liberal economic philosophy because they entail only very slight adjustments to debt loads, and in return require lowest-income countries to liberalise their economies even further.[4] NEPAD takes the African debate on HIPC backwards. Its proposed course of action – namely to prioritise the HIPC initiative and the Paris Club (where structural adjustment loans are negotiated) – will initially cement African debt peonage. Only when Africa is further weakened by additional slides down the HIPC slope, as more wretched countries sign up, will experiences be shared and the programme's neo-liberal conditions (perhaps) be contested. At the very time that Argentina was forced to default, a much more profound questioning of the ethics of foreign debt repayment would have been welcome.

Strengthening capital inflows
Regarding this issue, there are two kinds of capitals inflows worth considering: financial, and foreign direct investment (FDI). It hardly needs arguing that speculative 'hot money' capital flows into emerging markets such as South Africa do not by any stretch of the imagination qualify as 'a prerequisite for development'.

Nor do the vast majority of foreign loans granted to third world governments over the past 30 years, including concessional loans (at an interest rate of 0,75 per cent) through the World Bank's International Development Association and the African Development Bank. Those loans serve as the leverage for the imposition of neo-liberal conditions by borrowers. Repaying even concessional hard currency loans is extremely expensive once a country's currency collapses, as happens regularly in Africa. Yet NEPAD (2001: 106) calls for more such loans in its mandates to signatories.

Even if attracting further financial flows of the 'hot money' and multilateral types is a questionable objective, the second kind of potential capital inflow – plant, equipment, and machinery via FDI – is typically understood as an essential ingredient of any Washington-approved development strategy. But after having done everything in his power to attract FDI, not even Mbeki has succeeded. Good governance and political stability are not the key factors, he has learnt; otherwise oil-rich Angola and Nigeria would not be the main beneficiaries of FDI inflows.

NEPAD's main solution to the foreign investment drought appears to be the promotion of a foreign stake (public-private partnerships) in privatised infrastructure (106, 115). The lack of justification for this initiative – aside from Africa's capital shortage – is extremely unsatisfying, given that most infrastructure is of a 'natural monopoly' type, for which competition is unsuitable. Such natural monopolies include roads and railroads, telephone land lines (including optic fibre networks), water and sewage reticulation systems, electricity transmission, ports, and the like. NEPAD cannot make a case for competition in these areas; there is, in contrast, an extremely strong case, based on 'public good' and 'merit good' features of infrastructure, for state control and non-profit operation. In particular, the privatisation of infrastructure usually prevents cross-subsidisation in order to make services more affordable to poor consumers, as South Africa has learnt from price increases, the 'cherry-picking' of poor customers, and massive service cut-offs as privatisation proceeds in telecommunications, water/sanitation, electricity, and roads/transport/rail/air.

The more important financing challenges for Africa are establishing scrupulous, publicly owned, development finance institutions and tough financial sector regulations, including effective exchange controls, that would allow the circulation and reinvestment of the continent's existing financial resources, too much of which are frittered away on debt repayments, speculative projects, luxury real estate development, and capital flight via African branches of foreign banks (typically headquartered in London and Paris) and corrupt local *comprador* banks. NEPAD offers little or nothing to help Africa become more self-reliant in using such strategies, which were the basis of Korea's success, for example. One reason is that active state intermediation in financial markets remains out of favour in Washington.

Reforming the international financial institutions
Is there, as Mbeki seeks, an 'effective mechanism' for reversing the problem of scarce capital inflows? The standard mechanism to date has been the 'seal of approval' of the World Bank and IMF, yet huge controversies surrounded the late 1990s – and continuing – imposition of Washington Consensus macro-economic policy, dictated top-down, justified by Washington's need to rebuild the 'confidence' of international investors (via enormous bail-outs financed with huge cuts in living standards). Would reforming the international financial institutions constitute a viable strategy for changing investment patterns?

Trevor Manuel, chair of the IMF and World Bank during 2000, has described his reform agenda mainly in terms of 'democratising' the Bretton Woods institutions. As he explained in an interview in mid-1999:

> The power relations in these institutions need to change. This is a 'Catch 22' situation. Their Articles of Association go back to 1944, when the first shares were allocated. Voting is based on the amount of shares a country holds. The biggest problem that confronts us in relation to the Bretton Woods Institutions is that you need an 85 per cent vote to effect any change. With the United States holding about 17 per cent of all shares, no reform can take place without its agreement. Therefore, the kinds of reforms we are hoping for are not going to happen unless the world takes a very different approach to these institutions (*Global Dialogue* 1999).

The 'kinds of reforms we are hoping for' in global financial markets have never been publicly spelled out. Mbeki has not addressed this issue in any detail, and neither has NEPAD. From South Africa's standpoint, what would a reformed World Bank and IMF look like? One answer might be surmised by considering that, as Manuel put it, 'Our relationship with the World Bank is generally structured around the reservoir of knowledge in the Bank' (*Global Dialogue* 1999), and that the Bank itself considers its South African operations as the key pilot of its reinvention of itself as a 'Knowledge Bank'.[5] Yet, virtually without exception, development knowledge shared with post-apartheid South Africa – for example, missions and policy support in fields such as water, land reform, housing, public works, health care, and macro-economics, as shown in Hein Marais's chapter – has been excessively neo-liberal in orientation, and has failed to deliver the goods.

As a result, the ANC has had a schizophrenic relationship with the Bretton Woods institutions, which has, in the wake of the protests against these institutions in Washington on 16 April 2000, degenerated into defensiveness. 'It is very fashionable for people to say that the macroeconomic policy of the country was dictated by the IMF or the World Bank,' the ANC's general secretary, Kgalema Motlanthe, complained in a interview shortly after the protests (*Mail & Guardian*, 5 May 2000). The verb 'dictate' insinuates unwillingness, and may therefore be a red herring. In reality, Pretoria and Washington have constructed a revolving door, as witnessed not only by Manuel's job as chair of the Bretton Woods institutions during 2000 (and persistent rumours that he was going to take a permanent job there), but also the role of other bureaucrats who move seamlessly between the World Bank, the South African Department of Finance, and the Johannesburg commercial banks.

Suspicion of the World Bank and IMF involvement in South Africa is residual, against the background of its various bail-outs of apartheid in the 1950s and 1960s, and its sanctions-busting lifelines to the previous regime despite United Nations and global anti-apartheid pressure. It continued to supply the Nationalists with economic advice in the late 1980s and early 1990s, which included recommendations to privatise state assets, impose extremely high interest rates, enforce export-oriented strategies, and impose the unpopular Value-Added Tax.

But, claims Motlanthe, things have changed. 'We're not accountable to the IMF or World Bank, as we have not borrowed from them' (*Mail & Guardian*, 5 May 2000). This is incorrect, for in December 1993 an $850 million IMF loan was signed by the interim government, known as the Transitional

Executive Council (TEC), purportedly for 'drought relief' (18 months after the drought had ended). That loan bound Pretoria to cutting government deficit spending (from 6,8 per cent to 6 per cent of GDP in 1994), and reducing wages. The conditions were kept secret until they were leaked to *Business Day* in March 1994. In May, that newspaper's top financial journalist, Greta Steyn, concluded that 'the Reconstruction and Development Programme and the TEC statement of policies to the IMF are arguably the two most important clues to future economic policy . . . The ANC, in signing the statement of policies to the IMF, committed itself to promoting wage restraint' (*Business Day*, 30 May 1994). The progressive sections of the RDP were subsequently ditched in practice (Bond 2000: chapter 3). Motlanthe was also not told, apparently, about a $46 million World Bank loan to promote exports in 1997, nor of tens of millions of dollars invested in South Africa by the Bank's private sector subsidiary, the International Finance Corporation.[6]

Aid fatigue
Regarding foreign aid, Mbeki calls for 'more and better managed aid so as to deal with the basic needs that will have to precede any form of development in certain areas' (2000f). One problem is that Mbeki did very little in practice to dissuade Clinton and other international leaders from pursuing the classic neo-liberal maxim of 'trade, not aid', as a result of which the value of North–South aid during the 1990s fell by one third (*Financial Times*, 11 November 1998).

But what lessons does South Africa itself have to offer? Were foreign donors encouraged, under post-apartheid rule, to turn aid pledges into real programmes; sustainably provide for basic needs; promote civil society; and support good aid management (for example, via effective monitoring and evaluation, and regular collective consultations with government)? There is a strong case to be made that the Mandela and Mbeki governments were disastrous models in all these respects.

In one example, donor pledges of nearly $5 billion were made to Pretoria between 1994 and 1999. But just as the government failed to disburse much of its own domestically sourced development funding (80 per cent annual RDP-related budget 'rollovers' were typical in the early years, but even during the late 1990s the government's inability to spend poverty relief funding became a national scandal), the disbursement record of South Africa's largest donor, the European Union (EU), was also appallingly bad. Thus, in making the case for more international aid, Mbeki has not yet provided a convincing case that such aid won't exacerbate the well-known problems of bureaucratic capture and non-sustainability.

Trade rules
Mbeki wants to correct what he calls the 'rules and regulations that make the world trading system unbalanced and biased against the very countries that need a fair trading system so that these countries, which represent the majority of humanity, benefit from international rules of trade' (Mbeki 2000f). Even if the South African economy is on the margins of world trade, Pretoria won a high profile on the global circuits for at least three institutional reasons: Alec Erwin's 1996–2000 presidency of the UN Conference on Trade and Development; his controversial role at the 1999 WTO Summit in Seattle; and his subsequent attempt to bring together both a new middle-income bloc and African countries to restart WTO negotiations. The latter two functions – particularly Erwin's distaste for the Seattle social movement protesters, and his near-refusal to join the Africa bloc of trade ministers protesting against the abominable treatment meted out to them by the United States trade negotiator Charlene Barchefsky – have been addressed by other experts (see Tandon 1999 and Keet 2000).

Throughout, Erwin argued for less Northern protectionism for 'dinosaur industries' such as manufacturing and agriculture, but has done so meekly: 'In addressing the challenge of trade and development in UNCTAD IX, we were attempting to break with a conception of contestation by stressing partnership' (2000).

The efficacy of the stress on 'partnership' was made explicit not only in the 'What is in it for me!' attitude of the EU during free trade negotiations, as remarked upon earlier, but also in 1998–99 when the American vice-president, Al Gore, lobbied Erwin, the South African minister of health, Nkosazana Dlamini-Zuma, and Mbeki himself to roll back the 1997 Medicines Act, which promoted the parallel import and generic production of anti-retroviral drugs essential for fighting HIV/AIDS. The transnational pharmaceutical corporations threatened a constitutional lawsuit against the act, which they actively pursued for a month in March 2001 before international protests forced them to withdraw. This life-and-death case of technology transfer – blocked by corporations whose billions of dollars in profits overrode access to drugs that would save millions of lives – is an instructive example of the nature of political alliances that can, quite effectively, roll back the negative traits of globalisation.

Blocking access to drugs
It was not Erwin's philosophy of a fair and just trade partnership that persuaded Gore to halt his campaign against HIV-positive Africans. A vibrant Treatment Action Campaign emerged in South Africa during 1999 during

which grass-roots militants embarked on protests at American consulates in Johannesburg and Cape Town, and began networking with the Philadelphia, New York, and Paris chapters of the advocacy group ACT UP (Aids Coalition to Unleash Power). At the very outset of his presidential election campaign in mid-1999, Gore was confronted with repeated and aggressive protests in Tennessee, New Hampshire, California, and Pennsylvania. Numerous newspapers carried front-page reports on Gore's quandary. Within weeks, the vice-president's own cost-benefit analysis began to reveal the danger of siding with the pharmaceutical firms, whose millions in campaign contributions would not offset sustained damage to his image. In a September 1999 meeting with Mbeki in New York, Gore conceded the validity of the SA Medicines Act. With Thailand, Brazil, and India also taking strong non-partnership positions by establishing generic production facilities, and with tens of thousands of protesters in the streets, the American president, Bill Clinton, agreed at the Seattle WTO summit not to push for more stringent patent protection for American pharmaceutical companies.[7]

The South African government then failed to take advantage of the space won by the activists, as Mbeki searched for excuses – such as a controversial investigation into whether HIV is indeed associated with AIDS, the alleged toxicity of anti-retrovirals, and (artificial) fiscal constraints (which did not prevent Mbeki from authorising tens of billions of rands-worth of arms expenditures) – to *not* implement the parallel importation or generic production options. By the time NEPAD was launched, Mbeki's HIV/AIDS policies were routinely described as 'genocidal' in the local and international press, and in December 2001 Mbeki seemed to amplify his extraordinary image as South Africa's 'undertaker-in-chief' by authorising the state's appeal in the Constitutional Court against a hostile court judgement that required it to begin large-scale anti-retroviral treatment of mother-to-child-transmission. Mandela had very publicly demanded the same of Mbeki at the international AIDS conference in Durban in July 2000, but, notwithstanding the NEPAD document's brief mentions of a 'high priority given to tackling HIV/AIDS' (49), and leadership in a 'campaign for increased international financial support for the struggle against HIV/AIDS' (127), the latter continued to make arguments and policy that classified him as an AIDS dissident.

But even if, in retrospect, the victory was pyrrhic, the joint struggle by the South African government and AIDS activists against Gore and the pharmaceutical corporations was instructive. The David-versus-Goliath battle against pharmaceutical companies – and the White House – was won; yet Mbeki quickly grabbed defeat from the jaws of victory, and the broader war against AIDS took a turn for the worse.

In sum, progress on any of the five key issues Mbeki listed in Havana depends on who he is in partnership with. Speaking to an African-American congregation at the venerable Ebenezer Church in Atlanta during his trip to the United States in May 2000, Mbeki invoked the forces of social progress:

> In a world where no country can insulate itself from other parts of the same world, our success is highly dependent on your concrete support. This global solidarity between ourselves was part of the vocabulary of the civil rights movement... We are therefore saying that we should continue with this struggle of working together and striving for social and economic justice for the poor, for countries of the South, and come with practical ways of assisting Africa to pull herself out of the quagmire of poverty (2000a).

But with whom in the world does Thabo Mbeki really have an honest partnership, and with whom is he building genuine solidarity? Notwithstanding the eloquence of his Atlanta speech, the answers are not obvious.[8] Is there scope for an honest partnership with the world's progressive social movements?

Towards – or against – 'global solidarity?

One problem immediately arises, and must be openly confronted. In controversies surrounding Africa's relations with imperialism, as witnessed in numerous campaigns by South African labour and social justice movements, Mbeki and the ANC have repeatedly revealed repressive tendencies: against millions of anti-privatisation strikers in the trade union movements, against thousands of community residents in Soweto suffering from unaffordable services because of privatisation pressure, and against leading opponents of Mbeki's AIDS policies, who during 2000 were reportedly labelled by Mbeki as 'infiltrators' of the trade union movement and agents of pharmaceutical corporations and the American Central Intelligence Agency (CIA).[9]

Thus, on the eve of the anti-privatisation stayaway 29–30 August 2001, as insults flew between leaders of the ANC and the SACP/COSATU, *Business Day* ran a front-page report that contained the following:

> Cabinet ministers were subsequently dispatched to influential radio and television programmes first to 'clarify' government positions, but also to 'show COSATU members they are being urged to committing suicide', according to an official involved in the spin-doctoring offensive. Also part of the strategy – championed by trade and indus-

try minister Alec Erwin, transport minister Dullah Omar, and public enterprises minister Jeff Radebe – was to seek to caution COSATU members against the possible hijacking of their strike by outside elements such as those protesting at World Bank and IMF meetings (27 August 2001).

Bizarre as it sounded at first blush, the same newspaper demonstrated the valid underlying rationale for Pretoria's hijack phobia on the following day:

> SA needs to cut import tariffs aggressively, privatise faster and more extensively, promote small business effectively and change labour laws to achieve far faster growth and job creation. This is according to a World Bank report that will soon be released publicly and has been circulating in government (28 August 2001).

Under such circumstances, what kind of role did NEPAD envisage for civil society, aside from 'asking the African peoples to take up the challenge of mobilising in support of the implementation of this initiative by setting up, at all levels, structures for organisation, mobilisation and action' (2001: 56)? NEPAD contains no concrete actions to be taken by the African peoples, no offer of organisational resources, and no civil society implementation plan. The policy document itself has only been made available to African civil society via the internet – and then very obscurely. There have been no leadership-catalysed discussions of NEPAD within civil society organisations in South Africa itself – which is perhaps explained by the fact that Mbeki's alliance partners, COSATU and the SACP, have firmly opposed central neo-liberal NEPAD economic and infrastructure provisions via mass protests and stayaways, simultaneous to Mbeki's attempt to sell these at international and a few continental venues.

Instead, the spirit of grass-roots partnerships envisaged is captured in the vague mandate to 'promote community and user involvement in infrastructure construction, maintenance and management, especially in poor urban and rural areas, in collaboration with the New Partnership for Africa's Development governance initiatives' (106). In principle, this is a useful strategy. In practice, however, it has had the effect of placing financial and technical obligations that are the responsibility of the state in most civilised societies on the shoulders of Africa's most impoverished communities.

In South Africa, for example, the effect of requiring a greater role for communities in administering full cost-recovery rural water schemes was to leave most of them broken, because communities could not afford them. More than 43 000 children in this country die of diarrhoea each year as a result, mainly, of inadequate water and sanitation, which in turn is mainly an affordability problem. Similarly, the disconnection of (existing free) water supplies due to unaffordability occurred at the epicentre of the 2000–1 cholera epidemic, which affected more than 200 000 low-income people and killed more than 200.

The philosophy of user responsibility for maintenance and management – and the expenses thereof – already prevails in many African settings, notwithstanding the extreme levels of poverty, mainly because of policy-makers' and programme managers' ideological commitment to full cost-recovery. As the World Bank recently expressed its mandate to governments aiming to supply rural African villages in desperate need of water and sanitation: 'Promote increased capital cost-recovery from users. An up-front cash contribution based on their willingness to pay is required from users to demonstrate demand and develop community capacity to administer funds and tariffs. Ensure 100 per cent recovery of operation and maintenance costs' (World Bank 2000: appendix 2).

A subsequent World Bank initiative – the Kampala statement on urban water in February 2001 – was similarly naïve (or disingenuous) about the politics of water privatisation 'reform': 'Labour can also be a powerful ally in explaining the benefits of the reform to the general public. It is essential therefore that the utility workers themselves understand and appreciate the need for the reform.' The Kampala statement's bottom line: 'An increased role for the private sector in water/sanitation services delivery has been a dominant feature of the reform processes of African countries, as it has been recognised as a viable alternative to public service delivery and financial autonomy' (Water Utilities Partnership 2001). Finding an alternative to what states are ordinarily responsible for providing to their citizens is at the core of Washington's – and NEPAD's – notion of civil society empowerment.

What is revealed by these demands of African societies – made by both Mbeki and his Washington partners – is not only the counterproductive and illusory establishment of alliances and partnerships with the forces promoting global apartheid, but also the contradictory character of Mbeki's rhetoric concerning international social change. Notwithstanding the practical hostility Mbeki often shows when dealing with civil society opposition to his neo-liberal policies, he often makes rhetorical gestures to the enormously important role of social change activists. And as in Mbeki's own speeches, there is a high degree of empowerment rhetoric in NEPAD:

The New Partnership for Africa's Development seeks to build on and celebrate the achievements of the past, as well as reflect on the lessons learned through painful experience, so as to establish a partnership that is both credible and capable of implementation. In doing so, the challenge is for the peoples and governments of Africa to understand that development is a process of empowerment and self-reliance. Accordingly, Africans must not be wards of benevolent guardians; rather they must be the architects of their own sustained upliftment (27).

This is inspiring rhetoric. But NEPAD, in reality, shuns 'self-reliance' and the self-upliftment of Africans. To illustrate, none of the social justice 'achievements' that went against the grain of the then-prevailing features of globalisation – especially mass civil society protests that threw off the yokes of slavery, colonialism and apartheid – are specifically mentioned in NEPAD. It asks readers to 'reflect' – but only in an extremely blinkered way, so as to avoid a more thoroughgoing analysis and evolution of policy options. Thus none of the anti-imperialist ideas of the most progressive architects and analysts of twentieth-century African political and socio-economic liberation – such as Ake, Amin, Biko, Cabral, Fanon, First, Kadalie, Lumumba, Machel, Mamdani, Mkandawire, Nabudere, Nkrumah, Nyerere, Odinga, Onimode, Rodney, Sankara, Senghor, or Shivji – is considered worthy of reference, much less engagement and endorsement.[10]

Yet the radical rhetoric of self-reliance characterised some of Mbeki's discourses during 2000–1, as if to substitute for the top-down, elite-centred, non-consultative nature of NEPAD. For example, addressing an audience of social-democratic activists in mid-2000, Mbeki was resolute in his commitment to nurture challenges from the grass roots:

> All of us, but most certainly those of us who come from Africa, are very conscious of the importance that all tyrants attach to the demobilisation of the masses of the people. At all times, these tyrants seek to incite, bribe or intimidate the people into a state of quiescence and submissiveness. As the movement all of us present here represent, surely our task must be to encourage these masses, where they are oppressed, to rebellion, to assert the vision fundamental to all progressive movements, that – the people shall govern! (2000d).

Aside from not being implemented, one problem is that this kind of support – Mbeki generously citing demonstrators for raising consciousness – is not, in fact, mutual. For consciousness-raising is only a small fraction of the concrete challenge that many of the leading social justice movement organisations have set for themselves: the essence of that challenge is to *shut down* the WTO, World Bank and IMF. Mbeki's approach is the opposite: to gain greater admission. What, then, is the nature of the growing conflict over Africa's and South Africa's relations with the world economy, between leaders and progressive activists?

To understand how far the ANC government has gone to downgrade alliances with the left, consider a 1996 ANC discussion document, which concluded with these lines:

> The democratic movement must resist the illusion that a democratic South Africa can be insulated from the processes which characterise world development. It must resist the thinking that this gives South Africa a possibility to elaborate solutions which are in discord with the rest of the world, but which can be sustained by virtue of a voluntarist South African experiment of a special type, a world of anti-apartheid campaigners, who, out of loyalty to us, would support and sustain such voluntarism (ANC 1996).

The 1997 Medicines Act was, activists insist, precisely such a 'voluntarist experiment'. It was indeed *only* sustained by virtue of an appeal, by local activists, to 'a world of anti-apartheid campaigners' who 'out of loyalty', militantly demonstrated in favour of the act.

This is where the argument finally comes to a head. Thus far, we have taken seriously the extent to which Mbeki says he *wants* to change the world, even if the analysis is wanting, the rhetoric often confuses listeners, the strategy is dubious, and the tactics ineffective. Central to this problem is the issue of whom Mbeki most comfortably allies himself with. The social forces represented in the AIDS treatment example are emblematic of the challenge, for they evoke enormous potential for real solidarity, *for changing the balance of forces*.

This dilemma appears to be the case across Africa, notwithstanding optimistic NEPAD rhetoric:

> The present initiative is an expression of the commitment of Africa's leaders to translate the deep popular will into action . . . The political leaders of the continent appeal to all the peoples of Africa, in all their diversity, to become aware of the seriousness of the situation and the need to mobilise themselves in order to put an end to further marginalisation of the continent and ensure its development by bridging the gap with the developed countries (53, 55).

Some readers will find the hypocrisy in this passage breathtaking. Africans falling further into poverty as a result of leadership *compradorism* and globalisation may not need to 'become aware of the seriousness of the situation', compared to those elite rulers who generally live in luxury, at great distance from the masses. And when Africans in progressive civil society organisations express 'the need to mobilise themselves', they are invariably repressed by ruling elites.

Moreover, NEPAD could – but tellingly doesn't – document 'the deep popular will' to build a new Africa. That ambition certainly exists in various civil society initiatives, most of which explicitly oppose NEPAD. Across the continent, varied grass-roots organisations – community-based groups, HIV/AIDS support organisations, traditional and ethnic movements, progressive churches, women's and youth clubs, environmental groups and many others – have joined trade unionists and radical intellectuals in diverse struggles against neo-liberalism, for democracy and humanity. Many of the strongest expressions of popular will exist in South Africa, and involve Mbeki's alliance partners which fundamentally reject the same policies of alleged 'macroeconomic stability' (fiscal and monetary austerity) and privatisation that NEPAD promotes.

The same deep philosophical rejection of NEPAD and promotion of a genuine human rights culture exists across Africa. In the political sphere, this led in 2001 to mass demonstrations against unfree, unfair elections held in Tanzania, Zambia, and Zimbabwe. In the economic sphere, trade unions regularly protest against structural adjustment, and are joined by diverse citizens' movements. For example, branches of Jubilee Africa motivate strongly for full debt repudiation, cancellation, and reparations across the continent, and fundamentally reject Washington's debt relief strategies. African initiatives are also evident in the grass-roots campaign for the return of billions looted by the Nigerian dictator Sani Abacha and held by Swiss and London banks. Early success helped to break open bank secrecy, following similar campaigns over 15 years waged by citizens' groups and governments in the Philippines and Haiti in respect of the Marcos and Duvallier hoards.

Conclusion
The radical strategy is multifaceted, but is not merely destructive or protectionist, as Erwin and Manuel repeatedly posit. Recall the first great reformer of the IMF and World Bank: a key co-founder, John Maynard Keynes. When Keynes failed to persuade the dominant American negotiators of the need for a more politically neutral institution at the 1944 Bretton Woods and 1946 Savannah conferences, he was despondent. As one account has it, 'Keynes

had argued so bitterly at Savannah with US Treasury Secretary Fred Vinson and was so distressed by the course on which the Bank seemed to be set that his friends blamed the meeting for the heart attack he suffered on the train back to Washington, and for a second, a month later, which killed him at the age of 63' (Caufield 1997: 47).

It may be useful to conclude, as a result, with (an outline of) the kinds of changes to the world economy for which Keynes once firmly argued. For these words are – if one only added 'political solidarity' to the list of globalisation goods – perfectly consonant with the radical strategy referred to earlier:

> I sympathise with those who would minimise, rather than with those who would maximise, economic entanglement among nations. Ideas, knowledge, science, hospitality, travel – these are the things which should of their nature be international. But let goods be homespun whenever it is reasonably and conveniently possible and, above all, let finance be primarily national (Keynes 1933: 769).

Keynes was not only perhaps a more active, successful, and visionary shaper of global circumstances than Mbeki – albeit from a stronger power base in Britain, yet also ultimately a subservient and frustrating one. In that 1933 maxim he also captured the essence of a bumper sticker slogan that is often heard in the contemporary international social justice movement: 'The globalisation of people, not of capital!' It is that slogan which says so much more about analysis, strategy, demands, and alliances than Mbeki, and in turn hints more profoundly at why his initiatives, including NEPAD, have become 'an obstacle to the further development of our own revolution' (as Mbeki put it in his Tambo Memorial Lecture) and to global-scale and continental socio-economic progress. In sum, if international capital and its various institutional foundations, including the Bretton Woods institutions and the WTO, represent the chains of global apartheid, it is evident that Mbeki's project is shining, not breaking, those chains.

Notes
1. However, to do so would require two other corollaries: a collective repudiation of African and third world debt so as to again 'threaten the stability of the global financial system' and thereby gain leverage for genuine debt cancellation negotiations, and a prohibition of the use of funds invested in the IMF/World Bank by developing countries (for example, South Africa's 1 per cent share) to bail out

western investors, as ordinarily transpires in the case of a third world financial crisis. Tellingly, NEPAD does not mention that although poverty increased dramatically in the wake of the 1997–99 emerging markets crisis, foreign investors (especially New York and London financiers) generally recovered their funds, and new American investors in debt-ravaged Asian firms were able to pick up assets at fire-sale prices.
2. See especially the reporting by Mungo Soggott, *Mail & Guardian*, 6–13 December 2001.
3. For more information, see the Alternative Information and Development Centre's website at http://www.aidc.org.za.
4. In the main southern African pilot HIPC, Mozambique's conditionality requirements included quintupling cost-recovery charges (user fees) at public health clinics, the privatisation of urban and rural water supply systems, and the simultaneous liberalisation and privatisation of its largest agro-industry, cashew nut processing, which destroyed the industry. Mozambique's president, Joachim Chissano, publicly complained about the low levels of debt cancellation and the pressure being brought to bear on him by the Bretton Woods institutions to inappropriately liberalise the economy.
5. This is confirmed in World Bank (1999).
6. These include stakes in Dominos Pizza (which subsequently went bankrupt), for-profit health care, housing securities to make high-income people's homes more affordable, and the privatisation of infrastructure, none of which fight poverty (and all of which add a US dollar liability to South Africa's stressed current account).
7. The firms reacted with promises of cheaper, though not free, drugs, which in turn were spurned by activists as too little, too late. When faced with the prospect of local production, drug companies changed the subject by announcing offers of free medicines, which subsequently did not materialise.
8. Post-apartheid foreign policy examples – under Mbeki's influence – of areas where solidarity was *not* extended to democrats include the Indonesian and East Timorese people suffering under Suharto (recipient of a 1997 Cape of Good Hope medal), Nigerian opposition activists who in 1995 were denied a visa to meet in Johannesburg, the Burmese people (given the unusual diplomatic relations of the junta-controlled 'Myanmar' with Pretoria), and victims of murderous central African regimes which were recipients of South African arms. According to the National Conventional Arms Control Committee, in 1996–98 undemocratic regimes such as Colombia, Algeria, and Peru purchased more than R300 million-worth of arms from South Africa (Batchelor 1999: 17).
9. A more general level of paranoia was revealed in May 2001 when the then minister of safety and security, the late Steve Tshwete – a close ally of Mbeki – launched an extraordinary attack on three top ANC figures (all of whom had entered business) on the grounds that they were plotting to overthrow Mbeki.
10. We know from Mbeki's Oliver Tambo lecture (2000f) that he is well acquainted with the ideas of radical Africans. His failure to invoke these in NEPAD is revealing.

References

African National Congress (ANC). 1994. *The Reconstruction and Development Programme.* Johannesburg: Umanyano Publications.

———. 1998. The state and social transformation. Discussion document. Reprinted in *Umrabulo*, 5, 3rd quarter, www.anc.org.za/ancdocs/pubs.umrabulo.

ANC Alliance. 1999. The current global economic crisis and its implications for South Africa. Discussion document. Reprinted in *Umrabulo*, 6, 1st quarter, www.anc.org.za/ancdocs/pubs.umrabulo.

Batchelor, P. 1999. South Africa: an irresponsible arms trader? *Global Dialogue*, 4 (2). Johannesburg: Institute for Global Dialogue.

Bond, P. 2000. *Elite transition: from apartheid to neoliberalism in South Africa.* London: Pluto Press.

Caufield, C. 1997. *Masters of illusion: the World Bank and the poverty of nations.* London: Macmillan.

Erwin, A. 2000. Opening address to the tenth session of UNCTAD, Bangkok, 12 February.

Global Dialogue. 1999. Trevor Manuel. 4 (2), August. Johannesburg: Institute for Global Dialogue.

Gondwe, G and Madavo, C. 2001. New swipe at fighting poverty. *Financial Times*, 7 October.

Keet, D. 2000. South Africa's role in the WTO. Alternative Information and Development Centre occasional paper. Cape Town: AIDC.

Keynes, JM. 1933. National self-sufficiency. *Yale Review*, 22 (4).

Mbeki, T. 1999. Speech at the Launch of the African Renaissance Institute, Pretoria, 11 October.

———. 2000a. Address at the Ebenezer Baptist Church, Atlanta, 26 May.

———. 2000b. Address at the opening of the South Summit, Havana, 12 April.

———. 2000c. Keynote address to the National General Council of the African National Congress, Port Elizabeth, 12 July.

———. 2000d. *Vox populi* – is it real? Speech at the IUSY Festival, Stockholm, 28 July.

———. 2000e. *Ou sont ils en ce moment* – where are they now? Second Oliver Tambo lecture of the National Institute for Economic Policy, Johannesburg, 11 August.

———. 2000f. Address to the Commonwealth Club, World Affairs Council, and US/SA Business Council Conference, San Francisco, 24 May.

———. 2000g. Lecture at Georgetown University, Washington, 23 May.

Michie, J and Padayachee, V. 1997. The South African policy debate resumes. In Michie and Padayachee (eds), *The political economy of South Africa's transition.* London: The Dryden Press.

Mills, J and Oppenheimer, J. 2001. Partnerships only way to break cycle of poverty. *Financial Times*, 1 October.

New Partnership for Africa's Development. 2001. The New Partnership for Africa's Development (NEPAD). October. Online. http://www.nepad.org/AA0010101.pdf.

Tandon, Y. 1999. A blip or a turnaround? *Journal on Social Change and Development.* 49. December.

Toussaint, E. 2001. Debt in sub-Saharan Africa on the eve of the third millennium. Unpublished paper. Brussels: Committee for the Abolition of Third World Debt.

Water Utilities Partnership. 2001. Kampala statement. Washington, DC: World Bank. 14 March.
World Bank. 1999. *South Africa – country assistance strategy.* Washington, DC.
———. 2000. *Sourcebook on community-driven development in the Africa region – community action programs.* Washington.

CHAPTER 3

The logic of expediency
Post-apartheid shifts in macroeconomic policy

HEIN MARAIS

Analysts suffer from an understandable tendency to segment history and then, like so many railway coaches, hitch one period to another. After all, we divide history into centuries, so why not choose other markers and isolate a 'post-cold war era', or put an even finer point on things and speak of a 'post-Mandela era' in South Africa?

Such flourishes have generated something of a cottage industry in South Africa, with analysts dissecting alleged shifts in governing style, emphasis, and even character since Nelson Mandela's retirement from active politics.

It's a tempting approach to recent South African history, not least because it seems to have some virtue – as long as one ducks the rather elementary question of when exactly the Mandela era ended and the Mbeki era began. Certainly, the former was marked by activities that may be likened to a kind of grand national convalescence. It was during that period that South Africa was guided clear of the precipice, and nursed through perilous flux and confusion. Not for nothing is it associated with the person of Mandela. His historic and towering contribution was to help foster sufficiently broad-based consent for the 'new order', and carve out 'a breathing space where pulses could settle, enmities subdue, and affinities become recast' (Marais 1998: 265).

So the formative interlude of new policy-making, legislative overhauls, and trust-building between 1994 and 1997 seems to fit into what we might term the 'Mandela era', while the subsequent shift toward 'hands-on' political management, the firm emphasis on issues of governance, and the fine-tuning of political institutions seems distinct enough to warrant an 'era' and helmsman of its own.

Whereas Mandela's broad societal authority resembled that of the benign patriarch guided by the principles of inclusivity, Mbeki's is commonly associated with that of a visionary 'can-do' politician. Goals are spelled out, and the paths toward them more clearly mapped: switching metaphors, if Mandela's key accomplishment was to have rearranged the stage, then the role assumed by Mbeki has been to direct the actors. Hence the widely shared view that the two 'eras' have different characters, with the central reference points appearing to drift from appeasement, conciliation, and compromise toward a more forthright accent on some of the many contradictions and fault-lines that define South Africa.

The obvious appeal of conceptual maps such as these is that they turn complex processes into bite-sized chunks, and personalise (and thereby seem to illuminate) opaque and ambiguous dynamics. But how much they actually reveal is moot. It may be argued that, when we narrow our gaze to the alleged proclivities, styles, and visions of key political actors, we lose sight not only of the more extensive mechanics of change but also of the stout continuities that shape South Africa's transition.

Which is why this chapter takes the inverse approach. It concentrates on a definitive feature of post-apartheid South Africa – macroeconomic policy – and on the related and evolving set of state–capital relations situated at the heart of the wide-ranging modernisation project we tend to euphemise as South Africa's democratic transition.

This line of enquiry seems useful because, despite the cheerless results, the ANC government's macroeconomic policy remains one of the most crucial and consistent vectors of post-apartheid transformation;[1] in fact, it seems highly resistant to the kinds of episodic shifts mainstream analysis associates with different presidential 'eras'. To understand this, the sturdy foundations of a package of economic adjustments some observers have mistakenly regarded as a temporary idiosyncrasy of the new South Africa are probed in this chapter.

Evolving state–capital relations after 1994

As argued in the previous two chapters by John Saul and Patrick Bond respectively, the ANC has, like other social-democratic parties worldwide, become acutely sensitive to the shrunken horizon of economic options available in an era of globalisation marked by the ascendancy of neoliberalism. A party whose notions of economic transformation had hinged on a powerful state was soon left woozy by its awakening in a world in which the state's role in the economy seemed to have been drastically revised.

That awareness was pummelled home more than a decade ago when, upon his release from prison, Mandela assured supporters that 'the nationalisation of the mines, banks, and monopoly industry is the policy of the ANC, and a change or modification of our views in this regard is inconceivable' (*Sowetan*, 5 March 1990). The reaction was both swift and distraught, with JSE traders, as one observer put it, 'unceremoniously falling out of bed' (Duncan Innes, quoted in Kentridge 1993) to join an anxious bear run. It was a rude wake-up call for a party (then still in the guise of a liberation organisation) that had paid scant attention to economics during its long struggle to overthrow the apartheid system.

Business economists and leaders were quick to exploit this area of historical neglect. A barrage of briefings, seminars, and junkets ensured that ANC leaders were brought up to speed with the 'hard truths' that faced a developing country in a world that was being reshaped by neo-liberal globalisation. The print media joined this pedagogic exercise with sweaty enthusiasm.

Resistance to or incredulity over these prescriptions was drained further by the disappearance of the key signposts available to left-of-centre political movements. Having neglected the economic realm for decades, the ANC's resistance levels were low, particularly in an era advertised as the 'end of history'.

This disorientating discovery was hardly reserved for the ANC alone. Deprived of their respective development paradigms, progressive movements across the world were thrown into disarray as their ideological moorings snapped and the compass points of yesteryear faded. Vexing them was 'the apparent failure of all programmes, old and new, for managing or improving the affairs of the human race' (Hobsbawm 1995: 563).

During the 1990s corresponding sensibilities steadily congealed in the top ranks of the ANC (and among the sources of advice it drew on), hardening into articles of faith. Scanning the party's economic pronouncements from the early 1990s onwards, one discovers a markedly consistent drift toward orthodoxy – a trajectory it has maintained in office despite the frantic protestations of close political allies. By way of explanation, policy-makers and politicians have emphasised the extent to which post-apartheid economic strategy constitutes a compelled accommodation of a global economic system capable of fiercely punishing any 'deviance'.[2]

In fact, the penny had dropped early for some ANC leaders. In 1991 Mandela was already telling an audience of business people in Pittsburgh, United States, that:

> ... the private sector must and will play the central and decisive role in the struggle to achieve many of [the transformation] objectives ...

let me assure you that the ANC is not an enemy of private enterprise ... we are aware that the investor will not invest unless he or she is assured of the security of their investment ... The rates of economic growth we seek cannot be achieved without important inflows of foreign capital. We are determined to create the necessary climate which the foreign investor will find attractive (quoted in Gelb 1998: 13).

Seven years later, Thabo Mbeki, speaking as president of the ANC, would – correctly – remind SACP delegates that:

In clear and straightforward language, the RDP identified a high deficit, a high level of borrowing, and the general taxation level as, to quote the RDP again, 'part of our macroeconomic problem' ... It is because our movement as a whole understood clearly the economic challenges we face, that it refused, as it worked on the RDP, to fall victim to a subjective and populist approach to the economy (1998: 4).

What had remained consistent throughout that period – and subsequently – was an acute sensitivity to the weaknesses of the South African economy, the deepening conviction that the power and sovereignty of national states had wilted dramatically, and a dogged faith in the rewards of acquiescence to neoliberal ideology.

This culminated in the macroeconomic Growth, Employment, and Redistribution (GEAR) strategy unveiled in mid-1996. Indeed, GEAR responded quite emphatically to the frailties highlighted in the RDP white paper of 1994 – including 'falling rates of return', 'isolation from the world economy', 'excessive protection', 'primary product export dependence', 'excessive concentration of economic power', 'government dissaving', 'low exports and high import propensity', low levels of domestic savings and investment, and low skills levels (department of finance 1996: 9, 28, 29).

Underpinning GEAR's new 'integrated strategy' was the need to address some of these economic weaknesses on the one hand, and a truncated reading of the available remedial options on the other. As a result, the plan's logic hinged on a bid to build market confidence by introducing adjustments in line with the edicts of the Washington Consensus. 'The immediate aim of the GEAR strategy,' one of its drafters would later write, 'was to signal to potential investors the government's (and specifically the ANC's) commitment to prevailing orthodoxy' (Gelb 1998: 18). Both friend and foe were polite enough to disguise the class bias of post-apartheid economic policies with phrases such as 'business-' and 'market-friendly'.

Invoking the goals of the RDP, the strategy entailed a package of stern adjustments allegedly aimed at achieving higher and more labour-absorbing economic growth, thereby reducing poverty levels. At the heart of the plan lay the following logic:

> The higher growth path depends in part on attracting foreign direct investment, but also requires a higher domestic saving effort. Greater industrial competitiveness, a tighter fiscal stance, moderation of wage increases, accelerated public investment, efficient service delivery and a major expansion of private investment are integral aspects of the strategy. An exchange rate policy consistent with improved international competitiveness, responsible monetary policies and targeted industrial incentives characterise the new policy environment. A strong export performance underpins the macroeconomic sustainability of the growth path (department of finance, 1996).

'Many major indicators point to the excellent work that has been done to place our country on a strong growth path,' Mbeki told parliament in early 2000, before praising 'the resilience, the effective restructuring, and therefore the improved international competitiveness of our economy' (*Mail & Guardian*, 4 February 2000). Yet it is only with obtuse measurements that GEAR's failure to achieve its major stated goals – growth, jobs, and redistribution – can be concealed.

Save for a temporarily stabilised balance of payments situation, a very low inflation rate (in late 1999 headline inflation reached its lowest level in 30 years – 5,2 per cent) and a sub-3 per cent budget deficit, the evidence for Mbeki's cheery verdict has been lacking.

Applying a new accounting framework, Statistics South Africa revised the weighting of sectoral contributions to GDP, which in mid-1999 returned a marginally rosier picture of GDP growth.[3] Thus the 'strong growth path' referred to by Mbeki was in fact 1,2 per cent GDP growth in 1999 (GEAR had predicted 4,9 per cent), slightly up from 1998's 0,6 per cent (against GEAR's 3,8 per cent). The director-general of finance, Maria Ramos, quickly declared the economy to be more buoyant and resilient than had previously been believed, and added that the new figures proved that South Africa was benefiting from globalisation (*Business Day*, 22 June 1999). Most exciting to government officials was the deduction that the fiscal deficit would duck below 3 per cent of GDP (surpassing GEAR's 3,3 per cent target).

Glossed over was the fact that non-agricultural output growth had dropped from a rejuvenated 3,9 per cent in 1995 to 0,1 per cent in 1998, while manufacturing output had shrunk by 1,7 per cent in 1998 before growing by 0,2 per cent in 1999. GEAR's architects had hoped that private sector investment would rise by more than 9 per cent a year in 1996–98, before soaring by 13,9 per cent and 17 per cent in 1999 and 2000 – with heftier public investment occurring on the back of those surges. At this fundamental level, the plan failed dismally. Real private sector investment dropped sharply – from a 6,1 per cent growth rate in 1996 to –0,7 per cent in 1998; overall, the sector's share of total fixed investment fell from 73 per cent to 68 per cent (Adelzadeh 1999: 2).

Except in the mining and construction sectors, the Reserve Bank noted, 'the private sector held back its fixed investment spending in all the other major sectors of economic activity' (SA Reserve Bank 1998: 10). A decade-long 'investment strike' by domestic capital was showing no signs of abating.

As a result, foreign direct investment (FDI) acquired a new allure, especially after soaring to US$1,7 billion in 1997. Unfortunately, the agreeable climate crafted for private investors failed to sustain those inflows: in 1998, FDI plunged to dismal levels – at $371 million, little more than half the 1996 level, placing South Africa behind Nigeria, Egypt, Tunisia, Algeria, Zimbabwe and Angola as the continent's top FDI recipients (*Business Day*, 28 September 1999).

The composition of capital inflows had also changed dramatically. Since 1995 South Africa had witnessed a dramatic rise in net short-term capital inflows, most of it destined for the bond and equity markets. From 1996 to 1998 their value increased fivefold, overshadowing FDI. Their volatile nature hit home in 1998 when almost $1 billion left the country in the third quarter, triggering serious exchange rate instability[4] – an episode repeated in April 2000. In a trenchant summary, the ANC's trade union ally, COSATU, noted:

> The first three quarters of 1999 saw a net outflow of FDI of R3,3 billion ($550 million). During the same period, net portfolio investment inflows of R46,7 billion ($7,6 billion) occurred. Foreign investment flows outside the fields of FDI and portfolio experienced a net outflow of R21,6 billion ($3,5 billion) during this time. This transactions suggests that our policies, particularly the high interest rate regime, are attractive to volatile portfolio investment, but does not encourage FDI, which is much more valuable for technology development and job creation. This trend also raises questions around the efficacy of exchange control liberalisation in the stated goal of attracting productive investment (COSATU 2000; dollar figures are calculated at an average 1999 exchange rate).

The most traumatic failure occurred on the job front, where not just GEAR but the government's economic policies overall abetted rather than arrested the job-shedding dynamics in the economy. GEAR had touted specific job creation targets, predicting 1,35 million new jobs by 2000, of which 833 000 would be created through GEAR adjustments: 308 000 through higher economic growth, 325 000 through 'changes in the flexibility of labour markets', and 200 000 through 'government-induced employment' (mainly infrastructural development and public works programmes).

Continuing a trend dating back to the 1980s, more than half a million (non-agricultural) jobs were lost between 1994 and 2000, caused by the introduction of labour-saving technologies, increased outsourcing, and a determined turn towards using casual and contract labour. Several hundred thousand more jobs were believed to have been lost on South African farms in the 1990s.

The official (non-agricultural) unemployment rate – calculated by Statistics SA – stood at 22,9 per cent in 1999. Once unemployed workers who had not sought work in the month prior to being polled were included, the 'expanded unemployment rate' rose to 37,6 per cent (from 31,5 per cent in 1994). Hardest hit were the sectors that contribute about 80 per cent of total formal non-agricultural employment: manufacturing, mining and quarrying, construction, and transport and electricity. According to COSATU (2000):

> The service sector, particularly financial services, has experienced modest growth in employment. Gold mining alone accounted for some 40 per cent of all formal job losses between June 1996 and March 1999. In the six months to March 1998, job losses in the industry came to almost 100 000, or over a quarter of jobs lost throughout the economy in the two years to March 1999 . . . Manufacturing on the other hand contributed 36 per cent of job losses in the period. It experienced the sharpest decline in the year to March 1998, when it lost 75 000 jobs.

It requires the sunniest of dispositions and prodigious creative flair to interpret such data as proof of economic 'resilience', 'effective restructuring', and 'improved international competitiveness'. Yet an emphatic continuity has defined economic policy from 1993–94 through Mandela's presidential term and into that of Mbeki. Shortly after becoming South Africa's second democratically elected president, Mbeki had assured the SA–USA Business and Finance Forum of his government's commitment to maintain:

> ... fiscal discipline, achieved through deficit reduction; continued liberalisation of exchange controls; accelerated reduction in tariffs; tax incentives to fund training; accelerated delivery on the backlog of social infrastructure; maintenance of a stable and competitive exchange rate; labour market reform to increase the absorptive capacity of the economy; and the privatisation and restructuring of state assets. The rationale behind our macro policy is based on the simple reason that we believe that macroeconomic stability is a precondition for economic growth and development. Fiscal discipline and curtailing inflation are necessary to restore confidence and create the basic environment within which growth can occur (1999a).[5]

That the real world hardly bristles with supportive evidence for this claim must, one assumes, be as obvious to Mbeki as it was to James K Galbraith – who, at around the same time, summed up the effects of orthodox economic adjustment worldwide as follows:

> Where are the continuing success stories of liberalisation, privatisation, deregulation, sound money, and balanced budgets? Where are the emerging markets that have emerged, the developing countries that have developed, the transition economies that have truly completed a successful and happy transition? Look closely. Look hard. They do not exist (1999: 2).

How is one to interpret this continuity? When addressing business, the government has portrayed GEAR as a strategic package that reflects its economic philosophy. To ANC members and left-wing critics, it has preferred to call it a 'stabilisation package' impelled by the currency plunge in early 1996 and the need to quickly secure a platform of 'sound fundamentals'. On the balance of evidence, the latter claim lacks credence. Neither is there much substance to the lament that GEAR represents a U-turn in ANC economic thinking. On the contrary, it has consummated a remarkably consistent drift toward orthodoxy, a passage that began quietly in 1991 but had become overt by mid-1993.[6] At that stage, one study of economic policy debates could note persuasively that 'the language and tone [of ANC and business policy documents] are so similar that at times they appear interchangeable' (Kentridge 1993: 26).

Visions of the state
Much has been written in search of explanations for the emergence of and

subsequent loyalty to a set of economic adjustments that, by any humane standards, have failed in South Africa – as in the rest of the world. I will not even attempt to summarise them here. Instead, it seems more rewarding to focus on a conception that presumably stands at the heart of post-apartheid economic policy: the roles and power of the national state in an era of globalisation. It should be obvious that this, in turn, implies a particular conception of state–capital relations.

The presumed limits to state power have been a consistent theme in ANC discourse since 1994. Depending on the issue at hand, those limits have been attributed to the presence of 'old order' bureaucrats in the post-apartheid state, the power-sharing formula that made possible the 1993 negotiated settlement, the difficulties in modifying and aligning state structures to new values and practices ('transforming' the state), and 'counterrevolutionary' machinations occurring within the state. However, in the case of economic policy the limits of state power are seen to circulate formidably in a twilight zone of 'investor sentiments' and 'market dynamics'. In late 1996 Mbeki was telling business leaders that:

> ... the policies and objectives embedded in the GEAR [plan] are a pragmatic balance struck between our domestic economic demands and the realities of the international context. These policies and objectives emerged after a thorough analysis of global trends and the specific conditions in our economy.

And in his political report to the ANC's 1997 national conference, Mandela repeatedly referred to globalisation, particularly the integration of capital markets, which 'make it impossible ... to decide national economic policy without regard for the likely response of the markets' (1997). Opening parliament two months later, he declared that 'there is no other route to sustainable development' other than the market-led policies adopted by his government (1998).

South Africa's economic policies were being managed, as the *Financial Mail* (21 May 1999) approvingly put it in an editorial, by 'ANC politicians who have graduated from freedom fighters to the real new world'.[7] Their rhetoric still orbited around a 'developmental state' that would co-ordinate a national economic strategy aimed at creating jobs and redistributing resources to the poor. But, in reality, economic policy was apparently grounded in the certitude that national states no longer commanded the power to intervene decisively in the economy. Thus in 1999 the minister of trade and industry, Alec Erwin, stated in an interview that the route of rapid industrialisation via strong state intervention followed in, for example, South Korea and Malaysia was unavailable to South Africa:

> A country such as South Africa, which started its economic reform in the 1990s, was prevented from using such interventionist methods by World Trade Organisation rules. Accordingly, we therefore tend to implement policy packages that are similar to those of the other advanced developing countries (*Global Dialogue* 1999: 19).

Erwin was hardly speaking only for himself when he claimed that a 'fairly common package' of economic measures had worked 'for virtually all economies that have grown significantly over the last 10–15 years'. That assertion, of course, had little basis in reality. Erwin acknowledged the exceptions of Brazil, China and India, to which he could have added Malaysia, South Korea, Taiwan and Thailand – effectively emptying his claim of substance.

But such empirical nit-picking is, in fact, besides the point. For, in line with dominant ideology, the government has bowed to the dictum that the fates of individual economies can no longer be decisively shaped by national states that stand shorn of the powers that made possible the various state-led developmental strategies of yesteryear. Rather, economies are beholden to the opaque mechanics of financial markets, the profit-maximising migration of transnational corporations (TNCs), and the strictures and interventions of transnational institutions such as the International Monetary Fund (IMF), World Bank, and World Trade Organisation (WTO). The scope for risk-taking or even selective 'violation' of orthodoxy is deemed minimal for an emerging market such as South Africa.

Perched on such a vantage point, one encounters functionaries of the 'developmental state' in South Africa unsurprisingly protesting its impotence. 'I want someone to tell me how the government is going to create jobs,' the minister of finance, Trevor Manuel, told journalists in 2000. 'It's a terrible admission, but governments around the world are impotent when it comes to creating jobs' (*The Sunday Independent*, 9 January 2000, quoted in *SouthScan* 2000).

Such assumptions have annoyed leftist critics no end. They have accused the ANC government of treating the state as a 'neutral' referee between classes and between other contending social forces. These criticisms grew particularly shrill in response to an anonymous ANC discussion document entitled 'The state and social transformation', circulated in late 1996, which proposed that:

> The democratic state must also seek to forge a democratic and equitable partnership as well as a working relationship between labour and capital in the interest of social stability, economic progress, reconstruction and development. In the context of the South African situation, the tension between labour and capital demands special attention by the democratic state . . .[8]

In a mordant rebuttal, the SACP's Blade Nzimande and Jeremy Cronin (1997) wrote that the ANC document envisaged 'the new democratic state as essentially "regulatory" . . . it sees the new state as a mediator between different "interest groups" in society, and particularly between "capital" and "labour".' Instead, they argued, the state should promote and reflect the leading status of the working class in the 'national democratic revolution' – a perspective that formed part of 'a very long tradition in the ANC'.

But the post-apartheid state seems unfairly indicted for adopting a neutral and arbitrating attitude towards capital. The relationship is, in fact, considerably more intimate. There is nothing new about, or any mystery attached to, this phenomenon. Free market policies such as those introduced in South Africa require prodigious degrees of state intervention: applying economic and social adjustments, enforcing them through bureaucratic *fiat*, reorganising the body social and body politic, and defending the adjustments against the reactions of discontented social forces.

This, one could respond, might hold for earlier epochs, but not the current era of globalisation. Yet the importance of the state in safeguarding the reproduction and political cohesion of capitalist society has probably increased rather than decreased in recent decades. This is because, as Samir Amin (1997: 12) has reminded us, where neo-liberal adjustments have been followed 'the link between the arena of reproduction and accumulation and that of political and social control' tends to fray. While the reproduction and accumulation of capital is effected by an increasingly deterritorialised and integrated capitalist class, political and social control still resides at the national level (and is achieved and maintained mainly by the state). This places even greater responsibilities on the national state as the guarantor of stability, as well as the social and ideological reproduction of the economic system:

> [F]ar from dispensing with national states' functions and services, the extended reproduction of the accumulation of international capital is totally dependent on their constant intervention . . . [T]he political and ideological cohesion of social formations, still materialised only

> by and through states, provides the basis for reproducing the (interchangeable) coherent socio-economic and legal environments necessary for any productive organisation (Tsoukalas 1999: 67).

The notion of the impotent state is therefore as much a fiction as is the claim that it acts (or can act) as an aloof arbitrator or 'neutral referee' in a class society such as South Africa's. Rather than turn the national state into the proverbial 98-pound weakling on the global turf of pumped-up capital, the centrality of its role boosts its relative autonomy, and the capacity to engineer trade-offs with capital. In fact, the ability to introduce progressive labour legislation and affirmative action policies in South Africa since 1994 is best understood in this manner – especially when we recall that those measures stood at a sharp angle to orthodox injunctions (which, in other respects, were increasingly being heeded).

An alternative view has been promoted by Manuel Castells and Martin Carnoy (1999: 32); in their view, 'the relative autonomy of the state is fading away, to a large extent because relatively autonomous states chose their own historical demise' by adopting neo-liberal economic policies. But a less dismal and reductionist verdict seems more appropriate.

First, it is worth recalling Immanuel Wallerstein's reminder that state autonomy never was as rollicking and extensive as it is now being remembered. With reference to the past century and a half, he has noted that:

> All modern states, without exception, exist within the framework of the interstate system and are constrained by its rules and its politics. The productive activities within all modern states, without exception, occur within the framework of the capitalist world-economy and are constrained by its priorities and its economics ... Shouting that one is autonomous is a bit like Canute commanding the tides to recede (1996).

In short, a variety of shifting restrictions has limited and complicated the autonomy of the modern national state since the mid-nineteenth century. No doubt, in the era of globalisation, the relative autonomy of the state is circumscribed by new factors (most dramatically by the vast networks in which financial capital circulates), but the extent and character of those restrictions still vary from country to country. Moreover, they depend both on conjunctural global factors and on factors specific to individual countries. Thus Malaysia was able in 1998 to commit 'heresy' and reintroduce capital controls because of the extraordinary levels of savings in the country *and* the growing anxiety among the G7 industrialised countries (and supranational institutions such as the World Bank and IMF) about spreading financial instability triggered by the Asian crisis of 1997–98.⁹ Subsequent deepening tensions between the World Bank and IMF have (temporarily) widened the manoeuvring space of 'developing' countries such as South Africa. It was such space for shifting innovation and risk-taking that both generations of Asian 'tigers' so adroitly used from the 1960s onwards.¹⁰

All of which underlines the question of why macroeconomic policy in South Africa since 1994 has remained so consistently conservative. As argued elsewhere (Marais 1998), the need for a relatively stable social and political platform for revived accumulation in South Africa was a key factor in the 1990 thaw, and the country's eventual passage to democracy. The ANC government assumed and has steadfastly stuck to the task of building stability (which, after all, does not only benefit capital) and administering economic policies that correspond to the modernising imperatives of South African capitalism.

Here it is worth pausing to recall that it was not simply an abstract 'economy' that was withering on the vine from the late 1970s onwards, but a specific form of accumulation. The country's largest conglomerates had all but exhausted local avenues for expansion, having constructed huge and unwieldy corporate empires straddling any number of sectors. Imprinted in those pyramids of cross-ownership were the shrunken horizons of a besieged national economy. A comparative international isolation achieved by the anti-apartheid opposition on the one hand, and structured into an inwardly-biased economy on the other, was at odds with the liberalised, transnational routes of capital accumulation being threaded across the globe. South African capital had been shunted on to a neglected siding of the world economy. Many local corporations faced the prospect of the grave devalorisation of capital – a calamity as ominous as the political crisis, and, importantly, one intimately linked to it. For South African conglomerates (especially, but not only, those most active in the financial and mining sectors), economic liberalisation was essential if they were to wrestle free of a national economy that offered little scope for sustained expansion. In short, they had a pressing need to 'globalise'.

The ANC government's embrace of economic orthodoxy was designed precisely to help steer South African capital out of that *cul-de-sac*. Rather than a grudging surrender to the vagaries of the 'real world', its economic policies represent a conscious and expectant attempt to rescue – and, importantly, help restructure the operating conditions for – South African capital, and thereby hopefully enabling it to address some of the key demands and rights of the South African majority. In an era in which the markers of old have been all but erased, that recourse seems perfectly understandable (though not at all inevitable). It expresses specific choices that address the requirements of powerful sections of South African capital, and the perceived realities of the world economic system. Yet the alibi for the economic growth path followed has remained the ingenuous claim that denuded state autonomy and sovereignty preclude any alternative, prompting academic Philip Nel to note perceptively that the:

> ... emphasis on the loss of sovereignty makes it possible to shift some of the blame for domestically unpopular policies to faceless international forces (while convincing) doubters that what is happening is to a large extent inevitable (1999: 23).

Much as business leaders might grumble about the slow pace of privatisation, or the government's reluctance (at the time of writing, at least) to render the labour market even more flexible, they can hardly be oblivious to the extent to which their chief prerogatives have been answered since 1994. The globalising route of survival largely has been opened. More than 75 per cent of capital controls have been lifted, enabling corporations to extend their operations (and, more importantly, transplant their finances) beyond South Africa's geopolitical boundaries. Concomitantly, pressures to ensure productive, domestic investment (initially at lower rates of return) have been restrained. Substituting for those largely absent pressures has been an emphasis on luring foreign capital to South African shores – or, more accurately, to the JSE. The bulk of FDI since 1994 has gone towards mergers and acquisitions, thereby integrating South African corporations more deeply into the global circuits of capitalism. The penchant for public–private sector partnerships serves a similar function.

While all this has manifestly benefited the interests of white South African capital,[11] it would be wrong to understand it as a mere submission to those interests. Many of these liberalising measures have been meant to abet and propel the emergence of a black 'patriotic' bourgeoisie – an important, though seldom trumpeted, subproject of the 'national democratic revolution', as Mbeki told the 1999 annual conference of the Black Management Forum:

> As part of the realisation of the aim to eradicate racism in our country, we must strive to create and strengthen a black capitalist class. Because we come from among the black oppressed, many among us feel embarrassed to state this goal as nakedly as we should ... Accordingly, we walk as far and as fast as we can from the notion that

> the struggle against racism in our country must include the objective of creating a black bourgeoisie . . . indeed, the government must come to the aid of those among the black people who might require such aid in order to become entrepreneurs (1999b).[12]

Two-and-a-half years earlier, Mbeki had told the Cape Chamber of Commerce and Industry that 'the democratic government can and must play a significant role in the empowerment of black business. Through our procurement programme we should be in a position to provide markets for goods and services supplied by black businesses' (1997).

Vested in the rise of an African capitalist class is the expectation that racial solidarity (in this case with the African poor) would eclipse class solidarity and become the wellspring of a 'patriotic' capitalism. Its profit-seeking activities could be harmonised with an overriding commitment to help improve the living standards and opportunities of the African poor. Indeed, this African capitalist class is assigned a key role in enabling the post-apartheid state to meet its transformatory pledges to broader society.

It is difficult to reconcile the notion of an impotent state with such expectations and pledges. Moreover, it is not only through state tenders, contracts, and licenses that the black bourgeoisie's rise is being leveraged. Liberalising economic policies have been central. In a congested economy, the lifting of capital controls and approval of offshore listings has promoted a spate of 'natural' unbundling in the corporate sector as globalising firms sell off non-core assets in order to raise capital and streamline their operations. New black firms have been able to move into these economic spaces. Privatisation is opening new possibilities for the growth of black capital in conjunction with foreign capital and/or the state (in the form of private-public partnerships). Meanwhile, the prevailing dogma of wage restraint (which is demonstrably advanced by the state) and the steady pruning of the power of organised labour is helping to ease the conditions under which black firms operate.[13]

The hope that black capitalists will add a zealous and sustained sense of duty toward the African poor to their bottom line seems destined to be forlorn – a forecast that applies to the national bourgeoisie in general. This has little to do with the subjective will of individual capitalists, since the national bourgeoisie's attenuated role stems from its structural location in the global capitalist system which severely restricts its ability to muster an effective autonomy *vis-à-vis* international capital. In this regard, it is useful to reflect on Tsoukalas's description of the national bourgeoisie as:

the emerging and thereafter dominant fraction of a domestically operating capital which was already permeated by, and was thus reproducing, 'external' inter-imperialist contradictions . . . [I]t is now even more true that the contradictions between fractions of capital within national states are 'internationalised'. As a consequence, the disarticulation and heterogeneity of national bourgeoisies is further accentuated. Indeed, it may be doubtful whether the very term corresponds to a specific social reality (1999: 57, 60).

Paradoxically, such an analysis emphasises the importance of the state as a key variable in national economic and development strategies, since it befalls the national state to seek and achieve a 'reasonable' developmental, social, and political equilibrium between the needs of capital and those of other social forces.[14] Crucially, this does not demand a zero-sum equation; but it does entail choices about the extent, nature, and distribution of gains and costs. Bearing in mind the circumscribing context in which they were made, post-apartheid economic policies nevertheless represent specific choices or judgement calls by the ANC government. They can be related to a combination of related imperatives:

- the appeasement of South African and international capital in order to secure support for and the stability of the democratic transition;
- the (perceived) need to reverse economic stagnation by aligning economic policies to internationally dominant ideology;
- the improvement of the social and economic conditions of life of the African majority; and
- the objective of aiding the rapid rise of the African bourgeoisie – in order to address one aspect of the 'national question', and to assist the democratic state in its efforts to heed its pledges towards the African majority.

Therefore, the trajectory of post-apartheid economic policies seems too consistent to be explained as the result of momentary panic (GEAR as a stabilisation package, for instance), or a sudden awakening to the alleged 'realities' of the world (the impotent state). Rather, it tracks a selected series of adjustments with which political leaders and policy-makers have sought to reconcile a range of objectives. These adjustments fit on a continuum of ANC economic thinking that can be traced back to 1992. The notion of a sea change in June 1996 (when GEAR was introduced) enjoys little supporting evidence.

In the economic realm, the supposed shift from a 'Mandela' to an 'Mbeki' era in fact marks a remarkably consistent process of adaptation and refinement of policy. But that is not to say the two 'eras' are interchangeable. The qualitative difference lies in the *ideological* frames in which specific, more or less consistent, economic choices have been cast.[15]

Whereas in the so-called Mandela phase, post-apartheid South Africa's economic policies were promoted (or defended, depending on the audience) as stabilising measures; under Mbeki's presidency they have been given the status of long-term adjustments to new global realities. Indicative of this were his remarks to a meeting of the ANC's general council in July 2000:

> [W]e have to identify our global comparative advantages, to assist us in determining the sectors of the economy in which we have to focus; having done this, and considered all other relevant matters, we have to ensure that we attract the necessary investment into these sectors, without being shy of investigating such incentives as may be needed; this will have to be done in a manner that ensures that such productive establishments as are established are internationally competitive; such competitiveness requires that we remain at the cutting edge with regard to science and technology as well as management and work organisation . . .

This thinking closely matches the main themes of 'third way' experiments elsewhere in the world (including Brazil). On the one hand, it is self-consciously located on the left of the political spectrum; on the other, it claims that those categories are outmoded. As advertised, it is an attempt to salvage and update some of the values of the old left in a context where socialist and state-welfarist projects appear to be unattainable options, and where novel challenges have to be met. Hence, the ANC's propagation of a 'New Person' and a 'New Patriot' that are able to adapt trusted traditions and principles to the vagaries of the new global order.[16] Economic adjustments therefore become couched in a broader idiom of modernisation and adaptation that is aimed at reconciling rights and responsibilities, equity and enterprise.

The traditional left, meanwhile, is deemed to be an anachronism. According to dominant diagnosis, it is stricken with a lamentable lack of realism, and an inability to offer alternatives.[17] The world economy is seen to accommodate only one model of development: export-oriented production based on flexible labour markets, lower real and social wages, the privatisation of the public sector, freer trade, and unfettered capital flows.

Like other 'third way' fellow travellers, the ANC government under Mbeki's stewardship operates within a thought realm defined by 'an incapacity, self-induced or otherwise, to imagine autonomous forms of domestic planning and economic intervention' (Tsoukalas 1999: 62). As a consequence, economic policy debates occur strictly *within* the frame of the dominant ideology. Actual debate, as Greg Albo has noted, is 'limited to which specific constraints should be acted upon and the relative speed of flexible adjustment of market processes' (1997: 7).

During the 'Mandela era', conservative economic policies were promoted along with other 'compromises' as necessary ingredients for the stability and conciliation that could safeguard the democratic transition. Put differently, they were advanced as stabilising measures. The policies have remained consistent, but the official discourse surrounding them has shifted since 1997.

Although subject to periodic calibration, post-apartheid economic policies are now advanced as *fundamental* adjustments that form part of and correspond to an expansive bid to adjust South Africa to the imperatives of a new global order. Not only the democratic transition but the developmental fate of 'small states such as ours' (Mbeki 2000) is seen to depend on adherence to a set of policy prescriptions that are presumed to apply uniformly across the globe. Significantly, those policies are deemed to answer to the 'process of globalisation [which] is an objective outcome of the development of the productive forces that create wealth'.

The liberty to violate (some of) those prescriptions is no longer seen to be available to individual states: 'The globalisation of the economy resulting among other things in rapid movements of huge volumes of capital across the globe objectively also has the effect of limiting the possibility of states to take unilateral decisions,' in Mbeki's phrasing.

One of the main discursive shifts since 1997 has therefore been the secondary status accorded to the national state in the pursuit of a 'better life for all'. In fundamental respects, that quest is now lodged at the level of the global where the ANC government has to make its 'own input into the universal struggle for the establishment of a new world order that must work in the interests of the ordinary working people, including the billions in our country, Africa and the South who are poor and underdeveloped'. The global thereby replaces the national as a primary 'site of struggle' while, at the same time, functioning as an alibi for the domestic administration of economic (and social) policies that – on current evidence – demonstrably favour the accumulation of capital over the pursuit of socio-economic justice and equity.

Notes

1. This is underlined by the vehemence with which the policy is opposed from within the ANC and by its main political allies, the SACP and COSATU.
2. A charitable description of a compendium of adjustments that, in fact, lack the formative and coherent ingredients of a 'strategy'. For an explanation of this verdict, see Marais 2000, chapters five and six.
3. For the first time, government infrastructure provision (roads, bridges, dams, etc) were incorporated into calculations, while informal activities in the respective sectors have also allegedly been better measured. The latter include the (private) commuter taxi industry, the use of firewood, micro lending, and traditional health practices.
4. High interest rates act as a magnet for short-term capital.
5. At the time of writing, there was still no reason to doubt that pledge. The fixing of a very low inflation target band in early 2000 ensures that monetary policy will remain restrictive. There is no sign of fiscal policy being relaxed. More broadly, government has vowed that privatisation shall be accelerated and expanded, while the labour movement increasingly finds itself fighting rearguard battles to defend the legislative and regulatory gains since 1994.
6. This process and the debates that have accompanied it have been described in detail elsewhere – see, for example, Bond (2000) and Marais (1998).
7. The editorial labelled critics of GEAR as 'naïve believers in the ability of government intervention – even worse, activism – to get an economy moving'. Months later, the minister of finance, Trevor Manuel, parroted this sentiment in an interview with the *The Sunday Independent* (9 January 2000).
8. The document is believed to have been written by Vusi Mavimbela, a former adviser to Thabo Mbeki.
9. For more on this, see Wade and Veneroso (1998).
10. In their cases, of course, the space was created by their geopolitical importance during the cold war, the related support and indulgence of their development experiments by Washington, and access to Japanese investment capital, to mention only a few of the shifting factors at work.
11. It has done so in many ways, and sometimes to unexpected degrees. Thus the demise of apartheid saw Afrikaner firms' share of JSE capitalisation climb at its fastest rate in 30 years – soaring from 24 per cent in 1996 to 35 per cent in 1999; see *Business Times*, 30 January 2000.
12. This theme was stridently reaffirmed during the ANC's general council conference in Port Elizabeth during July 2000. For a terse look at the ANC's historical relationship toward black capitalists see Sipho Maseko's misleadingly headlined 'The real rise of the black middle class' (*Mail & Guardian*, 21 May 1999).
13. Until recently the purview of government leaders and (naturally) organised business, by mid-2000 such counsel was also being given by the ANC leadership – including the former trade union leader and current ANC secretary-general, Kgalema Motlanthe.
14. The pertinence of Amin's summary (1997) of the contradiction between the realms of the reproduction of capital and those of social and political control is obvious.

15. 'Ideological frames' are not meant to signify mere justification, but rather the frameworks of understanding in which policies are publicly couched.
16. In the words of the journalist John Matisonn (2000), 'this new person... has the political values of self-sacrifice and dedication to the poor' but will 'also study economics and enter the new information economy. He or she will develop industries based on a cold, hard look at our comparative advantage over other countries when it comes to producing specific products, and be able to take a tough line on destructive strikes that hurt SA's image and competitiveness.'
17. That this does not square with the facts does not seem to matter. Nevertheless, see www.cosatu.org.za for some economic policy alternatives.

References

Adelzadeh, A. 1999. The costs of staying the course. *Ngqo!*, journal of the National Institute for Economic Policy. Johannesburg. June.
Albo, G. 1997. A world market of opportunities? Capitalist obstacles and left economic policy. In L Panitch (ed), *Socialist register 1997: ruthless criticism of all that exists*. Suffolk: The Merlin Press.
Amin, S. 1997. Regionalisation in the third world – in response to the challenge of polarising globalisation (with special reference to Africa and the Arab world). Mimeo. Dakar: Third World Forum.
ANC. 1996. The state and social transformation. Discussion document. November. Reprinted in *African Communist*, 146, 1st quarter 1997.
Bond, P. 2000, *Elite transition: from apartheid to neoliberalism in South Africa*. London: Pluto Press.
Business Day. 1999. Foreign direct investment plummets. 28 September.
———. 1999. GDP defies expectations. 22 June.
Business Times. 2000. Black hold on JSE slips as Afrikaners strengthen. 30 January.
Carnoy, M and Castells, M. 1999. Globalisation, the knowledge society, and the network state: Poulantzas at the millennium. Paper, University of Athens, 30 September – 2 October.
COSATU. 2000. Public response by COSATU to the 2000/1 budget. Johannesburg. March.
Department of finance. 1996. *Growth, employment and redistribution: a macro-economic strategy*. Pretoria.
Financial Mail. 1999. Spare us from this collectivist twaddle. 21 May.
Galbraith, JK. 1999. The crisis of globalisation. *Dissent*, 46 (3), Summer.
Gelb, S. 1999. The politics of macroeconomic policy reform in South Africa. Symposium paper, 18 September. History workshop of the University of Witwatersrand, Johannesburg.
Global Dialogue. 1999. Interview with Alec Erwin. 4 (1), April. Johannesburg: Institute for Global Dialogue.
Government of South Africa. 1994. *RDP white paper*. Pretoria.

Hobsbawm. E. 1995. *Age of extremes: the short twentieth century*. London: Abacus.
Kentridge, M. 1993. *Turning the tanker: the economic debate in South Africa*. Johannesburg: Centre for Policy Studies.
Mail & Guardian. 2000. Mbeki bullish on economy, names top advisers. 4 February. Mail & Guardian Online. http://www.mg.co.za.
Mandela, N. 1991. Continuation lecture. University of Pittsburgh, 6 December 1991.
———. 1997. Address to the closing session of the 50th national conference of the ANC. 20 December, Mafikeng.
———. 1998. Address to parliament. 6 February, Cape Town.
Marais, H. 1998. *South Africa: limits to change – the political economy of transition*. Cape Town and London: University of Cape Town Press and Zed Books.
Maseko, S. 1999. The real rise of the black middle class. *Mail & Guardian*. 21 May.
Matisonn, J. 2000. ANC drags itself struggling into the new age. *The Sunday Independent*. 16 July.
Mbeki, T. 1996. Address by the deputy president, TM Mbeki, on the occasion of the annual president's award for export achievement. 26 November.
———. 1997. Address by deputy president Thabo Mbeki to the Cape Chamber of Commerce and Industry's annual banquet. Somerset West. 15 March.
———. 1998. Statement of the President of the ANC, Thabo Mbeki, at the 10th Congress of the SA Communist Party. Johannesburg. 2 July.
———. 1999a. Address to the SA–ISA Business and Finance Forum. New York. 23 September.
———. 1999b. Address to the annual conference of the Black Management Forum. Kempton Park. 20 November.
———. 2000. Keynote address to the National General Council. Port Elizabeth, 12 July. http://www.anc.org.za/ancdocs/history/mbeki.
Nel, P. 1999. Conceptions of globalisation among the South African elite. *Global Dialogue* 4 (1). Johannesburg: Institute for Global Dialogue.
Nzimande, B and Cronin, J. 1997. We need transformation, not a balancing act. *African Communist*, 146, 1st quarter.
SA Reserve Bank. 1998. *Annual economic report 1998*. Pretoria.
SouthScan. 2000. Left blamed for economic failures as Manuel woos foreign investors. 15 (1), 14 January.
Streek, B. 2000. Mbeki bullish on economy, names top advisers. Mail & Guardian Online. 4 February. http://www.mg.co.za.
Tsoukalas, K. 1999. Globalisation and the 'executive committee': reflections on the contemporary capitalist state. In L Panitch and C Leys (eds), *Socialist register 1999: global capitalism versus democracy*. Suffolk: The Merlin Press.
Wade, R and Veneroso, F. 1998. The gathering world slump and the battle over capital controls. *New Left Review*, 228. London.
Wallerstein, I. 1996. The ANC and South Africa: the past and future of liberation movements in the world system. Address to South African Sociological Association, Durban, 7 July.

CHAPTER 4

Does the emperor really have no clothes?
Thabo Mbeki and ideology

SAHRA RYKLIEF

There are a range of contradictory opinions of Thabo Mbeki. He has been described as liberal, imperial, enigmatic, ambiguous, opaque, and – most consistently of all, especially by his defenders – accommodating, pragmatic, and middle of the road. In a collection of comments in a recent analysis (Corrigan 1999: 75–85) he is described, *inter alia*, as consistent, inconsistent and/or ambiguous, chameleonic, and manipulative. He is also often described as primarily a strong manager, one who prefers technical solutions, and one who seeks accommodation without due regard to ideological fault-lines – all of these suggesting that he is ideologically and politically weak.

These incompatible and often unflattering opinions have been reinforced by Mbeki's own actions in the face of concerted opposition. Most significant is his stubborn defence of a non-orthodox position on the cause of HIV/AIDS, and his ambivalent/ambiguous stance on treatment of the disease. His government has introduced measures to lower the price of essential medicines through the Substance Control Amendment Act, aimed at making drugs more affordable and accessible, thereby invoking court action against it by the major pharmaceutical companies, yet proceeded to drag its heels over offering treatment to pregnant mothers suffering from HIV/AIDS, thereby provoking court action against it by domestic civil movements.

Mbeki has tacitly supported the undemocratic Mugabe government on the one hand, while agreeing to Zimbabwe's suspension from the Commonwealth on the other. In the case of the Ramaphosa/Phosa/Sexwale security débâcle, he responded with extreme paranoia to the slightest rumour of a challenge to the ANC leadership. Although much of the evidence that has shaped public opinion of Mbeki is purely anecdotal, it has undoubtedly had a negative impact on his image, and may well help to weaken popular support, from the left and the right, for the ANC presidency in general.

However, the strengths and weaknesses of political rule are not determined by the actions or even the integrity of political leaders alone. The ANC's suitability as a ruling party, as well as Mbeki's as party leader and president, depends more strongly upon the former's ideological consistency in respect of those issues that are most germane to the hegemonic role of capital in South Africa. The ANC's success (which is monumental, in terms of South African history) lies in the fact that it has, for the first time, brought about capitalist rule – with the economic and social power of the capitalist class remaining intact – based on overwhelming popular electoral consent.

In this chapter it will be argued that, like his predecessor, Nelson Mandela, Mbeki cannot be viewed in isolation from the ANC, and that any opinion of his ideology cannot be concretised without examining his role in the ideological development of the ruling party. Neither can an ANC government be viewed in isolation from the ideological development of ruling parties in general, whether popular or not, in this era of international neo-liberal hegemony.

Yet the relationship between a party and its leader is not a simple one. It is primarily affected by context – economic, social, and ideological pressures from without and within – but also by the leader's character, traits, and personal convictions. A case in point is the National Party of the late 1980s, which had to depose its own creation of that stormy decade, the 'strong man' PW Botha, before it could formalise negotiations for constitutional change. Perhaps a more pertinent example is Mandela himself, who personified the ANC in its carefully negotiated progression to government. The strength of Mandela's character, personal history, and ideology was crucially important for the maintenance of a stable capitalist economic system and class relations in the transition to a South Africa governed by the ANC. Throughout the transition, it helped to maintain working class trust in and loyalty towards the ANC as well as alleviate the fears of the white middle classes, pampered and pandered to during the decades of apartheid, and frightened of black majority rule. So the question becomes: is Mbeki a suitable leader for the ANC in the current context?

Mbeki has been president of South Africa since June 1999. As deputy president prior to that, he became increasingly prominent in the executive as Mandela prepared to retire. Within the first few months of his presidency, he introduced numerous changes: merging his former office into the president's office, restructuring the cabinet by clustering certain ministerial committees, appointing hand-picked directors-general, and setting up the

Policy Co-ordinating Advisory Services to screen all policies emerging from the ministries.

These changes have led to speculations of an 'imperial presidency' (Jacobs 1999), a charge facilitated by Mbeki's often high-handed response to criticism or conflicting political views, as well as by the craven praise and paranoid defence of him by his inner circle. However, we need to clarify whether this restructuring programme primarily emanated from Mbeki's own persona, or whether it was impelled by the ruling party's incremental evolution into a party of neo-liberalism, requiring greater centralisation of decision-making, and greater insulation from popular pressure. A brief look at the relatively recent ideological evolution of the ANC, and Mbeki's role in this respect, may shed some light on these issues.

Mbeki and the ideological regression of the ANC

In the latter half of the 1980s the success achieved by the apartheid state in crushing the mass internal uprising and arresting the ingress of guerrilla fighters via the frontline states caused the ANC in exile to focus increasingly on reaching a negotiated settlement. As a central figure in the ANC's diplomatic wing, Mbeki's stature in the ANC grew significantly as a result of the increasing prominence of the organisation's diplomatic activities.

As political secretary to Oliver Tambo, and head of the information desk of the ANC in exile, Mbeki was a core member of the party's international relations staff and of delegations that met representatives of a range of governments as well as South African business and government during the mid- to late 1980s.

He publicly spearheaded the ANC's search for a negotiated solution, at a time when the popular movement inside the country was intensifying its struggle against the increasingly repressive Botha regime. This necessitated a great deal of double-speak from the ANC, defended by Mbeki in an interview with the *Observer* in 1986 in which he explained that there was no contradiction in the ANC calling for an intensification of the offensive against the government while at the same time declaring a preparedness to negotiate, as the intent was not to overthrow the government but to effect a Lancaster House-type settlement (quoted in McKinley 1997: 87).

This was one of a series of newspaper interviews in 1986 in which he outlined an ANC strategy to work with business leaders, homelands leaders – whom he had described as 'parasites' in a Marxist-inspired speech in 1978 (Mbeki 1998a: 23–4) – and Afrikaner dissidents, in order to increase opposition to the apartheid state from within its own ranks (Waldmeir 1997: 66). Thus, from as early as the mid-1980s onwards, at a time when the internal anti-apartheid movement was still intent on insurrection and the overthrow of the apartheid state, Mbeki revealed, as spokesman of the ANC in exile, an ideological shift away from the revolutionary aspirations expressed in his 1978 speech, as well as an alienation from the general insurrectionary sentiment of the black majority inside South Africa.

Waldmeir even casts doubts on whether Mbeki was expressing a generalised position within the leadership layers of the ANC in exile. She claims that, with the exception of Tambo, most leaders were opposed to his position, favouring instead the seizure of state power, and that there were persistent rumours at that time that Mbeki was an 'enemy agent' (83). Whether this was so or not, the leadership of the ANC seemed to move fairly rapidly to a positive position on negotiations, perhaps spurred on by the persistent courtship by representatives of capital. PW Botha's disastrous 'Rubicon' speech in 1985 united embattled South African capitalists in their opposition to continued National Party rule, and sent them off on a frantic search for a credible alternative, which the ANC provided through its preparedness to negotiate on terms acceptable to the ruling class (Ryklief 1996: chapter 4).

Although Mbeki seems to have played a central role in preparing the ANC for this new role, the shift in strategic emphasis and the accompanying growth of conservative thought within its ranks were facilitated by several external factors as well. The most important was the weakness of mass organisations inside South Africa after successive states of emergency. An insurrectionary overthrow of the state no longer seemed viable to the exiled movement. Moreover, the ANC in exile depended heavily on international support, and was therefore susceptible to pressure from the increasingly hegemonic major capitalist states, strengthened by the disintegration of the Eastern bloc.

Despite the ANC's relatively early shift away from insurrection towards negotiation, the organisation enjoyed – in the years immediately following its renewed legality in the early 1990s – a brief historical moment of open debate and ideological diversity, and an immense growth in popularity. This was the inevitable result of the cultural impact on the ANC of the anti-apartheid movement inside South Africa, which had been strongly influenced by the socialist-inspired aspirations and traditions of the mass organisations and struggles of the 1980s. This culture coexisted uneasily with the middle-class-controlled, hierarchical, and clientelist exiled structures, but this coexistence was assisted by the 'spirit of *glasnost*', which strongly influenced left-wing organisations after the fall of the Soviet Union and the introduction of *perestroika*.

However, that moment of diversity soon passed. The protracted negotiations resulted in a growing convergence between the perspectives of the

ANC leadership and those of the ideologues of capital, most specifically on economic issues, which has been further consolidated during the ANC's period in government. In the space of a few years after the formulation of a social democratic programme at the Harare economic policy conference in 1990, the ANC beat a hasty retreat from the ideology underpinning its popular mandate, formulated in the early days of legality.

Popular faith in the ANC rested on the promised reconfiguration of South Africa's social and economic order in the interest of the impoverished majority. The party inspired a fierce and popular loyalty, given that it had proven its historical bona fides to the majority through decades of resistance to apartheid rule. This popularity and loyalty became entrenched through the idea, if not the much-reworked substance, of the Reconstruction and Development Programme (RDP), and especially its prioritisation of jobs, housing, education, health, and welfare in the new, democratic, South Africa.

Yet by 1994 the ANC took up the task of government fully committed to the ideological obligation of most capitalist governments in this period, namely to subsume the service of popular goals under the interests of global capitalism. This was consolidated in the commitment to fiscal and monetary austerity in the final draft of the RDP, the platform of the ANC in the 1994 elections.

During this period of negotiations, Mbeki's influence in the party become more decisive. He played a central role in formulating the Harare Declaration, which cleared the way for armed hostilities to stop and official negotiations to begin. More significantly, he presented the call for the suspension of the ANC's armed struggle to its consultative conference in 1990, and argued strongly for the suspension of sanctions at the 1991 Durban ANC conference (Mbeki 1998a: xx–xxi).

These measures were primarily responsible for proving to conservative political forces, nationally and internationally, that the ANC, despite its image as the main opposition force in the often bloody mass uprisings of the 1980s, could be reasonable and accommodating.

Despite his prominence during the pre-negotiation phase, Mbeki did not play a central role in thrashing out a settlement during the protracted, and often contentious, negotiations leading to the interim constitution. He participated in the working group on transitional government arrangements, and is cited as being responsible, in 1992, for first mooting the 'sunset clauses' and a government of national unity (Mbeki 1998a: xxi). He also led the ANC delegations that brought the Freedom Front, led by Constand Viljoen, and the IFP into the settlement. In 1996 Viljoen praised Mbeki as the person responsible for protecting the cultural and minority interests of all groups

(Corrigan 1999: 76). And the NP negotiator Tertius Delport has credited him with accommodating the NP's demands for checks and balances in respect of negotiated agreements on local government (77–8).

Given the above, it is clear that, during the past decade, Mbeki has played a key role in formulating and propagating a succession of strategic and tactical policy choices within the ANC. Ideologically, his preferred policies demonstrate, firstly, a strong inclination towards a conservative rather than a radical solution to mass insurrection, even at a time when the eventual outcome of heightened popular conflict against a discredited state was by no means certain.

Secondly, he has demonstrated a propensity for acceding to measures (such as the 'sunset clauses' and local government constraints) that, even in a capitalist framework, placed considerable and unnecessary constraints on the first, critical, phase of a new government struggling to prove its bona fides to a long-suffering majority population that had brought it to power. Mbeki's concern lay with proving the ANC's bona fides to a minority determined to retain as much power as possible, rather than to the majority. Undoubtedly, the necessity of securing the interests and winning the approval of the international capitalist powers was a strong element in these negotiations as well.

Thirdly, he has displayed a capacity to stick to and eventually push through highly ideologically charged and initially extremely unpopular positions in his party, and to patiently wear down opposition and create conditions that have facilitated consensus. As stated earlier, the rightward ideological progression of the entire ANC leadership did not result from Mbeki's efforts alone. However, his role in this progression does not display signs of personal weakness or inconsistency.

Lastly, the policy choices fronted by Mbeki in the newly constituted ANC structures inside the country in the early 1990s as well as in COSATU were by no means uncontroversial. From the constitutional guidelines – released by the ANC's national executive committee (NEC) in 1988 – onwards, they were strongly and widely resisted by activists. Yet Mbeki seldom took on the task of reconciling such resistance, leaving this persuasive role to leaders such as Joe Slovo, Chris Hani, Jeremy Cronin, Raymond Suttner, Cyril Ramaphosa, Tokyo Sexwale and, of course, Mandela. Mbeki was no populist leader, and seemed unable to make an impression on black South African militants steeled in battles against the apartheid regime.

Yet his rank in the party hierarchy remained undisputed, and the popular acknowledgement of his place in the leadership by the rank and file unquestionable. Since 1991 he has always featured at the top of the leadership elections at ANC conferences. His integral involvement in the evolution of these policies, his capacity to argue them coherently, and, moreover, his much-touted pragmatism and ability to listen carefully and respond soberly should have made him one of the primary candidates for openly and publicly defending the ANC's concessions in a range of popular and party discussion forums.

Why was this not so? Could it be that Mbeki could not discourse with South African militants on their home ground, in their own terms? Could it be that the language they spoke was too foreign to him, their aspirations too distant and unreachable?

If the answer to these questions is yes, then it suggests that Mbeki is not as much a pragmatist as a conservative, both politically and personally. His 'visionary' policies and reputed charm held little appeal to the militants of the early 1990s, whose memories of recent, brutal, repression by the NP government and the super-exploitation of the predominantly black working class by South African business inclined them to press forward whenever they held an advantage, and not concede defeat before everything had been lost. The real expression of this conservatism and its victory over the aspirations of the militants lay ahead, in the consolidation of neo-liberal orthodoxy in the 1996 macroeconomic Growth, Employment and Redistribution (GEAR) strategy.

Mbeki and GEAR

The litmus test for international capital's approval and support of governments in this era is the extent to which the latter conform to neo-liberal macroeconomic orthodoxy. Thus the first task facing the new ANC government was to prove its bona fides in this respect. This was by no means easy; in terms of the neo-liberal doctrine, the role of the nation state is redefined in such a way that popular socio-economic goals are subordinated to the international economic goals of the capitalist superpowers.

The nation state has become the official caretaker of the global economy; an agent of the so-called 'new world order'. Its role is to become 'integrated', to act within the international constitutional guidelines defined by the key institutions of global capital (the WTO, IMF and World Bank), which expand and consolidate corporate property rights and prohibit discrimination between the interests of national and foreign capital. The aim of a neo-liberal macroeconomic policy is to create economic growth by creating an investor-friendly environment. This requires, *inter alia*, the liberalisation of exchange controls that prohibit the movement of capital; tax cuts and wage freezes aimed at encouraging investments and maximising profits; fiscal austerity and rapid reductions in budget deficits, by means of cuts in state expenditure; and the sale of profitable assets to the private sector.

South African capital, thoroughly penetrated by international capital, and fuelled by expansionist interests in new markets in Africa, has provided the driving force in this regard. The South African neo-liberal state acts for foreign capital, within the interests of national capital, and, if necessary, against the development of its own domestic resources to meet popular needs. In so doing it fails to protect South Africa's resources against the rapacious short-term interests of international capital. It also resoundingly fails to meet popular socio-economic aspirations, specifically those that require any increase in the social wage, as this drives up state expenditure and calls for the retention and even increase of state-owned resources and state intervention in the economy.

Neo-liberal orthodoxy also requires a reconfiguration of political control. The political power of the state is shifted to those arenas controlled by capital, and specifically concentrated in those wings that are closest to the global economy, such as the ministries of trade and finance, and the central (Reserve) bank. The role of the executive is redefined so as to de-emphasise and disempower those areas of government with close ties to popular domestic interests, such as parliament, local government, and especially welfare and labour. This is accompanied by the increasing centralisation of political decision-making in order to ensure ideological consistency and 'policy harmonisation'. The streamlining of the executive and the drive for policy co-ordination under the Mbeki presidency fits in with this progression. Thus these aspects of an 'imperial presidency' do not reflect Mbeki's persona, but rather his ideological conformity to neo-liberalism.

This was graphically demonstrated by his role in the government's jettisoning of the RDP and adoption of GEAR in June 1996, which set the seal on the ANC's acceptance of an orthodox, neo-liberal economic framework. As is well known, GEAR is remarkably similar to the NP's Normative Economic Model, which the ANC and COSATU resoundingly rejected only three years earlier in 1993.

In his study of the evolution of ANC economic policy (1998), Hein Marais outlines the organisation's search in the early 1990s for an economic policy that would fall within a capitalist framework, but promote development. He sketches the vigorous ideological battle between the left and the right in this regard, and the 'short walk' to victory of a neo-liberal orthodoxy, capped by the emergence of GEAR (146–72).

Despite Trevor Manuel's high profile in propagating and defending the ANC government's new stance, Mbeki has been credited as the prime motivator for elevating it to the point where it has become the current economic orthodoxy within the ANC (Uys 1996). Whether this is true or not

– and Mandela's admission that he played no part in formulating the policy gives additional credence to this – Mbeki has certainly played a key role in introducing GEAR, and defending it ever since.

In an address to the Intergovernmental Forum's development summit in November 1995, Mbeki paved the way for GEAR by outlining a new strategic framework that would underpin the RDP's programmes and policies. Referring to the RDP's 'almost biblical character', he cautioned that its priorities would have to be subjected to realistic macroeconomic considerations. The strategy of 'growth with development' would underpin all RDP targets, to be streamlined into six pillars which would situate addressing poverty, employment, crime, and good governance within a 'powerful, competitive South African economy . . . [which would] . . . secure the wealth of the country and promote investment' (Mbeki 1998a: 82–5).

In a speech to a NEDLAC summit on 1 June 1996, two weeks before GEAR was presented to parliament, Mbeki announced that the government would table a macroeconomic policy framework before that consultative structure. Prefacing his speech with the dictum that 'however divergent our interests might seem, we are condemned to live together and interact with one another, both the unwashed and the perfumed. Divorce is not possible' (186), he referred to the sometimes adversarial nature of the consultative relationship, and appealed for a culture of co-operation. He warned against any one partner of NEDLAC treating the tabling of a point of view on economic growth, participation, and social equity 'as an act of hostility or a declaration of war' (188).

When GEAR was finally tabled in the national assembly in June 1996, it was Mbeki who introduced Manuel's presentation, positioning it firmly as an 'important part of government policy . . . which will guide all government actions' (140).

Despite the extreme unpopularity of GEAR among the ANC's alliance partners, especially COSATU, and throughout the ensuing furore, Mbeki has never retreated from his vigorous defence of the framework. While neither retreating from the ANC's commitment to development and redress, and in fact stepping up his rhetoric in this regard, he is implacable in subsuming all developmental policies under the priorities of GEAR, on the oft-repeated basis that there is no viable alternative.

In June 1998 he chided COSATU's central committee in a rather patronising manner, declaring that it had been misinformed and misled by those forces 'opposed to change' which claimed that the economy was stagnant and shedding jobs as a result of GEAR. Addressing an audience of trade union leaders, integrally involved in the reality of factory and mine closures, workplace restructuring and retrenchments, he placed the cause of their negative views of the economy on their susceptibility to misinformation. He cited the 'grey economy' and unregistered companies as the reason for the lack of accurate official information (Mbeki 1998b). A month later, in a widely reported speech at the 10th congress of the SACP, he humiliatingly – and with much less tact – slammed the party for its heightened criticism of ANC policies. Defending GEAR before the combined leaderships of the ANC's objecting alliance partners (COSATU and the SACP), he displayed an unambiguous conviction of the correctness of the ANC's ideological choice, and a capacity to stare down any opposition in this regard.

In the run-up to the general elections in 1999, certain COSATU and SACP leaders began to raise the possibility of a 'post-GEAR consensus' within the alliance, but this talk died down immediate after the elections. Three years hence, following a steady increase in job losses and rising pressures on wages, as well as the bitter public fracas between COSATU and the ANC over a national strike against the privatisation of essential services in 2001, the joint formulation of a new growth strategy is being mooted once again. Whatever may emerge from this new consensus, the Mbeki government is unlikely to jettison the interests of international finance capital.

Mbeki and African nationalism

Besides his idiosyncratic stance on AIDS, the one aspect of Mbeki that consistently seems to rattle the sensitivities of the still predominantly white South African capitalist and middle classes is his espousal of an African identity. Although his definition of 'African' in his 'I am an African' speech (Mbeki 1998a: 31–6) includes whites, his positioning of this identity within the discourse of the African Renaissance and his constant support for black empowerment and the creation of a black middle and ruling class raises the question of whether he casts his (capitalist) solutions for South Africa in a racial framework.

A brief scrutiny of the key instruments of Mbeki's support for the African Renaissance as well as the development of a black middle class reveals that the Africanness he refers to is regional rather than racial in character. He consistently locates South Africa in an African context, and calls for an African Renaissance, driven by economic development, that will unlock a new future for this formerly colonised, exploited, and fragmented continent.

According to Alison Bullen (1999), Mbeki's use of an African identity in this anti-colonial framework is problematic in several respects. Firstly, it is situated squarely in a Pan-African nationalist tradition; as a result, it does not rigorously challenge the existing power structures in most African countries, themselves products of colonial direct and indirect rule, but merely seeks to contain them within a neo-liberal paradigm of democracy acceptable to the international community.

Secondly, although situated within Pan-Africanism, the African Renaissance retreats from this tradition's aims of regenerating African economic enterprises by replacing individualistic methods of production with more socialist, communitarian methods. Instead, he believes the only way in which African countries can regenerate themselves economically is to become competitive in the global capitalist system. Moreover, he situates this in a framework of economic reform that regards foreign investment as the prime means of stimulating economic growth.

Thirdly, Bullen raises the ambiguities in this discourse around the role of South Africa in relation to the rest of Africa, and argues that Mbeki's Africanism plays a functional role in allowing South Africa to align itself with Africa – with all the attendant comparative advantages – while offering it little in terms of material support, ostensibly because of its own constrained resources.

Tracing the expansion of South African investment into southern Africa in the 1990s, Saliem Patel (2000: 7–10) argues that these trends have presented other countries in the region with serious problems, and calls for them to be carefully monitored. Firstly, he argues, they have led to the displacement of domestic enterprises. Secondly, the kinds of investments flowing into these countries will not help to create the conditions for long-term economic development. Thirdly, they increase the economic dependence of these countries on South Africa, thereby exacerbating existing historical disparities.

Mbeki's developmental vision of an African Renaissance is thus consistent with his solutions for South Africa. Development is refracted through the prism of neo-liberal economic reforms, aimed largely at attracting foreign investment – therefore, an extension of the 'redistribution through growth' strategy to all of Africa. He praises current trends in Africa to trim state assets and introduce privatisation. He emphasises acceptance of the 'global reality', and of the need for African countries to encourage investment partnerships with the west and Asia.

Even when he raises the exploitation of the continent's mineral resources, which he says cannot be the preserve of companies outside the continent, he refers in the same breath to the use of 'profitable and safe injections of international and private capital' (Mbeki 1998a: 203). Besides, given the fact that South African mining houses have played a prominent role in investments in southern Africa in the 1990s,[1] it is difficult not to question the intention of Mbeki's agenda in reclaiming Africa's minerals resources for Africans.

Neither can one doubt that NEPAD, the latest recovery plan for African development, with its encouragement of private sector investment, trade liberalisation, and the removal of restrictions, will promote the expansion of South African capital into Africa. NEPAD, like GEAR, subsumes both political reform and socio-economic development targets under neo-liberal economic tenets, and advocates the creation of appropriate conditions to attract FDI as the main developmental solution for African countries.[2]

Although only time will tell what this expansion will mean for the populations and economies of other African countries, it is resoundingly clear that Mbeki's African Renaissance is the best thing that has ever happened to South Africa's (still overwhelmingly white) capital in a long time. The question thus becomes: what is Mbeki doing about the whiteness of South Africa's capitalist class?

Mbeki and the creation of a black ruling class

There is little doubt that Mbeki is strongly inclined towards changing the racial composition of the South African ruling class, and expanding the black middle classes. In a speech entitled 'Is there a national agenda – and who sets it?' delivered at the University of Port Elizabeth in March 1995, he pledged to make government policy for 'the creation of possibilities for the (black) majority to obtain such education and training as would give them the capacity to compete for jobs as directors-general in the public service, as university professors, as judges, as financial managers in large corporations, as generals in the National Defence Force, and so on' (1998a: 106).

Yet the macroeconomic policy he fronted only a year later provides precious little leverage in this respect. Restraints on state expenditure limit any pouring of resources into higher education for black students. This – coupled with the obvious inability of the state's small bursary fund to solve the critical financial problems of an impoverished black working class, the only base from which a solid layer of black middle-class professionals can be built – has led to student enrolment in the historically black universities shrinking rapidly in recent years. Although the black student population has grown, it has not done so significantly.

Thus, in a hard-hitting speech at the University of Transkei in April 1998, only three years after his 1995 pledge, Mbeki sarcastically lambasted black students who 'know it as a matter of fact that they are entitled to government funding. If they do not receive such funding, they are obliged to be vexed, to be angry, to express that anger in any way they choose, to keep in their pockets the money they have to pay their fees, or better still, to spend it on the good things in life and to convey the message in the clearest terms: Deliverer, deliver!' (1998a: 156–7). It is clear that his intentions for the government to provide higher education to the *majority* has receded somewhat. These are not good precursors to the rapid expansion and eventual self-perpetuation of a black middle class.

Given this retreat, the major instrument for the creation of a black middle class has become the fast-tracking of black executives in the private and public sector. These options are limited firstly because the recruitment pool remains relatively small, and the corridors of executive power are tightly guarded. A recent survey of private sector companies conducted by the department of labour (2001) has revealed that blacks are still overwhelmingly located at lower management levels, and a huge majority of internal promotions still go to white managers. The fast-tracking of executives in the public sector is occurring more rapidly, despite the limitations placed upon it by constitutional guarantees for white public servants and the lean state GEAR aspires towards.

There is also the strategy of 'black economic empowerment'. This engineered phenomenon of unbundling South African companies and offering preferential shares and options to black empowerment investment initiatives, constituted solely for the purpose of buying into these offers, exploded in 1995–97, ensuring the rapid upward mobility of a number of black businessmen and women and creating a number of instant black (paper) millionaires. These initiatives were aided by state policies formulated to encourage the involvement of black economic groupings in all sales of state assets, and the setting up of a National Empowerment Fund in 1998 to provide loans to black empowerment groupings to buy shares in privatised enterprises.

However, black economic empowerment is occurring in highly volatile economic times, and its capacity to expand is very limited. South African capital has retreated from any further unbundling and/or investment in the risky practice of giving preferential options to black empowerment groupings purely because they are black. The main motor of black empowerment initiatives will therefore become the privatisation of state assets, at a time when the emergent black bourgeoisie is still a tiny fraction of the South African capitalist class.

Privatisation initiatives, and increased black employment and promotion in state and quasi-state structures, (including those NGOs favoured by the government for either service delivery or policy formulation) are thus set to become the prime vehicles for creating a black middle class in South Africa, and the prime springboards for the assimilation of blacks into the ruling class. Given the discretionary powers of the state in both areas, ideological uniformity, reinforced by strong links of patronage and loyalty, are virtually assured. It is clear that, even in respect of the urgent need to create a black ruling and middle class, Mbeki's government utilises instruments compatible with a neo-liberal framework. It is difficult to see what white South Africans have to be nervous about. No wonder that the rise in crime, a testament to the steady impoverishment and ideological alienation of the majority of the population, has become their biggest complaint.

The limits to the creation of a self-perpetuating black middle class means that the nascent black capitalist class will remain very small for some time to come. Its political advantage lies firstly in the fact that it is highly visible, as it is to both government's and capital's advantage to trot out the new black bourgeoisie at every opportunity as the face of transformation in the new South Africa. Secondly, given the way in which it is being created, it is inextricably tied to both white capital and state patronage.

The political disadvantage to the state of this strategy is that using patronage as a means of class perpetuation encourages corruption, secrecy, clientelism, and naked greed. The new black capitalist class is unlikely to elicit popular support and consent, and the buffer zone of a black middle class is still small, and likely to remain so as long as neo-liberal policies remain hegemonic.

Mbekism is alive and well, and is here to stay
In attempting to answer the question posed at the start of this essay, namely whether Mbeki is a suitable leader for the ruling party in the current context, we have applied a class-based analysis. In terms of this analysis, notwithstanding his (real or perceived) personal idiosyncrasies, Mbeki is eminently suited to lead a capitalist ANC. He boldly embraces globalisation and has skilfully positioned himself, both within South Africa and abroad, as a spokesman for and defender of its tenets. He is very comfortable with containing his African nationalist impulses within a neo-liberal paradigm. It must be emphasised that he has such impulses, and that they are a natural legacy of his association with the ANC. A conservative with such impulses and such a legacy as his will sound (and be) vastly different from one cast in the mould of Thatcher or Reagan. Neither would ever have been able to say, with conviction, as Mbeki did in his opening address of the ANC's 90th year celebration:

> Together we have travelled a long road to be where we are today. This has been a road of struggle against colonial and apartheid oppression. It is a

road along which we have suffered some defeats, and won many battles . . . (Mbeki 2002).

Mbeki's African nationalist impulses have been shaped by his party's long history of identifying with Africa, and the struggle against white colonial oppression. But this does not make his choices any less conservative. Thus Mbekism is a neo-liberal orthodoxy spiced with a 'liberal' dash of African nationalist impulses.

Many of the accusations of inconsistency levelled against Mbeki come from elements in the white conservative fold, who acknowledge his adherence to their neo-liberal inclinations but are unable to appreciate the subtle differences between him and their more rapacious selves. However, perhaps these accusations also have sinister undertones. The loud, banshee-like shrieking over every perceived deviation from orthodoxy plays a powerful role in containing a leader who has on more than one occasion displayed his readiness to accommodate capital's fears, out of his conviction that their goals are the same. It represents nothing more than the shaping of Mbekism, which has become less and less pronounced as Mbeki becomes more confident in his role.

Secondly, we have seen that, in the course of the careful ascendancy of Mbekism in the ANC and the alliance, Mbeki has displayed a capacity to not deviate from his chosen position, and to carefully and incrementally gain hegemony over time. It is not within the scope of this essay to cast an eye on his methods in this regard, but we do note a disturbing incapacity to relate to the masses. Mbeki displays none of the ambiguity that Mandela occasionally did when confronted by popular frustration, resistance, or just a sheer celebration of militancy and activism.

Lastly, we see the rise of a nascent black middle and ruling class, numerically small but ideologically cohesive, inextricably tied to white capital and Mbeki's government and policies, and willing and able to act as a consolidated and conspiratorial force in order to maintain itself.

Thus Mbekism is ideologically sound, gaining new converts every day, and intending to go the mile.

Notes
1. See table of South African investments in southern Africa in Labour Research Service (2000).
2. For an exposition of NEPAD's ideological framework, see Patel and Pretorius (2002).

References

Bullen, A. 1999. The African Renaissance: an assessment of the African Renaissance discourse as a unique strategy for development in Africa. Honours dissertation. School of African Studies, University of Cape Town. December.

Corrigan, T. 1999. *Mbeki: his time has come – an introduction to South Africa's new president.* Johannesburg: South African Institute of Race Relations.

Department of labour. 2001. Report of the commission for employment equity: 1999–2001. Pretoria.

Gumede, W. 2000. Modernising the ANC. *Financial Mail.* 31 March.

Jacobs, S. 1999. An imperial presidency? *Siyaya.* Summer, 4–9.

Labour Research Service. 2000. *The LRS report: bargaining indicators for 2000.* Cape Town.

———. 2002. *The LRS report: bargaining indicators for 2002.* Cape Town.

Lodge, T. 1999. *South African politics since 1994.* Cape Town: David Phillip.

Marais, H. 1998. *South Africa, limits to change: the political economy of transformation.* Cape Town and London: University of Cape Town Press and Zed Books.

Mbeki, T. 1998a. *Africa: the time has come.* Cape Town and Johannesburg: Tafelberg and Mafube.

———. 1998b. Speech at the inaugural meeting of COSATU's central committee, 22 June.

———. 2002. Address on the occasion of year 90 of the African National Congress, 6 January. The Mbeki Page, African National Congress. Online. http://www.anc.org.za/ancdocs/history/mbeki/2002/tm0106.html.

McKinley, D. 1997. *The ANC and the liberation struggle: a critical political biography.* London: Pluto.

Patel, S and Pretorius, L. 2002. NEPAD: a critical review. In *The LRS report: bargaining indicators for 2002.* Cape Town: Labour Research Service.

Patel, S. 2000. Investments in the Southern African Development Community: a review of the 1990s. In *The LRS report: bargaining indicators for 2000.* Cape Town: Labour Research Service.

Ryklief, C. 1996. The manufacture of chaos and compromise: an analysis of the path to reform in South Africa. MA thesis. School of politics and communications studies, University of Liverpool, United Kingdom. September.

Uys, I. 1996. The compelling future of Thabo Mbeki. *Millennium,* May. 32.

Waldmeir, P. 1997. *Anatomy of a miracle: the end of apartheid and the birth of a new South Africa.* London: Penguin.

CHAPTER 5

Thabo Mbeki, South Africa, and the idea of an African Renaissance

PETER VALE and SIPHO MASEKO

A note by Peter Vale

On Sunday 17 March 2002 my friend and collaborator, Sipho Maseko, died of cancer. He was only 36 years old. His untimely passing has deprived the political studies community in South and southern Africa of a major talent, and the world of a fine human being. I have paid tribute to Sipho elsewhere (Vale 2002), and will therefore not repeat myself here, but a word on procedure is necessary.

The first version of this essay appeared in the British journal International Affairs (Vale and Maseko 1998), and then in a number of other publications, sometimes in other languages. When we were invited to contribute to this volume, Sipho and I discussed a revision of the core text, and I prepared a draft that was sent to the editors. Quite correctly, the external reviewers asked us to devote some attention to the development of the African Renaissance via the Millennium Africa Recovery Plan (MAP), the New African Initiative (NAI), and the New Partnership for Africa's Development (NEPAD). Sipho was unable to contribute to such a revision.

As a result, the main text remains substantively unchanged, and I have added a short essay in which I take the story forward. In doing so, I have tried to remain faithful to both the structure and voice that Sipho and I established in our joint analysis of the African Renaissance; however, I am solely responsible for the final product.

Readers who have followed the argument on the African Renaissance will recognise that the intellectual structure of this piece has withstood the impact of major developments in quickly changing times to a remarkable degree. The greater credit for this is due to Sipho: it certainly suggests that our intellectual understanding of the present conjuncture of African events is infinitely poorer for his passing.

In this chapter we seek to interpret the idea of an African Renaissance, and to locate it within South African diplomatic practice. Our discursive interest, however, is with the emancipatory potential that the ideas unfolding around a resurgence of African self-assuredness, as articulated by South Africa's president, offer the continent's people. We are therefore interested in social theory, and this explains why we begin the argument with history.

Destiny
The notion that South Africa should play an assertive role in African affairs has featured consistently in the rhetoric of successive South African leaders, irrespective of their physical or ideological hue. Each political epoch has promised to open exciting possibilities of engagement across the continent's spatial and other divides; on each of these occasions, it has seemed as if the more economically developed South Africa could join – or even lead – Africa's people in the cause of modernisation and its technocratic twin, development. The logic of this belief has seemed unassailable, resting, as it has, on geopolitics and hierarchies: this made the idea of South Africa's continental destiny appear quite natural even to members of racial minorities accorded both South African citizenship and political leadership by dint of their skin colour.

Thus, in a speech in April 1940 to the country's premier agricultural and industrial show, South Africa's then prime minister, Jan Smuts, spoke of a far-reaching adjustment in the country's approach to African affairs. 'If we wish to take our rightful place as the leader in Pan-African development and in the shaping of future policies and events in this vast continent, we must face the realities and the facts of the present and seize the opportunities which these offer. All Africa may be our proper market if we will but have the vision, and far-sighted policy will be necessary if that is to be realised' (1942).

Caught up in the turmoil of the early stages of the Second World War, Smuts's concerns at that time were to stake out Allied interests in a nervous subcontinent, and to deal with domestic resistance to South Africa's declaration of war. However, he also announced the formation of the Industrial Development Corporation (IDC), which would build the country's wartime economy and, in the decades that followed, anchor South Africa's industrialisation. (The IDC remains a major force in modern South Africa, and has claimed a developmental role in the African Renaissance.) Thus Smuts's concerns reflected the increasingly economic logic of an assertive Africa-based foreign policy in which South Africa's surpluses could be used to benefit less well-endowed societies on the continent. This goal implied a mercantile trade-off: South African economic interests, particularly its more developed industrial and trading sectors, would be amply rewarded by the commercial potential the continent had always seemed to hold.

However, privileges accorded by race stood between South Africa and its achievement of this goal. The first decades of independence politics in Africa were certainly taken up with the idea that both development and nationalism would enable the continent to emerge as an equal global partner. The continent's leaders insisted that South Africa could form part of this 'African Revolution' (as many then called it); however, it would have to abandon apartheid. Successive South African minority governments could not accept this judgement, believing that it represented, at best, interference in the domestic affairs of a sovereign state, and, at worst, the end of the white man in Africa. Nonetheless, the thread of South Africa's destiny in Africa, with its themes of modernisation and leadership, reappeared several times during the apartheid years.

In the mid- and late 1960s, for instance, South Africa's then minority government initiated two linked forays into Africa. Known successively as 'dialogue' and 'détente', these sought continental approval for South Africa's racial policies, and diplomatic recognition of its soon-to-be-independent homelands (see Barber and Barratt 1990). But, as was invariably the case as far as apartheid South Africa was concerned, there was a further dimension: this was the heyday of modernisation theory, and the idea of South Africa actively developing Africa economically followed close on the heels of its diplomatic outreach.[1] As importantly, the rhetoric that accompanied these successive diplomatic moments was premised on substantial returns for South African business which, in turn, supported a range of additional initiatives to further the goals of apartheid's search for an African destiny. Both 'dialogue' and 'détente' failed, victims more of the cold war divide and the South African minority's blind faith in apartheid than the inability or unwillingness of the South African business community to support its government.[2]

Then, in the late 1970s, South Africa launched another African initiative, this time confined to the subcontinent, especially its immediate neighbourhood. It was crystallised in the proposed creation of a 'constellation of southern African states' (see Geldenhuys 1981) which would, it was hoped, join the states of the subregion in a common economic cause. At its base were immediate security concerns: the anti-apartheid threat to what the minority government called its 'domestic order', and a deteriorating regional security situation, driven – ironically – by apartheid's attempted destruction of its closest neighbours. Beyond these considerations, however, the regime's rhetoric around South Africa's African destiny, especially the mercantile benefits of the 'constellation' initiative (see Breytenbach 1980), did not differ greatly from that of Jan Smuts three decades earlier.

This patterning suggests why commonsensical policy outcomes invariably appear to flow from structural interpretations of South Africa's relations with the continent. Moulded by geography, and drawn to the idea of progress promised by economics, trade, and development, South Africa's natural hinterland (to borrow a phrase attributed to Cecil John Rhodes) lay to the north. And the country's destiny was clear: to lead the continent's people towards modernisation, and tap its market and other potential.

With apartheid ended, the country no longer bound by the rigidities of cold war logic, and no longer isolated, South Africa's capacity to fulfill its African destiny was a moment whose time, it seemed to many, had finally come. Moreover, the country's perceived ability to provide continental leadership was enhanced by its successful transition to democracy on a continent where social relations remain, in the opinion of equally as many, a Hobbesian 'nasty, brutish, and short'. The towering stature of former president Nelson Mandela – one of few Africans to have captured and retained the attention of the rest of the world – added to the allure of the future for the continent post-apartheid South Africa seemed to represent, and its role in creating that future. If these circumstances made the notion of an African Renaissance propitious, both within South Africa and in a wider theatre, it was the appeal of Mbeki's lyrical imagery[3] that turned the obvious – the commonsensical, almost – into a tryst with destiny. However, while analysts and commentators have trawled the idea of the African Renaissance for policy content, there seems to be very little of substance to anchor[4] an obviously fine idea.[5]

This particular interpretation suggests that, although rooted in structuralism, and buoyed by the same modernisation theory that inspired apartheid's African ambitions, South Africa's idea of an African Renaissance is abstruse, puzzling, even perhaps mysterious; more promise than policy. This explanation fits revisionist interpretations of some major policy initiatives in the twentieth century, whose authors have argued that Franklyn D Roosevelt's 'New Deal' and Lyndon Johnson's 'Great Society' were little more than invitations to social mobilisation in a common cause: openings around which, given the goodwill and energies of governments and citizens, significant policy initiatives might eventually take form.[6] The search for content complements a social-contractual reading of the African Renaissance. It suggests that the idea is a doubled-edged agreement, which commits the South African state to democratic concord with its own people on the one hand, and the cause of peace and democracy in Africa on the other.

Seen in this frame, some important policy developments have indeed followed on the African Renaissance idea. A good example is South Africa's assumption of a peacekeeping role in Africa.[7] Under this rubric, the country's defence force and foreign ministry have developed a comprehensive white paper on peacekeeping, based on the tenets of what political theorists commonly refer to as 'liberal internationalism'. This has, however, had unforeseen consequences, one of them being the opportunistic use of the African Renaissance as a means of justifying the maintenance of certain force levels in the South African military – a theme enthusiastically articulated by conservative defence analysts.[8]

These ideas mesh neatly with South Africa's own transitional experience, as well as its broad foreign policy stance. Therefore, South Africa is rhetorically committed to the development of liberal democracy at home and abroad: indeed, in his statements on the African Renaissance, Mbeki has insisted that 'the people must govern'. His predecessor as president, Mandela, was also vocal on the need to protect human rights in Africa (see, for example, Mandela 1997), and has subsequently continued in this vein as Africa's most respected elder statesman. On the other hand, South Africa's lively civil society organisations have often urged their government to be more interventionist in promoting democracy on the continent (see, for example, Vale 1997).

Notwithstanding claims that the idea of an African Renaissance now stands at the very centre of South Africa's entire diplomatic endeavour (see Mills 2000: 139–84), its essential features remain deliberately vague; it is high on sentiment, low on substance. Like Roosevelt's 'New Deal' and Johnson's 'Great Society', it exists as an unsettled policy goal propounded by a political leadership that faces particular sets of challenges, both domestically and internationally. In this reading, the historical roll call of successive South African initiatives in Africa, though not the immediate inspiration for South Africa's current policy-makers, offers perhaps the only reliable guide to future international relations. Simply put, the African Renaissance seeks to maximise South Africa's foreign policy options in Africa – including the country's quest to occupy Africa's permanent seat in the United Nations security council, should this come to pass.

Is there more than this simple utilitarianism to the African Renaissance? To answer this, we need to turn briefly to exegesis. Of course, the term 'renaissance' has been chosen intentionally, to denote an 'outburst of mental energy' (Rowland 1997: 30) aimed at promoting a spirit of awakening in Africa in the late twentieth century. With this look backwards, and again deliberately, Mbeki's rhetoric continuously draws attention to the significance of new technologies – computers, the internet, the worldwide web – to African development. In doing so, he confers on latter-day technological innovation the same power to trigger off quantum social changes as the evolution of printing had in speeding the passage from medieval to modern times.

Two streams

By casting the African Renaissance in expansive terms, political space has been opened within which a number of distinct interpretations of the future can be contested. For the purpose of the immediate argument, two deserve our scrutiny, because we believe that they reveal continuing cleavages in the social and economic fabric of the post-apartheid state, and may come to mirror the kinds of tensions that will follow South Africa's efforts to exercise a role in Africa.

The first interpretation is cast in the modernist tradition. This links South Africa's economic interests to Africa through the analytical register offered by the meta-theory devised by globalisation with its seemingly endless vistas, shrinking horizons, and economistic logic – we will call this the globalist interpretation. The second involves using the African Renaissance to unlock a series of complex social constructions that are more immediate, and turn on issues of identity:[9] we will call this the Africanist interpretation. While the former fits comfortably in accepted framings in contemporary international relations, the latter is less familiar, although we will argue that it offers footholds towards wider forms of emancipation, both at home and elsewhere.

In a globalist setting, the idea of an African Renaissance suggests a continental effort to advance the now familiar neo-Hegelian 'end-of-history' thesis associated with the work of Francis Fukayama. In this reading, economic globalisation – read the mix of free markets, privatisation, exchange control relaxation, and cuts in public expenditure – will erode the power of authoritarian governments to 'free' bedevilled polities from the restrictions of ideologically based control and resultant conflicts.[10] Polemicists, especially those in South Africa's foreign policy-making establishment, have been quick to seize on this celebratory interpretation and link it to the advancing vistas promised by an uncritical acceptance of globalisation as social progress.[11]

In this particular reading, South Africa's African Renaissance (the choice of words is important in this instance) is drawn towards a notion that the country will anchor a chain of Darwinian economies that may, in time, become the African equivalent of the largesse that the buoyant Asian Tigers once enjoyed. In his 1997 presentation to the Foundation for Global Dialogue (FGD), Mbeki's aide Vusi Mavimbela favoured this interpretation by declaring that '[t]he advent of the East Asian economic miracle is one of the most important socio-economic developments of the twentieth century... This miracle has offered hope to the people of Africa that economic development can be rapid and can be achievable without the annexation of foreign markets through imperial physical force.' In this rendition, the African Renaissance posits Africa as an expanding and prosperous market alongside Asia, Europe, and North America, one in which South African capital is destined to play a special role via trade, strategic partnerships, and the like. In exchange for South Africa's role as the agent of globalisation, the continent will offer this country a preferential option on its traditional promise of a largesse of oil, minerals, and mining. It is irresistible, but to make this further point: on any analytical register, this perspective is a decidedly northern understanding of development and progress.[12]

This globalist framing of the African Renaissance has been enthusiastically embraced by moneyed South African elites (of all races) whose understanding of modernisation is the generation of wealth – 'a world in which trade and global competitiveness are as important as the political dimensions of diplomacy', as Conrad Strauss, a South African banker and one-time chair of the South African Institute of International Affairs, has put it (1995: v). Thus South Africa's direct investment in Africa has increased from about R3,7 billion before the 1994 election to about R13 billion, while trade has increased by 52,6 per cent to R16,771 billion (Leftwich 1997: 7). This business confidence in Africa's globalisation has been carried forward on the financial markets, where South African companies trading in African markets have shown similar impressive growth. Seen from this perspective, there seems to be no end to the material benefits of the renaissance. As an anonymous South African entrepreneur has remarked: 'Africa is a huge market; it may sometimes be turbulent, but it eats and uses toiletries every day' (quoted in *Financial Mail* 1998).

The enthusiasm with which South African capital has embraced the African Renaissance may explain the deepening nervousness in other African countries over the country's goals on the continent, and helps to explain the reversals of early policy initiatives. The idea that 'what is good for South Africa is good for Africa' revisits a series of uncomfortable historical encounters between Africa and South Africa's traditionally powerful moneyed establishment: encounters which, despite the miracle attached to South Africa's transformation, have scarred Africa's political psyche. Moeletsi Mbeki, brother of South Africa's president, a former journalist and now a businessman, once captured this disquiet by suggesting that 'an increasing number of African countries would prefer us not to play a... [leadership]... role' (1997).

Wider experience suggests the wisdom of this scepticism: as the United Nations Development Programme (UNDP) reports annually, the solutions offered by the market tend to exacerbate, not narrow, the divides between rich and poor. Although the idea of the African Renaissance is rooted in the necessity to develop and sustain an African middle class, market solutions appear to only exaggerate, not ease, political and economic tensions, even if class is not the dominant mode of analysis. More immediately, there is no evidence to suggest that, for all the growing trade across the continent, there is any prospect of an end to history in Africa.

Indeed, the slew of reversals in instances of democratisation during the continent's 'third wave' – in addition to those already mentioned, recent events in Kenya, the DRC, and Swaziland make the point – suggest that transitions underpinned by the market, the military, and the ballot box have done little to dislodge traditional patterns of post-colonial control and the pre-eminence of elites. Africa's uncaptured peasantry (to use Goran Hyden's phrase) remains outside of, and alienated from, the state system. And in some places – such as Somalia, where there is still no effective state to speak of, and Rwanda and Burundi, where embers still simmer – the future of peasantry, people, and politics is wholly uncertain.

In contrast to this rendition, the second, 'Africanist', approach to the African Renaissance is post-structural. Africanists argue that globalist outcomes will 'amount to nothing more than an externally driven consumerist movement' that will leave Africans 'continuing to be valued only for an ability to absorb and popularise foreign ideas, trinkets, and junk' (Dladla 1997). They primarily (and sometimes with great militancy) aim to lay to rest 'the image of the perpetually dancing, skin-clad, African who is always smiling through ridicule and pain'; they are intent, rather, on developing a condition that would help Africans to 'contribute meaningfully to rescuing the world from barbarism that masquerades as civilisation'. These worries explain why Africanists call for a reinterpretation of both African history and culture away from its colonial construction and towards a consolidation of the 'wealth of knowledge that Africans are carrying around in their heads' (Dladla 1997). Seen through this optic, the idea of the African Renaissance draws on different strands of social theory and cultural history than those offered by utilitarian theories, such as globalisation, which are readily presented as common sense by the self-styled realist theory in international relations. Inspired by the legacy of Marcus Garvey, among others, Africanists eschew the modernising tendency represented by Africa's encounter with Europe – what Dladla has called the 'chasing of scientific glory and money'. In the course of this search, Africanists believe that '... identity is still in the making; there isn't a final identity that is African. But, at the same time, there is an identity coming into existence. And it has a certain context and a certain meaning' (Appiah 1992: 117).

From South Africa's perspective, this understanding of the African Renaissance is rooted in largely unexplored and hidden links – in culture, literature, and folklore – across the continent. This alone is not enough, of course. For these roots to take hold, they will have to be turned into policies that will touch the daily lives of people, especially the poor. The powerful appeal of black consciousness in South Africa, captured in the inspiring life and tragic death of Steve Biko, exposed but did not turn into lasting benefits the rich undergrowth of relationships – personal, social, and cultural – embedded in the Africanist framing.

But the challenge which the Africanist reading presents to the globalist interpretation offered by the modernising narratives has, we hold, opened the space for advancing alternative views of Africa's future. In this, the African Renaissance underscores an increasingly powerful appeal, strongly articulated by intellectuals,[13] for a new future for Africa. This partially parallels the Afro-American perspective in which 'Black Renaissance' refers to an insertion of the voice of the African diaspora into international relations. So, for instance, in late 1996 the journal *Black Renaissance/Renaissance Noir* invited the 'Black genius to apply itself to the realities of the twenty-first century with uncompromising, thoughtful, generous . . . commentary' (see Diawara 1996: 6). In the well provided by these overlapping interpretations of the spirit that carried black consciousness in South Africa, the Caribbean, and the United States, the African Renaissance offers multiple – and wholly unexplored – interpretations of South Africa's place on the continent.

While Africanist interpretations have been strengthened by the migration to South Africa of Africans from the rest of the continent (see Omotoso 1994), they remain largely outside the mainstream lexicon used to discuss interstate relations in Africa. This is why it seems difficult, beyond the rituals associated with the continental unity offered by African states, to turn these understandings into the cut and thrust of policy and its making. As Njabulo Ndebele, a leading South African intellectual and now vice-chancellor of the University of Cape Town, has argued (1997), 'the return to mythical roots ceases to be a compelling factor of mobilisation in the face of the sheer weight of existing socio-cultural realities that demand to be addressed on their own terms . . . the call for black roots has less effect than the provision of water and sanitation, electricity, telephones, houses, clinics, transport, schools, and jobs.'

But by critiquing the critique (to draw on an idea of the social theorist

Ernesto Laclau), exciting possibilities are opened up for the idea represented by the African Renaissance to change the lives of people across the continent. Most Africans consider themselves to be marginalised from the affairs of their countries, the continent, and the world. Without recognising this, there will be no renewal, no renaissance. This is why the inscrutable and unsettled nature of the African Renaissance can permit a plethora of alternative interpretations of the future. To succeed, an African Renaissance must end the economic discrimination the continent faces at the start of the twenty-first century, and blunt the anger that people of colour, not only in Africa but all over the world, feel towards an emerging international system that reinforces what has justifiably been referred to as a 'global apartheid'.

The keys to such a breakthrough may be found in the profound epistemological shift currently under way, involving a search for an understanding of human relations in the early twenty-first century that falls outside the limiting opportunities represented by race, and the politics – domestic and international – that these, and the discourse of the market, have engendered and celebrated. Such a shift must recognise both human worth and a diversity of cultural values. To play this role, a renaissance must discipline as well as liberate. The question is, how is this to be done?

Openings

Are there lasting opportunities for Africans that lie beyond the 'real game of international relations which has three basic rules: trade, trade, and trade' (*Business Report*, 15 January 1998)? Can the African Renaissance change the lives of ordinary Africans in the face of a world elite obsessed with the idea of globalisation? Can it draw politics closer to the productive energy of African literature, oral narratives, poetry, dance, music, and visual arts? To avoid answering these questions, as structuralists do, misses the emancipatory moment that Mbeki has captured, and avoids a careful consideration of deliberate nomenclature, particularly the renaissance metaphor, within which South Africa's African destiny now seems to be cast. What's to be done?

A beginning can be made by introducing mother-tongue education more widely. In South Africa this still remains an important arena for transformation; elsewhere on the continent, much has been achieved with this approach to education. Another beginning can be made in agriculture. There can be no African revival, let alone an epistemological shift, unless and until Africa can feed itself. The discriminatory conditionalities provided by the WTO have diminished the continent's capacity to take advantage of the one commodity – land – it has in abundance. As the respected African intellectual Yash Tandon has argued, power relations, not the neutrality of the market or technology, determine the daily diet of Africans (1997).

A third beginning can draw Africanist perspectives closer to the policy world so beloved by mainstream international relations scholars. The limitations of a neo-realist approach to continental relations – as South Africa's destabilisation of its neighbours during the 1980s tragically demonstrated – is clear, and the same logic suggests why neo-liberal economics offer Africa no hope, and will continue to force its great majority to live on the margins of its own and the global society.

But to carry the day, in policy terms, the African Renaissance will have to evince both a capacity to deliver the stuff of politics and a consciousness of the pain and humiliation of African people on a continent, and in a world, that remain entirely dominated by the cultural values of people who are not black. The search for an emancipatory democracy that will carry such a renaissance must begin with an affirmation that minorities and the values they hold are important. This has begun in small but significant ways – and South Africa has followed the lead of other countries in incorporating modes of traditional government at the third and second tiers of government. There are important parallel threads as well: could the African Renaissance help to wrest the debate over women away from the control of the patriarchal governments that dominate the continent?

Leaders and followers

South Africa's search for an African home in the aftermath of apartheid was to be expected. Exploring what kind of a home (see Adler 1998) – an imagined, real, or constructed community – Africa might become for South Africa lies beyond the bounds of this particular argument. But, given the great emotional distance that apartheid created between South Africa and the rest of the continent, and the resulting sense of expectation, the question of who leads is surely central.

In hierarchical understandings of politics, it appears natural – perhaps even predestined, as we have been at pains to note – that South Africa should provide such leadership. Because of this, South African commentators have been odious in their belief that their country and their experience of political transformation and managing market economics in particular has everything to teach Africa and, by implication, that Africa has nothing to teach South Africa. They have, to be fair, been encouraged to believe this by distinguished African figures, notably the former president of Tanzania, the late Mwalimu Julius Nyerere, who, in an address to the South African parliament in 1997, called upon South Africans to take up their responsibilities in Africa. These impulses have certainly fed wider international understandings that South Africa is the only country that can offer leadership to the countries south of the Sahara – a point, incidentally, enthusiastically embraced by the United States as it seeks to implement a version of the theory of pivotal states (Chase et al 1996) as a central plank of its post-cold war foreign policy.

The central paradox of leadership – that it requires willing followers – explains why, however desirable it might seem for South Africa to lead an African Renaissance, it cannot and dare not do so. This conclusion lies beyond an appreciation that traditional understandings of international relations remain, as drawn from the myth of the Peloponnesian Wars, 'largely the game of the powerful . . . the strong extract what they will, the weak must surrender what they cannot protect' (Tandon 1997: 390–1).

South Africa's leadership of Africa is condemned by its unhappy past. The country's residual power, particularly its economic muscle and military strength, skews, not balances, the prospects for sustainable and equitable development in southern Africa (*Sowetan*, 15 September 1997). And without equity, attempts to follow its leadership can only be reluctant and forced. There are numerous examples of this in post-apartheid southern Africa, perhaps the most tangible being the tension between South Africa and Zimbabwe over the former's use of its economic muscle in trade negotiations – a tension that was all too often portrayed as a simple personality clash between Mugabe and Mandela. But the extent and implications of the power imbalances in the region was also tragically displayed in the case of South Africa's invasion of Lesotho in 1998.

The leadership/followership dilemma have also emerged in other ways. Consider, for example, South Africa's unsuccessful bid to host the 2004 Olympic Games. Although the campaign was called 'the African bid', and was promoted as 'Africa's turn' to stage the games (this had been done on all four other continents), it seems that Cape Town lost the bid – to Athens – because, during the first round of voting, African delegates simply failed to support South Africa (Moeletsi Mbeki 1997). This is an important example, because it suggests the preponderant dilemmas of South Africa's relations with the continent in a very concrete way. Cape Town's Olympic bid was frequently flighted as integral to the African Renaissance; indeed, Thabo Mbeki (1997) argued that 'the time has come for the rest of the world to demonstrate its commitment to the African Renaissance by awarding the Games in the year 2004 to the African continent.' But was it truly an African endeavour? Or was it a South African effort to use its image of Africa for its own purposes?

This once again raises the issue of method. There is surely a danger that this discussion of the African Renaissance has relied too much on the perspectives offered by one politician: Thabo Mbeki. After all, there is a long and unsatisfactory history of foreign policy scholarship in South Africa that has relied on the role of personalities to carry understandings and build explanations. And yet the distinguishing feature of South African post-apartheid foreign policy is how obviously policy has moved from the ministry and department of foreign affairs into the president's office, and particularly into the hands of Mbeki, first as deputy president and now as president. Therefore, the place of the African Renaissance in policy terms cannot be appreciated without considering Mbeki's current location in the country's politics, and his goals for South Africa.

One possible interpretation of the personalisation of the renaissance idea is that it is integral to Mbeki's search for presidential status. A shrewd politician (see *Southern Africa Report* 1997), he faces an unenviable task; while the South Africa he has come to govern may well sustain a remarkable propensity for reconciliation – quite out of proportion to the horror of apartheid's long and crippling hold on the country's majority – the challenges of transformation remain daunting.[14] Added to this, the prospects for continued international interest – essential for the economic growth needed to transform South Africa into a modern, secular, state – have waned after Mandela's retirement.

Faced with this, is the African Renaissance little more than an effort to develop a presidential vocabulary that resonates with Mbeki's perceived political strength and interest: international affairs? Or is it simply an effort to further cultivate Mbeki's image as the quintessential renaissance man? To dismiss the idea of the renaissance in this fashion is, we believe, to misread the historical moment that Mbeki has seized, and to close off the political space for emancipation his initiative has secured.

From an immediate policy perspective, and following on our analysis, the important question is: is Mbeki an Africanist or a globalist? An astute observer of South African affairs, Vincent Maphai, who is said to be close to the president, has been reported as saying that Mbeki 'takes Africa seriously, and is emotionally and intellectually committed to proving Afro-pessimism wrong' (*Southern African Report* 1997). And yet, a reading of Mbeki's speeches, not only those that deal with the African Renaissance, suggest a strong commitment to the central tenets of globalisation. More significantly, too, his engineering of the neo-liberal GEAR strategy in the face of strong opposition from within his own party has led to him being marked out as a moderniser by South African business (see Marais 1997), much to the chagrin of the ANC's alliance partners, the SACP and COSATU.

One question remains to be answered: *cui bono*? Who will benefit from the African Renaissance?

Renaissance for whom?

The need for African states to shed their Hobbesian image remains important to members of African elites, irrespective of the colour of their skins. A negotiated settlement of protracted political conflict, followed by the election of a black-led government, has seen an African country, South Africa, attain unprecedented international status and recognition. (Besides its successful political transition, this rise in stature was also fuelled by the sound economic organisation – at least as perceived by the international financial institutions – South Africa's new government had inherited from its predecessor.)

These understandings explain why the idea of the African Renaissance has carried some weight with powerful groupings outside Africa, and outside the ritual pro-Africanist lobbies in western countries. But to believe, as many do, that South Africa alone should assume responsibility for the next wave of democratisation and economic liberalisation on the continent is absurd. On a structural reading, South Africa is undoubtedly well-positioned as a key player in these areas, because it appears to be the natural leader in political and economic affairs; a condition overwhelmingly confirmed by its military power, which it is determined to maintain.

This same reading of South Africa's African destiny explains why many believe the African Renaissance is no more than an effort to secure non-African (particularly American) interests on the African continent. By locking South Africa's transition into the basic tenets of the liberalism preferred by John Stuart Mill – or by rendering the narrative of the victory against apartheid on the same register – will secure the participation of South Africa's new elites in the globalist project. In this interpretation, Mbeki has had no choice – his contribution to history can only be made within this modernist framing.

Obviously, much more will need to be done if South Africa is to fulfill its destiny: the idea of an African Renaissance must primarily be raised in African forums, not only within South Africa but beyond its borders too. But, for Mbeki, the lasting problem may lie at home. South Africans need to be more Africa-literate; to make their country's experience part of a larger African history and reality,[15] they will have to twist Pliny's dictum that there can, indeed, be something new out of Africa that is not 'made in South Africa'. To succeed, South Africa's African Renaissance will have to draw together widely divergent ideas on what it means to be an African citizen early in the twenty-first century.

However, suggestions such as these, aimed at improving South Africa's prospects of realising its African destiny, rest on conventional interpretations of interstate relations, on structuralist understandings of power which, particularly in Africa, rely on the permanence of international boundaries and a return to the world described by Thomas Hobbes. This raises the most urgent question to be tackled on the African continent: whether the African Renaissance and its subsequent manifestations will have the intellectual mass to open and sustain an interrogation of the cardinal issue of what makes for community in Africa – states and people, or states or people. If it cannot do this, the renaissance faces the same unhappy fate as earlier efforts to rediscover Africa.

We believe there is much more at stake in the African Renaissance than the tuck and bob of policy and its making, as structuralist thinkers would have us believe. It remains a striking idea, with an appeal beyond the mundane business of politics, or the aspirations of business and politics. Efforts to codify it may well blunt its choral ring – but much of importance remains to be done in the space that Thabo Mbeki has opened.

Notes

1. For an example of this thinking, see Barratt et al (1974).
2. These issues are analysed in the late Sam Nolutshungu's fine study entitled *South Africa in Africa: a study in ideology and foreign policy* (1975).
3. On 8 May 1996, just before South Africa's new constitution was adopted, Mbeki, Mandela's chosen successor, opened an address to the country's constitutional assembly with the words: 'I am an African!' In a momentous speech, Mbeki drew together the diverse strands of the country's history, and outlined a new, unified, framework for a post-apartheid South Africa. The address provoked an emotional response in the assembly and outside it; across the political spectrum, South Africans strongly associated themselves with its spirit of reconciliation and outreach. See Mbeki (1996).
4. Despite – or perhaps because of – the earlier policy reversals, the visionary language of African Renaissance has been underpinned by five suggested areas of engagement: the encouragement of cultural exchange; the emancipation of African woman from patriarchy; the mobilisation of the youth; the broadening, deepening and sustenance of democracy; and the initiation of sustainable economic development.
5. On 31 July 1997 the Foundation for Global Dialogue (FGD), a South African NGO concerned with international relations questions, held a round table discussion on the African Renaissance which was addressed by Vusi Mavimbela, an aide to Mbeki. The event left participants confused; some reported that very little of substance was discussed. Nevertheless, Mavimbela's views on the African Renaissance are thought to closely reflect Mbeki's own. The text of the presentation was later published as an IGD occasional paper (Mavimbela 1997). However, according to Moeletsi Mbeki, Thabo Mbeki's brother, the analysis was initially prepared as 'an unpublished departmental paper'. See Mbeki (1998).

6. This analogy was suggested to me by Prof Richard Joseph of Emory University, Atlanta.
7. See De Coning (2000) and Vale (1997). Actually, Mbeki first raised the question of South Africa contributing to UN peacekeeping operations in Africa in a speech to the South African general assembly in June 1994 (quoted in SAIRR 1996: 422).
8. See, for example, Cilliers and Mills (1995); Institute for Security Studies (1997); and Romer-Heidman (1998).
9. Some of the wider debates around these notions are outlined in Appiah (1992: 284).
10. In July 1997 the business-funded South African Institute of International Affairs (SAIIA) held a conference entitled 'South and southern Africa: lessons from emerging markets', which reinforced globalist perspectives of the success of the Asian tigers.
11. Greg Mills, national director of the South African Institute of International Affaris, is a leading proponent of this perspective. Mills (1997) contains the following final paragraph: 'Yet, in an age of globalisation, it is important to leave behind academic and banal debates such as that around the definition of "African". If the Renaissance is to be kept alive in the face of intensifying conflict in many parts of the continent, the time for rhetoric and playing to the gallery is fast being supplanted by the need to put facts on the ground.'
12. For a class analysis of the African Renaissance, see Maloka (1997).
13. A 'Black Renaissance Convention' was organised at the former St Peter's Conference Centre at Hammanskraal on 13–16 December 1974.
14. Some of these issues are discussed in *The Economist*, 13 December 1997.
15. In 1997 it was reported that black South African diplomats preferred being posted to western capitals rather than African countries. AF Press Clips (1997).

References

Adler, E. 1998. Imagined (security) communities: cognitive regions in international relations. *Millennium*, 26 (2). 249–77.
AF Press Clips. 1997. Black South African diplomats do not want African postings. 3 August.
Africa Confidential. 2002. South Africa – crossing the Limpopo. 43 (2). 25 January.
Appiah, KA. 1992. *In my father's house: Africa in the philosophy of culture*. London: Methuen.
Barber, J and Barratt, J. 1990. *South Africa foreign policy: the search for status and security, 1945–1988*. Johannesburg: Southern Book Publishers.
Barratt, J, Brand, S, Collier, DS, and Glaser, K (eds). 1974. *Accelerated development in southern Africa*. London: Macmillan.
Breytenbach, W (ed). 1980. *The Constellation of states: a consideration*. Johannesburg: South Africa Foundation.
Business Report. 1998. Winning both ways in the inscrutable game of Chinese diplomatic checkers. 15 January.

Chase, R, Hill, E, and Kennedy, P. 1996. Pivotal states and US strategy. *Foreign Affairs*, 75 (1). January–February. 33–51.

Cilliers, J and Mills, G (eds). 1995. *Peacekeeping in Africa, vol 2*. Johannesburg: Institute for Defence Policy; South African Institute for International Affairs.

De Coning, C. 2000. Lesotho intervention: implications for SADC, military interventions, peacekeeping, and the African Renaissance. In H Solomon and M Muller (eds). *Contributions to the African Renaissance*. African Dialogue monograph series no 1. Durban: ACCORD. 39–75.

Diawara, M. 1996. To Toni Cade Bambrara. *Black Renaissance/Renaissance Noir*, 1 (1). Fall. 6.

Dladla, N. 1997. African Renaissance: teaching the past to find the future. *Mail & Guardian*. 1–7 April.

The Economist. 1997. The end of the miracle. 13 December.

Financial Mail. 1998. Mother Africa, mother niche. 16 January.

Geldenhuys, D. 1981. *The Constellation of Southern African States and the South African Development Co-ordination Council: towards a new regional stalemate?* Johannesburg: South African Institute for International Affairs.

Institute for Security Studies. 1997. The SA Navy and an African Renaissance. Selected papers, annual naval conference, 23 October. ISS papers no 27.

Leftwich, G. 1997. An African Renaissance? *South Africa: The Journal of Trade, Industry and Investment*. Summer.

Maloka, E. 1997. African Renaissance reactionary. *African Communist*, 147. 3rd quarter. 37–43.

Mandela, N. 1997. Statement as chairperson of SADC at the official opening of the summit of the SADC heads of states or governments, Blantryre, Malawi, 8 September.

Marais, H. 1997. The Mbeki enigma. *Southern Africa Report*, 13 (1). November. 6–11.

Mavimbela, V. 1997. *The African Renaissance: a workable dream*. Occasional Paper no 17. Johannesburg: Foundation for Global Dialogue. October.

Mbeki, M. 1997. The African Renaissance: myth or reality? Address to the South African Institute of International Affairs. 21 October.

———. 1998. The African Renaissance. In *South African Yearbook of International Affairs, 1998/9*. Johannesburg: South African Institute of International Affairs. 120.

Mbeki, T. 1996. I am an African! Speech in the constitutional assembly. *Debates of the Constitutional Assembly*, no 1, 29 March–8 May. Cols 422–7.

———. 1997. Address to Corporate Council on Africa's 'Attracting capital to Africa' summit, 19–22 April, Chantilly, Virginia, United States. http://www.anc.org.za/ancdocs/history/mbeki/1997/sp970419.html.

Mills, G. 1999. Understanding the African Renaissance. *Financial Mail*. 12 March.

———. 2000. *The wired model: South Africa, foreign policy, and globalisation*. Cape Town: Tafelberg.

Ndebele, N. 1997. The debate on eurocentricism risks degenerating into name-calling. *The Sunday Independent*. 28 September.

Nolutshungu, S. 1975. *South Africa in Africa: a study in ideology and foreign policy*. Manchester: Manchester University Press.

Nyerere, J. 1997. Speech to the South African parliament. 16 October. http://www.sardc.net/nyerere/speech.html.

Omotoso, K. 1994. *Season of migration to the south: Africa's crises reconsidered.* Cape Town: Tafelberg.

Romer-Heidman, H. 1998. Regional security: SA needs a power projection capability. *Finance Week.* 15–21 January. 38.

Rowland, ID. 1997. The Renaissance revealed. *New York Review of Books.* 6 November. 30.

Smuts, JC. 1942. *Plans for a better world: speeches of Field Marshall the Rt Hon JC Smuts.* London: Hodder and Stoughton.

South African Institute of Race Relations. 1996. *Race relations survey, 1994/5.* Johannesburg.

Southern Africa Report. 1997. African Renaissance (editorial). 13 (1). November.

Sowetan. 1997. Heavy load for SADC. Johannesburg. 15 September.

Strauss, C. 1995. Preface. In G Mills, A Begg and A van Nieuwerk (eds), *South Africa in the global economy.* Johannesburg: South African Institute of International Affairs, with the assistance of Standard Bank.

Tondon, Y. 1997. Globalisation and the South: the logic of exploitation. *International Politics and Society,* 4. 389–98.

Vale, P. 1997. Peace in Southern Africa – time for questions. In G Sorbo and P Vale (eds), *Out of conflict: from war to peace in Africa.* Uppsala: Nordic Africa Institute. 39–53.

———. 1997. The African Renaissance: it sounds wonderful, but what does it mean? *Election talk,* newsletter two. December. Johannesburg: Electoral Institute of South Africa. 1–2.

———. 2002. Obituary. *Politikon,* 20 (1). 123–4.

———. 2002. Presentation to the Goedgedracht Forum, Western Cape. 8 March.

Vale, P and Maseko, S. 1998. South Africa and the African Renaissance. *International Affairs,* 74 (2). 271–87.

Postscript
From the African Renaissance to NEPAD

Peter Vale

Looking back, it is easy to see the African Renaissance as the immediate curtain-raiser for Mbeki's ambitious and energetic campaign NEPAD. But the thrust towards NEPAD began with the millennium celebrations when the renaissance idea mutated into the Millennium Africa Recovery Plan (MAP), which was fully associated with Mbeki's earlier thoughts.

Moreover, the mandate to move further on the idea of reconsidering Africa's institutional arrangements came from elsewhere. Early in 2000 the OAU mandated Mbeki and his Nigerian and Algerian counterparts, Olusegun Obasanjo and Abdelaziz Bouteflika, to investigate how the continent could deal with its debt crisis. This engagement – a multilateral one, and focused on an economic issue – was the first thread in NEPAD's development.

The second was the OMEGA Plan proposed by president Abdoulaye Wade of Senegal, a latecomer both to office and to the idea of regenerating the continent: strong on regional infrastructural development and educational issues, OMEGA was – perhaps predictably – enthusiastically supported by Francophone African countries.

A third, and inadequately explored, thread was the Compact for African Recovery initiated by the UN Economic Commissioner for Africa, KY Amoako. Of the three, this was the most substantive; certainly, even though the compact initially lacked heavyweight political backing, the concerns it voiced have come to be prominently reflected in the NEPAD agenda.

These three threads were drawn together into the New African Initiative (NAI), at a meeting of African ministers of finance and economics in Algiers in May 2001. Two months later a meeting of the OAU, held in Lusaka, appointed an implementation committee of 15 heads of state to further manage the evolving process. Three months later, in October 2001, the process was renamed the New (Economic) Programme for Africa's Development, or NEPAD (pronounced as NêPAD, rather than KNEEPAD, as a number of satirists immediately insisted on calling it).

Some accounts have added a fourth thread to NEPAD's evolution: the peace and security relationship, traced backwards to the Conference on Security, Stability, Development and Co-operation in Africa (CSSDCA) – the Kampala Process – in which Obasango played an important role. If anything, this additional linkage masks the regenerative roots of NEPAD, and obscures the liberal internationalist claims to the value of peace-keeping that have come to mark international relations in the post-cold war era.

The drive towards NEPAD suggests Mbeki's (and now Africa's) determination to pursue a directed form of engagement with this neo-liberalism at home and abroad. In this process, any linkage between rich and poor, North and South, should be premised upon codes of institutional behaviour that have emerged in recent years.

In bullet form, these are:

- managing conflict non-violently, captured in NEPAD's discussion of a peace-keeping mechanism for the continent;
- enforcing the rule of law and exacting accountability, captured in NEPAD's frequent invocation of the idea of good governance; and
- creating the conditions for open competition, captured in the idea of equal access to global markets.

These suggest that any hope that this new agenda for Africa's regeneration would table a new, or an alternative, development paradigm to the dominant neo-liberal one has faded. Indeed, Mbeki and his colleagues clearly hope that Africans will accept these ideas as commonsensical ones, or as integral to the global public goods necessary for progress.

By accepting these as conditioning values, a series of ideological questions are embedded in the NEPAD process. Is NEPAD really just another way of rearranging Africa's elites? Are African states to be the local gendarmerie of international capital? Can agency be returned to African states, as they are presently constructed? And can this agency be used for emancipatory purposes?

Bonding

These (and other) questions raise the issue of the relationship between NEPAD and the long-cherished hope of African unity. On this front, evidence of what will happen next is flimsy, even though speculation around it has provided a rich seam of copy for the press. At the time of writing, a few things are clear, however. In early July 2002, the OAU was tranfromed into the African Union (AU). This transition was imbued with a great deal of symbolism. For all its entropy, the OAU did achieve a measure of success. It enabled African states to survive, if not flourish, as social institutions, and it did deliver the historically located dream of ending colonialism and white rule. These are no mean achievements, but Mbeki and his colleagues have clearly adjudged them to be inadequate for the twenty-first centuy.

On paper it seems as if the AU will bring to Africa a regularised and institutional mode of sovereign integration, with all the mundane presence of compromise and bureaucracy. So it has been proposed that 17 union institutions – from finance, to a court, to a parliament, to a social and economic council – should be established.

Sceptics and supporters alike, however, have pointed to the costs involved in an exercise of this magnitude, and alluded to the fact that the OAU itself is in arrears to the tune of $50 million. But if costs are one thing, the process for creating the AU has been another. Its constitutive act has not been thoroughly debated on the continent, neither by African parliaments nor by civil society. Like NEPAD, with which its relationship is entirely uncertain, the AU is a distinctly top-down exercise.

A third aspect of the AU initiative is that, for all its pious undertakings and its rhetorical location within the spirit of African unity, it may well become a political football. In this respect, two figures – Mbeki, and Libya's Muammar Gaddafi – symbolise distinctive positions. In September 1999 the latter proposed the immediate declaration of the 'United States of Africa'. By contrast, Mbeki's more cautious, even systematic, approach has seemingly gained the upper hand – but the potential for deeper divisions remain very high, in a situation complicated by the fact that an understanding of Libya's intentions are distorted by the media which, drawing on northern portrayals, insist on lampooning Gaddafi rather than analysing him and his country in a clear and objective manner.

However, the test of the new African multilateralism promised by NEPAD may lie elsewhere. While the immediate hope for NEPAD is that its commitments to good practice could enable African countries to modernise more quickly and more deeply, substantial concessions on, say, access to world agricultural markets may have to wait for the deliberations of increasingly complex multilateral forums such as the WTO.

To be seen to be working and effective, contemporary multilateralism must deliver, regularly and continuously. While successes such as the clearance of landmines (in which South Africa has played an important role) have demonstrated the success of post-cold war multilateralism, more recent examples have been found to be wanting. Thus the International Criminal Court has been ignored – no, spurned – by the current American administration, while other treaties, such as Kyoto, have been ignored, and the Anti-Ballistic Missile Treaty unilaterally reversed. Delivering on what NEPAD has promised Africa's people would certainly give credence to the claims of Africa's leaders, including Mbeki, to represent a new spirit of accountability, but the outcome of the G8 meeting in Canada in late June 2002 suggests that the proverbial jury is out.

The beguiling question

What is NEPAD? The plan rests on a simple leitmotif: no political and social world is possible beyond the market. The central argument for NEPAD (one used ceaselessly by state-makers and the liberal press) is this: those who play the game of markets and its derivative, globalisation, will be presented with great opportunities. The corollary of this argument is that efforts to counter globalisation can only be weak and episodic.

The hope of those who wish to engage with NEPAD, as opposed to the many that will resist it, is simple: in the absence of alternatives, can NEPAD be improved? This moment has a clear contemporary chime. Elsewhere, the challenge of drawing people closer towards the market–globalisation agenda has been a blend of effective rhetoric around economic and social governance, with a sustained and passionate commitment to democracy, and an intense interest in human rights. This is the 'third way' – proclaimed by the eminent British social theorist Anthony Giddens, and championed by Britan's prime minister, Tony Blair.

So here lies the answer to the question posed at the beginning of the section: NEPAD is a creature of the times. But is this enough of an answer? No, it is not, because the times are also marked by an intense interest, mainly academic, but increasingly political, in the nature of knowledge and its making.

This brief narrative has pointed to the instrumentalism implied in both the theory and practice of NEPAD as a new form of social organisation. Given that Mbeki – as Sipho Maseko and I note in the preceding analysis – is more of a policy politician than a people politician, it should not be surprising that his presidency has been marked by a concern with the managerial and procedural aspects of social organisation. This has certainly been accompanied by a focus on institutional and bureaucratic efficiency and accountability. NEPAD is an excellent example of this approach, a narrowing of the social basis of popular participation within a disciplinary code represented by market economics. It represents the confluence of new constitutionalism and neo-liberalism cast within the culture of technical-rationality that marks these times.

Underlying any unfolding series of social perspectives is the question: for whom? It seems easy to answer – but, on reflection, any answer is confused and confounded by the welter of managerial and economic logic that has infused the debate on NEPAD. Is NEPAD a new moment in the emancipation of Africa and its people? Or is it, like the 'third way', upon which its plainly rests, simply a new authoritarianism?

PART TWO

Politics

CHAPTER 6

Remaking the presidency
The tension between co-ordination and centralisation

FAROUK CHOTHIA and SEAN JACOBS

When, in May 1994, Nelson Mandela began to serve as South Africa's first democratic president, his office was considerably smaller in size than that of his predecessor, FW de Klerk. However, the demands on it were probably far greater. For one, Mandela had to share it with his two deputy presidents: De Klerk, and Thabo Mbeki. For another, given his job description of head of state, with a heavy international schedule, as well as head of a government setting out to review every aspect of government policy, overhaul the apartheid statute book, and implement new systems of provincial and local government, Mandela's own workload was probably heavier than that of his predecessor. Therefore, it is hardly surprising that, soon after his installation, a process was set in motion to expand his office.

The official vehicle for doing so was a presidential commission on the reform and transformation of the public service. As its name suggests, it had a broad mandate to restructure executive government, but concentrated mainly on restructuring the president's office (1998: chapter 2). A second impetus for restructuring the presidency (as the office subsequently became known) was the work of Mbeki, first as first deputy president and later as president. During the commission's public hearings, it soon emerged that there was widespread uncertainty about the president's role. Dr Jakes Gerwel, then director-general of Mandela's office, bluntly told the commission:

> What is the role of the President's Office in the initiation, formulation and co-ordination of policy; what is the filtering down process of policy from cabinet to departments; how is the work of directors-general co-ordinated, and by whom? It does seem . . . from the

questions posed as well as other signs that we, who are working at the centre of government, pick up that there is a concern at times, even a preoccupation, with what is described as the co-ordination of government, or actually a lack of co-ordination of government (1997).

The commission eventually made a series of recommendations that transformed the presidency in a way that would have profound implications for the way in which Mbeki would govern South Africa after Mandela had departed. Most significant was the presidency's central role in detailed policy-making and day-to-day governance. Surprisingly, there has been little, if any, serious public engagement over the changing role of the presidency and its place in the post-Mandela power nexus. Analyses of the workings of the presidency are largely confined to the mainstream media, as no academic scholarship exists on presidentialism in the new South Africa.[1]

In this chapter we will explore the genesis of the restructured presidency, and its implications for an Mbeki politics; notably, we trace the roots of the restructuring to moves by Mbeki and his closest advisers – while he was still deputy president[2] – to build a power base in and around the office of the president in anticipation of his rule, particularly in the context of leadership rivalries within the ANC.

We further suggest that the Mbeki presidency is characterised by tensions between a quest for better co-ordination of policy to achieve the government's stated aims of economic growth, job creation, and social development on the one hand, and a tendency to centralisation on the other.

Finally, we locate these developments in a general trend in this direction among governments worldwide, particularly those led by historically left-of-centre political parties. We particularly point to parallels between the institutional restructuring surrounding the Mbeki presidency and those surrounding Tony Blair's prime ministership in the United Kingdom, which has served as a model for Mbeki's advisers.

Preparing to rule
There were no historical precedents for the positions of deputy president or presidents that came into force with the 1994 transition; they were first created by the interim constitution of 1993, a product of the negotiations of the early 1990s, which culminated in the Government of National Unity (GNU) that assumed power under Mandela's leadership. As its name suggests, the GNU essentially worked on the basis of consensus, and was made up of the three most powerful parties in South African politics: the ANC, NP, and IFP. In terms of the interim constitution of 1993 (s82) every party with at least

80 seats in (or 20 per cent of) the national assembly – the lower house of parliament – could designate an executive deputy president from among members of the assembly (s84).

Flowing from the results of the 1994 elections, the ANC and NP each nominated a deputy president, resulting in the appointment of Mbeki and De Klerk. When it came to decision-making, the interim constitution required the president to consult the two deputy presidents on the development and execution of government policies. Consultation involved 'all matters relating to the management of cabinet and cabinet business, in the delegation of functions to the deputy president, in the appointment of ambassadors, diplomats and consular staff, and before exercising any of the competencies as president under the interim constitution' (s82). The constitution also required that deputy presidents could '. . . if the president so instructed, chair cabinet meetings, taking turns to do so, unless exigencies of government dictated otherwise' (s82). However, any decision by a cabinet meeting presided over by a deputy president had to be ratified by the president.

While publicly Mandela and Mbeki observed all the constitutional rules, privately De Klerk was being sidelined. In any event, the NP and De Klerk soon became peripheral to succession politics surrounding the presidency. Following the 1994 elections, the NP's power and influence declined rapidly. De Klerk's popularity also declined, while Mandela's support among all population groups grew to an all-time high. Among whites – its traditional constituency – the NP faced stiff competition from the more assertive DP under its new leader, Tony Leon.

Mandela delegated little authority over the day-to-day running of the country to De Klerk; the latter was left with nothing to do except chair the cabinet committee in charge of security and intelligence affairs, and travel abroad to receive honours for his role in the negotiated settlement. It therefore came as no surprise when, in May 1996, De Klerk announced his intention to lead the NP out of the GNU, thus effectively ending his deputy presidency. The walkout – at end June – coincided with the date on which the final constitution came into effect, and was well ahead of the GNU's formal expiry date of 1999.

Mbeki now served as deputy president all by himself. Crucially, around this time Mandela began to publicly endorse Mbeki as his successor. Following the NP's withdrawal from the GNU, Mbeki's role increased even further *vis-à-vis* that of Mandela. The latter assigned more and more functions to the former, including that of co-ordinating the work of ministers. *Inter alia*, Mbeki announced his intention to check progress made with implementing white papers – official government policy statements – by the different ministries. This gave him and his allies an opening to build a separate deputy president's office – thus developing the power of the deputy presidency, and preparing for an expanded presidency.

Mbeki's office started from a zero base, with no extra space and no staff (Davis 1999: 3). The initial establishment of the office was therefore tentative, and relied heavily on advisers with minimal support staff. By July 1994, however, the deputy president's office had 50 posts, and was headed by a chief director, Dr Frank Chikane (a former anti-apartheid cleric). Administrative support was initially provided by the president's office, but it was subsequently decided that these offices should have their own administrative structures. Personnel in the deputy president's office included four advisers, as well as administrative staff needed to maintain offices in the legislative capital, Cape Town, and the executive capital, Pretoria. The office was also expanded to include communications staff. Despite being the second most important political office in the country, it had a smaller budget than most ministries; in 1996 it was R9,3 million, six per cent more than in the previous year. This would soon change; the budget for 1997–98 was 29 per cent bigger, while that of Mandela's office was 11 per cent smaller.

By April 1997 Mbeki's office was staffed by 96 people (up from the 50 of three years earlier), and his intention to appoint 65 more had been reported in the press. Mbeki began to make a number of crucial appointments. His first after 1994, apart from Chikane, was to make Essop Pahad, a close associate during his days in exile, his parliamentary councillor. In this way Mbeki established a direct link with the legislature, its committees, and the ANC's parliamentary caucus. He also appointed four other advisers, the most important being Moss Ngoasheng as economics adviser, and Vusi Mavimbela as political adviser.[3]

A key factor in the evolution of the office of the deputy president, however, was the closure in April 1996 of the RDP office following a cabinet reshuffle forced by the resignation of the minister of finance, Chris Liebenberg (Davis 1999: 5). A task team that included Ngoasheng, the cabinet secretary, Jakes Gerwel, and senior RDP officials thoroughly reviewed the activities of the RDP office. The RDP ministry was scrapped (Jay Naidoo, minister without portfolio responsible for the RDP, was shifted to telecommunications and broadcasting in place of Pallo Jordan, an intellectual rival of Mbeki's), and was absorbed into Mbeki's office. A number of other offices and institutions were also established in the deputy president's office. Politically, the most important of these was the Government Communications and Information

Service (GCIS), for which Pahad assumed political responsibility as a deputy minister, and whose director was Joel Netshitentzhe, then a close ally of Mbeki. The GCIS, set up to co-ordinate and modernise government communications, has since effectively become the propaganda arm of central government and the presidency in particular.

In June 1997 the cabinet approved the establishment in Mbeki's office of an important new unit designed to 'equip government with the strategic planning and management capacity it required': the Co-ordination and Implementation Unit (CIU) (Davis 1999: 6). It was this unit that – following many different reincarnations, including a diminution of its powers and responsibilities – evolved into the Policy Co-ordination and Advisory Service (PCAS). At the time, the establishment of the CIU was not formally announced. However, in October 1997, in a rare comment on the organisation of his office, Mbeki mentioned this in an interview with the *Financial Mail* (Bruce and Laurence 1997). Asked what the CIU was, he declared:

> It's an economic, a socio-economic co-ordinating unit. There has been a difficulty in the separation of departments, with each doing its own thing. When people think about foreign affairs, they normally think of the department of foreign affairs. But trade and industry is in foreign affairs, finance is in foreign affairs, defence is in foreign affairs, safety and security are in foreign affairs – a whole number of departments. You could have a situation where each one is pulling in different directions. So you need a co-ordinating unit, particularly with regard to economic questions. It is a unit of co-ordination.

Asked whether this meant that he would become an 'economic superminister', Mbeki replied:

> No... the deputy presidency has this function of co-ordinating government policy, and we have been trying to carry out that function on economic matters with two people, myself and Moss Ngoasheng, that's all. And it's quite impossible.

Despite Mbeki's public pronouncements on the CIU, and the spin placed on its formation by his ministers, the unit has had a mixed reception. On the one hand, its formation underlined the government's intention to improve the co-ordination of its programmes, and its perceived need for improved delivery ahead of the 1999 elections. On the other, it raised the issue of whether the provincial governments and line ministries were being sidelined (Davis 1999).

Centralisation or co-ordination?

Despite his numerous speeches and articles on a range of policy and governance issues, Mbeki himself has rarely referred publicly to the reorganisation of the presidency (the interview mentioned earlier is an exception). When representatives of his office embark on public relations exercises, the reason they give for the restructuring is that it will improve policy co-ordination, and thus help to ensure economic growth, job creation, and social development. 'It's about better co-ordination and implementation', is what Mbeki's aides have said on the few occasions that they have spoken publicly or written about this issue. They have also emphasised that the restructuring process has flowed from the work of the Presidential Review Commission.[4] The commission's final report, presented to then president Mandela in May 1998, suggested that the president's office was inadequately resourced and badly structured. Most importantly, the commission argued that policy formulation and decision-making by the cabinet were 'unsatisfactory': decisions were too often taken without the necessary co-ordination across departments, and between national departments and their provincial counterparts. It called for a 'radical appraisal' of the functions, structures, personnel, and management of the office of the president, and insisted that the presidency should be 'the core of the system of governance' (chapter 2). It also recommended the creation of seven new offices under the umbrella of the presidency. In making these recommendations, the report emphasised that centralising power in this manner was a growing trend among governments around the world. It argued that there was a need to deliver on election promises, and that the purpose of centralisation was to give heads of government the means to play a strong co-ordinating role in achieving this objective.

The media questioned the reforms, on the grounds that they represented an excessive concentration of power. However, Mbeki's defenders responded that the restructuring of the presidency was not the outcome of a whim, or a predilection for power, and stressed that the commission was a public process of inquiry and consultation headed by two respected South African political scientists, Vincent Maphai and Norman Levy.

But the questions have persisted. The central one is: how much of the restructuring is about improved co-ordination, and how much about power? It could be argued that, whether or not this was their primary motive, the silence of Mbeki and his advisers on this question lends weight to the perception that the restructuring process has primarily been aimed at concentrating enormous power in his hands. The fear is that, however benign their intent may be, such centralisation could presage an imperial presidency:

powerful, imposing, and impenetrable. This is the charge levelled by critics of the president (*Financial Mail*, 28 May 1999), who suggest that the centralisation of policy- and decision-making power in the president's office is the last piece in a jigsaw of consolidated control over every aspect of government.

The main features of the transformed presidency are:

- the amalgamation of the formerly separate offices of the president and deputy president into a single entity known as 'the presidency';
- 38 more staff members than those employed in the previously separate offices, bringing the total complement to 334 people;
- a deputy president with a limited brief to 'fulfil tasks delegated by the president', and act as the 'leader of government business' in parliament;
- a minister without portfolio in the presidency, reporting to the president and controlling all government communications;
- a beefed-up cabinet office, which makes policy recommendations to the cabinet and vets policy proposals made by it. Based on the British cabinet office, it consists of three sections: research, operations, and a cabinet secretariat, which oversees and co-ordinates policy implementation and delivery strategies across various ministries;
- the clustering of cabinet ministers into committees around key policy and delivery areas;
- directors-general who are contracted to the president rather than by their own ministries; and
- a five-unit agency entitled Policy Co-ordination and Advisory Services (PCAS), which shadows the ministerial cluster committees, vets new policy, and drafts legislation for tabling at cabinet meetings (Jacobs 1999: 4–5).

As the features of this new system emerged, critics focused on two themes: a lack of accountability to elected representatives, and a centralisation of power in the hands of a few individuals.

On the face of it, they have a point. For example, neither the minister without portfolio (currently Essop Pahad) nor the PCAS is accountable to any legislative body. And it is the PCAS – if it works effectively – that will exercise a crucial gate-keeping function in the policy-making process, as ministries are now required to refer all new policy documents and draft legislation to the presidency for scrutiny by PCAS officials. They will decide whether proposals fit in with the government's broader policy framework, and whether the fiscal implications are acceptable.

An advantage of the reforms is that it establishes a team of experts to check legislation, thus avoiding, in theory at least, the passage of an ambitious but inadequately conceived or drafted act that would otherwise have infringed the constitution. During the term of the first democratic government, this function was left to underresourced parliamentary committees and cabinet members, who possibly lacked the necessary expertise outside their own portfolios.

The PCAS consists of five chief directorates: economic sector, intergovernmental co-ordination, social sector, criminal justice system, and international relations. The chief directors of the five units within the PCAS are at least as powerful as cabinet ministers. While each minister controls a single portfolio, each chief director is responsible for a cluster of ministries. Since October 1998, cabinet committee clusters reflect the structure of the PCAS chief directorates. Thus they are:

- the economics cluster (the ministries of finance, trade, labour, and water);
- the social services cluster (the ministries of education, health, housing, and welfare);
- international relations (the ministries of foreign affairs and defence);
- intergovernmental relations (the ministry of provincial and local government); and
- criminal justice (the ministries of safety and security, justice, and correctional services).

In some cases at least, this system will probably result in battles for turf as ministers compete against the PCAS for control over policy-making. The suspicion is that, while the formal policy-making process seems well entrenched, the PCAS will have the upper hand. The likely outcome is that the PCAS will take the decisions behind the scenes, while ministers will sell the resultant policies to the public. The sense is that only strong ministers will challenge this new regime, and even they will have to weigh their dissent against the possibility of being dropped from the cabinet when a new cabinet is chosen or the existing one reshuffled. Most are likely to accept being reduced to managers.

Another troubling scenario is the possibility that unpopular or unsuccessful policies will become the site of accountability battles between individual (or clustered) ministries and the PCAS. Accountability issues arise in relation to other elements of the new system. It is clear that more integrated policy – a need most obvious in respect of the criminal justice system – should be one of the benefits of the clustering of cabinet committees. But who will be responsible for implementation, and who will fight the fires?

This problem is compounded by the fact that the president has the power to create posts that cut across ministries, with the incumbents reporting directly to him rather than to ministers or ministerial committees. One example is that of director of public prosecutions (a kind of super attorney-general), whose staff includes the newly established Scorpions unit, charged with investigating serious high-priority crimes. Similarly, while cabinet ministers are accountable to parliament, the chief directors of the PCAS are not. No portfolio committee can summon them to explain their decisions; they are accountable only to Mbeki.

Also accountable to the president are the new directors-general, who now sign contracts with the presidency rather than with their own ministers. Not only does this erode the traditional power of ministers to make the most senior political appointments in their departments; it also opens up the possibility of divided loyalties. Who will directors-general serve in the first instance: their ministers, or the president? On the positive side, this system means the president can move directors-general more easily should they and their ministers prove unable to co-operate.[5]

A potentially problematic – and beneficial – outcome of the reorganisation of the presidency is the modification of the relationship between the different levels of government, with the centre strengthened at the expense of the provinces. The policy-making powers of the provinces – which was extensively debated during the constitutional negotiations – has already been considerably curtailed in that their budgets are now determined by the national ministry of finance and, to a lesser extent, the nationally located Financial and Fiscal Commission (FFC). The latter is effectively controlled by the department of finance.

The rationale for further strengthening the centre in this case is again largely one of improved efficiency. This is backed by the undeniable need to address management and institutional dysfunction in some provinces.[6] The aim was to improve policy co-ordination among different levels of government. The major new mechanism is a chief director of co-operative governance in the PCAS. Previously, policy made at the national level would be referred to the provincial level for implementation, without the necessary regard for provincial contexts and conditions. The hope is that PCAS vetting will remedy the gap.

The major losers in the restructuring of the presidency, and its effects on policy-making and the exercise of political power, are parliament and the ANC. While the government has shifted to the cluster approach, parliamentary committees still oversee separate government departments, The committees not only lack the resources to effectively monitor the government, but also do not have the powers to oversee the decisions of the PCAS and the minister in the office of the president. But it is the position of the ANC as a political entity relative to the presidency that has been the most negatively affected. As the president builds the capacity of his executive office, so the ANC's capacity dwindles. Mbeki wants officials at ANC headquarters to be managers, dealing with organisational matters such as errant branches and building election machinery rather than with political issues.[7] As we argue below, at the same time as he has downgraded the role of officials at ANC headquarters, Mbeki has consolidated his grip on the party apparatus.

An African Tony Blair?
In many ways, Mbeki's office and his politics are a replica of those of Tony Blair. Not only has Mbeki embraced Blair's 'third way' ideology; he has also modelled the presidency on Blair's prime ministerial office. Mbeki has more influence in government than Mandela ever had – just as Blair has more power than any of his predecessors, including Margaret Thatcher. Both Blair and Mbeki were somewhat insecure while rising to the pinnacle of power, as their new vision for social democracy based on privatisation, fiscal discipline, and fewer rights for workers was strongly challenged by left-wingers within their parties.

Both Blair's Labour Party and Mbeki's ANC had historically been the political home of the trade union movements in their respective countries, which had helped to shape policies, finance party activities, and lead their electoral campaigns. As newly styled social democrats, Blair and Mbeki set out to challenge the traditional natures of their parties. They were starting a 'revolution', and for this they needed to strengthen their hold over their respective parties and governments on a larger scale than their predecessors. Otherwise, the centre, which they occupied, would collapse, bringing their political careers to an end.

In August 1999 *The Economist* described the British prime minister's style of rule as follows:

> Blair tightened his grip on Whitehall in the same way he tightened his grip on the party. Policy development and decision-making, which were scattered throughout departments in Whitehall, have been centralised around the prime minister's office.

Mbeki has done the same. After becoming ANC president in 1997, he set about building a power base at Luthuli House, the party's headquarters in Johannesburg. One of his first initiatives was to restructure the president's office, bringing departments that were close to his heart – such as international affairs and information and publicity – under his direct control.

He appointed SACP member Smuts Ngonyama as the head of the president's office, and made him responsible for information and publicity. At the same time, Mbeki deployed his parliamentary councillor, Mavivi Manzini, at Luthuli House to head the international affairs section, and later appointed her to the key post of ANC chief whip in the national assembly. These appointments neutralised two prominent critics of Mbeki: the independent socialist Pallo Jordan, who lost the media post to Ngonyama, and Blade Nzimande, now secretary-general of the SACP, who, while heading the international affairs desk, was critical of government foreign policy.

After president and deputy president, the two most significant posts in the ANC are those of national chairman and secretary-general. When Jacob Zuma – now deputy president of South Africa – and Cyril Ramaphosa, now a prominent businessman, filled these posts, they built up substantial public profiles. Mbeki's reign has changed this: the new party chair, Patrick Lekota, seems to have less influence within the ANC than Zuma had when he held the post (Lekota's appointment is part of his managed rehabilitation after he was deposed as premier of Free State province), while, under Kgalema Motlanthe, the secretary-general's post has lost its image of the Ramaphosa era as a rival power base within the ANC.

In government, Mbeki has been consolidating his power in a similar fashion. The deputy presidency has lost its independent status. Zuma does not have a separate office with its own director-general; his office falls under that of Mbeki, and his staff under Mbeki's director-general, Frank Chikane.

The downgrading of the deputy president's post is understandable. It had clout when Mbeki occupied it precisely because Mandela was grooming the former for the presidency. It has now reverted to its natural role: that of supporting the president. In most governments, the posts of deputy president or deputy prime minister are empty shells, and this is now also the case in South Africa. Deputies tend to bide their time, waiting for their political bosses to vacate office so that they can take over with their blessing.

However, while Zuma is a long-standing ally of Mbeki, it is doubtful that he will be the next president; the post is likely to go to a leader from the post-Mbeki/Zuma generation.[8] Zuma – previously member of the executive committee for economic affairs and tourism in KwaZulu-Natal – secured the deputy presidency by default. Mbeki had planned to give the post to IFP leader Mangosuthu Buthelezi, but the latter refused to accept the conditions under which it was offered: that the premiership of the strategically important KwaZulu-Natal be surrendered to the ANC.

Of the significant public functions that Mbeki performed as deputy president, only one has gone to Zuma: chairing the South African delegation to the various binational commissions formed with foreign governments. But Zuma's role appears to be a titular one, as control over foreign policy rests firmly in Mbeki's hands. Zuma does not seem to be held in high regard by western governments – the best example being Washington's desire in 1999 that Mbeki (when he became president) continue chairing the binational commission with its then vice-president, Al Gore. Mbeki refused; he regarded Washington's demand as arrogant. Not only did it imply a lack of faith in Zuma, but would also have suggested that Mbeki remained Gore's equivalent rather than becoming president Bill Clinton's.

On the domestic front, Zuma has been appointed as 'leader of government business'. This captures the extent to which the deputy presidency has been downgraded, as, during the Mandela era, an ordinary cabinet minister (then the minister of sport, the late Steve Tshwete) fulfilled this function. It is largely an administrative one, with the incumbent responsible for ensuring that legislation flows smoothly from the cabinet to parliament.

While Mbeki has downgraded the deputy presidency, he has upgraded the post of his trusted aide, Essop Pahad. Mbeki took Pahad with him to the president's office, and elevated his status from that of deputy minister (which excluded him from cabinet meetings) to that of minister. The two of them are very close; their relationship dates back to the days when they studied at Sussex University in the United Kingdom. Pahad has retained political responsibility for most of his previous functions, including the National Youth Commission, the Office on the Status of Women, and the Office for the Disabled.

Pahad comes across as a belligerent politician, so it is ironic that Mbeki is hoping to build an image of a caring president, one who champions the cause of socially marginalised groups, with Pahad's assistance. At the same time, Pahad stays in touch with and wields influence over two powerful (and previously troublesome) constituencies: youths, and women. Pahad also exercises political responsibility for the GCIS as well as the African Renaissance, the central theme of Mbeki's presidency. Pahad has appointed the former journalist Tony Heard as his adviser. Another former journalist in the presidency is Mbeki's political adviser, Titus Mafolo.

Despite this, Mbeki, Pahad, and Zuma generally have poor relations with the media. They tend to be secretive, suspicious, and hostile towards the media – the most vivid example of this being the ANC's hard-hitting submission to the South African Human Rights Commission's (SAHRC) inquiry into media racism (ANC 2000; see also SAHRC 2000).

After assuming the presidency, Mbeki showed a commitment to improving his media profile, *inter alia* by appointing Parks Mankahlana (now deceased) as his media spokesperson. The latter was the only member of Mandela's team to be retained by Mbeki. Mankahlana had built a healthy and open relationship with journalists while working for Mandela (Jacobs 1998), and one would have expected him to continue with this approach in order to improve Mbeki's image. Instead, he appeared to withdraw, and adopted a belligerent stance, particularly on the issue of HIV/AIDS. Mankahlana's new persona possibly captured the nature of advisers in general: they are created in the image of presidents, rather than the other way around. Advisers who differ sharply with their presidents or advocate a radical shift in policy seldom survive, and Mbeki's presidency is no exception.[9]

Pahad has a reputation of being his master's voice. When he expresses a controversial view, he is probably doing so on behalf of the president. In this way, he shields the president from counterattack, and keeps the latter's reputation unsullied. He is also the president's eyes and ears in the SACP. When Mbeki relinquished his membership of the party in the 1980s, Pahad kept his. And, despite efforts by the Nzimande-led faction within the SACP to marginalise him, Pahad was re-elected to the SACP's central committee at the party's last congress. Among Mbeki's closest advisers are SACP members who fall outside the Nzimande faction. The president's parliamentary councillor is party chair Charles Nqakula, who, at the congress, was forced to relinquish the more powerful post of general secretary to Nzimande. Three other SACP central committee members close to Mbeki are the cabinet ministers Geraldine Fraser-Moleketi, Jeff Radebe, and Sydney Mufamadi.

These appointments were a clever move on Mbeki's part, as they placed SACP members in the front line of the government's campaign to privatise state assets and essential municipal services, and retrench public servants. This considerably weakens COSATU, led by a left-wing general secretary, Zwelinzima Vavi, who, unlike his predecessor Mbhazima Shilowa, is close to Nzimande and not Mbeki. Vavi leads COSATU as the union federation tries to win the moral high ground in opposing the government's economic policy. Mufamadi, a COSATU office-bearer in the pre-1994 era, is particularly reputed to belong to Mbeki's inner circle. Some cabinet ministers battle to get a one-to-one audience with Mbeki, but Mufamadi, who, like the president, tends to shun the public spotlight, has no such problems. Reputed to have a good analytical mind and to accurately read the balances of forces at any given time, he is often called in by Mbeki to offer advice.

Compared with the Mandela era, Mbeki is playing a more direct role in government and has demanded greater accountability from cabinet ministers and public servants. As *The Economist* noted (1999), this is something Blair also did after rising to the top job in government. He created two units, the

Social Exclusion Unit (SEU) and the Performance and Innovation Unit (PIU). To their supporters, the purpose of the SEU and PIU is not centralisation but (in the ugly phrase favoured by Blair) joined-up government. As *The Economist* observed, their job is to prevent policies being pulled out of shape by interdepartmental tugs of war, or problems disappearing into the cracks of departmental boundaries.

Mbeki has also beefed up two structures in the presidency: the cabinet office, and the policy co-ordination and advisory services unit. Controlled by Chikane, the most powerful public servant in government, their brief is similar to those of Blair's policy units: 'to join up government', or, in Mbeki's words, 'to integrate government'. Blair's units are achieving their objective – but at a price. 'Undoubtedly, these units are helping to co-ordinate departments' efforts to tackle difficult problems, but equally clearly they are sucking away power from individual departments,' *The Economist* asserted. And Blair is running his government along the lines of a business in an attempt to improve service delivery, something Mbeki is also trying to do. Blair shook up the public service, forcing permanent secretaries (the equivalent of South Africa's directors-general) to sign 'personal objectives' with their line function ministers.

Most mandarins in the British government have spent their careers as policy advisers to ministers, not as operational managers. Some are adapting well to change. One permanent secretary now says she thinks of herself as a chief executive reporting to a board chair in the guise of a minister. According to *The Economist*, others are being trained. Mbeki has done the same thing, making directors-general sign 'performance contracts' with their line function ministers. Those who are not up to their job are either being retrained, or being pushed out of the public service. On paper, Mbeki's units are as powerful as Blair's, but it is too early to tell whether this will be the case in practice. The presidency is still taking shape, with advisers coming and going. Until the staff settles down, it is difficult to see the presidency performing its overarching role within the government. The influence of the PCAS (discussed earlier) is unclear. There was a lot of media hype around it (Haffajee 1999), but its head, the economist Pundy Pillay, quit less than a year into the Mbeki presidency. It was a clear indication that he had fallen out with Mbeki, and that the president was not heeding his advice on economic matters. After resigning, one of Pillay's first public engagements was to address a COSATU-aligned think-tank, the National Labour and Economic Development Institute (NALEDI). He sharply criticised government policy, declaring it was overly obsessed with inflation and cared too little about fighting unemployment, poverty, and inequality (*Business Day*, 13 March 2000).

Conclusion

For now, the minister of finance, Trevor Manuel, and his director-general, Maria Ramos, both of whom are serving second terms, appear to be playing the role identified for the cabinet secretariat and PCAS. If the policy of any department is out of sync with government's macroeconomic policy, they send out orders for it to be redrafted. A good example of this is the Property Rating Bill, which was drafted by Mufamadi's department of local government. Once the Manuel–Ramos team had rejected it, the department, despite the fact that its minister is a Mbeki confidante, was forced to revise the bill. After the president, Manuel is possibly the most influential person in government. He has grown in confidence, and also in arrogance. He has criticised (albeit indirectly) cabinet colleagues, questioning the outcome of the 1998 presidential job summit, and has called for an overhaul of labour legislation. This is despite the fact that protocol dictates that cabinet members do not publicly express views on the policies of colleagues. That Manuel escaped censure shows that he commands Mbeki's respect, and is in tune with the president's thinking.

And the power of the department of finance is increasing. Manuel has publicly mooted the possibility of downgrading the Finance and Fiscal Commission, a move that will give his department a greater role in determining the budget allocations of the three spheres of government (*Business Day*, 24 August 1999). And, following a cabinet green light for a new policy and legislative framework aimed at boosting the private sector's role in service delivery, he has established a Public-Private Partnership Unit (PPPU) within his department. The unit's brief includes ensuring that the various departments at the national and provincial level come up with projects that are viable and sustainable – a clear sign that they are losing their autonomy to Manuel's department (Gumede and Haffajee: 2000).

The department's ascendancy has gained momentum under Mbeki's presidency, but started during the Mandela era when the RDP office was closed down, and Manuel was given the responsibility of ensuring that it was implemented within the framework of macroeconomic policy. And Manuel, through his strong emphasis on budget austerity and fiscal discipline, has struck against the decentralisation of power. Deeply concerned that the provincial governments were not remaining within budget, Manuel eroded their autonomy by instructing them on how to spend their money, and demanding regular report-backs on expenditure patterns. In a nutshell, Manuel is the greatest disciple of Mbeki's three Cs: centralise, co-ordinate, and control. While – at least for now – South Africa does not have an imperial president, it already has an imperial minister of finance.

Notes

1. See, for example, Keeton (2001), and Jacobs (1999). For the apartheid period, see Schrire (1994). One of the better journalistic analyses is that of Pottinger (1988). Other (scattered) insights can be gained from a series of impressionist, and mainly fawning, biographies of apartheid's presidents by mainstream apartheid-era South African (especially white Afrikaans-speaking) journalists.
2. Mbeki's official title was 'First Deputy President'.
3. Ngoasheng has since gone back to running his business, but remains a close ally of Mbeki's, providing him with a link to the growing black middle class. Mavimbela has been appointed by Mbeki to head the country's security and intelligence services.
4. See the exceptionally informative but relatively un-analytical government publication entitled *Democratic governance: a restructured presidency at work, 2000/2001*. While no author is given, the publication has been attributed to Chikane.
5. This will prevent the loss to the public sector of much-needed policy and management capacity, as happened, for example, when Leila Patel, director-genereal of welfare and population development, clashed with the former minister of welfare, Geraldine Fraser-Moleketi, and Dr Olive Shisana, director-general of health, came to grief against the former minister of health, Dr Nkosazana Zuma.
6. There have already been some instances of national ministers trouble-shooting for their provincial counterparts. For example, as minister of public service and administration, Fraser-Moleketi has sent national teams to KwaZulu-Natal, Eastern Cape, and Northern Cape to draft management plans and identify spending priorities.
7. The delayed establishment of a policy unit at the ANC's headquarters in Johannesburg illustrates the point. It was supposed to have been run by Tito Mboweni; in the two years since his departure to become governor of the South African Reserve Bank, no replacement has been mooted.
8. No candidates have openly staked their claim to succeeding Mbeki, although Ramaphosa is probably the strongest challenger. A leading industrialist, and a key figure in the quest for 'black economic empowerment' (which Mbeki facilitates through his economic policies), Ramaphosa is a former trade union leader and chairperson of the constitutional assembly that wrote South Africa's final democratic constitution in 1994–96. In 2001 Ramaphosa, along with two other leading ANC politicians turned businessmen – Tokyo Sexwale and Matthews Phosa – was accused of plotting to unseat Mbeki. All three were later cleared following an official government investigation (despite this being an internal party-political squabble over leadership ambitions). The 'plot' only had the effect of further embarrassing Mbeki and his backers. However, stronger speculation surrounds the candidature of Joel Netshitenze, head of GCIS. His inconspicuous public service posting belies his influence. One of the ANC's top intellectuals (he edited its publications *Mayibuye* and *Sechaba* in exile), Netshitenze commands the respect of all factions within the party, and is a symbol of continuity in government. He has been an influential adviser to both democratic presidents, and has had access to the inner workings of both their cabinets. Few ANC leaders have been in such a privileged position.
9. Sadly, Mankahlana died in 2000 and was replaced with Bheki Khumalo, who had

previously worked as media liaison officer for the minister of education, Kader Asmal, and had developed a reputation for good 'spin'.

References

African National Congress (ANC). 2000. Submission to the South African Human Rights Commission Inquiry into Racism in the Media.

Bruce, P and Laurence, P. 1997. The rational heir. *Financial Mail*. 3 October.

Davis, G. 1999. The shaping of governance: the deputy president. Research report prepared for the Centre for Development and Enterprise.

The Economist. 1999. Britain: the cafetiere theory of government. 21 August. 47–9.

———. 2000. Thabo Mbeki – micro-manager. 15 July.

Gerwel, J. 1997. Evidence before the Presidential Review Commission. 25 September.

Gumede, WM and Haffajee, F. 2000. Minding his business. *Financial Mail*, 11 February.

Haffajee, F. 1999. Backroom brigade. *Siyaya*. Autumn. 10–12.

Jacobs, S. 1998. Communicating Mandela: the news organisation of the South African president. Paper delivered at the 26th joint session of workshops of the European Consortium on Political Research, University of Warwick, Coventry, United Kingdom, 23–28 March.

Jacobs, S. 1999. An imperial presidency. *Siyaya*. Summer.

Keeton, C. 2001. A work in progress. *Leadership*. March.

Pottinger, B. 1988. *The imperial presidency: PW Botha – the first 10 years*. Johannesburg: Southern Books.

The Presidency. 2001. *Democratic governance: a restructured presidency at work, 2000/2001*. March. http://www.gov.za/reports/2001/president/01.pdf.

Presidential Review Commission on the Reform and Transformation of the Public Service in South Africa. 1998. Developing a culture of good governance. Report presented to the President of South Africa, NR Mandela. 27 February. http://www.polity.org.za/govdocs/reports/presreview/chap2.html.

Republic of South Africa. 1993. Constitution of the Republic of South Africa (Interim Constitution), Act 200 of 1993. Pretoria: Government Printer.

Schrire, R (ed). 1994. *From Malan to De Klerk: leadership in the apartheid state*. London: C Hurst & Co.

South African Government. 2001. Integrated democratic governance: a restructured presidency at work. http://www.gov.za/reports/2001/presidency01.pdf .

South African Human Rights Commission. 2000. *Faultlines: interim report of inquiry into racism in the media*. August.

CHAPTER 7

Thabo Mbeki and the South African Communist Party

VISHWAS SATGAR[1]

On 1 July 1998 there was an expectant – perhaps even anxious – mood among delegates to the 10th conference of the SACP as they waited for then deputy president Thabo Mbeki to enter the hall and step on to the stage.

The fact that Mbeki would address the conference – held at the Shaft 17 Conference Centre at Crown Mines, just south of Johannesburg – was not unusual in itself. Given their long-standing alliance, it is customary for the ANC to send strong delegations to SACP conferences as a mark of solidarity. In fact, then president Nelson Mandela had addressed the conference the day before.

However, over a considerable period, deep differences had built up within the tripartite alliance – and specifically between the SACP and COSATU on the one hand and the ANC on the other – around the ANC-in-government's GEAR strategy. Given that Mbeki was regarded as one of GEAR's main sponsors, delegates sensed that the simmering tensions might well come to a head.

When Mbeki eventually arrived, he was swept through a side entrance, flanked by aides and senior party leaders. Tackling the situation head-on, Mbeki (1998) delivered a highly defensive speech, inlaid with sharp counter-attacks on the SACP. Through its political engagements around macro-economic policy, Mbeki declared, and its assessment of the general state of the South African revolution,[2] the SACP was trying to '... pose as the [only] genuine representative of the progressive movement of our country', and to 'propagate the understanding that our government has failed, as all other African governments have failed'. In the process, the SACP was 'ready to use the hostile messages of the right, and thus join forces with the defenders of reaction to sustain an offensive against our movement'. Ultimately, he accused the party of engaging in 'fake revolutionary posturing so that our mass base, which wants speedy transformation and the fulfilment of its material needs on an urgent basis, accepts charlatans, who promise everything that is good, while we all know that these confidence tricksters are telling the masses a lie'.

Journalists generally presented Mbeki's speech as a 'verbal bludgeoning' of the SACP, and a humiliation of the party (see ka'Nkosi and Desai 1998). In this moment, Mbeki was constructed as the unchallenged heir to the Mandela presidency, and enemies of the SACP had a field day advertising this.[3]

Mbeki's comments alienated many SACP leaders and supporters. However, rather than interpreting them as a victory for the former in a clash with the party, many regarded them as the result of a failure by the party's leaders to find a way of consolidating the tripartite alliance, and working constructively with the deputy president in particular and the ANC in general in the context of the ANC having gained state power.

The 'Mbeki factor'

When, almost a year later, Mbeki was inaugurated as president, this challenge to the SACP was still unresolved,[4] and has remained so ever since. Many SACP members have reinvented themselves as Mbeki loyalists, with a blind reverence anchored in realised ambitions of serving in his cabinet or 'kitchen cabinet' (see chapter 6). Others are totally anti-Mbeki, and have gathered together in a tendency made up of three threads. The first is an opportunistic one, composed of those who were not given cabinet posts, and have therefore been forced to deflate their political egos. These elements are chameleon-like and can swing easily between extremes, depending on how they believe they can best safeguard or promote their careers. Thus they could easily adopt a feigned pro-Mbeki stance if they thought this would advance their political careers, and betray those they have converged with in opposing Mbeki.

The second thread comprises those who ascribe to a determinist theory of neo-colonialism – i.e., that African petit bourgeoisie leaderships are intrinsically disposed to sell out the masses, and evolve into what academics refer to as neo-colonial elites. The third thread is dogmatic and ultra-leftist, prone to pontification and self-righteous puritanical claims. It clings to an extreme sectarian position, fed by intolerance and an explicit hatred of the ANC – and, of course, Mbeki, who is seen as an agent of monopoly and transnational capital.

The third thread, a more serious one with greater intellectual depth, is neither anti- nor pro-Mbeki, but recognises that a sound working relationship with the president is important from a wider strategic perspective. Most of those located in this tendency would argue that 'we need to deepen and strengthen our relationship with the president of the ANC without relinquishing our power and independence'.[5] In practice, this tendency is defined by a commitment to debate, a critical interrogation of ideas, a commitment to the notion of unity (the advancement of a working-class-led transition within a multi-class alliance), a modest or minimalist socialist agenda, a grass-roots-based activism, and self- and mutual criticism without malice.

Mbeki's cabinet contains nine ministers or deputy ministers said to be communists.[6] The most prominent of them are Geraldene Fraser-Moleketi, Essop Pahad, Jeff Radebe, Alec Erwin, Ronnie Kasrils, and Sydney Mafumadi.[7] Since the advent of GEAR, and particularly since Mbeki became president, many journalists have argued superficially that the implementation of neo-liberal economic policies by these ministers signals the ideological confusion in and bankruptcy of the SACP. They use these arguments to discredit and delegitimise the SACP, while presenting Mbeki as the nationalist leader who 'tamed' the party.

This perspective is highly inaccurate. In fact, the SACP has maintained a firm and principled opposition to GEAR, and has struggled consistently alongside organised workers in the process. The media and most political analysts have consciously skirted the struggles against GEAR waged from below since 1996. Organised workers have fought against privatisation, and have secured the National Framework Agreement, negotiated between organised labour and the government. When this framework has failed to secure gains for workers, the anti-privatisation struggle has been advanced at the parastatal or local government level. In addition, labour market reform has been pushed in the direction of re-regulation, and projects and processes agreed to at the national job summit of 1999 have been used to bring pressure to bear on fiscal deficit reduction targets.

The tripartite alliance – stormy waters

The impasse over macroeconomic policy poses a serious challenge to Mbeki's presidency, and may yet prove to be his most important biographical moment. Embedded in this impasse is a vexed question, namely: what is the future of the tripartite alliance? In 1996 Mbeki himself suggested that the alliance was not cast in stone, and could be broken up if this became necessary or desirable (Lodge 1999: 113). However, under his stewardship of the ANC and the country, it has become increasingly clear that he seeks an alliance capable of cohering around a minimum consensus, which implies room for disagreement. Ironically, he hinted at this in his speech to the 10th congress (1998) when he said:

> There is one other matter I would like to raise, speaking with the full authority of the leadership and membership of the African National Congress. This relates to the important question of how we handle differences and contradictions that will necessarily and inevitably arise among ourselves as members of the alliance and members of the mass democratic movement.

Two important initiatives have opened the way to steering the alliance through the crises it has had to contend with. The first was the SACP's strategy conference held in September 1999. In the midst of a sea of red t-shirts and caps was the visible presence of a very powerful and high-ranking delegation of the ANC, including its secretary-general, Kgalema Motlanthe; the deputy president, Jacob Zuma; and other stalwarts such as Joe Nhlanhla, then minister of intelligence, and even Winnie Mandela. It had come to engage in a constructive dialogue with the SACP. Zuma was very explicit on the need for the SACP to play a role in South African society, and assert its voice publicly on important questions.[8] According to the SACP's assistant general secretary, Jeremy Cronin, 'this was an acknowledgement that the party was a force in its own right, and their presence was clearly a peace offering' (interview with author, October–November 2000).

The second important initiative was the ten-a-side meeting of the tripartite alliance held in December 1999. While this meeting did not resolve the impasse on macroeconomic policy, it helped to overcome the hurdle of open hostility and public head-butting. In some senses it continued the rebuilding of relationships begun at the strategy conference. According to Cronin, 'the ten-a-side reminded the movement as a whole of its tradition of debate. There was an acknowledgement that labelling comrades and declaring hunting seasons on them did not assist the movement. We acknowledged that the way in which we conducted debates might not have been helpful. In the end, the meeting opened channels and set the basis to conduct intelligent debate in order to build the alliance.'

The Mbeki presidency and the alliance

For the greater part of the first year of Mbeki's presidency (June 1999 to June 2000), the tripartite alliance displayed signs of a more overt – if still fragile – unity. Then, in May 2000, COSATU embarked on mass action and a general strike in support of demands for a review of macroeconomic policy. While these actions were primarily aimed at putting pressure on the private sector to invest in the domestic economy and create jobs, pronouncements by COSATU leaders nonetheless had an inflection aimed at Mbeki's government. The SACP marched alongside COSATU during these mass activities. All of this served to unsettle the alliance. By 2001 the divisions were palpable, and sharpened around two issues. The first was a mass strike by COSATU against privatisation, which coincided with the World Conference Against Racism (WCAR). Publicly, the ANC stated that it was opposed to the timing of the strike, not the strike per se. Towards the end of the year the ANC's NEC raised temperatures to unprecedented levels by alluding to an 'ultra-left and immature leadership tendency' at the helm of the ANC's alliance partners. This prompted a public spat of attacks and counterattacks among leaders of COSATU and the SACP on one hand, and certain ANC leaders on the other. Numerous alliance leaders declared these tensions to be the worst in the history of the national liberation movement.

Fortunately, in 2002 these tensions began to dissipate via bilateral meetings as well as ten-a-side meetings among all the alliance partners, which culminated in the National Alliance Summit held in Ekurhuleni on 3–7 April. This summit gave members of all three alliance partners an opportunity to address all their differences, including those over economic policy. Following this summit, the alliance (plus the South African National Civic Organisation – SANCO) has been intent on securing a new economic consensus via the proposed growth and development summit announced by Mbeki in January 2002. The agenda being developed for the summit takes on board numerous concerns raised by the ANC's alliance partners. These include the need for a more active industrial policy; the need to redirect local savings to drive economic growth and development; the need for active labour market policies and strategies to create jobs; the need to strength the training system; the need to develop a strong co-operative movement; and the need to emphasise spatial and local economic development (SACP 2002: 5–7). All this is meant to inform the growth and development summit, due to be held in 2002. Most importantly, the build-up to this summit is regarded as an opportunity to build a mass movement for economic transformation led by the alliance (5). In short, the Ekurhuleni summit resolved to advance an alliance agenda for transformation that reaffirms and requires as a necessary precondition a united and organisationally capacitated alliance (1, 7–8).

The media's appropriation of the Mbeki presidency
The media, both local and international, have consistently fed off tensions in the alliance, often amplifying them in the process. The renewed unity achieved at the Ekurhuleni summit, which requires active consolidation, is also being threatened by the media. This incipient unity can easily be aborted by media that have consistently tried to portray Mbeki as the hard-nosed

'Boris Yeltsin' of South Africa. The media are quick to write an anti-worker or anti-communist script for the president and his cabinet;[9] for instance, the restructuring of state assets is presented as full-blown privatisation, and the recent labour market review as deregulation. At their most astute, the media argue for more liberalisation of exchange controls on the grounds that this will attract foreign investors, when in fact this is merely about opening the escape hatch for local capital. In the end, a 'caretaker' imperial presidency of South African capitalism, with extremely centralised powers, is being nurtured in the media.

However, Mbeki seems to be cut from a different cloth, and refuses to assume the Yeltsin cloak. He is fervent about making multiparty democracy work, and links this to his calls for a new world order and an African Renaissance. Like all politicians, he is schooled in the primacy of power. Many acquire power for its own sake, while others regard it as a means to an end. For many media analysts, Mbeki's real project is obscured by his political dominance, and they therefore provide him with an enigmatic mask, thus turning him into a figure shrouded in mystery. The most cynical reading of this mask is of a puppeteering, conniving, manipulative, and dangerous person. At the other extreme, the enigma is imbued with the mythical powers of an omniscient political chess player who is constantly ahead of any competing political intelligence.

'African Renaissance capitalism' and the SACP

Through immersion in the mass struggles of the 1980s, which later paralleled and coincided with the mass wave of militant direct democracy that brought down tyrannical rule in the former second world/Soviet empire, my generation of communists shrugged off its Stalinist breeding. We carried the red flag into the 1990s and then the start of the twenty-first century with a clarity of political consciousness marked by a deep aversion to the 'cult of the personality', either with a dark or enlightened aura of authority. Hence, for me, the Mbeki enigma is revealed and transparent. Decoding his political dominance unearths a 'moderate multiclass capitalist project' that can be teased out into a serious and concerted strategic initiative. Three important elements provide the strategic chemistry. The first is the notion of an African Renaissance, which provides the ideological veneer for a version of modernisation in which multiparty democracy and market economies are meant to evolve on the African continent, rooted in the imagination of modernity. The political centre within South Africa of this renaissance would be a multiclass alliance held together by a 'class compromise' in which an African bourgeoisie would be nurtured into becoming one of the key 'motive forces' of catch-up 'African Renaissance capitalism'. Initially, this bourgeoisie was promoted via equity holdings in public companies on the JSE. This strategy has failed, and the restructuring of state assets, the multi-billion-rand arms deal, and 'black economic empowerment' (see the recent report of the Black Economic Empowerment Commission) are increasingly being used to foster this new bourgeoisie.

A second critical ingredient, which is both novel and visionary, relates to the global positioning of the South African nation state in several global forums, including the Non-Aligned Movement (NAM), the Southern African Development Community (SADC), the Commonwealth Head of Governments Meeting (CHOGM), as well as its strategic bilateral alliances with several countries via presidential binational commissions and other face-to-face diplomatic initiatives. In essence, Mbeki's international relations project is an attempt, in a post-cold war context dominated by the United States, to carve out a space in which South Africa can develop 'African Renaissance capitalism' on its own terms. The recent unveiling and championing of NEPAD and the recently launched African Union are consistent with this approach. The third ingredient, for me, is a 're-engineering' and conversion of the ANC from a liberation movement into a modern political party. Electoralism has increasingly become the lifeblood of ANC politics, with policy agendas and political decision-making being driven from within the state, particularly Mbeki's cabinet.

In short, Mbeki's presidency is about ensuring that this project is consolidated, and it forms the overarching strategic umbrella under which the tripartite alliance is intended to operate.

My daily interactions and debates with comrades have convinced me of the validity of one basic wisdom: in practice, no political project can ever be pure. In the twentieth century, the African revolutionary process is ornamented with a junkyard of wrecked and mangled experiments. Vanguards steering radical nationalist projects in Zambia or Egypt, for instance; African socialism in Tanzania; or scientific socialism in Angola and Mozambique all crashed into the stone wall of imperialism. The invisible hand of counter-revolution, guided by imperialism, put the brakes on any attempt to go beyond capitalism or even achieve a successful third world capitalism. During his 30 years of exile, Mbeki witnessed and encountered this harsh reality at first hand, and it is in this rich experience that a 'moderate African Renaissance capitalism' has been incubated. So, even if the 'two nations' cleavage in South Africa is to be resolved via a prudent but reformist 'moderate African Renaissance capitalism', then its progeny, an African bourgeoisie, can only be decisively formed with elements of anti-imperialism and – ironically – anti-capitalism, at the cutting edge of this project.

It is at the intersection of the anti-imperialist and anti-capitalist edges of 'moderate African Renaissance capitalism' that a renewed unity among the ANC, COSATU, and the SACP can be welded into place. This is also the opportunity afforded by the outcome of the historic Ekurhuleni summit. However, can the SACP really achieve this? Can it advance a transition that straddles 'African Renaissance capitalism' and its own socialist agenda?

Mbeki and the struggle for a socialist South Africa

Many analysts believe the time for the SACP to have a decisive influence is past, and that it lacks the strength and capacity to advance a socialist alternative for South Africa (see, for example, Adams 1997). As limiting factors, they cite a competitive and sophisticated policy-making environment that is supposedly beyond the reach of the SACP; a declining membership; the exodus of key leaders; dwindling numbers of intellectuals involved in the party; and the collapse of eastern Europe and its ostensible discrediting of 'socialism'. In this context, many have concluded that the SACP will founder in the same way many communist parties in Latin America in the twentieth century have done. Most of these parties became irrelevant onlookers, and were replaced by new political agents either influenced by Guevarism or a kind of Maoist vanguardism that brought together the political and military in one formation, very much like the FSLN in Nicaragua or the FMLN in El Salvador. In the case of South Africa, many argue that the 'onlooker status' of the SACP requires the creation of an alternative political formation that could champion the cause of the poor, the working class, and the excluded.

Other analysts (Adams 1997) have concluded that the SACP is evolving a strategic role and approach akin to those of the Euro-communist parties,[10] and is therefore, like most of those parties, becoming reformist and social-democratic.

Then there are those at the other extreme of paranoia and exaggeration who believe that the SACP's relationship with the ANC is a fetter on 'free market capitalism', and that the presence of communists in the ANC (and government), and the latter's alliance with the SACP, give the communist left a disproportionate influence.

This was recently argued by the late Peter Mokaba. In October 1997 he called for a review of the ANC–SACP relationship, and went on to say that the SACP should end its secrecy, come out of the closet, and stop hiding behind the cloak of the ANC. He said the SACP operated as a 'cabal or a tribe within the ANC influencing policy, and, where they can't get their way, they go out and criticise the ANC' (Cronin and Nzimande 1997). According to Mokaba, 'nobody knows the policies and programmes of the SACP. We hear the SACP criticising GEAR, but do we see them coming up with any alternative?' (Mbhele 1997).

There is a simple answer to Mokaba. The SACP has an alternative for South Africa: socialism. This is not a 'barrack or bayonet' kind of socialism. Since its unbanning a decade ago, the SACP has been preoccupied with rethinking socialism and extracting lessons from the Soviet experience. Two important conclusions form the premise for the SACP's advancement of socialism in South Africa. Firstly, it believes socialism here will have to define itself within South African realities, and not transplant a bureaucratic and centrally planned model from the past. Secondly, democracy, not just in a liberal multiparty sense but more radically in a participatory and direct democracy, is also crucial for the construction of socialism.

Since the SACP's ninth congress in 1995, this has been the basis for its strategic slogan: 'Socialism is the future! Build it now!' Not only did this represent a break with the two-stage theory of transition (a bourgeois stage followed by a socialist stage); it also placed socialism on the agenda of the national democratic revolution. Put differently, the SACP has not shied away from the challenge of advancing socialism as an integral part of the national democratic revolution. In addition, since its ninth congress, both the 10th congress and two strategy conferences have attempted to provide programmatic content to this slogan. To my mind, notwithstanding the uncompromising assertion of a socialist alternative for South Africa, the SACP has failed to pin down the socialist alternative in programmatic terms in a way that will allow it to get to grips with the challenge of finding a consensus with Mbeki, and ultimately the ANC. Recent SACP strategy documents point to an increasing maximalism in its thinking. Underlying this is a serious gap in how the SACP understands a socialist transition on a democratic terrain, both in theory and in practice. While it has moved away from a conception of a socialist transition involving the classical Leninist schema of two-stagism and a dictatorship of the proletariat, it has still not adequately theorised a socialist transition in contemporary South Africa. Without this, it is likely to fall into defeatism or irrelevance – or, even worse, it could become an instrument for containing and controlling the organised movements of the working class and the poor.

Perhaps it is time for party members to consider a conception of socialist transition that maintains a principled commitment to socialism (or a society that predominantly represents the interests of the poor and the working class), but recognises that this will take a long time to achieve. Expressed in another way, the socialist transition is going to be a long one. This means, at a programmatic level, that a minimum or modest socialist programme has to be developed – one that can be asserted and employed to build a consensus within society, and, most importantly, a sound working relationship with Mbeki and the ANC. In this regard, hard and real strategic choices have to be made. For instance: should the SACP focus on championing and developing a state-led industrial policy, or a welfare net? Should it focus on democratising the banking sector, or nationalising numerous sectors of the economy? Should it focus on building a co-operative movement, or struggle for more labour standards? Should it advance land reform from below, or should it focus on tax reform? Should it focus on southern Africa, or try to solve all of Africa's problems? In short, I believe it is possible for the SACP to negotiate a consensus with Mbeki that identifies three or four socialist solutions for South Africa, for which it would take responsibility and struggle for democratically and openly.

Many would argue this is a dead end, and that the tripartite alliance should be laid to rest in the cemetery of history. Others strengthen this argument by asserting that, given its own long and valiant contribution to the national liberation of the black majority and Africans in particular, the SACP has as much of a right as the ANC to contest for political power.

This perspective is dangerously short-sighted, and displays a failure to understand the high stakes involved in trying to consolidate a third world democracy. South Africa's political 'miracle' has leap-frogged our country over a 'Congo scenario', but it would be reckless to believe that some eight years of multiparty democracy has steered us clear of renewed violent conflict between white and black South Africans – a scenario that would merely produce a lose–lose outcome. In fact, the much-vaunted 'trickle down' of economic benefits under neo-liberal structural adjustment is not materialising among the workers and the unemployed poor. Jobs are not being created, income patterns are becoming more skewed in favour of the rich, and more and more people are becoming even poorer.

The short story of economic transformation in post-apartheid South Africa points to a deepening of social polarisation, growing discontent, and the increased likelihood of volatile social conflict bursting out into the open. Democracy in South Africa is fragile and tenuous. Ironically, it is the SACP that takes this situation as its starting point, and has been arguing its case within the alliance based on this appreciation of conditions in South Africa (SACP 2001). In the words of the SACP's general secretary, Blade Nzimande, 'globalisation does undermine national sovereignty in that it narrows the options for progressive development and creates dependency on (if not subjugation to) the mainstream global economy that favours developed countries. This subjugation tends to reproduce the class and consequently national patterns of inequalities characteristic of the colonial era. It is therefore a myth to think that the national question can be addressed, whether racism or access to land, without simultaneously challenging imperialism' (Nzimande 2001: 10).

From this standpoint, working towards a long socialist transition would mean that, in the short term, the SACP would have to promote a socialist tendency in South Africa that would coexist alongside a capitalist and a statist tendency – i.e., amounting to a mixed economy. These tendencies would collide and struggle for space and amplification, but this is the stuff that a new democratic left politics is made up of, at least in theory.

Challenges for the SACP under Mbeki's presidency

However, if the SACP is to actively advance a modest or minimalist socialist alternative for South Africa, it has to develop beyond a mere propagandist presence in society and the tripartite alliance. In 2001 the SACP was 80 years old. From the time of its formal inception in the early 1920s, until it was banned in 1950, the then Communist Party of South Africa (CPSA) worked hard to build strong trade unions, contest municipal elections, and help build non-racial unity in the broader liberation movement. Even after this the SACP enriched the ideological development of the Congress Movement, culminating in the Congress of the People in Kliptown, at which the Freedom Charter was adopted. In the early 1960s the party has its own military units that merged with those of the ANC to form Umkhonto weSizwe, and so on. The abridged story of the SACP, in the 80 years of its existence, is one of independent and practical political action, in the context of building a wider movement. In the 1990s, while it has had to face itself in the mirror of history, and painfully shed its Stalinist skin, it has taken on the psychology of an impotent grouplet in terms of decisive political action.

The unity that has to be built with Mbeki, and the ANC more broadly, requires the SACP to engage actively and constructively with the dominance that drives a 'moderate African Renaissance capitalism'. The Italian Marxist theoretician Antonio Gramsci is instructive here, because he gave the communist tradition important conceptual tools with which to bring about democratic consensus. In his words,

> We must not conceive of a scientific discussion as if it were a courtroom proceeding in which there is a defendant and a prosecutor who, by duty of his office, must show the defendant guilty. It is a premise in scientific discussion that the interest lies in the search for truth and the advancement of science. Therefore the most 'advanced' thinker is he who understands that his adversary may express a truth

which should be incorporated in his own ideas, even if in a minor way (Forgacs 1988).

This is the lesson of theory and practice that is grounded in humility, sobriety, and probity. If the SACP starts here, the dominance underpinning 'moderate African Renaissance capitalism' could perhaps be transformed to involve the interests of all class forces, and thus evolve into a truly hegemonic societal project. In addition, from the side of the SACP the challenge is to ensure that the interests of the working class and the poor predominate, even, in the short term, via a minimalist socialist programme. This is the only rational alternative for the SACP if it is to avoid the danger of becoming a co-manager of a reformed capitalism, either of a corporatist or social welfare capitalist variety, or a commandist third-world one.

To rise to this challenge in the twenty-first century, the SACP has to fundamentally renovate itself and become a serious strategic political force. This means it has to shrug of its narrow intellectual vocation, and reconnect theory to a transformative practice that promotes new working-class-led social movements for reconstruction and development. It has to get back to the basics of grass-roots work and activism among the people to build co-operatives as part of sustainable local economic development, and promote a new kind of transformative unionism to ensure, for example, that workers respond proactively to economic restructuring and organise the unemployed. A new generation of communist activists have to be developed through immersion in the practical and theoretical challenges of economic transformation in which class relations are transformed to the advantage of the working class, the forces of production are developed (or, as some would prefer, South Africa becomes part of the information and communication revolution), and the state plays a leading and directive role in the development process.

To ensure that this happens, the SACP has to learn what has to be undone. The Stalinist ghost within the party has to be buried and a 'new vanguardism', embracing a political culture of vibrant and open internal political debate in which the collective intellectual in the SACP is allowed to flourish, must become crucial. Relationships with mass forces such as social movements have to be recast into a 'party movement' mould that allows a dynamic journeying alongside each other, without the vanguard controlling and bending the political will of these forces. Thirdly, the young – 'the best sons and daughters', as Amilcar Cabral, one of Africa's greatest revolutionaries, put it – have to be harnessed and nurtured without the old guard feeling threatened.

The transition in the SACP to a post-Stalinist vanguard has begun, and this is an internal strength that can be harnessed to consolidate the affirmation of the political, strategic, and programmatic unity achieved at the Ekurhuleni summit. However, it can easily be lost in the course of a slide back into the certainties of dogma and/or ultra-leftism. A few unreconstructed Stalinists within the SACP might easily view the defence of a jaded ideological canon as more fundamental than a bold engagement with existing realities in order to find necessary and appropriate socialist solutions. On the other hand, 'entryist ultra-leftists' who came into the SACP at the height of the tensions in the alliance around economic policy to try and achieve a split in the alliance or take over the SACP might also reassert their historical mission of undermining the revolutionary unity and outcomes of the Ekurhuleni summit.

If these political and ideological tendencies in the party are not realigned, the historical gains and opportunities achieved at the summit will be squandered. Most importantly, the opportunity to engender a dialogue and constructive relationship between Mbeki and the SACP will be lost – with dire consequences for the future of the South African revolution.

Notes

1. While I am the Gauteng provincial secretary of the SACP, I have written this chapter in my capacity as a political and policy analyst based at the Co-operative and Policy Alternative Center (COPAC). Being a member of the SACP has enabled me to draw on insights gained through 'participant observation'. I joined the party after its unbanning in 1990. Prior to this I had a vicarious relationship with it via the most radical Indian political tradition in South Africa, of which not much is known, and little has been written. This tradition had its roots in the underground structures of the SACP within the country, and the political-military infrastructure linked to Operation Vula. Ironically, its legal expression was the Natal Indian Congress (NIC), an organisation founded by Mahatma Gandhi. This tradition found and influenced me in the NIC, but more strongly and directly in my family. A dear uncle was deeply immersed in the underground structures of the SACP and Operation Vula, and this organised our entire family into a survival network. He and his comrades were extremely purposive, and were prepared to sacrifice everything in order to build a fighting machine that could take on the South African Defence Force. I grew up politically around these people, and as a result the militant 1980s graduated me not just into activism but also into an encounter with Marxism-Leninism. In the 1990s, after the SACP was unbanned, it was a mere formality for me to become a card-carrying member.
2. Mbeki was referring to a draft discussion paper prepared by the SACP's central committee for the 10th congress – see *African Communist* (1998). The paper also

dealt with the perceived shortcomings of the liberation movement *vis-à-vis* the 1994 democratic breakthrough. According to the authors, these included a misunderstanding of the ANC's location in global realities, macroeconomic policy, a lack of consistency in building a strong developmental state, and an exaggerated tendency towards demobilising the mass popular movement.
3. Mbeki's speech was broadcast on SABC TV, CNN and BBC World, and was prominently covered in all the leading financial newspapers and magazines in the country.
4. In the past, these tensions were always resolved by mature and respected leaders such as Moses Kotane, Yusuf Dadoo, and Joe Slovo, who were trusted by the top leaders of the ANC, and had close links with the latter. While some of them (notably Moses Kotane, who was both the treasurer-general of the ANC and general secretary of the SACP) served in the highest echelons of the ANC, this merely served to cement communists and nationalists around the imperative of unity, and ultimately a cohesive collective leadership of the national liberation movement.
5. Leaders of and activists in the SACP have shared this perspective with the author during various conversations and discussions.
6. In terms of a long-standing tradition, the party does not publicly identify individual members.
7. The SACP forms part of a formal alliance with the ANC and COSATU. This means it does not participate in elections on its own, but only as part of the alliance. Only the ANC puts forward candidates from alliance structures. SACP members elected to office subject themselves to the ANC's leadership, its organisational discipline, and, in the case of members of parliament, its caucus. A significant proportion of the ANC's 60-member national executive committee are SACP members. In 1994, of the 18 ministerial posts open to ANC members, at least six went to communists. One of these, Joe Slovo (appointed as minister of housing), has since died of cancer. The SACP component in parliament is said to have grown from 50 MPs in 1994 to just under 80 in February 1998. At least three of seven ANC provincial premiers – Makhenkosi Stofile in the Eastern Cape, Sam Shilowa in Gauteng, and Manne Dipico in Northern Cape – are said to be SACP members. It is estimated that at least 50 per cent of ANC representatives in provincial legislatures are SACP members. A dozen mayors are said to be SACP members, many others serve as local councillors, and many more serve in senior posts in the civil service.
8. Zuma made these comments during a plenary session at the conference; they did not form part of a formal speech.
9. The journalist who has done so most consistently has been Howard Barrell, in writing on GEAR and related issues for the *Mail & Guardian* before becoming its editor.
10. Since the 1960s, the Spanish, French, and Italian communist parties have been referred to as the Euro-communist parties.

References

Adams, S. 1997. What's Left? The South African Communist Party after apartheid. *Review of African Political Economy*, 24 (2). June. 237–48.

African Communist. 1998. A socialist approach to the consolidation and deepening of the national democratic revolution. No 149. Second quarter.

Black Economic Empowerment Commission. 2000. Integrated national black economic empowerment strategy. October.

Lodge, T. 1999. *South African politics since 1994*. Cape Town: David Philip.

Cronin. J and Nzimande, B. 1997. ANC Thatcherites want a party of black bosses. *Mail & Guardian*. 10 October.

Forgacs, D (ed). 1988. *The Antonio Gramsci reader*. New York: Lawrence and Wisehart.

ka'Nkosi, S, and Desai, R. 1998. Moment of truth for the SACP. *Mail & Guardian*. 1–6 July.

Mbeki, T. 1998. Statement at SACP 10th congress. Unpublished mimeograph. 1 July.

Nzimande, B. 2001. Political report to the central committee of the SACP. 2 February.

Rostron, B. 2002. South Africa: the new apartheid? *Mail & Guardian*. 21 February.

SACP. 2001. Economic policy challenges facing the SACP and alliance in 2001. Central committee discussion document. 2–4 February.

South African Communist Party. 2002. Ekurhuleni Declaration of the Alliance Summit. 7 April. http://www.sacp.org.za/docs/summits/ekurhuleni0407-02.html.

CHAPTER 8

From 'Madiba magic' to 'Mbeki logic'
Mbeki and the ANC's trade union allies

SAKHELA BUHLUNGU

The history of the tripartite alliance – comprising the ANC, the SACP, and COSATU – has been well documented by academics and others. More recently, observers and commentators have predicted the break-up of the alliance in the light of a perceived decline in the power of its trade union and communist components on the one hand, and the ANC's shift towards free market economic policies on the other. These debates have been useful insofar as they have shed light on the contradictions and tensions among the three components of the alliance. However, they have been sterile and predictable insofar as they have failed to provide a framework for understanding the dynamics of the alliance. In part, this weakness stems from a failure to locate the alliance – and particularly the ANC – in the historical context of the mass democratic struggle.

Thabo Mbeki's ascent to the South African presidency has once again brought these issues to the fore. Not only does it represent a shift away from the era of reconciliation and consensus-building in post-apartheid/post-transition South African politics; it also represents an era in which new configurations of power and political relations are being established and entrenched. While the Mandela era was about allaying the fears of minority groups and other powerful interests on the one hand while maintaining the cohesion and unity of the liberation forces on the other, the Mbeki era is about building and consolidating powerful social forces that will finally cohere into the ruling bloc in a democratic South Africa. The unions and the broader working class movement will not form part of it.

There are two ways in which this goal can be achieved: by silencing all opposition forces, or by adopting a more sophisticated strategy of containing and co-opting them by means of a deliberately vague discourse of nation-building, developmentalism, and an African renaissance.

The discussion in this chapter is based on a set of assumptions, some of which suggest new approaches to understanding alliance politics in a democratic South Africa. Firstly, an assessment of the role of Mbeki as leader of the ANC and head of the South African government should be based less on his role as an individual and more on the dynamics of leadership in nationalist movements that assume power after a protracted struggle against an unjust and unequal social order. If this approach is adopted, Mbeki ceases to be the sole architect of politics in the post-Mandela era, and becomes the personification of the politics and outlook of the leadership of the ANC as a whole. Indeed, his approach to issues is shared by many other ANC leaders.

Secondly, Mbeki's approach to alliance politics is rooted in the history of the liberation struggle and the power relations among the different networks or strands of the liberation movement. For example, his ability to chastise delegates at the SACP's congress in 1998 did not derive solely from his stature as ANC president and deputy state president; it derived more from historical notions of an 'ANC-led alliance', loyalty to the ANC, and the fragile nature of the liberation movement during the years of illegality that made the expression of dissent a luxury which the movement could not afford.

Thirdly, all liberation movements that assume state power after the collapse of a colonial and/or repressive regime are inclined to be intolerant of bases of power that are independent of the new state and its agencies. The new state attempts to eliminate potential or actual bases of independent opposition either by repressing them outright, or by co-opting and manipulating them. Winning state power gives the former liberation movement unlimited access to sources of coercive power and patronage, which enables the new ruling group to fashion a carrot-and-stick strategy for dealing with its potential and actual opponents. Talking specifically about authoritarian post-independence regimes, one analyst has in fact referred to the phenomenon of the absorption of civil society and other interest organisations as the 'post-colonial state' (Akwetey 1994: 21).

Fourthly, the victorious liberation movement does not become the ruling party in an unproblematic way. More often that not, it also becomes the agency through which a new class asserts and consolidates its power, or inserts itself into an existing class of power and privilege. In the process, the boundaries between politics and business become permeable as the liberation activists-turned-politicians increase their interaction with business, and develop or expand their business interests. Even the most revolutionary movements have found this to be one of the most intractable problems of the post-liberation era, as some in their own ranks find it difficult to resist this temptation.

Fifthly, in a highly polarised society the achievement of liberation creates the base for a more legitimate state. However, this is often accompanied by the demobilisation of organisations of civil society, as they come to believe that they can trust the legitimate state to promote their interests and take care of their future well-being. This inadvertently creates a situation in which the new state is able to centralise power and become increasingly intolerant of opposition, because it believes it is the sole custodian of 'the national interest'.

Finally, and flowing from the above, any liberation movement that becomes a ruling party tends to appropriate the 'glory' of the cultural symbols, political traditions, and achievements of the liberation struggle to the exclusion of any other movement that was part of that struggle. In fact, these symbols, political traditions, and achievements are often invoked to justify blatant abuses of power. The above assumptions are based on a reading of a broad range of experiences in the developing world, particularly in those societies that have emerged from decades or even centuries of colonial rule. The post-colonial experience is particularly germane to understanding the trajectory of alliance politics and political and economic power relations in post-1994 South Africa.

These issues are discussed in greater detail below. The analysis draws on interviews and discussions with a number of COSATU officials; for reasons that are discussed later, they asked not to be identified. Besides general sources in the form of books, journals and newspapers, books and other documents emanating from leading figures or structures of the three alliance partners were also studied in the course of researching this chapter.

The alliance and the legacy of struggle politics

Mbeki's approach to the trade unions in particular and the tripartite alliance in general cannot be understood in isolation from the history of the liberation movement, and the ANC's role in the liberation struggle. There are several dimensions of current ANC policy towards the alliance that are consistent with its approach to the liberation struggle since it was formed in 1912. Two of these deserve particular mention, as they continue to shape the organisation's thinking on its relationship with its allies.

The first is the notion of the ANC as a 'broad church' that accommodates various class forces within its ranks. Over the years, this has enabled the organisation to claim to represent all classes in a struggle that was intended to liberate all of them from national oppression. Under apartheid, this claim made a lot of sense as it sought to achieve the greatest possible unity of all the oppressed people. This, together with the fact that the ANC is the oldest liberation organisation, accounts for its appeal among all the black sections of South African society.

The second dimension, which also goes back many decades, is the organisation's status as 'leader of the liberation movement' and, more recently, 'the tripartite alliance'. This leadership also implies the primacy of national liberation over any other political programme that articulates the specific interests of a particular class in the struggle. For the ANC's allies, this means subsuming their political programmes under a broad, multiclass, programme that seeks to transfer power to 'the people'. Again, this approach was very effective during the years of the democratic struggle, as it eliminated some of the factionalism and infighting seen in other movements here and in other countries.

However, as will be shown later, these approaches have come to serve a different purpose, and may engender an intolerance of political competition and opposition. Thus one analyst has referred to the post-colonial trend of subsuming workers' claims under universally defined rights and entitlements forming part of a project of 'nation-building' as 'the tragedy of Africa's mode of decolonisation' (Cooper 1996: 468–9).

During its years underground and in exile, the ANC was made up of three strands, which continue to function as discrete networks in the democratic South Africa. The first comprised its leaders in prison, notably Nelson Mandela, Walter Sisulu, and Govan Mbeki. Although they successfully maintained contact with the leadership in exile, their ability to remain in contact with and influence internal struggles was extremely limited. However, within the internal mass movement they were regarded with the same respect as those leaders in exile.

The second strand comprised those in exile. Among them were those leaders – such as the late president of the ANC, Oliver Tambo, and the late Alfred Nzo – who issued commands to underground structures and ANC-aligned structures of the Mass Democratic Movement (MDM) as a whole. Although Mbeki belonged to a younger generation of exiled ANC leaders, he nevertheless worked closely with these veterans and was socialised into their political and leadership culture from an early age.

The third strand comprised those in MDM structures. Although these structures avoided associating openly with the then outlawed ANC, many of their members and leaders were engaged in underground activities. Moreover, many of the MDM structures were ANC structures under other names, and many of the current leaders of the ANC emerged from the struggles waged by these organisations. The conditions under which the ANC operated during the struggle were dictated by the political situation of the time, and it is difficult to imagine how things could have worked differently. The legacy borne of these conditions still needs to be fully interrogated and understood.

But there are elements of that legacy that have come to the fore in the current practices of the leadership and membership of the alliance that are worth noting. They are particularly relevant when discussing Mbeki's leadership of the ANC and the country, as his political style epitomises the style of one of the three strands of the movement discussed above, namely the exile strand. Firstly, the prison and exile strands of the ANC presented themselves, and were also seen by many 'internal' activists, as bearers of the true culture, traditions, and symbols of the movement. Although there were thousands of internal activists who undertook various tasks in the name of the struggle, many of them felt it was necessary to defer to 'the leadership' by seeking its endorsement of their plans and activities. Thus, to many internal activists, exile and prison seemed to confer a status and authority onto certain leaders that could not be obtained by remaining active in 'mundane' activities within the country.

A second, and related, consequence of this phenomenon is the way in which internal activists and ANC-aligned movements surrendered the symbolism of the traditions of the ANC to the exiled and imprisoned strands of the movement. To many, the mystique of the ANC in Lusaka, Zambia, or Robben Island was associated with a commitment to, sacrifice for, and knowledge of the struggle that ordinary activists were assumed not to have. In the 1980s it was particularly customary for internal activists to take trips to 'get the line from the leadership' in neighbouring countries such as Swaziland, Lesotho, and Botswana. Those involved in mass or military actions would feel particularly proud of being officially acknowledged in statements emanating from Lusaka, or some other base of the exiled leadership. In other words, the ANC in exile validated and acknowledged those deemed to be loyal members of the organisation, while the struggling masses continued to sing the leadership's praises in songs, poetry, and other cultural forms.

Thirdly, the strategic choices made by the exiled leadership had a profound impact on the internal movement, particularly the youth. For many of these 'internals', militarism became an increasingly important way of demonstrating a commitment to the struggle. After 1990, dealing with this militarism was to become a serious problem for the leadership of the movement. It also took long for other forms of struggle, such as mass unionism, to become part of the liberation movement's repertoire of strategies for confronting the apartheid regime, precisely because they were non-militaristic and entailed operating within the existing framework.

Fourthly, many in the dominant exile strand of the ANC had no experience of democratic and independent unionism. They had lived for too long in host countries that had no respect for independent trade unions, and in environments where there were very few examples of democratic unionism. Their instrumental approach to unions – the 'transmission belt' approach, which was prevalent in the collapsed socialist countries in eastern Europe and in developing countries – has remained highly influential among activists and leaders.

Finally, it is important to note that waging a struggle against a repressive regime when the liberation movement is forced to operate clandestinely (underground and in exile) limits the practice of democracy within a liberation movement. Under these conditions it is hard for a liberation movement to live up to its democratic ideals. Dissenting views are often silenced by means of manipulating, labelling, or marginalising those who express them. This tendency is also present in the ANC, and there have been occasions when it has been used against individuals or groups. Of course, the legacy of the liberation struggle is complex. If the tendencies identified above are part of this legacy, it is equally true to say that there are countervailing tendencies in the liberation movement. The final shape of the ANC's thinking on and approach towards its allies is determined by the balance of power among various groups and factions within the organisation. Suffice it to say that an assessment of the organisation's policies and leadership should take account of this legacy and its complexity.

COSATU's loss of influence and power since 1990

Alliances between trade unions and political parties in South Africa date back to the early years of the twentieth century when white unions formed an alliance with the white Labour Party. But it was only in the 1950s, with the formation of the South African Congress of Trade Unions (SACTU), that a strong alliance was established between a trade union federation and the ANC. During its time, SACTU established a strong tradition of 'political unionism', a notion based on the view that under the specific conditions of apartheid South Africa the trade union and political struggles could not be separated (Webster 1994: 268). After the re-emergence of black unions in the 1970s, union engagement in politics and in alliances with political parties was the subject of heated debates within the emerging MDM. This led to the 'populist' – 'workerist' division in the 1980s, the former being unions that preferred engagement in politics and alliances with liberation movements, and the latter being those that opted for political non-alignment and a strategy of building a strong shop-floor base (Lambert and Webster 1988). 'Workerist' unionists were those who were suspicious of nationalist politics that liberation movements such as the ANC were seen to represent (see, for example, Foster 1982). The formation of COSATU in December 1985 represented a change in strategy by the unions affiliated to the new federation. Besides its shop-floor struggles, the new federation took an overtly political stand. Jay Naidoo, its general secretary at the time, explained why political involvement was imperative:

> Experience has taught us that it is not enough to simply concern ourselves with factory issues. Non-political unionism is not only undesirable, it is impossible. And this basic truth has become increasingly clear to the organised worker movement (1986: 34).

This position led the new federation to explore the possibilities of alliances with other organisations within the liberation movement. In March 1986 it met with the leadership of the ANC and the exiled SACTU to discuss issues of common interest. These discussions brought COSATU much closer to the ANC than any of the other liberation movements. Although no formal agreements were reached, the meeting noted that COSATU was 'an essential component of the democratic forces of our country', and had a task of engaging workers in 'the general democratic struggle'. It was also agreed that 'the advancement of the interests of the workers and the democratic struggle of our people requires that COSATU, in working together with other democratic mass organisations, seek to build disciplined alliances so as to ensure the mobilisation of our people in united mass action' (ANC-SACTU-COSATU 1986). But these talks, and the tentative agreements they resulted in, did not immediately lead to the formalisation of the alliance, as COSATU had to accommodate the concerns of those within its ranks who were opposed to alliances with nationalist movements.

This issue threatened to split the federation; however, delegates to its second national congress in 1987 managed to reach a 'strategic compromise' whereby the 'integrity of the "shop-floor tradition" was acknowledged while the new federation committed itself to participating in the national democratic revolution under the leadership of the ANC' (Webster 1996: 146). The history of ANC–COSATU relations before 1990 is well documented (see Lambert and Webster 1988; Baskin 1991; Webster 1996; Eidelberg 1997). However, three issues warrant attention at this point.

Firstly, COSATU's acknowledgement of 'the leadership of the ANC' was reciprocated by the ANC's acceptance of COSATU as 'an essential component of the democratic struggle'. Even though there was no formal alliance at this time, the federation's adoption in 1987 of the Freedom Charter strengthened its credentials as part of the democratic movement. In a situation where the ANC was exiled and the United Democratic Front (UDF) forced to operate underground, COSATU effectively became the only visible representative organisation of this movement that had direct access to the masses. Secondly, COSATU experienced a dramatic growth in membership; for example, between 1985 and 1991 its membership increased from 462 359 to 1 258 853.[1] These members were organised into vibrant structures across the country, an achievement which neither the exiled movements nor the other internal opposition groups could match. This strength significantly enhanced the stature of the federation within the democratic movement.

Thirdly, in the late 1980s mass action by COSATU and the ability of its leadership to provide direction to the MDM tended to overshadow the ANC's armed struggle and the political campaigns of internal organisations such as the UDF, thus earning it the *de facto* leadership role of the struggle. Thus COSATU played a decisive role in this phase of the struggle. This put the federation in a powerful position from which it would not be easy for the ANC to dislodge it. The unbanning in 1990 of the ANC and SACP resulted in the alliance being formalised the following year. Although the ANC was regarded by its two partners as the leader of the alliance, this leadership did not necessarily translate into a 'consolidation of ANC hegemony', as some have suggested (see, for example, Eidelberg 1997). Given that the ANC was still preoccupied with re-establishing itself as a mass-based organisation and with getting the negotiation process off the ground, it was not easy for it to simply reoccupy its leadership of the democratic movement in general, and the alliance in particular. In other words, the displacement of COSATU as the *de facto* leader of the internal movement was more gradual than many analysts realise.

Up until 1994, the ANC found that it had to renegotiate the terms of its leadership of the alliance. For its part, COSATU made sure that it tied the ANC to a radical programme of transformation which the Reconstruction and Development Programme (RDP) came to embody. Thus, while it is accurate to suggest that the displacement of COSATU started in this period, moves by the ANC to sideline the trade union federation were tentative at first because the ANC was aware that its leadership of the alliance was still extremely tenuous. Notwithstanding the popular appeal of the movement and its national leadership, the ANC could ill afford to antagonise or alienate COSATU, given the federation's strong influence at the grass roots.

Analyses of the alliance also commonly fail to pinpoint key moments of this process of COSATU's marginalisation. It is argued here that there are key identifiable moments which mark the reassertion of the ANC's leadership of the alliance. Firstly, the conceptualisation of the alliance as one 'led by the ANC' is important to note in this regard. But this in itself did not result in the marginalisation of the other alliance partners. Secondly, COSATU's exclusion from the constitutional negotiations solidified the ANC's leadership and relegated the former to the status of a bit player dependent on the latter's goodwill. However, this should not be overstated, as COSATU retained the ability to use mass action to 'unlock the transition process when it seemed to stall' (Buhlungu 1994).

Thirdly, the fact that the RDP became the ANC's election platform even though it was a COSATU initiative allowed the ANC to get the credit for the programme, thus boosting its credibility among the grass-roots memberships of all the alliance organisations. Finally, and most crucially, the ANC's election victory and the fact that it captured state power was the final act in the consolidation of its hegemony within the alliance. State power gave the ANC the freedom it needed to take decisions without having to refer them to the alliance. For COSATU, this was the beginning of a new phase in which its influence began to slip away. In the post-1994 period the ANC–COSATU alliance had several advantages for the organisations concerned. For its part, COSATU could count on an ANC government that was more sympathetic to the concerns of its constituency. This allowed the trade union federation to have greater influence over government, and to win significant policy and legis-lative victories, such as the Labour Relations Act (LRA) of 1995.

However, over the past few years there have been signs that, beneath the semblance of cohesion among the alliance partners, serious tensions and strategic differences exist and continue to grow. These have surfaced particularly around the government's announcement of its intention to privatise state assets, as well as its macroeconomic GEAR strategy. Since the 1994 elections, alliance activities have been less prominent, while the ANC and its leaders have been concentrating on consolidating their power as the ruling party. The ruling party has found itself having to respond to a much broader range of constituencies and interests than those of the alliance. What is being argued here is that the post-1994 period has resulted in a marked decline in the role and influence of COSATU within the tripartite alliance, and that this decline has coincided with Mbeki's ascent to power, both within the ANC and in government. This is explored further in the next section. A 1996 COSATU discussion document acknowledged that there were serious problems in the way in which the alliance was operating. It made a number of revealing observations which support the view that 1994 was the decisive moment for the federation's marginalisation within the alliance. The document lamented the fact that

> ... In the pre-election period, the alliance partners consulted one another on major issues ... Since 1994 there have been very few substantial meetings of the alliance. Even those that have taken place have been *ad hoc*, sporadic or crisis meetings. Further, issues agreed at those meetings have largely not been followed through ... The alliance never sat down to systematically look at the challenges of the transition and formulate a strategy, and what role our various formations should play in that strategy (COSATU 1996: 3).

The document then noted other problems linked to the non-functioning of the alliance, including weak organisational structures, the lack of a common vision on how the RDP should be implemented, and the fact that COSATU had to rely on individual views emanating from certain government ministries. It also lamented the fact that policy-making was becoming the domain of consultants, conservative economists, bureaucrats who had been prominent in the old order, international financial institutions such as the World Bank and International Monetary Fund (IMF), and a few progressive people in government. It noted that a range of forces had undermined the RDP.

Finally, the document noted its concern about 'the demobilisation of our people', and observed that 'most activists are no more sure of what the strategic objectives are' (COSATU 1996: 4). Thus the changing balance of power in the alliance since 1994 resulted in a gradual but sustained reconfiguration of relations at organisational and strategic levels, in the course of which political alignments that existed before liberation began to break down, making way for new ones. Although South Africa was unlikely to witness a dramatic break-up of the alliance, there was no doubt that the ANC had been using its hegemonic position within the alliance to reconfigure the relationship in a way that gave it space to bypass the alliance when deemed necessary. When the ANC was criticised for the manner in which it had introduced GEAR (by bypassing the alliance), the then president, Nelson Mandela, responded by articulating what appeared to be a redefinition of the terms of the alliance. He did so by identifying three ways in which the alliance operated in relation to policy issues:

> There are matters where we will agree. The second category is matters where we disagree among us, but compromise. The third category is where there is no agreement at all, and the government will go on with its policy (*Sunday Times* 1997).

Thirdly, the debate on the alliance does not take into account the rapid changes in the leaderships of both the ANC and the alliance. In particular, processes of class formation that have accompanied democratisation and deracialisation are not examined. On the one hand, the ANC leadership has been shifting to the right, as evidenced by the organisation's adoption of the GEAR strategy. The priorities of this leadership have changed significantly since 1994, and the project of radical transformation is being overtaken by a conservative one based on neo-classical economic policies. A growing number of these leaders, including many ex-unionists who have gone into politics on an ANC ticket, are using politics as a launching ground to get into the world of business. On the other hand, COSATU's leadership has been restrained in its criticism of these shifts. Thus its sixth national congress held in September 1997 noted what it termed as a 'shift on the part of the ANC in government', but resolved to dedicate more resources and leaders to ensure an electoral victory for the ANC in 1999 (COSATU 1997).

For some in the unions, the alliance has become an avenue for upward mobility into politics. Thus, in the context of democratisation and deracialisation, the alliance has come to serve another purpose, namely that of a breeding ground for the emerging middle class. Meanwhile, the unions are facing their toughest challenges since 1994; only a few of these will be highlighted. Firstly, COSATU's influence has diminished significantly, and it could be argued that the only reason why the ANC wants it in the alliance is because it brings votes and is easy to contain. COSATU no longer commands the same respect it used to in the past, and, in certain quarters of the ANC, there is a growing irritation with, or even hostility towards, the federation. Secondly, the leadership drain that accelerated in 1994 continues, and threatens to deprive the unions of an entire generation of leaders. The haemorrhage has hit unions at all levels, from the shop floor up to the national level. Many previous shop-floor leaders are now managers and local government councillors, while scores of full-time officials and national leaders have moved on to become managers, consultants, civil servants, business people, and politicians. The impact of this on the unions has been examined elsewhere (Buhlungu 1999). Suffice it to say that an added dimension of this leadership exodus is the loss of organisational memory by the unions.

Few unionists still remember the early history of the unions, and those who understand how its organisational and political traditions were established are fewer still. This loss would be less severe if most of these ex-unionists had remained sympathetic to the labour movement. However, interviews with current and past unionists have revealed that their outlook changes as soon as they leave the union ranks; they reinvent themselves so that they can project an image 'appropriate' to their new positions. Indeed, it appears that, in their efforts to outgrow their union history, many ex-unionists try to present their union years as an adolescent stage, and their lives since leaving the unions as an adult and responsible stage. As a result, many ex-unionists no longer maintain links with their former unions, and, according to some unionists, many have adopted an unashamedly anti-union stance since leaving the unions. They regard the current crop of union leaders as an immature and reckless lot who are desperate to develop a national profile. Whether this view is justified or not is difficult to judge. What is clear, though, is that very few ex-unionists continue to support the union movement. Thirdly, the failure of the union movement to position itself as the core of a broader civil society movement has diminished its clout in society.

Although the unions still retain some capability to pull off major mass protests, such as the anti-privatisation strikes and protests of May 2000 and August 2001, they are increasingly becoming isolated from other grass-roots movements. As they become more marginal within the tripartite alliance, it is becoming easier for their detractors (including some within the alliance itself) to dismiss them as representatives of the sectional interests of a small and privileged section of society. During the acrimony generated by the 2001 general strike, the government placed advertisements in all the major newspapers in the country, arguing that the strike was unnecessary and that the government was 'restructuring', not 'privatising', the parastatals. The advertisements sought to present 'restructuring' as a 'mandated policy arising from the RDP', and the government as a custodian of the workers' best interests. By contrast, COSATU was presented as a spoiler intent on 'sacrificing' workers' wages, undermining the economy, and obstructing transformation by striking a few days before the start of the World Conference Against Racism (see GCIS 2001).

In October 2001, in the aftermath of the strike, the ANC released a briefing document that accused 'ultra-leftists' in COSATU of 'subverting' the national democratic revolution (ANC 2001). And, during a meeting between COSATU and the ANC in early January 2002, Mbeki accused COSATU leaders of working with international left-wing forces to 'topple' him.

Fourthly, the labour movement is experiencing two major problems that have the potential of drastically reducing its power and influence. On the one hand, it remains highly fragmented, and there is evidence that fragmentation is now taking on a new form as splinter groups take advantage of weaknesses within the larger unions affiliated to the different federations. The past few years have witnessed the emergence of splinter groups from unions in the food, mining, metals and auto, and commercial and catering sectors, to mention just a few. On the other hand, unions are losing thousands of members through retrenchments as the structure of the economy continues to change under the impact of new trends in global capitalism. Meanwhile, union have remained incapable of adapting their organising strategies and structures to confront these conditions. One example is the failure of unions to develop strategies and structures to organise informal sector and casual workers. Finally, there has been a qualitative change in the orientation of workers and leaders towards their unions.

Since 1994 many workers have adopted a more instrumental orientation towards unions, which means they see them as agents supposed to deliver immediate material benefits rather than as agents working for the radical transformation of society. As a result, membership participation in union activities has diminished, except in those cases where workers' jobs and other bread and butter interests are concerned. Many union leaders' orientation towards unions has changed as well. Today, many shop stewards see their positions as platforms for seeking better jobs and other benefits. The same applies to other leadership positions within the unions. This has given rise to intense competition for jobs, and debilitating infighting and factionalism among union leaders. However, this should not be taken as suggesting that the unions are collapsing; indeed, they will continue to exist as relatively strong organisations. But union organisation and struggles will assume a different form from those in the past.

Mbeki and the unions: the birth of a strategy
There is little doubt that, since the ANC assumed power in 1994, unions represent the single strongest source of political support of as well as potential opposition to the governing party. During this time, the tripartite alliance has been central to the ANC's strategy for dealing with this potential threat. Essentially, this strategy is about keeping the unions 'inside the tent' rather than outside, and under Mbeki's government this approach will probably be refined rather than jettisoned. Thus there is some continuity between Mandela's and Mbeki's approach to dealing with the unions, the more so because Mbeki assumed leadership of the ANC and the country long before the presidency was officially handed over in 1999.

During the early years of Mandela's presidency, it appeared that the new government's strategy was to view unions as partners in reconstruction and development. The elevation of Jay Naidoo to a ministerial position responsible for the RDP was a symbolic gesture to the union movement, acknowledging its importance as a partner of the ANC in governing the country. Among the gains the union movement made at this time was the progressive labour dispensation that began with the enactment of the LRA in

1995. However, in 1996 a shift occurred in ANC strategy, punctuated by the abolition of the RDP ministerial portfolio and the government's adoption of GEAR, and coinciding with the time when Mandela began to hand over the reins of government to Mbeki.

This shift was accompanied by a greater assertion by ANC leaders of the government's 'duty to govern the country'. The government and the party increasingly solicited advice and ideas on policy issues from a circle of experts beyond the traditional network of advisers and trusted activists. One example is the 'kitchen cabinet' that Mbeki set up to advise him on a variety of policy issues. This informal advisory body included business people, lawyers, academics, and unionists, many of whom were drawn from outside the normal network of ANC activists. The unionists whose advice was sought in this fashion were not selected on a representative basis, but were hand-picked by Mbeki himself. Mbeki's strategy at this time had the effect of removing labour from its privileged position and reducing it to one of the many social actors which he could approach for ideas and advice. In parliament, the ANC had succeeded in discouraging former unionists from organising themselves into a labour caucus, and this forced them to become loyal to powerful figures in the party. Thus, in the period 1996–99, labour as a movement, and via its ex-leaders in national, provincial, and local government, gradually lost a lot of the influence it had enjoyed before and just after 1994.

Many unionists in the provinces and local areas began to discover that a career in the unions did not guarantee them a position in ANC structures. However, it must be pointed out that Mbeki is not the sole inventor of the strategy of keeping unions inside the alliance as junior partners. In the provinces and local areas, activists who perceive unionists as competitors for positions are adept at playing the games of power. They know the unions have many members who can be relied upon to vote for the ANC, but when issues of position and power arise, they invoke the notion of 'an alliance led by the ANC' to get ahead in the power stakes. Union activists say there is a growing hostility to unionists at the local and provincial level, with COSATU shop stewards attending ANC branch meetings often being reminded that these meetings are 'not union meetings' and that they should not dictate to the leadership how these proceedings should be conducted. And, during the 1999 parliamentary election campaign, some ANC leaders in the Eastern Cape expressed their unhappiness about the fact that there were 'too many shop stewards' on the ANC's provincial list – meaning that they resented the number of unionists due for election. Thus the period up to 1999 saw the birth of a new ANC strategy towards the trade union movement which sought to produce a pliant movement that did not pose a threat to the party.

Although Mbeki had a hand in crafting this strategy in his period of apprenticeship during the Mandela era, it has resonated with many other leaders at different levels of the ANC.

From 'Madiba magic' to 'Mbeki logic'

Mbeki has served as president for nearly three years. It could be argued that this period is not long enough to allow a full assessment of his performance. Besides, during this time he has rarely referred to trade unions and their relations to the ANC and the government. However, as has been suggested earlier, his approach to unions developed long before he became president. Many unionists interviewed argued that a new approach to unions by Mbeki's government was gradually taking shape. 'Some comrades are saying that we have moved from Madiba magic to Mbeki logic,' one unionist remarked. This shift is characterised by a move away from the accommodating style of Mandela, which sought to *win the voluntary co-operation* of all interest groups, towards one that *demands co-operation* by different groups.

Mbeki's style is a sophisticated combination of coercion and political persuasion, dressed up in a logical and intellectually compelling political discourse. His celebrated speech at the SACP congress of 1989 illustrates this. On the one hand he called the SACP to order, while, on the other, he presented a very eloquent case that the ANC had not 'sold out'. After he had spoken, the direct criticism of the ANC that had emerged at the congress was muted, because the critics were unable to refute Mbeki's logic. Before discussing how 'Mbeki logic' has shaped his strategy for dealing with the unions, it is important to say something about how some unionists view the president. During the interviews conducted for this study, many unionists were less charitable in their comments about the new president than they were about Mandela during his presidency. Comments such as 'he is anti-union', 'he does not like unions', and 'he has no respect for unions' were frequently made. Some suggested that these views were shared by more people in the unions, including ordinary members. 'Many workers sing songs about Mandela. Have you ever heard workers singing songs about our new president?' asked one activist.

Others argued that Mbeki's so-called anti-union disposition was due to the fact that he was 'an intellectual with a middle-class background', and that this caused him to be aloof from unions and their members. Notwithstanding these views, none of those spoken to were prepared to go on record. This has a lot to do with 'Mbeki logic', and how it impacts on the unions. One aspect of the government's approach to unions is the use of patronage to gain loyalty. Loyal unionists are often rewarded with party-political positions and civil service or parastatal jobs, while those who display disloyalty run the risk of being bypassed or ignored for such positions. Thus patronage has become an extremely powerful weapon for disciplining the unions. This involves a carrot-and-stick approach: those unionists who would like a well-paid political or government job are unlikely to antagonise the president and the ANC. At present there is a pervasive fear that discourages unionists from expressing dissenting views about political issues in the country insofar as they have a bearing on the ANC and the government.

Many unionists say they fear being marginalised within their own unions and within ANC structures. Since 1994 many unionists have been silent about ANC–COSATU relations, for fear of destabilising the relationship. However, over the past three years or so this silence has been replaced by a fear of being marginalised. It is in this atmosphere that 'Mbeki logic' becomes effective, because it means that, as long as there is fear, there is no need to use coercion. The combination of coercion and persuasion is also used to deal with 'difficult' union leaders. Some of these leaders have been called in for 'tea' or a 'braai' with the president, only to find that these sessions are intended to discourage certain actions by unions and their leaders, and to demonstrate to those summoned why those actions are wrong and undesirable. Mbeki's comments on the situation at the Volkswagen plant in Uitenhage in 2000 (where a faction of the COSATU-affiliated National Union of Metalworkers of South Africa (NUMSA) led a strike without informing the union leadership), made during his speech at the opening of the 2000 parliamentary session, also hints at the crux of his future strategy towards worker action. He warned that:

> Jobs, a better life for our people in the context of a growing economy, and our standing in the eyes of the investor community cannot be held hostage by elements pursuing selfish and anti-social purposes. Accordingly, the government has worked with the management at Volkswagen as well as NUMSA to ensure that the problem created by some irresponsible elements at this plant is resolved. The government will not waver from this position (Mbeki 2000).

These are probably the strongest words yet uttered on this topic by a head of state in the democratic South Africa, and they are, in many respects, reminiscent of speeches made by government ministers under the old order. They contain a multiple message. On one hand, they position the government on the side of the jobless against 'selfish elements' who still have jobs; and on the other, they suggest that strikes diminish the standing of the government in the eyes of investors. Also, striking is equated with anti-social behaviour, and therefore as undesirable. Finally, the president referred to efforts by the three 'social partners' to try to resolve the problem. It is not clear what he meant when he said that the government would not 'waver from this position'. What is clear, however, is that operatives of the National Intelligence Agency (NIA) have been monitoring events at Volkswagen. One of the operatives I spoke to in Uitenhage in 2000 said such monitoring was essential as the strike 'posed a threat to national security'.

But at this point there is insufficient evidence to sustain the argument that Mbeki and his government are anti-union. The ANC has continued to draw in leading unionists either as civil servants or as politicians. Recent high-profile examples include Mbhazima Shilowa, former general secretary of COSATU, who has become premier of Gauteng; Enoch Godongwana, former general secretary of NUMSA, who has become a member of the executive council of the Eastern Cape; and John Gomomo and Connie September, former president and vice-president of COSATU respectively, who are now members of parliament. The available evidence suggests that what we are seeing is a sophisticated strategy of containing the unions within the alliance. Some senior ex-unionists play a vital role in this strategy because of their links with union leaders and their knowledge of union organisational strategies; Godongwana is still close to NUMSA's leaders, while Gomomo has been playing a part in trying to resolve the crisis surrounding Volkswagen in the Eastern Cape.

However, there are some unionists who resent attempts by ex-unionists to use old union ties and credibility for currying favour with their new political bosses, by keeping the unions within the political parameters defined by the government. One unionist interviewed referred to the minister of labour, Membathisi Mdladlana, as an example of how ex-unionists are being used against labour. He argued that Mdladlana was like a wind instrument (*ixilongo*): 'You know, an *ixilongo* will not make sound of its own. When it makes a sound, then you know there is somebody who is blowing it to make that sound. That is how that comrade is.' Part of this resentment stems from the fact that the ex-unionists in politics always preach caution and moderation whenever they meet their old comrades. Many seem to have lost much of the power and influence they enjoyed in the unions, and have little regard or respect for democratic processes. These days they do not talk about 'debates in structures', but are more likely to be heard telling unionists that their issues and concerns are still being 'cooked in the pot' ('*indaba isebhodweni, isaphekiwe*') – which means that the issue has been passed on to the president for his consideration and decision.

How, then, do we characterise Mbeki's strategy towards COSATU in particular and the union movement in general? To label it as authoritarian would be too simplistic. It appears as if his approach to unions fits in with his approach to governance in general, which is about winning as many people as possible to his side and then isolating or marginalising those who cannot be won over (Hadland and Rantao 1999). Those who are won over remain beholden to the ANC or to him personally, so they do not pose a further challenge. Thus there are two sides to the government's union strategy: to contain or co-opt the majority, and to marginalise its remaining opponents.

The success of this strategy is based on two factors: the first is the support the ANC enjoys as the largest liberation movement which has successfully appropriated the symbolism associated with the liberation struggle. The second is patronage. This strategy will remain in place as long as the ANC continues to invest intellectually and ideologically in preserving the aura and symbolism of the liberation struggle, and as long as there are political and civil service positions to be given to loyalists and pliant and ambitious supporters.

But these are not the only reasons for Mbeki's success in maintaining a reasonably stable ANC–COSATU relationship despite some controversial ANC policies in recent years. This must also be ascribed to his ability to interpret and reinterpret the history and traditions of the ANC and the liberation struggle to suit his current policy approaches. In addition, he has proven to be extraordinarily adept at interpreting the history, identity, culture, and destiny of South Africa's people in such a way that they mesh with ANC policies and objectives, and the struggle which the ANC fought.

It is this ability to weave all these elements into a single narrative of the struggle that has enabled him to earn the reverence, if grudging, of many in the unions. However, it must be added that this rendition and reinterpretation can also take the form of political manoeuvring to achieve certain political and ideological objectives. It is this attribute that many, including unionists, find logical and unassailable, the more so because it is intended to persuade people to accept a particular political narrative and to discourage certain forms of political behaviour. Hence the term 'Mbeki logic'.

In the period from 1996 to the present Mbeki has emerged as the key person in government who has pronounced on questions of the history, identity, culture, and destiny of South Africa's people. In all these pronouncements, the ANC has featured as a central player. This has served to cement the ANC's hegemony as the leader of the alliance representing the interests of all South Africans irrespective of forms of social cleavage such as race, ethnicity, class, or gender. Meanwhile, the unions have not been able to match Mbeki's extraordinary intellectual 'logic'. This is partly due to the crisis of ideas – or intellectual crisis – the labour movement is facing because of the lack of a coherent political and ideological programme.

During the Mandela years COSATU was seemingly happy to follow that legendary leader's lead, because he was always prepared to incorporate others' contributions in his narrative of the liberation struggle. What they did not realise, however, was that, as Mbeki was gradually being handed the reins of power, the narrative of the struggle was also being redefined, and that Mbeki was asserting the ANC's right to make key policy decisions alone. The unveiling of GEAR was a wake-up call to the unions, which alerted them to the change in the ANC's attitude. Today, unions are in a difficult situation, as their influence within the alliance continues to decline. However, leaving the alliance at this point is not an attractive option, as it would amount to walking into a political wilderness.

Learning from post-colonial experiences in developing countries

The dilemma facing COSATU today has been faced by many other union federations in other newly independent countries in Africa and the rest of the developing world. It is therefore important to take note of these precedents, as they help us to understand developments in ANC–COSATU relations. One observer has remarked that, in other post-colonial societies, the achievement of 'the unifying objective', namely independence, resulted in a breakdown of the 'harmony' of union–party alliances (Bienefeld 1975: 242). Nationalism of the variant that propelled many societies to liberation sought to totalise political thought and action under the ruling party, and any alternative locus of power and political expression represented a threat to the nationalist elite and its project of nation-building. In his discussion of labour–state relations in post-colonial Africa, Bill Freund referred to this trend in the attitude of the new rulers towards civil society organisations in general and trade unions in particular:

> Virtually without exception, African states moved towards as great a control over local social institutions and potential power bases as they could manage regardless of their formal ideological stance. The trade union was potentially a nest of rivals to the ruling party, and party and state were anxious to ferret out any potentially dangerous leaders (Freund 1988: 94–5).

But a more significant point is that a set of class interests are embedded in the ideology of national liberation that contradicts those of trade unions and the working class. These are the interests of the middle classes that in most colonial societies occupied leading positions in the national liberation movements. In this situation, many leading unionists have tended to lose their revolutionary impulse and have subordinated the interests of the union movement to those of the new political elite, because there were personal rewards to be reaped. For example, one observer has noted that union leaders in post-independence Kenya 'took advantage of their positions to further their own ambitions in the political sphere, where the greatest personal rewards can be obtained' (Sandbrook 1975: 182).

Experiences in other developing countries help us to understand current party–union relations in South Africa. Already, some of the patterns identified by observers in those countries are beginning to emerge in this country as well. The fact that party–union relations here are similar to those in other developing countries has got nothing to do with any innate tendencies among the people of these countries, nor do they suggest the existence of some iron law of authoritarianism. The similarity stems from the common colonial experience that all these countries have undergone, as well as the character of the national liberation movements which have sought to eject the colonial powers and install a new political order led by a coalition of bourgeois elites. Many studies of decolonisation and liberation have emphasised the moment of rapture that independence appears to represent, and have neglected the continuities with the colonial era. Thus they fail to grasp some of the similarities in the ways in which political and economic power are distributed and exercised after liberation.

Yet post-colonial governments mirror the old orders in many respects, including a tendency towards the authoritarian use of political power, and organising political and economic power in a way that does not favour subordinate classes and their organisations. Another way in which these regimes mirror colonial rulers is their ideological claim that presents government as a benign use of political power for the benefit of 'all the people', thereby positioning themselves as champions of the poor and the powerless. In a nutshell, the reality is that once the symbolic changes have been made, and the political rituals completed, post-independence regimes inherit a considerable amount of political baggage from the colonial past, including trappings of power, a tendency to authoritarianism, repressive state agencies and laws, a fear of opposition, a cynicism towards the poor, and a readiness to protect the interests of the rich and powerful. Space does not allow me to elaborate. Suffice it to say that Mbeki's strategy towards the union movement will not differ vastly from other experiences in the developing world that are characterised by attempts to subordinate unions. This strategy will succeed for as long as the ANC is able to present itself as a leader of the liberation forces, and its government is still able to provide patronage.

Note
1. Macun and Frost (1994). According to Filita (1997), COSATU currently has about 1,8 million members, distributed across 19 affiliates, with memberships ranging from 6 520 to 357 198.

References

Akwetey, EO. 1994. *Trade unions and democratisation: a comparative study of Zambia and Ghana*. Stockholm: University of Stockholm.

ANC National Executive Committee. 2001. Briefing notes on the alliance. October.

ANC-SACTU-COSATU. 1986. Joint statement of the executive committees of COSATU, SACTU, and the ANC, Lusaka, 5–6 March. Reprinted in *South African Labour Bulletin*, 11 (5).

Baskin, J. 1991. *Striking back: a history of COSATU*. Johannesburg: Ravan Press.

Bienefeld, MA. 1975. Socialist development and the workers in Tanzania. In R Sandbrook and R Cohen (eds). *The development of an African working class*. London: Longman.

Buhlungu, S. 1994. COSATU and the elections. *South African Labour Bulletin*, 18 (2).

———. 1999. Generational transition in union employment: the organisational implications of staff turnover in COSATU. *Transformation*, 39.

Cooper, F. 1996. *Decolonisation and African society: the labour question in French and British Africa*. Cambridge: Cambridge University Press.

COSATU. 1996. A draft programme for the alliance. November.

———. 1997. Resolution at the sixth national congress on political strategy and vision (tripartite alliance).

Eidelberg, P. 1997. The tripartite alliance on the eve of a new millennium: the Congress of South African Trade Unions, the African National Congress, and the South African Communist Party. Paper presented to a seminar at the Institute for Advanced Social Research, 3 March 1997. Seminar paper no 413, University of the Witwatersrand, Johannesburg.

Filita, T. 1997. COSATU: marching forward. *South African Labour Bulletin*, 21 (1).

Foster, J. 1982. The workers' struggle – where does FOSATU stand? *South African Labour Bulletin*, 7 (8).

Freund, B. 1988. *The African worker*. Cambridge: Cambridge University Press.

Government Communication and Information System (GCIS). 2001. 'Privatisation' strike – the facts. Advertisement in *The Sunday Independent*, 26 August.

Hadland, A and Rantao, J. 1999. *The life and times of Thabo Mbeki*. Rivonia: Zebra Press.

Lambert, R and Webster, E. 1988. The re-emergence of political unionism in contemporary South Africa. In W Cobbett and L Cohen (eds), *Popular struggles in South Africa*. London: James Currey.

Macun, I and Frost, A. 1994. Living like there's no tomorrow: trade union growth in South Africa, 1979–91. *Social Dynamics*, 20 (2).

Mbeki, T. 2000. State of the nation address at the opening of parliament. 4 February.

Naidoo, J. 1986. The significance of COSATU. *South African Labour Bulletin*, 11 (5).
Sandbrook, R. 1975. *Proletarians and African capitalism: the Kenyan case, 1960–1972.* London: Cambridge University Press.
Sunday Times. 1997. Mandela ponders some home truths. 25 May.
Webster, E. 1994. The rise of social movement unionism: the two faces of the black trade union movement in South Africa. In E Webster, L Alfred, L Bethlehem, A Joffe and T Selikow (eds), *Work and industrialisation in South Africa: an introductory reader.* Johannesburg: Ravan Press.
———. 1996. Trade unions, economic reform, and the consolidation of democracy. In S Friedman and R de Villiers (eds). *Comparing Brazil and South Africa: two transitional states in political and economic perspective.* Centre for Policy Studies, Foundation for Global Dialogue, Idesp.

CHAPTER 9

Down to business, but nothing to show

WILLIAM MERVIN GUMEDE

Thabo Mbeki, 'the business-friendly president' (Gumede 2001), has given business leaders unprecedented scope to shape government policies. His government has pursued pro-business reforms such as lowering taxes, reducing the budget deficit, reducing exchange controls, privatising state companies, and reducing inflation.

He also styles himself as the pillar of 'third way' politics in the developing world, and an advocate of the cause of the poor, both at home and internationally as a leading spokesperson for the nations of the 'South' (Gumede 1999). Mbeki has worked hard at changing the image of the ANC from that of a liberation movement associated with radical socialist economic policies into a governing party with centrist policies. His government and ministers have also worked hard to reassure the market and investors that the ANC is a sensible governing party. This is in contrast to other former liberation movements, such as Zimbabwe's ZANU-PF, which, once in government, messed up their economies through 'mismanagement and graft' (*Financial Mail* 2000c).

Despite the fact that a number of studies, including one by the International Labour Organisation (ILO), has shown that the South African labour market is already highly flexible, the government has proposed amendments to labour laws to meet business demands for greater flexibility in hiring and firing (Manuel 2000). The ANC's trade union and civil society allies have strongly opposed this, but in vain. The ANC government has been reluctant to consider providing a social safety net, such as a basic income grant, for those left destitute as the government liberalises the economy. In public, Mbeki has consistently distanced himself from the ANC's traditional left allies, COSATU and the SACP. And in meetings with representatives of these two organisations, he has made it clear that the government is going to stick to its economic reforms despite their protestations.

So far, though, Mbeki has got little in return from local business. Local business confidence – as measured on the monthly index of the South African Chamber of Business (SACOB) – remains perilously low, and local business people remain highly reluctant to invest in their own economy. Mbeki and key government economic reformers, such as the minister of finance, Trevor Manuel, regularly criticise local business people for not investing in their own economy: 'Sometimes we in government have to wonder whether our own business people, our own citizens, believe enough in our country,' Manuel has complained.[1]

The president of COSATU, Willie Madisha (2000), has referred to this drop in domestic investment as an 'investment strike'. Foreign investors, seeing the reluctance of local business people to invest their money in South Africa, have followed their example.

Policy-making and business

Mbeki draws heavily on business advice. He has gathered around him a select group of prominent people, mostly business leaders, divided into five working groups (dealing with black business, 'big' business, labour, agriculture and religion) and three councils (dealing with international information technology, international investment, and international marketing) which he consults on key economic and social policy issues.

His international investment council is undoubtedly the plum. Joel Netshitentzhe, CEO of the Government Communications and Information Service (GCIS), and the government's chief spin doctor, emphasised the importance of this council when he said: 'The council provides many insights which help to inform the evolution of government's approach to things' (*Financial Mail* 2001).

Mbeki has presented his inflation target policy and his economic growth plan, as well as the government's new 'Marketing South Africa' campaign intended to attract more direct foreign investment, to his international investment council. Its members include the chair of Mitsubishi, Minoru Makihara; the chief executive officer of Unilever, Niall Fitzgerald; the chair of Commerzbank, Martin Kohlhaussen; the chair of D-Group, Sir Robin Ross; the chair of ABB, Percy Barnevik; the chair of Alliance Capital, Frank Savage; the vice-chair of Citibank, William F Rhodes; the chief executive officer of Ashanti Goldfields, Sam Jonah; the chair of Tata Enterprises, Ratan Tata; the chief executive officer of Petronas, Hassan Marican; the chief executive of

DaimlerChrysler, Jürgen Schrempp; the chairperson of Independent Newspapers, Tony O'Reilly; and the international financier George Soros (*Financial Mail* 2000b).

Soros is a particular favourite of Mbeki's, notwithstanding criticisms by the Hungarian-born financier of Mbeki's 'quiet diplomacy' in response to human rights violations by the president of Zimbabwe, Robert Mugabe (*The Sunday Independent* 2000). Senior executives of the United States-based computer manufacturer Dell Computers and the networking equipment manufacturer Cisco have been influential in advising Mbeki on information technology strategy.

Closer to home, the counsel of local captains of industry is very important to Mbeki, who consults both white and black business leaders on policy matters. Although organised labour, both COSATU and the more conservative Federation of Unions of South Africa (FEDUSA) are also consulted, COSATU's general secretary, Zwelinzima Vavi, has complained to Mbeki at a meeting of the labour working group that the voice of business seemed to carry more weight than that of labour.

Civil society groups, the National Economic Development and Labour Council (NEDLAC), and some members of the ANC's parliamentary wing have also privately complained about marginalisation. NEDLAC's chief executive, Phillip Dexter (2000), has expressed his alarm over perceptions that Mbeki's regular policy discussions with business leaders were upstaging this tripartite negotiating forum, established after apartheid, aimed at reaching consensus among business, labour and government on economic, development, and social policies.

The director of the South African Non-Governmental Organisation Coalition (SANGOCO), Abie Ditlhake, has bemoaned the strong influence of business on government policy-making (*Financial Mail* 2000d). And Mbeki's economic adviser, Wiseman Nkuhlu, has stated that Mbeki has gone to great pains to understand business's concerns (*Financial Mail* 2000f).

Mbeki has acknowledged that neither 'the market' nor the state on their own can tackle the vast poverty and inequality among the black population left by 300 years of colonial and apartheid rule. He regards business – with its skills base, access to capital, resources, infrastructure, and delivery mechanisms – as a key partner in meeting South Africa's development objectives. This has been the driving philosophy behind his efforts to establish a 'hot-line' with business. The proximity of business and government is clearly visible at NEDLAC, where these two parties frequently agree on issues at the expense of labour and the civil society groups. Before, it was common for business to complain that the government had a close relationship with labour; lately, it has been the other way round.

However, the problem has been that few South African business leaders share Mbeki's and the ANC's national development objectives – and that, despite the ANC's efficient economic management record, business leaders still distrust the government. The common belief – and a correct one – among many South Africans (especially blacks) is that white business benefited from apartheid to the detriment of black business and labour. As a result, many people in the ANC government, as well as members of the public – especially blacks – have harboured strong expectations that white business (or, on another level, white society) would contribute to 'transformation'. However, since the 1994 transition most corporates have reverted to a 'business as usual' attitude: many business people argue that, now that legalised apartheid has ended, there is no further need for them to contribute to social change (Mackay and Shubane 1999). Mbeki and ANC strategists have also naïvely thought, and still do, that, as the government is implementing the liberalisation that business wants – which is causing even greater poverty, inequality, and hardships among blacks – business would reply in kind; the more so since the economic liberalisation requested by business leaders to 'create an environment for investors' has allowed South African business to prosper as never before. Productivity is up, and corporate profits are at their highest levels in a decade.

However, instead of expressing its appreciation, business has complained that the government is making excessive demands for contributions to development programmes. Moreover, local business is slow to observe new legislation, such as those on equity and affirmative action, aimed at redressing the apartheid-induced imbalances in South Africa's workplaces. The skills levies introduced by the government to try to boost the skills levels of black workers are rarely paid. Also, when local business leaders are called upon to explain their low rate of domestic investment, they frequently cite the slow pace of privatisation as a stumbling block.[2]

In the course of its attempts to appease business, the Mbeki government has been 'soft' on financial regulatory frameworks, which former World Bank chief economist Joseph Stiglitz (2001) has identified as a key ingredient for any market economy to function. Mbeki has allowed key South African companies to shift their primary listings from the JSE to foreign exchanges. The government has been slow to tackle banks that are costing the treasury billions of rands in revenue because of low tax payments (*Business Day* 2002c).

Neither has it acted against banks that still discriminate against blacks in their lending practices, or continue to 'redline' black areas (i.e., refuse to grant mortgage bonds secured against the property). The government has promised to take tougher action against the banks (*Business Day* 2001), but has been reluctant to scrap apartheid debts to South African financial institutions for fear of alienating the business community. It has also refrained from implementing the key recommendation by the Truth and Reconciliation Commission (TRC) that business, in order to 'empower the poor', should contribute to a wealth tax, comprising a once-off levy on corporate income, or a once-only donation by listed companies of 1 per cent of their market capitalisation. Moreover, the government meekly relented to business pressure to postpone the implementation of its capital gains tax from 1 April 2001 to 1 October 2001.

Mbeki's cosy relationship with predominantly white 'big business' took a dip over his handling of the land grab crisis in Zimbabwe, as well as HIV/AIDS. However, he managed to patch it up after a charm offensive which included reassuring South African business groups, in a closing address to the SACOB convention in Cape Town in October 2000, that he would not tolerate similar attempts by disenfranchised blacks in South Africa to reoccupy land taken from them by colonial powers and the apartheid government. He privately gave business leaders similar assurances during a meeting of his big business working group on the same day (*Financial Mail* 2000f).[3]

According to some who attended the meeting – who have chosen to remain anonymous – there were sharp exchanges between Mbeki and business leaders. The latter demanded that Mbeki should adopt a tougher approach to Mugabe, and publicly condemn the Zimbabwean leader in the strongest terms. Mbeki apparently first retorted that he had already done this six times, and then spent close to an hour explaining why he had opted for quiet diplomacy in dealing with Zimbabwe. He expressed his horror at the 'doom and gloom' perceptions of the country's economy which was prevalent in business circles. This meeting restored the Mbeki–big business relationship, with the latter promising to tone down its persistent criticisms of Mbeki's handling of the Zimbabwe crisis, and to kick-start a domestic investment drive. In turn, Mbeki undertook to allay white fears of a Zimbabwe-style land crisis in South Africa. Mbeki also promised that he would make an even greater effort to communicate with and consult business on key policy shifts.

Following the meeting, the big business working group placed half-page adverts in domestic and international newspapers pledging support for Mbeki's handling of the Zimbabwean crisis. This was probably the first time that business had responded so tangibly to overtures by Mbeki. After the meeting government and business expressed warm feelings for each other, prompting some observers to speculate that government–business relations had not been as cordial since the 1960s. However, the political analyst Robert

Schrire warned that big business's backing still seemed tentative (*Financial Mail* 2000f).

While Mbeki's emphasis on delivery and implementation is valid, he often fails to distinguish between management and leadership. Being a CEO is not only a matter of having a vision, but also of communicating it. A good CEO gets out and about, and tries to keep his shareholders informed of what he is doing and thinking. Despite Mbeki's accommodation of business, he has been unable to persuade business leaders that it is in their own interests to contribute to positive change – that rising poverty and inequality could be the end of South Africa's market economy. Thus he has failed to draw business into a shared understanding of the social and economic problems left by the apartheid government. This will be a key challenge for Mbeki, as most nations that have rapidly reduced poverty have shared a common understanding among business, labour, and government about how to tackle society's problems.

Black Economic Empowerment (BEE)

Black business people, like their white counterparts, also have their special place at Mbeki's fireside. He meets regularly with a select group of black business people in the form of a presidential black business working group. Things have come a long way since the ANC's days in exile when it had a strongly socialist orientation, and was inherently suspicious of the 'capitalist' local black business community.[4] Soon after the ANC was unbanned in 1990, its leadership decided the time had come to establish closer links with the relatively small black business community. At a historic three-day conference held at Mopane Lodge in the Kruger National Park in late October 1993, the two groups decided to establish a mechanism to help forge a more 'dynamic' relationship between black business and the ANC at both national and provincial levels. More interestingly, the ANC and black business groups decided to work together to promote what they then vaguely called 'black economic empowerment' (BEE). The meeting also noted that black business should get more 'organised' if it was to make a greater impact on the country's mainstream economy (Mopani Memorandum of Undertaking 1993). However, since that historic rendezvous, black business organisation is still chaotic, beset with endless internecine struggles. In addition, black business organisations are still viewed with scepticism by many in the ANC fold.

Thus far, BEE has mainly been measured in terms of the size of black holdings in blue-chip companies on the JSE – the 'black-chip' shares. This happens every time a black group acquires shares in previously white-owned companies, establishes joint ventures with white businesses, or secures an equity stake in government-initiated businesses, such as casino licenses. It has therefore had the unfortunate effect of linking the success of BEE to financial volatility.

At the end February 2001 black companies accounted for 4,9 per cent of the JSE's total market capitalisation – a decline of 6 per cent over the 5,2 per cent in November 2000. During this period the JSE All Share Index rose by 22 per cent, buoyed largely by non-gold resources (BusinessMap 2001). If measured by how many blacks own shares in blue-chip companies, the BEE experiment so far must rank as a great let-down.

In 1999 this same trend caused an alarmed Mbeki (1999) to declaim that, five years after the arrival of the democratic order, not much progress had been made in this field, and that BEE may well be marching backwards. He sees BEE as a crucial route to the formation of a black capitalist class which he sees, in turn, as a key aspect of deracialising South African society. Speaking at the annual national conference of the Black Management Forum in late 1999, he said:

> As part of the realisation of the aim to eradicate racism in our country, we must strive to create and strengthen a black capitalist class. A critical part to create a non-racial society, is the deracialisation of the ownership of productive property (Mbeki 1999)

He went so far as to equate the failure of BEE with the ANC failing to achieve its historic mission, namely eradicate racism. Thus, to Mbeki a failure on the BEE front means a failure in the fight against racism. Thus it is equally damaging to him that BEE has come to be associated with a small elite intent upon making as much money as it can at the expense of the broader black society.

The state and black economic empowerment

Mbeki is a big fan of the way in which economic empowerment was pursued in Malaysia and Singapore (Friedman 1997); the governments of both these countries acted aggressively to provide capital and open up opportunities.

For Mbeki, state procurement is an important means of hastening the formation of the black bourgeoisie. While BEE may be running away in the sands of the JSE, it has powered on through contracts awarded by the government to black companies for goods and services. The government awards contracts worth up to R80 billion a year. From a zero base in 1994, when the ANC assumed power, black business went on to bag more than 40 per pent of the state's national and provincial contracts between 1997 and 1999. This trend accelerated further in the first three quarters of 1999.

Between July and September of that year, five of South Africa's nine provinces bought more than 75 per cent of their procured services from black-owned companies (*Financial Mail* 2000a). The department says the government's effort to promote the participation of black entrepreneurs is paying dividends. After a slow start, the government has beefed up its procurement policy. Tenders for government contracts now score additional points if they involve participation by blacks, females, or disabled people, or meet RDP goals (*Financial Mail* 2000a). New regulations are planned that will expand the services of tender advice offices to 'match-making' between large white-owned corporations and small or medium-sized businesses.

However, critics of the government's procurement strategy abound. For example, at public hearings on the workings of the system held in the Northern Cape in summer 1999, black small businessmen complained that the tender forms were too complicated. They also accused the state of being a poor payer; indignant entrepreneurs reported that many small black businesses had gone under while waiting for payment. Black professionals argued that the department of state expenditure's statistics were skewed by huge state contracts with significant black participation, which diverted attention away from the private sector. Black accountants and lawyers, for example, got little business. The government only monitored procurements by state tender boards, but most government departments also entered into their own contracts, which were rarely monitored (*Parliamentary Bulletin* 1998).

'Comrades in business'

Many new black business leaders are former (usually materially poor) activists turned ANC politicians, who, following their migration from politics to business, have become extremely wealthy.

The path from battlefield to boardroom has become well worn since Cyril Ramaphosa quit as the ANC's general secretary to join the largely black investment corporation New Africa Investments Limited (NAIL). It was not long before the premier of Gauteng, Tokyo Sexwale, left the public sphere to carve out a career in the diamond industry. Another former provincial premier, Mathews Phosa, has turned to business and holds numerous directorships, including one in Madiba Mills, which has vied for a stake in South Africa's state forests. In 2000 Moss Ngoasheng resigned as Mbeki's economics adviser and joined Safika Investment Holdings, a R500-million technology and telecommunications company which now has a controlling stake in NAIL.[5]

This stampede so horrified the president that he prompted the cabinet into debating a code of ethics for government executives heading for the private sector; among other things, it was proposed that they be prohibited from using privileged information to further their business careers. A 'cooling-off period' during which politicians and senior civil servants may not take private sector posts in the same spheres they dealt with during their public careers was also mooted. However, the debate on the code has fallen flat.

Much has happened to fuel the increasingly negative perceptions – beyond the cynical criticisms heard in the white community – of the way in which BEE is unfolding. In particular, the actions of the new breed of black entrepreneurs continue to reinforce the notion that, instead of benefiting the previously disadvantaged black community, BEE has degenerated into the self-enrichment of a few.

These excesses seemed to reach a high point in April 1999 when the media revealed that the chair of NAIL, Nthato Motlana, and executive directors Dikgang Moseneke, Zwelakhe Sisulu, and Jonty Sandler were planning to transfer shares worth R130 million in African Merchant Bank to themselves. The plan was dropped following a public and shareholder outcry.

The most recent scandal surrounding BEE involved Safika and Makana Trust (an organisation set up to help former Robben Island prisoners). It centred on R120 million-worth of MTN shares which Makana said it had temporarily transferred to Safika, and which it wanted returned. However, Safika had refused to do so.

Both groups sought the help of the courts, and tore each apart in public. The conflict was even more embarrassing because two of the three leading adversaries – Ngoasheng, chair of Safika, and Sotho Ndukwana, a Makana trustee – had both been imprisoned on Robben Island.

Ndukwana asked the High Court to order an investigation under section 258 of the Companies Act into the share transfer, as well as alleged improper payments of R2 million each to Ngoasheng and Vuli Cuba, Safika's chief executive officer. In turn, Ngoasheng and Cuba sued the Makana trustees for defamation of character. In March 2002 a High Court judge agreed to the investigation, saying grounds existed to believe Ngoasheng and Cuba had acted 'dishonestly and dishonourably' (Templeton 2002; Msomi 2002).

The conflict was eventually settled out of court in May 2002 (Petros 2002), in a deal said to be brokered by ANC heavyweight Tokyo Sexwale.

Moreover, many supposed BEE companies are little more than facades. While blacks typically serve as non-executive directors, whites hold the top executive jobs, and also control operations and management. Examples abound of black businessmen who rent their faces to white businesses so that the latter can satisfy the requirements for government tenders.[6] Given these trends, proposals that the state should use privatisation to kick-start BEE should turn on the warning signals; unless such a system is strictly monitored, it could lead to a situation in which state corporations are transferred to a few members of the black elite – or, even worse, black business people fronting for whites.

Another criticism has been that BEE companies are often the worst industrial relations violators. Many black entrepreneurs are enthusiastically 'downsizing' the workforces in companies under their control. The president of COSATU, Willie Madisha, has condemned black employers for failing to comply with labour legislation, or maintain progressive labour relations. Madisha charged that black business people were joining the 'chorus of whining white business' which called for more labour flexibility, forgetting that poorly skilled workers in South Africa could already be hired and fired with ease (Madisha 2000). At COSATU's national congress in 2000, Thami Mazwai, CEO of Mafube Publishers (which publishes the business magazine *Enterprise*) and a leading supporter of BEE, was voted among the 10 worst employers in the country.[7]

Once successful, former black politicians turned business people seem to quickly forget about the 'struggling masses'. When the TRC demanded that white business contribute to apartheid reparations, much of white business balked – but so did newly successful black business people. Saki Macozoma, a former Robben Island political prisoner and now chief executive officer of NAIL, said: 'Dishing out money [to victims of apartheid] would be futile' (*Financial Mail* 2001a).

'Narrow' BEE

The ANC has never agreed internally on the definition of 'black economic empowerment'. As a result, the question of how BEE should fit into broader government economic policy, such as GEAR, has also not been worked out in detail.

However, since the words 'black economic empowerment' were first used in South Africa in the early 1990s, this notion has been interpreted in roughly two ways. The first is a rather narrow view which sees BEE as purely about creating a new black capitalist class in post-apartheid South Africa. Once this has happened, the argument goes, benefits will trickle down to the black poor. This approach emphasises an increase in the 'proportional' representation of previously disadvantaged groups, and focuses on the advancement of blacks in managerial, professional, and business ranks. Therefore, it largely involves the promotion of a new class of wealthy and powerful African movers and shakers.

This view has been particularly promoted by sections of the South African media and 'big business', and has become the 'accepted' public view of BEE.

Supporters of this 'narrow' view of BEE defend it with statements such as 'there is nothing wrong with being filthy rich' (Edigheji 1999).

Mbeki's statement that there is no need for blacks to be embarrassed about the emergence of successful and prosperous black bourgeoisie has been embraced with glee by some elements of the 'new black elite'. Addressing a conference of black business leaders, Mbeki (1999) declared:

> This is the real world. As part of our continuing struggle to wipe out the legacy of racism, we must work to ensure that there emerges a black bourgeoisie, whose presence within our economy and society will be part of the process of the deracialisation of the economy and the society.

However, frustrated that his call for the formation of a black capitalist class has been used as a defence by elements of the black elite bent on enriching themselves, Mbeki has repeatedly rebuked those using BEE to acquire 'a grand house, a grand car, and a grand salary' (ANC Economic Transformation Committee 2001).

Many have argued that, despite its flaws, 'narrow' BEE has at least boosted the black community psychologically in that it has shown that blacks such as Ramaphosa or Motlana can also become successful business people. However, this approach consigns the rest of black society to being spectators, celebrating the success of a small elite, without benefiting from increased employment opportunities, skills development, start-up finance, or development in their communities.

COSATU leaders in particularly have been scathing in their criticism of this 'narrow' BEE. In 1999 Zwelinzima Vavi, general secretary of COSATU, told an ANC workshop:

> We do not see BEE narrowly as the enrichment of a few black individuals. Rather, we see it as empowerment of the black majority in the context of dealing with the legacy of apartheid. We accept that the process of dealing with (economic) discrimination may ultimately lead to the development of a new black bourgeoisie. Our approach, however, is that, for BEE to make sense for the majority of our people, the emphasis must be on blacks as a whole (*Financial Mail* 1999).

Opposition parties, such as the conservative Democratic Alliance (DA) and United Democratic Movement (UDM), but also black left parties such as the Azanian Peoples' Organisation (AZAPO), have been quick to capitalise on negative perceptions of BEE. Arguing against BEE, the DA and especially its leader, Tony Leon, wrongly contend that wealth and income disparities between black and white has nothing to do with colour, but is class-based, as it would be in a country such as Germany or Sweden (ANC Economic Transformation Committee 2001).

'Broad' BEE

In the second approach, the black empowerment process is interpreted far more broadly to include the economic and social development of the whole of black society. In May 1998, in an attempt to find an acceptable definition of BEE, and determine how it could be achieved, the Black Economic Empowerment Commission (BEECom) was set up under the auspices of the Black Business Council – an umbrella body representing 11 black business organisations. It had the support of Mbeki and Ramaphosa was appointed as its chair. The idea of the BEECom came from the Black Management Forum, whose members, worried about the slow pace of BEE, adopted a resolution at its national conference in November 1997 calling for the launch of such a body.

Regarded by Mbeki and black business leaders as a national priority, the BEECom started off rather as a national disappointment. Commissioners consistently failed to meet deadlines, and became embroiled in a leadership struggle when one faction, led by the deputy chair, Gavin Pieterse, attempted to oust Ramaphosa. Ramaphosa wanted the BEECom to come out with tough recommendations, including putting pressure on white businesses to contribute more concretely towards economically empowering blacks. However, Pieterse and his supporters called for moderation, fearing that being 'too tough' on white business would scare them away. They argued they needed to get white business to 'buy in' to BEE.

After a long delay, the BEECom produced a report that accepted the 'broad' definition of black empowerment (*Financial Mail* 2000e). Key government economic mandarins received it with scepticism; the minister of finance, Trevor Manuel, initially dismissed it as short on detail and as reading 'like out a text out of the Communist Manifesto'. And the minister of trade and industry, Alec Erwin, said the proposals demanded too big a role for the state in BEE. He foresaw a minimal role for the state, and wanted to know what black business was doing to promote empowerment (ANC Economic Trans-formation Committee 2001).

In March 2002 the National African Federated Chamber of Commerce (NAFCOC) rejected the report, declaring that the BEECom had 'betrayed black people' (*Business Day* 2002). Its former CEO, Sabelo Macingwane, claimed that the organisation had not been given a chance to contribute towards the report. NAFCOC is now working on its own report. Its decision is likely to delay government BEE plans even more, and also further tarnish its public image.

Despite NAFCOC's criticisms, Mbeki and the ANC have accepted key recommendations in the BEECom report, particularly the suggestion that the state should play a bigger role in promoting BEE. The BEECom proposed setting up an empowerment commission or council in Mbeki's office to drive and monitor BEE, to which Mbeki has agreed.

Another BEECom proposal that has met with the ANC and government's approval is its suggestion for an 'investment for growth accord' among business, labour, and government, involving consensus on a strategy to raise the level of fixed investment. It remains to be seen whether government and business will accept the other part of the proposal, namely that the Government Employees Pension Fund as well as the private financial sector – particularly life and retirement funds – should invest 10 per cent of their assets in productive enterprises in areas of national priority for an adjustment period of five to seven years, as part of a targeted development investment (TDI) strategy. The report suggested that the banking sector should set targets for and disclose its investment in underdeveloped areas. It also urged the trade unions to use joint employer–employee pension contributions to increase worker ownership of industries.

At a tripartite alliance policy workshop in March 2001, organised by the ANC's powerful Economic Transformation Committee, the alliance adopted the BEECom's 'broad definition' of BEE, especially its call for a bigger role for the state, and for an empowerment council to be based in the presidency.

The meeting heard input from BEECom commissioners. Alliance leaders expressed their alarm over the public perception that BEE was only enriching a selected black elite, and that BEE in general had been a failure. The ANC's Economic Transformation Committee noted that: 'BEE has been hijacked by others who [have] sought to promote a narrow definition for their own purposes and agendas' (ANC Economic Transformation Committee 2001).

The adoption by the alliance of the 'broad' definition of BEE ended the confusion around this notion, and gave the BEECom proposals new credibility. The ANC's transformation committee asserted that BEE should be placed firmly within the ANC's new economic growth strategy.[41] The 'broad' definition of BEE proposed by the BEECom, and which the ANC's Economic Transformation Committee adopted, reads:

- An integrated and coherent socio-economic process, which is located in the context of the country's national economic, social and development transformation, programme;

- It must be aimed at redressing the imbalances of the past by seeking to substantially and equitable transfer ownership, management and control of South Africa's financial and economic resources to the majority of its citizens;
- It seeks to ensure broader and meaningful participation in the economy by black people to achieve sustainable development and prosperity (BEECom 2000).

The ANC's national executive committee adopted the transformation committee's proposals at its January 2002 *lekgotla* (strategic meeting).

Looking ahead
In his state of the nation address to parliament in February 2002, Mbeki announced that he would establish a BEE council in his office, as proposed by BEECom and the tripartite alliance. This was the government's first public response to the BEECom report since it had been handed to Mbeki six months earlier.

Although Mbeki has not disclosed the details of this, he is planning sweeping changes, including introducing laws that will require companies to set targets and submit reports on the progress they have made thus far in promoting BEE.

A strategy that is being discussed at cabinet level is to extend the BEE model used in the liquid fuel industry to other sectors. In November 2000, top players in the fuel industry – including the South African Petroleum Industry Association, BP Southern Africa, Caltex Oil, Engen Petroleum, Sasol, Shell South Africa, Tepco Petroleum, Excel Petroleum, and Total South Africa – agreed to transfer 25 per cent of the industry to blacks within 10 years, this giving the government its first major BEE success.

If this model is extended, it will mean that different industries will adopt BEE charters and commit themselves to certain targets. The deputy minister of finance, Mandisi Mpahlwa, has urged the main players in the South African economy to go this route (*Business Day*, 31 January 2002).

As part of the new BEE programme, the Companies Act will be amended to require listed and other large companies to disclose and report on their BEE programmes. Progress made by businesses will be monitored and evaluated by a BEE advisory council, which will be formally established in July this year. The council will be chaired by Mbeki, and will consist of a broad spectrum of stakeholders nominated by the cabinet.

The council is to implement a reporting and monitoring framework for the public and private sectors, which will enable the government to continually evaluate BEE, and intervene where necessary. Progress on BEE will be measured in terms of four indicators: ownership, control, skills, and income.

However, according to Andy Brown, BEE director of the department of trade and industry, the council will only have the authority to ensure the compliance of state-owned companies, but not of private companies, which would operate on the basis of 'a self-regulatory mechanism'.

Conclusion

Despite these developments, it is clear that BEE is faltering. ANC intellectual Pallo Jordan's hope that the emerging black bourgeoisie will set a 'new agenda for corporate social and civil responsibility' (*Mail & Guardian* 1997) seems further away from fulfilment than ever. Yet it is clear that higher levels of economic growth – which is so desperately needed – cannot be achieved unless blacks participate meaningfully in the country's economy.

John Friedmann, a professor of urban planning at the University of California (Los Angeles), has defined empowerment as an alternative development that aims to redress a historical process of systematic disempowerment. This disempowerment, according to Friedmann, denies the 'human flourishment' of the disempowered, as their lives are characterised by 'hunger, poor health, poor education, a life of back-breaking labour, a constant fear of dispossession, and chaotic social relations'. Empowerment, he argues, aims to humanise the system that shut out the disempowered, and its long-term aim is to fundamentally transform the whole society, including the structures of power. BEE in South Africa falls far short of this framework.

The fact that Mbeki's government has accepted the BEECom's 'broad' definition of BEE has given it the space to pursue genuine economic empowerment that will reduce poverty, unemployment, and inequality.

There are already signs that the government is starting to play a far more proactive role in promoting broad-based BEE; the planned setting-up of a BEE council to be chaired by Mbeki being a case in point. However, its efficacy of the council will be compromised if it does not have powers to enforce BEE targets in the private sector. Importantly, the BEE process needs to be strictly monitored.

The current government and black business approach to BEE also seems to underplay the development of skills. Mbeki will also need to refocus BEE on small, medium, and micro enterprise (SMME) development, and make it easier for blacks to access capital and education. There are plenty of examples where governments have used privatisation revenue to distribute the wealth among the poor, among other things via voucher and collective investment schemes, public offerings, and capitalisation (Edigheji 1999).

It is clear that Mbeki's pro-business strategy has not yet borne fruit. Its success will be measured in terms of whether he will be able to convince the South African business community that it is in its own interests to buy into transformation – and the ultimate barometer will be the extent to which local business will invest in the domestic economy. Although Mbeki seems to have a good relationship with the captains of industry, this has not filtered down to the middle managements of their corporations, and not to the leaders and managements of smaller businesses. Invariably, it is at middle management level where key investment decisions are made.

Mbeki's cultivation of international business leaders has also yet to deliver – despite the fact that members of his international investment council regularly sing the Mbeki government's praises for its prudent economic management.

To some extent, the problem is of the ANC's own making. Before the ANC assumed power, its policy was nationalisation. In preparing for possible nationalisation, local business leaders were quick to start programmes aimed at redressing the imbalances left by apartheid. Thus the insurance industry mooted an investment development unit which was supposed to finance employment and infrastructure creation in the lower-income groups. The obvious route then for the ANC would have been to press the advantage, and encourage more such initiatives from a business community on its back foot.

However, after the ANC came to power it quickly dropped nationalisation in favour of a market- and business-friendly approach. It did not want to put too much pressure on business, lest it risked a backlash from 'the markets'. One governing term later, it is much more difficult to get business to buy in to transformation policies, especially as the transition seems relatively peaceful, with Malaysian-style riots not yet on the horizon, lulling business into believing that all is well.

In Malaysia, the local business community only bought into 'transformation' after riots in the streets. Mbeki's challenge is to persuade local business to buy in to transformation before the riots of the disadvantaged appear on South Africa's streets. For that, he and his government need a strong dose of political will (Crouch 1996).

Notes
1. In a speech to PSG Online Securities in Johannesburg on 6 September 2000, Manuel unveiled treasury figures which showed that the level of domestic investment, as a proportion of gross domestic product (GDP), had declined from 16,5 per cent in 1998 to 14,9 per cent in 1999.

2. For example, at a meeting between Mbeki and business leaders in November 2000, the latter again cited slow privatisation as a stumbling block to investment (*Financial Mail* 2000f). And the South African Chamber of Business (SACOB) regularly decries the slow speed of privatisation in its press statements; see, for example, SACOB (2002).
3. *Financial Mail* (2000f). Business leaders who attended the meeting at the SACOB convention were the chair of Murray and Roberts, Dave Brink; the deputy chair of the Anglo American Corporation, Leslie Boyd; the chair of Barlows, Warren Clewlow; the chair of Absa Bank, Danie Cronje; the chair of Sanlam, Marinus Daling, the chief executive of FirstRand, Laurie Dippenaar; the chair of De Beers, Nicky Oppenheimer; the chair of Rembrandt, Johann Rupert; the chair of Stannic, Conrad Strauss; and the chair of Johnnic, Cyril Ramaphosa. It was also attended by the heads of two key parastatals: the chair of Eskom, Reuel Khoza; and the managing director of Transnet, Saki Macozoma.
4. Alarmed by the liberation movements' questioning of its commitment to the 'struggle', the National African Federated Chambers of Commerce (NAFCOC) sent a delegation to meet the then president of the ANC, Oliver Tambo, in Lusaka. On 27 May 1986 the president of NAFCOC, Sam Motsuenyane, met Tambo in Lusaka, Zambia, to express the commitment of local black business people to the struggle to end apartheid. See ANC/NAFCOC (1986).
5. After being fired by Safika, the American businessman Eric Phillips – who owned a 10 per cent stake in the company – wrote a letter to Mbeki complaining that Ngoasheng had been involved in the firm while he was still a public servant. This issue emerged again in January 2001 when Ketso Gordhan, Johannesburg's city manager, left to join FirstRand Bank, which had done business with the city council.
6. Not surprisingly, large mining companies, such as De Beers and the Anglo American Corporation, have created 'empowerment portfolios' in their stables. The government has drafted a Minerals Development Bill which seeks to give especially black small entrepreneurs a slice of the mining cake. However, when the bill becomes law, it may have the effect of favouring wealthy blacks who are already established in the industry, as well as those big companies with 'empowerment portfolios'.
7. This came after Mazwai had publicly criticised trade unions for protesting against business calls to limit employees' rights in the workplace. What infuriated COSATU most was Mazwai's statement that he was not paying his employees for Sunday work, on the grounds that small companies should be exempt from labour legislation.

References

ANC Economic Transformation Committee. 2001. Black economic empowerment policy workshop report. March.

ANC/NAFCOC. 1986. Joint communique. Lusaka, Zambia. 27 May.

Black Economic Empowerment Commission. 2000. Integrated national black economic empowerment strategy. October.

Business Day. 2002a. NAFCOC unhappy with report on empowerment. January 18.
———. 2002b. Empowerment charters called for. 31 January.
———. 2002c. Measures in pipeline to tighten noose on evaders. 21 February.
BusinessMap. 2001. Low share prices continue for black-controlled companies on the JSE. Press release, 22 March.
Crouch, H. 1996. *Government and society in Malaysia*. Ithaca and London: Cornell University Press.
Dexter, P. 2000. Interview with author. 21 May.
Edigheji, O. 1999. Rethinking black economic empowerment in post-apartheid South Africa. Tips Annual Forum. Johannesburg.
Financial Mail. 1999. Executives braced for a little bonanza. 16 April.
———. 2000a. Fast-tracking black economic empowerment. 28 January.
———. 2000b. Top-flight advisors to raise SA's investment rating. 11 February.
———. 2000c. SA may not be ready to bin the old ideologies. 3 March.
———. 2000d. New seeds of opposition. 19 May.
———. 2000e. Whose fight is it anyway? 6 October.
———. 2000f. Scratch here, rub there. 17 November.
———. 2001a. The perils of ruling-class amnesia. 26 January.
———. 2001b. Lead more, manage less. 9 February.
Friedman, S. 1997. The Mbeki era and South African business. Unpublished paper. Johannesburg: Centre for Policy Studies.
Gumede, WM. 1999. The triumph of style over substance: the influence of British and American campaign methods on the professionalisation of South African political campaigns. MA dissertation, Cardiff University, Wales.
———. 2001. The Mbeki presidency. Lecture given at St Antony's College, Oxford University, 25 October.
International Labour Organisation (ILO). 1999. Restructuring the labour market: the South African challenge. ILO country review. Geneva.
Mackay, S and Shubane, K. 1999. *Down to business: government-business relations and South Africa's development needs*. Research report no 69. Johannesburg: Centre for Policy Studies.
Madisha, W. 2000. Speech at a rally to celebrate Workers' Day. FNB Stadium, Johannesburg. 1 May.
Mail & Guardian. 1997. ANC must cultivate the new elite. 28 November.
Manuel, T. 2000. Speech to PSG Online Securities. 6 September.
Mbeki, T. 1999. Speech at the annual national conference of the Black Management Forum, Kempton Park. 20 November.
Mopani Memorandum of Undertaking. 1993. 31 October. http://www.anc.org.za/ancdocs/pr/1993/pr1031a.html.
Msomi, S. 2002. Safika appeal bid pitched liberation heroes into battle. *Sunday Times*. 31 March.
Parliamentary Bulletin. 1998. SA is still suffering from inequalities from racial capitalism. No 31. 14 April.
Petros, N. 2002. Safika, Makana finally reach a deal on shares. *Business Day*. 21 May.

South African Chamber of Business (SACOB). 2002. SACOB welcomes 'growth' budget, but stresses the need for measurable delivery. Media release, 20 February.
Stiglitz, J. 2001. Interview with author. 27 March.
The Sunday Independent. 2000. Soros dumps three top Mbeki aides. 17 December.
Templeton, A. 2002. 'Dishonesty and dishonour' haunt the dreams of Safika and NAIL. *The Sunday Independent.* 31 March.

CHAPTER 10

State and civil society in contemporary South Africa[1]
Redefining the rules of the game

KRISTA JOHNSON

> Where the people are no longer the enemy of the state, the question arises as to what role the people play with regard to state matters.
> – Thabo Mbeki (ANC 1996)

The restructuring of state–society relations has emerged as a primary goal of the ANC government led by Thabo Mbeki. Like most post-transition political leaders, he confronts the challenge of reasserting the political authority of the new democratic state while drawing a clear distinction between the new social order and the *ancien regime*. In South Africa this process is further complicated by the need to reconcile the history of popular politics and mass mobilisation with the institutions of liberal democracy. Many organisations deemed part of civil society historically had a close relationship with the ANC during the anti-apartheid struggle. Indeed, during the transition the traditional boundaries between government and civil society became blurred as large cohorts of civil society activists moved into government, and powerful constituencies of civil society, such as the trade unions and civic associations, forged formal alliances with the ANC ahead of the 1994 elections.

Mbeki's ascent to power, first within the ANC and then to the South African presidency, has prompted considerable speculation on how state power is being internally reorganised, how the state agenda is being redefined, and how the relationship between civil society and the state is being recast. There is a sense that South African politics is moving into an era of normalcy in which more conventional forms of politics are being consolidated, and key relations between social and political actors permanently fixed. This chapter assesses, in very broad terms, the ways in which the ANC's leadership, with Mbeki at the helm, has sought to define the rules regulating state–society relations, and the implications of this for participatory democracy and people-driven development.

State–society relations are being recast at a time when the ANC government has adopted much of the neo-liberal logic of global capitalism, leading some critics to bemoan the ANC's 'tragic leap to the right' (Saul 2000). Its emphasis on democratic forms of rule and good governance, the institutionalisation of individual rights and capitalist market economics via a constitutional dispensation, and the scaling down of the state's role in the economy have prompted other analysts on the left of the political spectrum to proclaim that 'it is the ANC that has now become the standard-bearer of liberal democracy in South Africa and the African continent' (McKinley 2000: 2). Indeed, in step with the dominant liberal ideologies of our time, clear boundaries are being drawn between the political and the economic spheres, and between political society and civil society.

In this chapter I will seek to demonstrate the dominance of the liberal conception of state–society relations in post-apartheid South Africa, but I will also examine the extent to which the dominant liberal paradigm conforms to the ANC leadership's own perceptions of state–society relations and the relationship between rulers and ruled. Mbeki and his followers in the ANC leadership, most of whom are former exiles and were trained in the radical Leninist school of thought that gives primacy to the role of the vanguard party and revolutionary intellectuals, are finding that the reorganisation of state–society relations along conventional liberal lines is quite compatible with their own hierarchical understanding of the relationship between rulers and ruled, and the primacy of leadership over mass action during processes of revolutionary change. Given South Africa's history of mass mobilisation and popular participation during the anti-apartheid struggle, when civil society was politicised from below and focused not only on opposing the state or seizing state power but also redefining the form of the state and its relationship to society, the dominant approach currently promoted by Mbeki and the ANC leadership remains highly contested. It is also important to note that, while this perspective is not shared by all the leaders of the ANC or the tripartite alliance, it is also not confined to those members of the new elite who have gone into government, as many leaders within civil society share this perspective. By reflecting on the broad underpinnings of the ANC leadership's recasting of state–society relations, and its implications on participatory forms of democracy, I hope to contribute to these continuing debates.

Liberal versus popular conceptions of state–society relations
Civil society and its relationship with the state have already sparked heated and lengthy debates in South Africa; in fact, despite its rather ambiguous meaning, this term has become something of a buzzword. While space does not permit the many contributions to this debate to be analysed in detail, it is useful to begin by briefly outlining two broad frameworks for conceptualising the relationship between the state and civil society. The first can be characterised as the liberal perspective, and coincides with the understanding of state–society relations found in most liberal democracies. The key characteristics of this approach are the clear boundary drawn between political and civil society, the designation of the state as a neutral arbiter, and – in its neo-liberal version – the promotion of the deepening of civil society, enabling it to act as a counterweight to the state.

Wary of most Africanist scholars' uncritical absorption of western perspectives of civil society and its relationship to the state, the second approach – the popular-democratic school – focuses on those organisations and movements in Africa that actually emerged during struggles for democracy; it seeks to understand the ways in which the anti-colonial struggle, and indeed the anti-apartheid struggle, attempted to recast the relationship between state and society and between ruler and ruled (see, for example, Mamdani 1990; Neocosmos 1998). While both perspectives share the view that statism is one of the primary obstacles to Africa's socio-economic and political development, they propose different solutions to the problem. Whereas liberal analysts emphasise the need to reinforce the boundary between the state and civil society, and strengthen civil society so as to provide a counterweight to the state, popular-democratic scholars push for a reconceptualisation of the very basis of state–society relations in order to make it more democratic.

In South Africa the liberal framework has been the dominant perspective. Often pre-occupied with the promotion of a one-sided anti-state ideology, it counterposes civil society – seen as positive, homogenous, and coherent – with the state, which it characterises as inherently authoritarian and bureaucratic. Liberals and socialists alike have supported the idea of a vibrant and independent civil society, serving as a 'watchdog' *vis-à-vis* the state (Atkinson 1992; Mayekiso 1992; Swilling 1991). In the context of transitional South Africa, scholars working in the liberal framework have effectively advocated the withdrawal of the popular movements from the political realm to the private and apolitical realm of civil society, where they should serve as interest groups or channels for community interests. Mimicking the dominant liberal perspectives emanating largely from western and eastern Europe, these scholars have stressed the need for a vibrant and independent civil society as the basis for ensuring democracy and holding the state accountable. The end result of this approach is to reduce democracy to pluralism plus an accountable state tasked with balancing the various particular interests in civil society.

While the liberal perspective on state–society relations is problematic in numerous respects, I will only point out a few of them here. Firstly, scholars working within this framework fail to recognise that, given the depoliticised nature of civil society in the liberal account, a vibrant civil society is perfectly compatible with an authoritarian and bureaucratic state (Gibbon 1993; Neocosmos 1999). The liberal perspective fails to explain how the state will be held accountable if the people are once again removed from the public realm. In addition, by relegating to the state the role of regulating relations among voluntary organisations, capital, and local government, this framework leaves open the possibility that the state will become the exclusive definer or guarantor of a general or national interest. Furthermore, given the fact that many of the strongest institutions in civil society are market-related, there is a danger that the people-driven approach which these authors see emanating from civil society may be overwhelmed by a market-driven approach to growth and development.

In contrast, the popular-democratic approach is far less celebratory of civil society, and cautions against equating pluralism or multiparty political systems with democracy. Scholars working within this framework adopt as their starting point the popular-democratic struggles that emerged in many African countries, and the unique form of politics they espoused. They suggest that, far from advocating the demise of a particular regime or colonial system, these groups sought to challenge the very basis of state politics and state power, and in the process redefine the nature of relations between the state and society, and ruler and ruled. By developing alternative structures of power and government, these organisations planted the seeds of an 'emancipatory politics' (Wamba Dia Wamba 1993) – revolutionary, liberating, progressive, and fundamentally rooted in the masses of the people.

In South Africa, Neocosmos (1998) has argued that the 'organs of people's power' and 'the kinds of politics which were developing within the mass movement in South Africa [provided] some of the fundamental elements of a genuinely emancipatory politics'. He suggests that, 'in the 1980s, the dominant trend of popular nationalism corresponded to the politicisation of civil society and the democratisation of the state from below, while in the 1990s we are witnessing the statisation of civil society or its politicisation from above' (234). Neocosmos likens recent developments in South Africa to processes of nation-building in many African countries after independence in the 1960s. He follows Mamdani's argument that the origins of statism and the reduction of nation-building to state-building lies in the 'defeat of popular movements in the period of transition from colony to independent state' (234).

According to Neocosmos, part of this process was one whereby such popular organisations that had, during the struggle for independence, entered the realm of political society (by addressing explicitly political questions, through interpellating their supporters as citizens) were gradually restricted to the realm of civil society (where they were to address the narrower concerns of 'interest groups' defined by the division of labour), before losing their independence altogether (197).

Although examining this argument in any detail is beyond the scope of this paper, it is worth noting that, in every genuine revolution during the nineteenth and twentieth century, popular-democratic institutions (councils, soviets, or *Räte*) emerged which, if the revolution was not defeated, were eventually defeated by the revolutionary parties themselves – or members of those parties – who failed to give any serious thought to the new form of government these popular institutions represented.[2] Yet the central distinction between the popular institutions and the revolutionary party, or – as Neocosmos defines it in South Africa's case – between popular and state nationalism, lies in different notions of state–society relations, and different conceptions of the relationship between leaders and led: 'While the former stressed popular democracy and control, accountability and direct mandating of leaders, the latter stressed the independence of leadership, top-down prescriptions, and statist arguments of various kinds' (234–5).

Clearly, this issue is more basic than the contradictions brought out by democratisation. It gets to the heart of the crisis of governance and the fundamental problem of all modern politics, namely how to reconcile equality and authority. Scholars working within the popular-democratic paradigm suggest that what is required is a redefinition of the relationship between ruler and ruled whereby the practices of government are no longer considered to be the privilege of the few, and the majority of citizens are not excluded from the public realm. By advocating the politicisation of civil society, 'whereby their members are addressed as equal citizens and not simply as members of an interest group', and the democratisation of the state (Neocosmos 1998: 232), the popular-democratic approach provides a viable basis for the emergence of popular democracy, or a democratisation process that will be meaningful for the majority of working people.

Establishing a new social contract

In establishing a new social contract, Mbeki and the ANC leadership face multiple pressures and formidable challenges. On the one hand, the ANC government faces widespread domestic pressures for democratisation and development. At the same time, it confronts pressures from powerful international and national interests to liberalise the economy, downsize the government, and grow the economy via export-oriented niche development.

During the first few years of South Africa's democracy, the rules for regulating state–society relations in the post-transition era were still rather fluid; state–society relations were largely defined within the framework of the RDP that had set out to establish a new social contract, intended in turn to break down the adversarial relationship between the state and society and bind the state to redistributive policies aimed at meeting the basic needs of South Africa's majority. With the introduction of GEAR, the discourse has shifted from an emphasis on a new social contract to one on building new social partnerships. In this section I examine one of the first and most detailed attempts to lay out the justification and parameters of this new social partnership for post-apartheid South Africa: an ANC discussion document entitled 'The state and social transformation', drafted in November 1996 by then deputy president Mbeki.

He did so in response to emerging tensions within the ruling tripartite alliance and broader democratic movement, especially over the government's new macroeconomic strategy. The document's aim was to 'sell to the more left-wing alliance partners the rationale for government's economic programme' (*Business Day*, 27 November 1996). At the same time, it sought to define the roles of the state and civil society in the process of social transformation, and establish the rules that would regulate state–society relations in the post-transition era.

The importance of this document does not derive from a belief that these are Mbeki's personal opinions, or that he has the last word on all policy matters within the ANC. This document generated considerable debate within the ANC and the tripartite alliance. But it has become clear that it has been adopted by most ANC leaders, as its authorship is no longer ascribed to Mbeki, and its ideological and philosophical underpinnings are evident in much of the ANC's recent policies. Thus the document is significant because it illustrates the most characteristic elements of what appears to be the governing philosophy or 'rules of the game' espoused by the ANC's leaders.

In it, Mbeki advocates a more technocratic approach to governance that removes politics from the picture and bases decision-making on rational calculations of 'subjective and objective factors in the national and international environment' (ANC 1996). The governing philosophy presented represents a hybrid of dominant liberal precepts, such as an impartial state, and prominent features of liberation or anti-apartheid politics, such as participatory democracy and people-driven development and an interventionist state. Given the consistent understanding of the role of leadership, the relationship between rulers and ruled, and, above all, the shared concern for stability and order, significant aspects of the two frameworks are quite compatible.

Therefore, Mbeki accepts the liberal notion of the democratic state as a neutral referee responsible for balancing competing social interests. He explains the rationale behind such a characterisation as follows:

> To the extent that the democratic state is objectively interested in a stable democracy, so it cannot avoid the responsibility to ensure the establishment of a social order concerned with the genuine interests of the people as a whole, regardless of the racial, national, gender and class differentiation. There can be no stable democracy unless the democratic state attends to the concerns of the people as a whole and takes responsibility for the evolution of a new society.

Furthermore, by virtue of its impartiality, the democratic state is seen as the only legitimate expression of the interests of the whole nation, becoming coterminous with the 'national interest' or 'public will'. At the same time, all other demands or proposals for social change emanating from civil society are viewed as partial, subjective, or sectarian, regardless of the legitimacy of the demands. As far as the most powerful, organised, and popular voice in civil society is concerned, Mbeki warns that:

> The instinct towards 'economism' on the part of the ordinary workers has to be confronted through the positioning of the legitimate material demands and expectations of these workers within the wider context of the defence of the democratic gains as represented by the establishment of the democratic state . . . If the democratic movement allowed that the subjective approach to socio-economic development represented by 'economism' should overwhelm the scientific approach of the democratic movement towards such development, it could easily create the conditions for the possible counterrevolutionary defeat of the democratic revolution.

As an alternative, Mbeki proposes to reconstruct the terms of relations between civil society organisations and the state in a hierarchical and highly institutionalised fashion. For him,

> the issue turns on the combination of the expertise and professionalism concentrated in the democratic state and the capacity for popular mobilisation which resides within the trade unions and the genuinely representative non-governmental popular organisations. The democratic state therefore has a responsibility to ensure that this independent and representative non-governmental sector has the necessary strength to play its role in the ensuring that the people themselves, and in their own interest, become conscious activists for development and social transformation.

In other words, Mbeki ascribes to the state the role of knowledge producer, able to develop policy and set the agenda for social transformation. He restricts the role of civil society organisations to that of mobilisation, and the implementation of directives from above. Mbeki attempts to draw a clear distinction between the government or party experts who 'know', and the mass of the people who are supposed to apply this knowledge, leaving out of the equation the capacity of the average citizen to act and form his or her own opinion.

Mbeki does take seriously the issue of popular participation and people-driven development. However, given his understanding of the role of leadership and the vanguard ruling party, he leaves no room for popular *political* participation outside the state or the ruling party. For example, he defines popular participation as 'the process of the people becoming their own governors'. He goes on to explain that:

> This is one of the central reasons why the democratic movement must resist the liberal concept of 'less government', which, while being presented as a philosophical approach towards the state in general, is in fact, aimed specifically at the weakening of the democratic state. The purpose of this offensive is precisely to deny the people the possibility to use the collective strength and means concentrated in the democratic state to bring about the transformation of society.

Mbeki is correct to argue that powerful vested interests in society threaten the empowerment of the people and the attainment of meaningful democracy, and that what is required is the empowerment of the majority of the people in their public capacity. However, his solution is to incorporate popular organisations into corporatist arrangements with the state, thereby reducing all politics to state politics.

In sum, Mbeki's governing philosophy on state–society relations is one that clearly distinguishes between the political and economic spheres, and between political society and civil society. His approach to building new social partnerships with civil society is premised on hierarchical and elitist understandings of the relationship between rulers and ruled. While he clearly supports grass-roots participation and people-driven development, his technocratic or ready-made formulas for social transformation simply require execution on the part of citizens or communities, rather than pro-action. Thus the ruling party is given a commanding role in relation to all autonomous social forces, which are denied leading roles in processes of change, instead serving mainly as reservoirs of popular support for the centralised and corporatist project of transformation.

Liberal framework, or liberation framework?

In 'The state and social transformation', Mbeki appeals to the liberation alliance and the broader national democratic movement to appreciate the limitations as well as the possibilities imposed by contemporary global realities on the conduct of the democratic struggle. Furthermore, he suggests that it would be foolhardy to put forward a more radical programme of transformation that does not conform to the contemporary international environment. Thus Mbeki ends the document as follows:

> The democratic movement must resist the illusion that a democratic South Africa can be insulated from the processes which characterise world development. It must resist the thinking that this gives South Africa a possibility to elaborate solutions which are in discord with the rest of the world, but which can be sustained by virtue of a voluntarist South African experiment of a special type, a world of anti-apartheid campaigners, who, out of loyalty to us, would support and sustain such voluntarism.

On the economic front, this entails the ANC government adapting itself to the imperatives of the global capitalist economy. In the political sphere, it requires that democracy be limited in its scope and disengaged from the idea of social progress, and that popular organisations within civil society be demobilised. Indeed, liberal democracy has been put forward as the global panacea for securing order and stability in fragile and deeply divided societies. This limited form of democracy shows 'concern for the sensibilities of capital' (Saul 1999: 43) by deflating the state and limiting the scope of democratic gains to the political sphere. Saul points out that even left-leaning scholars such as Adam Przeworski subscribe to the notion that:

> A stable democracy requires that governments be strong enough to govern effectively but weak enough not to be able to govern against important interests ... [D]emocratic institutions must remain within narrow limits to be sccessful (46).

Particularly in 'transitions from below' that have entailed the mobilisation and politicisation of a broad section of society, a key source of instability is said to be democratic forces within society that continue to push for more substantive changes. Thus much of the literature on democratic transitions has tended to echo the sentiments of powerful global interests, and prescribed the demobilisation of popular forces within civil society and the adoption of elite pacts and negotiated settlements. Some have depicted this as a rather benign process whereby

> some individuals and groups depoliticise themselves again, having run out of resources or become disillusioned, and as others deradicalise themselves, having recognised that their maximal hopes will not be achieved. Still others simply become tired of constant mobilisation and its intrusion into their private lives (Donnell et al 1986).

In reality, however, the very notion of elite pacting and negotiations is premised on the assumption that negotiations cannot be conducted by the masses themselves, at venues other than the bargaining table, but must be entered into on their behalf by a leadership that ostensibly speaks for them (Ginsburg 1996). The end result is that the elite negotiations 'sideline many of the bearers of popular resistance who had done so much to place negotiations on the table in the first place' (Saul 1999).

Saul describes the extent to which the ANC was pressured into moderating its aspirations for a more substantive democratic transformation in order to conform to powerful international interests as a precondition for achieving a smooth transition (58). However, he also warns the ANC that its efforts to avoid 'chaos' during and after the transition by demobilising the popular forces may in fact create new forms of instability. Rather than falling into lethargy and popular indifference, he asks:

> Might not any 'demobilising' of popular constituencies for purposes of consolidating 'inter-elite accords' make such constituencies available for other forms of mobilisation than developmental ones? ... Might not the 'chaos' that negotiations are said to have pre-empted merely be found to be bubbling up again, within the electoral arena and elsewhere, in new and even more dangerous forms? (60).

Of course, Mbeki and the ANC leadership are fully aware of this possibility; hence their emphasis on the incorporation of popular groups in civil society rather than outright demobilisation.

But to what extent do the dominant global prescriptions for stability, law and order, and good governance coincide with the ANC's own perceived needs to consolidate its power base, and assert its role as the uncontested leader of the broad democratic movement? In what ways do liberal, representative, notions of democracy and western conceptions of state–society relations overlap with the ANC's own understandings of the place of leadership in a national liberation struggle, and the relationship between rulers and ruled? As a liberation movement largely in exile, and faced with enormous military pressures and dangers of infiltration by the apartheid regime, the ANC's commitment to a vanguard Leninist strategy of democratic centralism was successful in co-ordinating, disciplining, and directing the anti-apartheid struggle. Ironically, this same strategy also suits the need perceived by many in government to build autonomous state agencies directed from above and capable of carrying out complex and politically controversial economic reforms.

The reassertion of the practices of democratic centralism, tight internal discipline, and strong central co-ordination has provoked accusations that the boundaries for opposition and debate within the government, the ANC, and the tripartite alliance have narrowed (see McKinley 2000; *Mail & Guardian* 1996, 2001a). Pressure to toe the party line and not be too critical of the leadership and its decisions has also been brought to bear on various organisations of civil society. Indeed, it was Mandela (1997) who led the public attack on those organisations of civil society that seek to play the role of 'critical watchdog' over the movement, and serve as channels for grass-roots communities to voice their grievances and wishes. Referring to similar calls made in 1990, when the ANC was unbanned, to retain the grass-roots structures of the UDF as an independent movement alongside the ANC, Mandela described such past and recent proposals coming from popular organisations within civil society as posing an 'illegitimate challenge' to the leading political role of the ANC and the government (Greenstein 1998).

At a basic level, the tensions between the state and these popular organisations in civil society boil down to a struggle over power and resources. During the anti-apartheid struggle, these organisations created alternative sources or bases of power that directly challenged the authority of the state. Thus it is understandable that the ANC saw these organisations as something of a threat once it had assumed power.

However, more importantly, these tensions tell us something about the complex interplay within a national liberation struggle between the imperatives of leadership, organisation, and co-ordination on the one hand, and spontaneous decentralised mass action on the other. During the 1970s and 1980s the anti-apartheid struggle was clearly driven by the imperatives of spontaneous mass action, characterised by the Durban strikes of 1973, the Soweto student uprisings of 1976 and the activities of the UDF in the early 1980s (see Neocosmos 1998; Saul and Gelb 1981). Yet, while spontaneous mass action provided the energy needed for revolutionary transformation, it also had the destructive potential of leading to increased violence, political intolerance, and ungovernability, and often lacked a clear political vision.

When the ANC assumed power, there was an understandable need to shift the focus to strong co-ordination and leadership. However, there is a tendency within the ANC to see these two processes in dichotomous and often contradictory terms, pitting the forces in the 'camp of revolt' against the forces in the 'camp of law and order'. For those deemed part of the camp of law and order, the substance of politics is not action but administration. While it is true that many within civil society underestimate the extent to which the government machinery in modern societies must indeed perform the functions of administration, it is folly to assume that management or administration in the public interest can replace the participation by citizens in public affairs.

A related tendency within the ANC leadership is to view the process of mass action or popular participation solely as a process of tearing down rather than of building up. Similarly, many people in leadership positions in the ANC and the broader democratic movement believe the need for mass action was transitory, and in the contemporary context either unnecessary or subversive.[3] Thus all calls for mass action or participation are characterised as destructive, regardless of the legitimacy of the demands.

This tendency can be observed in the ANC leadership's concern that mass action will probably lead to ungovernability and instability. For example, in an internal ANC document entitled 'From resistance to reconstruction: tasks of the ANC in the new epoch of the democratic transformation – unmandated reflections', drafted in December 1994 in preparation for the ANC's 49th national conference, Mbeki makes the case for controlling dissent and opposing political views within the democratic movement by labelling opposing views as necessarily destructive and inherently negative. He also warns against the use of mass action, as it is likely to lead to instability and ungovernability. As regards the trade unions – one of the most organised sectors of civil society – Mbeki writes: '... to encourage the launching of a major and sustained mass campaign ... while addressing various legitimate demands would, at the same time, pose the spectre of ungovernability' (quoted in McKinley 2000: 6). Such positions, however, remain hotly contested and debated within the ruling alliance.

The result of this vanguardist approach that privileges co-ordinated and centralised leadership over decentralised mass action is a governing strategy that – despite the continued official rhetoric of participatory democracy and people-driven development – systematically limits the public spaces for people to participate outside the highly regulated and institutionalised settings defined by the state. One of the first examples of this was the defeat in 1993 of the civic movement's proposals to include popular assemblies into the decision-making mechanisms of government at the local level (see Seekings 1999). The party governing structure of representation, premised on a hierarchical relationship between a ruling elite and the people, prevailed over the popular governing institutions of participation, founded on a much more egalitarian understanding of the relationship between rulers and ruled. Further implications of this approach for state–society relations and opportunities for popular participation, particularly in the new Mbeki era of 'delivery', are taken up in the following section.

Reconfiguring state–society relations in the era of delivery

Mbeki has come to power with an overwhelming mandate to 'speed up change' and 'deliver' on the ANC's programmes (see ANC 2000). He has unveiled a clear and detailed vision of South Africa that includes reducing poverty, stimulating economic growth and development, developing human resources, and creating jobs. Some of his specific proposals include stepping up the fight against crime by restructuring the criminal justice system, right-sizing the public service, creating a business–labour–government investment council, changing the labour law regime to promote job creation, forming a government partnership with grass-roots citizens' groups in order to promote development, and building partnerships between the public and private sectors. His reputation as a doer and someone who can make things happen has won him the title of the 'kick-arse president' (Barrell 1999).

But to what extent does this new 'delivery' approach come into conflict with the 'people-driven development' approach that emphasises opportunity for popular participation in government decision-making? As Friedman (1999) has noted, in the course of the drive to deliver, 'the technical aspects of securing economic growth, implementing social programmes to reduce poverty and inequality, and deracialising the society are likely to take precedence over democratic goals like respecting political diversity or extending representation through strengthened provincial and local government'. Broad consultation and participation may become more perfunctory in light of 'fast-track delivery' (Marais 1997).

A study of executive policy-making in South Africa has revealed that:

> Public participation in its broadest sense may have, in relation to many of the departmental and ministerial policy- and law-making processes, come to be viewed as something of a time-wasting procedure. The political need to be seen to act and act quickly to address the needs of the electorate has taken precedence as the term of office of the present parliament has progressed (IDASA 1999a).

There is growing concern in the voluntary sector that, as politics in South Africa begins to fall into a routine, the opportunities for broad consultation and influencing government are swiftly declining as decisions are increasingly being made within very small, closed, circles at the top. In many government departments, economically and politically powerful interests such as big business have had the largest input into the policy process. The main point of access to policy-making for the general public and most non-govermental organisations (NGOs) is the parliamentary portfolio committees; however, it is unclear how much power they actually have. In a thoughtful article, the national legislation monitor of the Black Sash has expressed concern that 'the role of parliament in holding the executive accountable has become more and more problematic':

> Our experience is that opportunities for advancing social justice in the context of parliament are no longer frequent. Further, it is difficult to influence issues in the parliamentary context if there is resistance at executive level to accepting input from civil society (Tilley 1997).

The current focus on rapid reforms and service delivery has shifted the government's focus away from the broad consultative inclusion of popular organisations to more limited solicitations of 'technical' services with specific expertise. Another indication of this is the increased use of consultants or experts by governmental departments, that has alarmed many within the NGO sector as well as in parliament. For example, a 1999 report on executive policy-making in the department of housing concluded that:

> Both the national department and provincial departments of housing do use consultants to perform specific pieces of work for them as additional capacity to the departments. These persons would be the only outsiders who contribute to executive decision-making. NGOs and CBOs [community-based organisations], which during the time of the National Housing Forum had considerable voice and input into policy-making, are feeling marginalised (IDASA 1999b).

ANC MPs have also charged the executive branch with relying too heavily on consultants. Government departments have increasingly turned to accounting firms offering consultancy services, such as Deloitte & Touche and Ernst & Young, to help them formulate and implement policy. For example, ANC MPs objected strenuously when Deloitte & Touche was tipped to win a R1 million contract for the transformation of the department of correctional services. Thus one MP wrote: 'This contract, should it go to Deloitte & Touche, may be the last straw on the camel's back for many MPs who are dissatisfied that high-flying consultants have moved into ministries, eclipsing the party's traditional advisers: NGOs, academics, and the Shell House policy unit' (Edmonds 1996). The parliamentary committee on defence had already probed the awarding of a contract to Deloitte & Touche for transforming the South African National Defence Force. Similarly, Ernst & Young was awarded a contract to manage the department of health's primary school feeding scheme at a cost of R7 million in 1996 alone (*Mail & Guardian* 1997).

Again, turning to consultants or experts to plan and implement development programmes is largely premised on the assumption that knowledge and expertise flow from the top down. NGOs and communities supposedly have little to contribute to the design of development programmes, but are simply supposed to implement the plans handed down from above. This trend has increased with the growing emphasis on delivery that has not been matched by a similar emphasis on sustainability. Edward Breslin, health manager of Mvula Trust, an NGO that has historically had very good working relations with the department of water affairs, has questioned the sustainability of South Africa's 'water miracle' without greater community control and involvement in decision-making. He explains that:

> Emphasis has been placed on adherence to guidelines rather than on what is practical and affordable to communities. Community involvement in designing the scheme or choosing the technology has been non-existent in the vast majority of cases. In a recent case, in an isolated, impoverished area of the country, letters from community members and NGOs operating in the area state that the scheme could never be sustained and that alternative systems should be considered. The written response from the department was clear – spend the money on the proposed scheme now, or the project will lose its funding (quoted in Smith 1999).

However, the drive to deliver is also taking place in a macroeconomic context that seeks to spur economic growth by reducing state expenditure and promoting fiscal responsibility. GEAR has severely reduced the government's ability to lead a process of socio-economic transformation, as it has largely shifted the responsibility for social transformation into domestic and even foreign business hands. As Hein Marais (1997) has explained, 'The state's lack of capacity to deliver is certainly a factor in government's greater reliance on the market to generate wealth and resources.' This, he says, is due largely to the fact that, following the transition, the new ANC government was still required to operate in the context of the old state structures and a bureaucracy with an institutional culture and practices that were largely inimical to people-driven development and genuine social transformation. As a result, under Mbeki's leadership, greater emphasis has been placed on building public–private sector partnerships.

The new approach to economic growth and development embodied in GEAR also poses considerable challenges in respect of state–society relations and popular participation. Whereas the RDP sought to define social objectives, and then devise measures to meet them in macroeconomically sound ways, GEAR outlines the macroeconomic framework and then determines which social objectives are economically feasible within it. In the policy formulation arena, this approach tends to diminish opportunities for broad consultation, particularly with non-governmental and community-based organisations, and a role for civil society actors in government decision-making, as the parameters for social development are already set by the GEAR framework.

This was perhaps first witnessed in the 1997 debates over the department of welfare's new child support grant, a test case of the ANC government's new approach to social security and social development.[4] It was the first instance of social policy that tried to comply with the restriction of government expenditure according to GEAR. Furthermore, it was the first ANC policy on a broad social issue that drew sustained and vocal public criticism from numerous popular organisations outside of government, as well as internal opposition from the ANC-led parliamentary portfolio committee on welfare and other key members of the party. Extra-parliamentary groups criticised the policy-making process resulting in the grant as 'a high-handed, technocratic, "expert", consultant-driven approach that simply assumes what people want or need (and will get) with little or no consultation or participation by the people to be affected' (Barberton et al 1998: 6). Even members of the ANC welfare study group (i.e. the ANC members of the portfolio committee) expressed concern that the minister was 'trapped' by high-level executive advisers, 'whom she listens to regardless of whether they are arguing a good case or not' (Calland 1999: 38).

On the policy implementation front, the GEAR scenario may lead to many popular organisations of civil society being reduced to 'piecemeal providers of social services that only mitigate the worst excesses of poverty and inequality' rather than true 'catalysts of broad social change' (Marais 1997: 99). Indeed, notes Marais, in the new era of social partnerships, the voluntary sector is confronted with a vexing dilemma:

> On the one hand, capacity-building at the community level inevitably implies boosting the ability to express demands, pursue interests, claim social entitlements and resist unpopular policies. On the other hand, financial pressures forcing the voluntary sector to act as a delivery agent of government programmes – or to pick up the pieces where government cannot provide – may confine them to 'welfarism' (100).

The drive to turn all popular organisations in civil society into welfare organisations servicing the needs and interests of particular communities has gained even more momentum in recent months with the formation, by former NP and UDM politician Roelf Meyer, of the Civil Society Initiative (CSI). In 2001 the initiative hosted a conference attended by prominent national and international leaders, including former presidents Nelson Mandela and Bill Clinton. The theme of the conference as well as the overall initiative was one of encouraging the spirit of volunteering and self-help, promoting social partnerships between government and civil society organisations, and defining an apolitical role for civil society organisations as assistants to government in service delivery. In his address to the conference, Meyer explained:

> The CSI holds the view that in South Africa civil society forms part of a social partnership with the state and with business. It works alongside government and business to further the common national interest in a non-political arena (National Civil Society Conference 2001).

Other speakers, many of whom are leading figures in the ANC, either inside government or outside of it, reiterated the basic message that civil society had to recast itself, move out of the political arena, and focus on voluntary service to communities.[5]

On the surface, the development language of 'social partnership' seems appropriate to South Africa's continuing transition, and even supportive of a process of people-driven development. However, it cannot be allowed to sweep aside the concept of a 'social contract' between government and the people, whereby citizens can hold the state accountable for meeting the particular social needs and expectations of the majority. The ability of citizens to do so is diminished when they are relegated to the non-political realm of civil society. Furthermore, the seemingly benign language of new social partnerships and apolitical civil society simply reinforces existing power relations within the private realm, and privileges those already powerful interests over grass-roots groups and constituencies. In contrast, popular democracy and people-driven development require that the state's approach to development has an evident bias towards the working people.

Conclusion

As this chapter has sought to demonstrate, in their search for a 'third way' out of the complex and vexing dilemma of positioning the South African economy and the state in the international world order while addressing demands for development and democratisation at home, Mbeki and the ANC leadership have embraced liberal conceptions of state–society relations within a broader discourse of new social partnerships. In the context of a growing reliance on the market, a declining developmental role for the state, and an emphasis on good governance, new social partnerships with the private sector and an apolitical civil society are being put forward as the magic formula for development and democratisation in South Africa. If Mbeki and the ANC leadership are truly committed to popular democracy and people-driven development, they should reflect very hard on this language and the policies and practices it produces. One needs only be reminded of who within the international and domestic arenas are advocating such positions to know that this approach to development at best supports the status quo. While it may serve the ANC leadership's concerns in respect of stability and order, it is unlikely to spur genuine transformation or fundamental change.

I have outlined the broad terms in which state–society relations in contemporary South Africa are being redefined. I have suggested that, while these terms conform to conventional liberal paradigms of state–society relations, they are also consistent with the ANC leadership's own understanding of the relationship between political and civil society, and between rulers and ruled. Therefore, the challenge confronting those concerned with promoting popular democracy and participatory forms of development is not simply to oppose the liberal paradigm and promote a leftist or socialist alternative. Popular democracy requires nothing less than a redefinition of the form of the state, and how it relates to social forces. To fail to do so would ensure the reassertion of the old dichotomy between rulers and ruled against which the anti-apartheid struggle was fought, in terms of which the few constitute a public space and the many live their lives outside it, in obscurity.

Notes

1. I would like to thank Mike Neocosmos and Raymond Suttner for their comments on an earlier version of this paper.
2. For a thorough analysis of this global phenomenon, see Arendt (1963).
3. Jeremy Cronin, one of the main theorists of the SACP, has identified three different 'strategic outlooks' within South African liberation politics, 'the boat, the tap and the Leipzig way' (1992). He hints that 'the tap' strategy was the dominant position within the ANC, whereby mass action should be controlled like a tap one can turn off and on.
4. For a detailed analysis of the debates on the child support grant, see Johnson (2000).
5. The CSI conference was not welcomed by everyone within civil society or the government. COSATU and SANGOCO, two of the largest and most powerful progressive constituencies in civil society, boycotted it after claiming that they had not been consulted on its planning, and that it lacked transparency. See *Mail & Guardian* (2001b).

References

ANC. 1996. The state and social transformation. Discussion document. November.
———. 2000. Together speeding up change. Manifesto for local government elections.
Arendt, H. 1963. *On revolution*. New York: Viking Press.
Atkinson, D (ed). 1992. The state and civil society. Special issue of *Theoria*, 79. May.

Barberton C, Blake M, and Kotze H. 1998. *Creating action space: the challenge of poverty and democracy in South Africa.* Cape Town: IDASA and David Philip Publishers.

Barrell, H. 1999. A seriously kick-arse new president. *Mail & Guardian.* 28 May–3 June.

Calland, R. 1999. *The first 5 years: a review of South Africa's democratic parliament.* Political information monitoring service. Cape Town: IDASA.

Cronin, J. 1992. The boat, the tap, and the Leipzig way. *African Communist*, 3rd quarter.

Donnell, GA, Schmitter, PC, and Whitehead, L. 1986. Tentative conclusions. In *Transitions from authoritarian rule: prospects for democracy.* Baltimore: Johns Hopkins University Press.

Edmonds, M. 1996. ANC MPs peeved about consultant's power. *Mail & Guardian.* 4 October.

Friedman, S. 1999. South Africa: entering the post-Mandela era. *Journal of Democracy*, 10 (4).

Gibbon, P. 1993. Civil society and political change, with particular reference to 'developmentalist states'. *SIAS mimeo.*

Ginsburg, D. 1996. The democratisation of South Africa: transition theory tested. *Transformation*, 29.

Greenstein, R. 1998. *The state of civil society in South Africa.* Johannesburg: Community Agency for Social Enquiry (CASE).

Institute for Democracy in South Africa (IDASA). 1999a. Executive policy-making in the new South Africa: justice.

———. 1999b. Executive policy-making in the new South Africa: housing.

Johnson, K. 2000. The trade-offs between distributive equity and democratic process: the case of child welfare reform in South Africa. *African Studies Review*, 43 (3). December.

Mail & Guardian. 1996. Authoritarian leadership alarms ANC politicians. 4 October.

———. 1997. Private solutions for public problems. 27 June.

———. 2001a. ANC puts party before democracy. 6 February.

———. 2001b. Clinton, Mandela face boycott. 23 April.

Mamdani, M. 1990. State and civil society in contemporary Africa: reconceptualising the birth of state nationalism and the defeat of popular movements. *Africa Development*, 15 (3/4). 47–70.

Mandela, N. 1997. Report by the president of the ANC. Paper read at the 50th national conference of the African National Congress, Mafikeng, 16 December.

Marais, H. 1997. The voluntary sector and development in South Africa, 1996/97. *Development Update*, 1 (3).

Mayekiso, M. 1992. Working class civil society: why we need it, and how we get it. *African Communist*, 2nd quarter.

Mbeki, T. 1994. From resistance to reconstruction: tasks of the ANC in the new epoch of the democratic transformation – unmandated reflections. Cited in D McKinley. 2000. Democracy, power and patronage: debate and opposition within the ANC and the tripartite alliance since 1994. Paper read at the conference on opposition in South Africa's new democracy, 28–30 June, Kariega Park, Eastern Cape.

McKinley, D. 2000. Democracy, power and patronage: debate and opposition within the ANC and the tripartite alliance since 1994. Paper read at the conference on opposition in South Africa's new democracy, 28–30 June, Kariega Park, Eastern Cape.

National Civil Society Conference. 2001. www.idasa.org.za/csi/default.htm.

Neocosmos, M. 1998. From peoples' politics to state politics: aspects of national liberation in South Africa. In A Olukoshi (ed), *The politics of opposition in contemporary Africa*. Uppsala: Nordic Africa Institute.

———. 1999. Intellectual debates and popular struggles in transitional South Africa: political discourse and the origins of statism. Paper read at the Centre for African Studies, 21 April 1999, University of Cape Town.

Saul, J. 1999. 'For fear of being condemned as old-fashioned': liberal democracy versus popular democracy in sub-Saharan Africa. In K Mengisteab and C Daddieh (eds), *State building and democratisation in Africa*. Westport, Connecticut: Praeger Press.

———. 2000. SA's tragic leap to the right. *Mail & Guardian*. 27 June.

Saul, J and Gelb, S. 1981. *The crisis in South Africa*. New York: Monthly Review Press.

Seekings, J. 1999. After apartheid: civic organisations in the 'new South Africa'. In G Adler and J Steinberg (eds), *From comrades to citizens: the South African civics movement and the transition to democracy*. Basingstoke: Macmillan Press.

Smith, C. 1999. Too poor to pay for services. *Mail & Guardian*. 26 March.

Swilling, M. 1991. Socialism, democracy and civil society: the case for associational socialism. *Work in Progress, 76*. August.

Tilley, G 1997. Is parliamentary advocacy all it's cracked up to be? *Black Sash National Newsletter*.

Wamba Dia Wamba, E. 1993. Democracy, multipartyism, and emancipative politics in Africa: the case of Zaire. *Africa Development* 18 (4).

CHAPTER 11

Mandela's democracy[1]

ANDREW NASH

> This should be taken as a general rule: that it never or rarely happens that any republic or kingdom is ordered well from the beginning or reformed altogether anew outside its old orders unless it is ordered by one individual.
> – Machiavelli, *Discourses on Livy*, Book 1, chapter 9

In his speech from the dock at his trial in 1962 for inciting African workers to strike, and leaving the country without a passport, Nelson Mandela described the initial formation of his political ideas as follows:

> Many years ago, when I was a boy brought up in my village in the Transkei, I listened to the elders of the tribe telling stories about the good old days, before the arrival of the White man. Then our people lived peacefully under the democratic rule of their kings and their 'amapakati', and moved freely and confidently up and down the country without let or hindrance.
>
> Then the country was ours, in our own name and right. We occupied the land, the forests, the rivers; we extracted the mineral wealth beneath the soil and all the riches of this beautiful country. We set up and operated our own government, we controlled our own armies and we organised our own trade and commerce. The elders would tell tales of the wars fought by our ancestors in defence of the fatherland, as well as the acts of valour performed by generals and soldiers during those epic days. The names of Dingane and Bambata,

among the Zulus, of Hintsa, Makana and Ndlambe of the Amaxhosa, of Sekhukhuni and others in the north, were mentioned as the pride and glory of the entire African nation . . .

The land, then the main means of production, belonged to the whole tribe, and there was no individual ownership whatsoever. There were no classes, no rich or poor, and no exploitation of man by man. All men were free and equal and this was the foundation of government. Recognition of this general principle found expression in the constitution of the Council, variously called *Imbizo*, or *Pitso*, or *Kgotla*, which governs the affairs of the tribe. The council was so completely democratic that all members of the tribe could participate in its deliberations. Chief and subject, warrior and medicine man, all took part and endeavoured to influence its decisions. It was so weighty and influential a body that no step of any importance could ever be taken by the tribe without reference to it . . .

In such a society are contained the seeds of revolutionary democracy in which none will be held in slavery or servitude, and in which poverty, want and insecurity shall be no more. This is the inspiration which, even today, inspires me and my colleagues in our political struggle (1965: 182).

Mandela briefly returned to this theme in his speech from the dock during the Rivonia trial of 1964, as well as in his autobiography, drafted on Robben Island in 1974. In that work he described what he had learnt from the proceedings of the tribal meetings at the Thembu Great Place at Mquekezweni. He expanded on the earlier account, personalised it, and drew from it an account of the role of the democratic leader:

It was democracy in its purest form. There may have been a hierarchy of importance among the speakers, but everyone was heard: chief and subject, warrior and medicine man, shopkeeper and farmer, landowner and labourer. People spoke without interruption, and the meetings lasted for many hours. The foundation of self-government was that all men were free to voice their opinions and were equal in their value as citizens. (Women, I am afraid, were deemed second-class citizens.) . . .

At first, I was astonished at the vehemence – and candour – with which people criticised the regent. He was not above criticism – in fact, he was often the principal target of it. But no matter how serious the charge, the regent simply listened, not defending himself, showing no emotion at all. The meetings would continue until some kind of consensus was reached. They ended in unanimity or not at all. Unanimity, however, might be an agreement to disagree, to wait for a more propitious time to propose a solution.

Democracy meant all men were to be heard, and a decision was taken together as a people. Majority rule was a foreign notion. A minority was not to be crushed by a majority. Only at the end of the meeting, as the sun was setting, would the regent speak. His purpose was to sum up what had been said and form some consensus among the diverse opinions. But no conclusion was forced on people who disagreed. If no agreement could be reached, another meeting would be held . . .

As a leader, I have always followed the principles I first saw demonstrated by the regent at the Great Place. I have always endeavoured to listen to what each and every person in a discussion had to say before venturing my own opinion. Oftentimes, my own opinion will simply represent a consensus of what I heard in the discussion. I always remember the regent's maxim: a leader, he said, is like a shepherd. He stays behind the flock, letting the most nimble go on ahead, whereupon the others follow, not realising that all along they are being directed from behind (1994a: 614; cf 610).

These two passages set out the basic elements of a model of democracy that is clearly distinct from those outlined in conventional treatments of the topic. It is not the only conception of democracy to be found in Mandela's writings, but it is the one most extensively described, and most explicitly claimed as his own. According to this model, democracy consists of giving everyone a chance to speak on those matters that concern his or her conditions of life, and allowing the discussion to continue until sufficient consensus has been reached, with due regard for the standing of the people concerned, for the community to proceed without division.

The role of the leader is to interpret the arguments and viewpoints put forward in debate in such a way as to make that consensus possible, drawing from expressions of difference a 'tribal wisdom' that reaffirms their essential unity. The model requires that the leader who assumes this role should be accepted, but not necessarily elected. What is crucial is that the question of leadership be settled beforehand, and kept separate from the question of how the popular will is to be interpreted.

In calling this the tribal model of democracy, I am seeking mainly to describe a current in the ideological history of modern capitalism, and am not taking a position on the extent to which pre-colonial Africa conformed to this ideology or not.

The pre-capitalist character of the tribal model
There are at least four features of pre-capitalist society – all of which distinguish it from capitalism – that are integral to this tribal model of democracy. None of them implies a rigid dichotomy between capitalist and pre-capitalist societies, or a linear mode of progression from one to the other. On the contrary, the thrust of the argument that follows is to show how past and present interpenetrate precisely in the context of capitalism, and in resistance to its political forms.

First, in pre-capitalist society (including the context that Mandela describes), the place of each person in the system of production is fixed by custom and tradition. Acceptance of such custom and tradition is essential for the stability of such a society. As a rule, these customs and traditions will evolve relatively gradually. In some cases, their evolution will be circumscribed by what nature allows. And as long as all people accept their place in the social order, it will almost always be possible to achieve some kind of consensus. But it will necessarily be a consensus based on that acceptance of the place of each within production. By contrast, in the context of capitalist society, the major decisions that must be taken can have no such common premise of a social order in which everyone knows his or her place, and there is place for all.

Second, accepting the customs of the tribe provides the individual with a certain degree of security. With no system of wage labour, there is also no incentive to cut off anyone's access to the means of production, as there is under capitalism. The chief cannot increase his wealth by removing people from the land; on the contrary, the more people who live on the land, the stronger the tribe in relation to its neighbours, the more tribute is paid to the chief, and the more hands are available for collective projects. In capitalism, wage labour is the principal method of accessing the means of production, and profits depend on not paying more for it than the capitalist can help.

Third, the pre-capitalist context provides the basis for an ethic of communal solidarity, in which, for example, the chief makes sure that those in need are helped, and that no one goes hungry while the resources of the tribe are sufficient to prevent that. This ethic helps to make tribal consensus possible, as the well-being of the tribe is genuinely in the interest of its members. Within capitalism, such an ethic is an economic irrationality. Accordingly, huge numbers of people go hungry, although the resources of society are sufficient to prevent it. The consumerist ethic of capitalism works against the very idea of there being a common wisdom that can be formulated through discussion.

Fourth, there is no separation of politics and economics in pre-capitalist society. Those who have any say in the life of the tribe can also discuss what is to be done with its resources. This makes it possible to have a council that, in Mandela's formulation, is 'so weighty and influential a body that no step of any importance could ever be taken by the tribe without reference to it'. By contrast, capitalism depends on a separation of politics and economics, which ensures that basic decisions about the use that society will make of its productive resources are removed from the public sphere.

Although Mandela's tribal model of democracy is essentially pre-capitalist in character, it is articulated as an alternative to liberal or capitalist democracy. It is a reconstruction for the purposes of political advocacy. In some respects, it might be considered to lag behind bourgeois democracy: leadership is decided by birth, not election; part of the adult population is excluded from public debate and decision-making; those who participate do so on the basis of a hierarchy of property and prestige, rather than of formal equality; there is little prospect of the poorer members of society organising themselves on the basis of their own aspirations. But it also differs from bourgeois democracy in ways that may be considered as advances on it: it sustains a way of life in which all are concretely involved in deciding the direction of society; it brings all issues concerning society within the sphere of public discussion; its structures of leadership and governance are not distorted and alienated by the creation of a professional layer of politicians.

The tribal model as a critique of capitalism

There might be a sense in which the tribal model 'contains the seeds of revolutionary democracy', as Mandela suggests. But this does not answer the question of whether those seeds could sprout in the soil of capitalist society. Although the tribal model of democracy depicts pre-capitalist society, it could not easily have emerged in that context. Indeed, this conception of the pre-colonial past emerged in South Africa only in the 1940s, after the integrity of tribal society itself had been destroyed, making any real return to its conditions impossible. The tribal model began life as a protest against the exclusion of urban, educated Africans from what they saw as their rightful place in the class hierarchy of capitalist society. At the same time, it served to mobilise a dispossessed proletariat around democratic demands.

The idea of an African past whose heroes transcended ethnic division was first developed by liberal educators and missionaries in the 1920s and 1930s. It was aimed at showing African students the sphere of their own potential contribution to the linear, world-historical march of progress championed and exemplified by the British Empire. But this idea was put to a very different use by the next generation of African intellectuals. The crucial figure in the initial development of the tribal model of democracy was Anton Lembede, philosopher of Africanism, and first elected president of the ANC Youth League. Until his early death in 1947, Lembede's defence of the 'glorious achievements of the heroes of our past' was uncontested among that generation, and hugely influential. It was coupled with an argument that 'ancient Bantu society' was radically democratic in that it enabled 'any citizen' to participate equally in the affairs of government, and 'naturally socialistic' in that 'land belonged to the whole tribe'. Mandela's later recollections of his childhood experience often follows Lembede's formulations *verbatim*. Lembede called on Africans to recover this legacy in their own time. This exhortation depended on a cyclical view of history according to which the 'ancient glory' of Africa was to be revived (1945, quoted in Karis and Carter 1987: 315; 1946a, quoted in Karis and Carter 1987: 330; and 1946b, quoted in Edgar and kaMsumza 1996: 94).

But in this version the tribal model of democracy remained in a fundamentally ambiguous relationship with capitalism. While it rejected capitalism, it could never provide a real analysis of it. Instead, it saw capitalism as the product of the philosophical outlook of European civilisation, against which an African philosophy of harmony and unity might prevail. Invoking a precapitalist past as the basis for a call for racial equality within the capitalist present, it was unable to generate a real critique of capitalism on the one hand, or reach an effective accommodation with it on the other.

Mandela's transformation of the tribal model
Soon after Mandela arrived in Johannesburg from the Transkei in 1943, he met Lembede and fell under his influence. But by the 1950s Mandela had abandoned his Africanism, and become one of the ANC's main proponents of non-racialism. His writings of the 1950s look to the African townships, not the pre-colonial past, for inspiration. It is likely that Mandela shared the view articulated in 1952 by Chief Albert Luthuli that 'tribal organisation is outmoded, and traditional rule by chiefs retards my people' (1963: 42). There is, then, nothing self-evident in Mandela's exposition of the tribal model in his speech from the dock in 1962. And yet we can see how that exposition transformed the tribal model in such a way as to make it an ideological instrument for a democratic accommodation of capitalism in the 1980s and 1990s.

First, Mandela emphasises the moral basis of tribal political institutions rather than the institutions themselves, and does so in a way that mostly draws them closer to the formal ideals of western liberalism. Thus 'all men were free and equal, and this was the foundation of government' (1965: 147);

'all men were free to voice their opinions, and equal in their value as citizens' (1994a: 20). The hereditary position of the chief is lost from view in this version of tribal democracy, and his tolerance of criticism and commitment to open debate comes to the fore.

Second, Mandela's evocation of the tribal past is made to serve as the basis of the moral stance taken by himself as an individual; it forms part of a moral dramatisation of the South African conflict of which Mandela is both a central protagonist and an active interpreter. For Lembede, by contrast, the tribal model of democracy served as a source of values for the ideal society. Mandela repeatedly traces his own political vocation to his hopes, as a boy listening to the tales of the elders, that he could continue the legacy of the African heroes. In his trial speeches, in particular, he sets out the moral requirements of that vocation: he and his comrades must 'choose between compliance with the law and compliance with our consciences'; they must act as 'men of honesty, men of purpose, and men of public morality and conscience' (1965: 149); 'if I had my time over,' he declares, 'I would do the same again, and so would any man who dares call himself a man' (152). Above all, as he states in the final words of his speech from the dock at Rivonia, he is 'prepared to die' for the ideal of a free and democratic society that animates 'the struggle of the African people' (189).[2] Through all of this, the tribal model is extended significantly, in such a way as to make it a model of the democratic virtues, and in some moments a model of democracy constituted by such virtues.

Third, at the same time as stressing the need for these democratic virtues, Mandela constantly returns in his speeches and writings to the collective context in which his major decisions are taken, and in which these virtues are generated. His position as volunteer in chief during the Defiance Campaign, and convenor of the organising committee of the national strike to protest against the white referendum on the Republic; his decision not to surrender himself after a warrant for his arrest had been issued; his decision to leave South Africa illegally, and return; the decision to form the armed wing of the liberation movement, Umkhonto weSizwe – on each occasion, the display of virtue is made to depend on the collective decision (see, for example, Mandela 1965: 109, 158, 166, 167, 169.) The democratic virtues, in effect, are embodied in the courageous and self-sacrificing leader, who embodies them only on behalf of the larger collectivity. The moral integrity of the leader (whether it be an individual or an organisation), rather than the principle of heredity, becomes crucial in legitimising the interpretation of the larger consensus allocated to such a leader by the tribal model.

Fourth, to a greater degree than any other African leader appealing to the tribal past, Mandela's model of that past is differentiated. Its essential harmony is achieved not through the negation of differences, but through the development of moral codes for overcoming them. In his accounts of the tribal past, he switches at crucial moments from the singular on which Lembede and Africanism depended ('the African people', 'the fatherland') to the plural ('under the democratic rule of our kings'; 'our own armies') (Mandela 1965: 147). This recognition of different African communities raises the question of their relations with each other. Within the Africanist framework, this is not insignificant; for as long as the organic solidarity of 'the African people' was presupposed, no such question could occur. Once it does occur, it leaves space for an account of the role of the democratic leader in enabling different communities to reconcile their differences harmoniously.

Shifts in the political strategies and thought of the ANC during the 1950s helped to fill this newly created space. Co-operation between the ANC and the South African Indian Congress, and then the establishment of allied organisations for coloureds and whites, required a move away from the Africanist idea of national identity being rooted in a distinctive philosophical outlook. The fundamental premise of the 'four nations' thesis of the Congress Movement was the possibility that identities could change and develop along lines that were 'national' in a larger sense. While the tribal model never explicitly informed the ANC's ever more inclusive nationalism, it increasingly formed Mandela's own role within it – and, through his example, the model of democratic leadership within the ANC.

Fifth, as the result of the conceptual shifts and developments outlined above, the tribal model of democracy comes to be removed from the cyclical conception of history in which Africanists have most often – though never quite consistently – located it. The tribal past now serves to personally inspire the heroic individual, not to summons the African people to relive their former glory. Mandela appears never to have doubted that the larger historical process was linear and progressive. His admiration of the African past presented no barrier to his admiration of the Magna Carta, the United States bill of rights, the British parliament, and the American congress (1965: 182–3). For him, these did not belong, as for Lembede, to a fundamentally different philosophical outlook. In this sense, Mandela can be said to have returned the conception of the unified African past to its liberal and missionary origins.

The result of this fivefold transformation was to create a moral framework for South African politics in which Africanist and western liberal elements were integrated in so instinctive and original a way that Mandela himself could probably not have said where the one ended and the other began. This framework had disabling effects in some respects, and enabling effects in others. Although it was a powerful mobilising tool, it set limits to political clarity.

Mandela on capitalism and socialism

Above all, this moral framework required a fatal ambiguity on the question of capitalism and socialism. For, to the extent that this question divides society, the leader who is to take on the consensus-interpreting role required by the tribal model of democracy can give his allegiance to neither without endangering the tribal model itself. The need to avoid such an allegiance is, I believe, the only way to explain the extraordinary and persistent confusion of Mandela's views on capitalism and socialism. A brief account of his economic views will show how the tribal model made room for the capitulation of the ANC to capital.

This capitulation is often located in the 1990s, in the aftermath of the collapse of Stalinist regimes in eastern Europe and the Soviet Union. In Mandela's case, the ground for it was laid in his earliest economic writing, a defence of the nationalisation clauses of the Freedom Charter published in 1956. The Freedom Charter, Mandela argued, was 'by no means a blueprint for a socialist state but a programme for the unification of various classes and groupings amongst the people on a democratic basis ... [It] visualises the transfer of power not to any single social class but to all the people of this country, be they workers, peasants, professional men or petty bourgeoisie' (1965: 57). The curiosity of the argument is that it neither avoids the existence of classes (as a liberal democrat would, emphasising individual rights instead), nor draws any conclusion about their relationship (as would a Marxist). It acknowledges the existence of classes, but assumes that each can pursue its aims in harmony with the rest. The model of democracy that enables class relationships to be harmonised is surely the tribal one; just as the chief extracts a consensus from the differing opinions of the tribe, so the democratic state extracts a consensus from bosses and workers, enabling each to pursue their interests without impeding the interests of the other.

The same premise is needed in order to understand the views on capitalism and socialism set out in Mandela's autobiography. On the one hand, he praises Marxism as a 'searchlight illuminating the dark night of racial oppression', and socialism as 'the most advanced stage of economic life then evolved by man' (Mandela 1994a: 112–13, 455.). He is also fiercely critical of the 'contemptible' character of American imperialism (307; cf 216, 424; cf 1965: 85). But at no stage does he draw the conclusion that it is necessary to fight against capitalism or imperialism. And, upon his release from prison, when the then president of the United States, George Bush, telephones to tell him he has included him 'on his short-list of world leaders whom he briefs on important issues', Mandela immediately accepts his *bona fides*; the entire problem of imperialism is undone at a stroke (1994a: 575). For the tribal model can be extended across the globe, as long as leaders can find a way of recognising each other's proper status, and allowing them to speak for their followers.

Mandela's shifting positions on economic policy since his release from prison are well known. His memorandum to PW Botha of March 1989 reaffirmed the words of his Rivonia speech on 'the need for some form of socialism to enable our people to catch up with the advanced countries of the world and to overcome their legacy of poverty' (Mandela 1989, quoted in Johns and Davis 1991: 223). Until the meeting of the World Economic Forum in Davos, Switzerland, in 1992, he continued to defend nationalisation as an instrument of economic policy. But upon his return from that event, he remarked: 'We have observed the hostility and concern of businessmen towards nationalisation, and we can't ignore their perceptions ... We are well aware that if you cannot co-operate with business, you cannot succeed in generating growth' (quoted in Waldmeir 1997: 256). The policies of the ANC moved rapidly towards privatisation, fiscal austerity, and budgetary discipline. By the time Mandela addressed the Joint Houses of Congress of the United States on 6 October 1994, he was ready to proclaim the free market as the 'magical elixir' which would bring freedom and equality to all (1994b: 16–17).

It appears both to those who praise Mandela as a realist and those who denounce him as a traitor that he has abandoned all he stood for before. But there is no betrayal in his record. He has simply remained true to the underlying premise that has animated his economic thought all along: the need for the leader to make use of his prestige to put forward as the tribal consensus the position that is most capable of avoiding overt division. Once it became apparent that 'the hostility and concern of businessmen towards nationalisation' was more than even the prestige of Mandela could alter, his prestige had to be used for the cause of privatisation; the capitalist market had become the meeting place of the global tribe. Even then, Mandela would continue to claim impartiality in the conflict of ideologies, holding, in a lecture delivered in Singapore in March 1997, that South Africa was 'neither socialist nor capitalist, but was driven rather by the desire to uplift its people' (*Cape Times* 1997). For him, the character of the economy, and through it the movement of history, is defined on the basis of the consensus that the leader can interpret at a given moment. Thus a hidden consistency in his political thought holds together a dual commitment to democracy and capitalism, and legitimates a capitalist onslaught on the mass of South Africans who sustained the struggle for democracy for decades.

Mandela's democracy

The new South Africa – inaugurated by the election victory of the ANC, led by Mandela, in April 1994 – is, to a greater extent than is often realised, what he has made it. To some extent, the limits of social change in South Africa were established by the global context. But the tribal model of democracy which I have outlined here was crucial at an ideological level in legitimating the negotiation process that led to democratic elections, the negotiation strategy of the ANC, and the settlement that emerged from it.

Mandela's transformation of the tribal model had legitimated the ANC's role as interpreter of the African consensus on the basis of the sacrifices of its leaders, in a context where the original principle of heredity no longer applied. By the time the apartheid regime was ready to negotiate, it was Mandela himself, the world's most famous political prisoner, and the living symbol of sacrifice, who had adopted that role. This is already evident in his letter to PW Botha in July 1989, proposing negotiations between the ANC and the National Party as the country's 'two major political bodies'. Mandela emphasises that he acts on his own authority, not that of the ANC, and implicitly confers the same authority onto Botha (quoted in Johns and Davis 1991).

Once Mandela had been released from prison, and negotiations had begun, the crucial idea that made it possible for the ANC to organise the oppressed majority around the tribal model was that of society being made up of 'sectors' – youth, women, business, labour, political parties, religious and sporting bodies, and the like – each with a distinctive role to play. This idea has emerged from the organisational needs of the struggle against apartheid when repressive conditions prevented them from mobilising around directly political demands. It was now used to insulate the leadership of the liberation movement from critical questioning. In this vein, Mandela explained to the Consultative Business Movement in May 1990: 'Both of us – you representing the business world, and we, a political movement – must deliver. The critical questions are whether we can in fact act together, and whether it is possible for either of us to deliver if we cannot or will not co-operate' (1990: 57–8). In calling upon business – and, in their turn, labour, youth, students – to act within the limits of a 'national consensus', the question of the basis of that consensus could be removed from sight (58, 65, 66). In effect, the 'tribal elders' of South African capitalism were gathered together in a consensus that could only be 'democratic' on the basis of capitalism.

The tribal model of democracy has come to form the ideological contradictions of the new South Africa. It is nowhere to be found in the constitution of the new South Africa, nor in the programmes and policies of the ruling ANC. But it informs many of the institutions of the new South Africa, and, above all, the real relationships of power behind the façade of formal democratic procedures. In its many institutional embodiments, and, above all, in the hugely symbolic presence of Mandela, it calls upon the oppressed majority in particular to sacrifice in the cause of building a new society. They respond with a recognition of the ties of solidarity and common struggle which that call presupposes, and which they so immediately recognise in the record of Mandela himself. But the society they are called upon to build – the basis of the only consensus that can preserve the role of the chief intact – is one that will respect the cash nexus rather than any other ties.

Mandela has played a crucial role in forming these contradictions, as well as sustaining them. They will live on long after he has left active politics, and outside the South African context in which he has been most active in forming them. His ideological legacy – in South Africa and globally – is startlingly complex. He has inspired the struggles of oppressed people throughout the world, and has made himself a symbol of reconciliation in a world in which their oppression continues. To understand his historical role, and come to terms with his legacy, we need to see how his greatness and his limitations stem from the same source.

Notes

1. This is a revised version of an article that originally appeared in *Monthly Review*, 50 (11), April 1999. 18–28.
2. The theme of leadership legitimated through sacrifice was already prominent in the writings of Albert Luthuli; cf 1952.

References

Lembede, A. 1945. Some basic principles of African nationalism. In T Karis and G Carter (eds). 1987. *From protest to challenge: a documentary history of African politics in South Africa*, vol 2. Stanford: Hoover Institution Press.

———. 1946a. The policy of the Congress Youth League. In T Karis and G Carter (eds). 1987. *From protest to challenge: a documentary history of African politics in South Africa*, vol 2. Stanford: Hoover Institution Press.

———. 1946b. National units. In RR Edgar and L kaMsumza (eds). 1996. *Freedom in our lifetime: the collected writings of Anton Muziwahke Lembede*. Athens: Ohio University Press.

Luthuli, A. 1952. The road to freedom is via the cross. In T Karis and G Carter (eds). 1987. *From protest to challenge: a documentary history of African politics in South Africa*, vol 2. Stanford: Hoover Institution Press. 486–9.

———. 1963. *Let my people go*. Johannesburg: Collins.

Mandela, N. 1965. *No easy walk to freedom*. London: Heinemann.

———. 1989. Statement to president PW Botha. In S Johns and RH Davis Jr. (eds). 1991. *Mandela, Tambo, and the African National Congress: the struggle against apartheid, 1948–90*. New York: Oxford University Press. 216–25.

———. 1990. *Intensify the struggle to abolish apartheid*. New York: Pathfinder Press.

———. 1994a. *Long walk to freedom*. Randburg: Macdonald Purnell.

———. 1994b. *Invest in peace: addresses to the UN General Assembly and the Joint Houses of the Congress of the USA*. Pretoria: SA Communication Services.

Waldmeir, P. 1997. *Anatomy of a miracle: the end of apartheid and the birth of the new South Africa*. New York: Viking.

CONCLUSION

Thabo Mbeki
Politics and ideology

RICHARD CALLAND and SEAN JACOBS

Thabo Mbeki's legacy is in danger; tragically, 'the president with inexplicably contrary views on HIV/AIDS' would be most apposite at this stage. This is not a legacy that his central role in the ANC's struggle for democracy and human rights deserves, nor one that his part in the quest for African redemption and justice implies. However, his presidency has been dominated by poor or crude political management – in the case of the arms deal controversy and the farcical 'plot' allegations against three of the ANC's most senior members – and an ill-considered obsession with dissident theory, in the case of his government's HIV/AIDS policy. His policy on Zimbabwe has failed, and – while the damage in this case is not self-inflicted, as it is in that of HIV/AIDS – his strategic approach to Robert Mugabe has not borne fruit. Underestimating the need to reaffirm his own commitment to good governance and the rule of law, however distasteful such an exercise might be for him, Mbeki has further threatened to undermine the one visionary goal he has thus far branded as his own: the 'African Renaissance', and NEPAD.

While debunking the mythology enveloping Mbeki is no easy task, defining his ideology and politics is, in this context, an even more elusive one. Yet these perplexing and curious inconsistencies in strategy and politics help to explain Mbeki, a man defined not by true vision or ideology but by the contradictions of his history and his pragmatism. This book claims to do no more than declare an honest intent to start an incisive and constructive public discourse about Mbeki's presidency, his government's policies, and what they mean for the future social and economic development of South Africa. Mbeki is not alone among modern leaders in appearing to have no ideology – all of them symptoms of a relatively non-ideological era. It is certainly not easy to attach any ideological label to Mbeki; it is perhaps easier to say what his ideology and politics are not than to describe their actual content.

His early writings and speeches, including the speeches he wrote for Oliver Tambo when the latter was president of the ANC, show that he is not and never was a socialist. John Saul (chapter 1) reminds us of Mbeki's assertion in 1984 that 'the ANC is not a socialist party. It has never pretended to be one, it has never said it was, and it is not trying to be. It will not become one by decree for the purpose of pleasing its "left critics".' Mbeki's rhetorical commitment to poverty alleviation, articulated most clearly in his 'two nations' speech (1998), suggests a classical social democrat. His belief that the market will serve the social goals of such a philosophy indicates that his social democracy is a modern, Clintonian/Blairite, 'third way' social democracy – more liberal than social.

As we noted in the introduction, the political and economic backdrop to Mbeki's presidency is a demanding one. The current South African transition has its roots in a historical deadlock achieved between the then ruling bloc (the state and capital, whose interests – despite their apparent differences – were both served by the structure of the apartheid political economy) and the democratic forces of the late 1980s. Mbeki himself participated actively in the initial stages of this rapprochement, via his role in the proto-negotiations in various capitals around the world with emissaries of the apartheid government as well as capital.

The 'era of negotiations' (principally the Convention for a Democratic South Africa, or CODESA, and the subsequent Multiparty Negotiating Process, or MPNP) resulted in a remarkable transition from an authoritarian and racist dispensation to a hybrid form of liberal democracy, incorporating the principle of one person, one vote. This electoral democracy was supplemented by a number of unique institutions designed to impose checks and balances on the democratic state and its representatives as well as protect the rights of citizens – obvious examples being the constitutional court and the 'chapter 9' institutions 'supporting constitutional democracy', such as the Human Rights Commission and the public protector. At the same time, the terms of the political transition that Mbeki inherited from Nelson Mandela privileged reconciliation, multiracialism, and consensus ahead of a bold engagement with the past or its structural legacies (Steenveld and Strelitz 1998). The very negative reactions within the white community to the economic subtext of Mbeki's public speeches since his 'two nations' speech in June 1996 confirm this precarious legacy.

Because the political dimension was emphasised during the negotiations, little attention was paid to the 'economic CODESA'. The terms of the economic negotiations were clearly laid down: the most favourable economic strategy for South Africa was to fall in behind the prevailing neo-liberal consensus (as discussed by Hein Marais in chapter 3). That meant 'redistribution through growth', and the state's withdrawal from the social sphere. At worst, this has resulted in what John Saul (chapter 1) has described as 'the stabilisation of capital relations'. The result is that the much-vaunted political compromises concealed, and continue to conceal, substantive continuities with the past in social and economic power and policy orientations. The 'transformation' of South Africa's economic and political life increasingly coincides with the formation of new elites that incorporate most of the old ones. White capital has, of course, been an active accomplice in this process. In addition, both white capital and the new state have actively encouraged the strategic formation of a sizeable black middle class in order to ensure stability and a stake in the deracialised capitalist system for the new political elite, and act as a shock absorber between the black masses and the regime.

This 'balance of forces' not only determines the limits of change, but also the opportunities for the economic and social restructuring of African society. Moreover, global economic forces now impose themselves on the world's democratic leaders as never before. As Jeremy Cronin, an ANC MP and assistant general secretary of the SACP, argued in the national assembly in early 2001, as a democracy South Africa is emerging 'in the shadow of powerful, typically unelected, forces in the North' (Cronin 2001). As Noreena Hertz (2001) shows, many transnational companies now enjoy bigger revenues and more power and influence than most nation-states or their governments. 'Propelled by government policies of privatisation, deregulation and trade liberalisation, and the advances in communication technologies of the past 20 years, a power shift has taken place . . . 51 of the hundred biggest economies in the world are now corporations, only 49 are nation states . . . Whatever way we look at it, corporations are taking on the responsibilities of government' (7).

However, as Patrick Bond points out in chapter 2, merely to characterise the balance of global forces as inherently inequitable is pedestrian. It is more useful to express the problem as a call for action, rather than an excuse for paralysis or malaise (the 'There Is No Alternative' view of macroeconomic policy-making). The ultimate measure of any leader – whether in the North or South, whether Blair or Mbeki – is how they respond to the unelected and largely unaccountable forces of global capitalism, and the extent to which they are able to forge a strategic policy path towards substantially reducing inequality and poverty in their countries.

This is a test. Moreover, it is one to which Mbeki has responded in a confusing and apparently ambiguous way. On the one hand, as the effective economics tsar of his government, he has steered South Africa's transition away from a potentially radical Keynesian approach to macroeconomic management – represented by a brief flirtation with the RDP[1] – towards a policy – GEAR – that abides by the rules of the modern international macroeconomic heterodoxy. This is Mbeki the conformist – Mbeki the unadulterated conservative, as Sahra Ryklief (chapter 4) characterises him – a leader neither prepared nor willing to take on the neo-liberal ascendancy that underpins the global status quo.

While we largely agree with Ryklief, there is perhaps an element of nuance. There *is* an ambiguity in Mbeki's approach, and, beneath this, a fundamentally schizophrenic relationship with capital and the global elite of what Mbeki has, with growing persistence, referred to as 'global apartheid'.[2] This has been done in a tone of growing outrage: Mbeki has confronted world leaders (Clinton and Blair) and international institutions (such as the United Nations) with brilliant and incisive expositions of the moral injustice of the contemporary world order. This is Mbeki 'the redemptionist', determined to play a leading role in the fight for justice for Africa and Africans.

We detect that Mbeki sees himself as a historical figure with an important international role to play. There is a certain conceit to his politics (which also finds expression, unfortunately, in his disastrous flirting with AIDS dissidents). As John Saul argues (chapter 1),

> But Mandela's was not a politics that the younger generation (with Mbeki at the lead), and epitomised by Mbeki, either could or would choose to play. Their sense of self-importance bore no quasi-traditional markings. It was auto-produced: having pulled off the impossible, the overthrow of apartheid, they are very pleased with themselves indeed. Too smart now to be mere ineffectual lefties, they expected to play the only game in town – capitalism – successfully.

Perhaps Mbeki's sense of history derives partly from his outrage at the way in which Africa and Africans have been treated by the North and by non-Africans, and partly from his recognition that South Africa has, at this moment in history, a disproportionate degree of influence in world affairs – that it 'punches above its weight' – offering it an unprecedented and perhaps unique opportunity to acquire greater justice from the rest of the world.

If these were the points of departure for this book, its overall intention is to shed light on Mbeki's philosophy and ideology. Despite, or perhaps because of, his ideological ambiguity, Mbeki is more radical and progressive at the global level (although even these bona fides must be questioned, as Bond points out in chapter 2), and much more conservative at home. This, however, is at best diagnostic rather than explanatory, as is Bond's identification of Mbeki's 'dual elision'(chapter 2):

> . . . on the one hand, a displacement of the South's problems from the (untouchable) economic to the moral-political terrain, which in turn evokes calls for the reform (not the dismantling) of existing economic systems and institutions; and on the other . . . a relentless campaign to persuade his constituents that 'There Is No Alternative' to globalisation.

Why is this? One way to understand Mbeki is to locate his politics in the political compromises of the late 1980s and early 1990s. The argument made by John Saul and Hein Marais (chapters 1 and 3) in this respect is very instructive: by the late 1980s the 'cooler heads in the camp of capital' had begun to develop a counterrevolutionary strategy designed to shape a socio-economic transition that would parallel the political one. In the face of lower growth rates, and a possible recession, capital prepared itself to sever the marriage between the structures of capitalist exploitation and those of racial oppression that had proven to be so profitable in the past. Capital realised that the capitalist system in South Africa had to be 'modernised' – in both economic and political terms in short, South Africa had to become a 'normal' capitalist society. Despite its haphazard reform efforts of the 1980s, the NP had proved unequal to the task.

Increased interaction with Mandela in prison and Mbeki and others in exile helped to confirm a growing sense that the ANC might be a potential participant in (and even possibly the best guarantor of) a transition that safeguarded the essentials of the established economic system.[3] Well into the new South Africa, this same tendency of capital to align itself with moderate ANC leaders in the new government (and Mbeki is certainly seen in that light by business) was illustrated by the Centre for Development and Enterprise (CDE). In mid-1999 – shortly after Mbeki was elected as president – this conservative think-tank, which is largely funded by big business, published a lengthy review of the activities of the ANC government, and its future challenges. In a summary of the report written for *Business Day*, Ann Bernstein, CDE's executive director, blamed South Africa's failure to embrace market-friendly policies on '. . . internal ANC documents, or certain government policy positions or actions by the labour movement, which directly undermine the president's commitment to make South Africa the "world's most exciting emerging market"' (1999). She went on to argue that 'it was . . . critically important that the new cabinet stay "on message". If we want South

Africa to become the world's most desirable emerging market, we have to persuade investors – domestic and foreign – that this is the case. We have to take the actions necessary to become a competitive market, and we have to communicate first to ourselves as a country (including within the ANC itself) and then to the outside world what we are doing, and why this is important for South Africa and the future of all its citizens.'

Bernstein (undated) also had some advice for Mbeki himself. It was important, she argued, that Mbeki build a new coalition that excluded the ANC's old partners, the unions and the communists, in favour of a new embrace:

> ... the country's president should act to harness and strategically strengthen new partners for government, who are committed to sustainable market-based growth, development, and a strategic approach to poverty alleviation.

The same desire smoulders in the capital cities of the North. An unguarded comment, made to one of the authors at a cocktail party by a (Republican) member of the United States Congress during a visit by its foreign affairs African subcommittee to South Africa in the mid-1990s, was revealing: 'We like Mbeki very much,' he said, 'because we know he will screw the labour unions.' Sakhela Buhlungu's chapter supports such an analysis, though with greater subtlety.

One should not underestimate the cumulative effect of attempts by big business, its acolyte think-tanks, and lobbyists – both in South Africa and the North – to impose their own agenda on Mbeki's approach to policy-making.

Despite the robust rhetoric of his redemptionist view of the world, Mbeki sends out confusing signals in response to the barrage of information and lobbying emanating from these quarters. In April 2001 South Africa enjoyed a rare moment of warmth in the sun as the international media provided extensive coverage of a Pretoria High Court case. Thirty-nine pharmaceutical companies retreated from their legal challenge to the government's Medicines and Related Substances Control Amendment Act of 1997, agreeing that the act be implemented without amendments (as it stands, it allows the government to import or allow the production of cheaper, generic medicines). What was striking at this rare moment of victory for people over global economic might was the conspicuous absence of Mbeki. The South African government then failed to take advantage of the space won by the activists as Mbeki searched for excuses – such as the outcome of a controversial investigation into whether HIV is indeed associated with AIDS, the alleged toxicity of anti-retrovirals, and (artificial) fiscal constraints (which did not prevent him from authorising tens of billions of rands-worth of arms expenditures) – *not* to implement the parallel importation or generic production options. Instead, the government took the activists to court on the grounds that it does not have the infrastructure to implement the policy, and even censured those provincial governments (most of them controlled by the ANC) that wanted to roll out public treatment programmes.

This was (moral) justice prevailing over (economic) injustice – the central theme of the Mbeki redemptionism – so why not seize the moment, for yourself and for your message? Is Mbeki so shy, and/or so contemptuous of modern political public relations? Or can his stance be explained by referring to the history of his engagement with HIV/AIDS activists specifically – and his dissident stance in the face of 'orthodox' thinking around the link between HIV and AIDS – or to his more general discomfort with grass-roots campaigns? Or is there another explanation? Is it that his relationship with international and local capital is too intricate, too nuanced, for him to associate himself too closely with what was obviously a public relations disaster for the pharmaceutical companies?

Is Mbeki's redemptionist rhetoric just that: rhetoric, albeit laced with a strategic thinking which convinces itself that it represents a viable path towards radical reform? We suspect that Mbeki may well think, in an intellectual sense, and may even *believe*, that his interventions in global politics and his projection of an 'African Renaissance' are strategies of revolution through evolution. All he must do, in this strategic wonderland, is remind the North of the extent of their oversight, and articulate the work that still needs to be done, for remedial action to follow. If this analysis is correct, Mbeki is either strangely naïve or unable or unwilling to confront the basic structural defects of the global economic system. This, then, is strategic thinking based not on ideology but pragmatism. As Vale and Maseko put it (chapter 5), while the African Renaissance has been a 'propitious notion', it has been the appeal of Mbeki's 'lyrical imagery' that has turned the obvious – 'the commonsensical, almost' – into a 'tryst with destiny'. However, they continue, it offers 'more promise than policy', and seeks to maximise South African foreign policy options in Africa – including the country's search for a seat on the United Nations Security Council.

In other words, Mbeki's 'African Renaissance' is entirely strategic, and neither philosophical nor ideological in its genesis. On this basis, one can come to see Mbeki's brand of pragmatism for what it is: not the superficial repackaging of Blair's New Labour third-wayism, but rather the manipulation of power and organisations that is Mbeki's greatest skill as a politician. It derives from his mentorship under Oliver Tambo, whose giant triumph in holding the ANC together both in exile and during its emergence from exile should be shared with Mbeki. This core strength belies and betroths a weakness: to hold together an organisation as convoluted in its breadth and diversity as the ANC often requires a fudge, a 'muddling-along', and bureaucratic solutions to decisions of philosophical and ideological principle.

As one ANC MP, who has known Mbeki for a long time, told us: 'Although Mbeki is marked by the ANC's tendency to do this, and moulded by the trajectory of the ANC, he wins bureaucratically. He chooses bureaucratic methods to resolve contradictions.' That is why the ANC in government is so poor at the political management of crisis, and also why the unity of adversity – in the apartheid days – is imperilled now by the absence of a clarity of vision and values, because the enemy lies within. Mbeki and his closest supporters would argue, no doubt, that he has given full expression to South Africa's adversity at home, namely the inequality of the 'two nations'. Yet, ironically, his adroit control of factions and manipulation of bureaucratic power creates its own internal problems, and serves only to eclipse any possibility of building a collective ideological vision or national consensus. There is no better example of this style of leadership than his unwarranted demonising of a justified disquiet within the unions and the SACP over the ANC's rightward economic shift, contained in the significant and controversial 'Briefing notes on the Alliance', prepared for the ANC's NEC in October 2001, in which he accused 'the ultra-left' of staging a 'class struggle against capitalists in the ANC' (COSATU 2001).

Unlike his mentor, Tambo, Mbeki cannot get away with running the ANC in a secretive and dictatorial manner, with all kinds of undemocratic excesses being frowned upon but tolerated. He presides over an ANC operating under very different conditions than those in Tambo's time: a political universe dominated and mediated by the media, one in which every action of the ANC is scrutinised, reported on, and analysed (Jacobs 1999).

The post-1990 period marked the convergence of two main political traditions in the ANC. The one is found among former exiles and Robben Island prisoners, characterised by a greater devotion to loyalty, and a 'Stalinist' instinct for organisational discipline; the other is found among members of the internal anti-apartheid movement, and is marked by a greater affection for consultative decision-making, and a greater ability to practise it. The exile politics that has come to dominate the post-1990 ANC (and has cemented that position since Mbeki assumed power in 1999) is uncomfortable with a tradition of consultative decision; and understandably so. In exile – given the danger of state terror and assassination, and the imperative to maintain a united front[4] – absolute loyalty to the ANC leadership was required. However, the organisational and political consequences for the ANC of this style of leadership have been devastating.

As Vishwas Satgar (in a more sympathetic account in his chapter on the SACP) and Sakhela Buhlungu (in his contribution on the trade unions) point out, the Mbeki leadership probably faces more alliances and factions than Mandela's did, and – despite the space afforded to it by operating in the open – the ANC seems intent on reverting to its Stalinist ways. The Mbeki presidency also unfolds in the context of the ANC's transformation from liberation movement to political party, and its ability to mobilise 'the masses'. The negotiations of the early 1990s had a dissipating effect on mass organisation; this was a time that saw the ANC's broader constituency relegated to the role of spectators as leaders took decisions without consultation.

One example of the tension between Mbeki's ability to manage factions and manipulate bureaucratic power and the need to build a collective ideological vision is the contest over macroeconomic policy in the ANC. Mbeki and his predecessor as president, Mandela, have managed to ensure that the ANC adopt GEAR as its economic framework, but have done so at the cost of shattering a collective vision on economic policy. From the outset the GEAR document – although never publicly debated – was declared to be 'non-negotiable'. The tone adopted by both Mandela and Mbeki in defending it is also notable of the anti-democratic and elitist decision-making patterns within the ANC, as Marais, Saul, Satgar, and Buhlungu all point out.

Within the ANC there are those who oppose not so much what Mbeki does, but the way in which he does it. They complain about his politics, his tendency to gather around him people who will do his bidding and not ask critical questions, and the shift in decision-making from alliance and ANC forums to a small group located in and around his office. A former policy adviser to Mbeki, Vusi Mavimbela, has described this apparently pragmatic approach as follows:

> He's a consensus-seeker, but he moves from the premise that the ANC has many different strains within it; hence it is more of a movement than an organisation. It can have different ideological persuasions within it, but it is important for the ANC to reconcile all perspectives within it. If you seek a purist approach, you can forget the ANC as an organisation (quoted in Davis 1998: 37).

This is why Andrew Nash's creative analytical approach to understanding

Mandela (chapter 11) also helps to explain Mbeki. Nash describes a moral framework that integrates Africanist and western liberal elements in much the same way in which they have melded in Mbeki's own philosophical and ideological approach to power. The fundamental problem with what Nash describes as the 'consensus-interpreting' role required by this framework is that it fails to fully recognise inequalities of power. Some people have louder voices than others; some have the means to add to the weight of their persuasion. This is a metaphor for the new South Africa, where powerful capitalists, old and new, white and black, yield the most influence.

So, as Nash says, while this tribal model of democracy 'acknowledges the existence of classes . . . [it] assumes that each can pursue its aims in harmony with the rest' (chapter 11). Thus: 'This framework has disabling effects in some respects, and enabling effects in others. Although it was a powerful mobilising tool, it set limits to political clarity' (chapter 11). One could also argue that the difference between Mandela and Mbeki is that, whereas Mandela may have believed that the consensus would be consistent with greater equality, Mbeki knows that it cannot be, but is willing to accept the perpetuation of inequality between classes which it permits. Either way, and at the very least, we agree with Nash as to the outcome: a 'fatal ambiguity on the question of capitalism and socialism', an ambiguity which, we believe, both defines and constrains Mbeki.

Winning by means of bureaucratic control is therefore an inevitable product of Mbeki's approach to politics and ideology, and, equally inevitably, his prime instrument of power. This is Mbeki the manager rather than Mbeki the leader. However, great leaders offer a vision, and a sense of common values. The questions now are: has Mbeki, as president, captured and articulated a clear vision and collective sense of values? Does he truly trust his own organisation? Beyond that, does he truly trust the people? Is his discomfort in the face of mass politics and grass-roots struggles a product of his years in exile, or does it define him more fundamentally as a bourgeois thinker and intellectual? Is he the right person to lead the ANC and South Africa?

Most of the contributors to this volume suggest overwhelmingly that the answer to most of these questions is no. Mbeki does not appear to trust his organisation, even less the people. Ideologically, he appears to be a bourgeois thinker informed by the predominantly social and liberal-democratic ideology of western Europe. This means that Mbeki cannot change the world – however much he may want to – unless he transcends the shackles of his own and the ANC's past.

This would require a more radical strategy. The challenge for Mbeki is to see a more critical engagement with globalisation and its adherents as a meaningful alternative, and to forge new alliances with the post-1990 social movements, both global and, especially, domestic. These movements are engaged in a new struggle: to reclaim power and authority for the democratic state, and thus real politics for its citizens.[5] Such alliances can enable Mbeki to help change the world by offering a new ideological vision, one that provides a voice for the poor, and articulates a radical agenda for social, political, and economic rights and substantive equality.

Mbeki has adopted NEPAD as his vision of engaging with global capital. Conceived by economists close to South African business (and drawing on the political weight of Nigeria's Olusegun Obasanjo and Algeria's Abdoulaziz Bouteflika), NEPAD has been well received in the west (most notably by the G8 leaders and the political and economic elites of the World Economic Forum). The attraction is not surprising, as Bond illustrates. NEPAD is big on rhetoric and symbolic commitment on the part of the west, but not so big on specifics in the key areas of reform: falling levels of assistance and aid, a more favourable trade regime, and reversing the over-reliance on private investment to kick-start economic growth. In keeping with Mbeki's elitist, top-down, decision-making style, NEPAD has been short on involving civil society organisations or direct representatives of ordinary people in its decision-making, or even the founding document's formulation (to enforce NEPAD, it will rely on governments with their not-too-proud records of accountability and delivery).

Inside South Africa, the cornerstone of Mbeki's policy is GEAR; this is considered to be his clearest policy statement, one to which he commits himself religiously at every annual opening of parliament. Introduced in 1996, GEAR is in many respects a free marketer's dream come true. It is based on fiscal discipline, a tight monetary policy, free trade, capital account liberalisation, privatisation (especially of essential municipal services such as electricity, water, and housing), flexible labour markets, skills development, and public service reform (mainly trimming down the size of government, especially the civil service). It also calls for jobs to be created by fostering a stable environment conducive to growth and foreign investment.

Conservative observers have lauded the 'successes' of GEAR (the budget has been overhauled, debt and cash flow management radically reformed, and the deficit brought down from about 10 per cent of GDP under apartheid to 3,5 per cent in the 2000 financial year). However, the majority of South Africans are worse off socio-economically than they were ten years ago. If this policy continues unchanged, the expected positive changes in living standards and quality of life are not likely to materialise soon, particularly in key areas such as water, electricity, land reform, and housing.

Thousands of people still contract cholera every month; more than 40 000 children die each year from diarrhoea caused by dirty water; and financial problems have resulted in many local governments forcibly disconnecting supplies to people who are too poor to pay their water bills (which have risen dramatically since 1994). The government makes much of the fact that since 1994 at least 3,5 million new households have gained access to electricity, yet it neglects to mention those whose power has subsequently been switched off because they cannot pay for it. The soon-to-be privatised electricity utility, ESKOM, finds it cannot profitably link far-flung rural areas to the national grid. It disconnects low-income urban consumers – often because of artificially inflated bills – in most working-class townships, making a mockery of the government's promise during the 2000 municipal election campaign to provide affordable 'electricity for all'.

Land reform is also desperately needed, in the wake of apartheid's bantustan system of reserving the vast majority of good arable land for white farmers, achieved by forcibly removing indigenous residents by the millions. The ANC's 1994 election promise was that by 1999 a total of 30 per cent of arable land would be redistributed; in fact, less than 3 per cent has been redistributed. The 'willing seller, willing buyer at market-related prices' strategy is at the core of the land reform programme, virtually disqualifying (and discouraging) many potential land claimants, most of whom settle instead for small, once-off state payouts. Cumbersome procedures and resource constraints further constrain any progress. Anger at the slow pace of land reform – even slower than during Zimbabwe's first decade of independence – has been reflected in land invasions such as the internationally publicised Bredell community's squat and forced removal outside Johannesburg in July 2001.

What about housing? The government makes much of the 1,2 million 'housing units' it has built since 1994, or 'has under construction', yet Mbeki's own minister of housing has issued public statements condemning the very low quality and location of the new homes. The tiny, poorly built units are sometimes termed 'kennels' because they typically comprise 20 square metres in floor space. They are invariably further from cities and jobs than even the apartheid-era townships. Meanwhile, state spending on housing has been cut, and the backlog keeps on rising – it is estimated that more than three million families are still without adequate shelter.[6]

Mbeki has sharply criticised popular forces and those within his organisation (with an ear to the ground) that have pointed out this state of affairs. When COSATU decided to protest against the government's privatisation programme just a day ahead of the United Nations' World Conference on

Racism in Durban in early September 2001, Mbeki accused the labour movement of turning its back on the morality of the liberation struggle, and its leadership of lying about the privatisation process. 'One of the lies they tell,' Mbeki wrote in a contribution to his special page on the ANC's website, 'is that our government has betrayed policies agreed upon by the broad democratic movement with regard to the restructuring of state assets' (2001). What is remarkable is that, as Mbeki retreats into elite-style politics, and builds alliances with business and a base among the small black middle class, a popular movement is emerging. Drawing on South Africa's long history of protest and resistance, this movement finds its expression among sections of the union leadership and some of its affiliates, particularly in the municipal sector; in community-based resistance to the privatisation of services; and in the local affiliates of the global anti-debt movement.

Trade unionism in South Africa has a long history. In recent decades, though, one can highlight three decisive moments: the first two were the 1973 strike by industrial workers in Durban, and the recommendation by a government commission on trade unionism to accept the formation of black trade unions as fait accompli. The final, and probably most decisive, moment was COSATU's formation in 1985.

This signalled a significant departure from the way in which unionism in South Africa had operated until then. For one, unlike other contemporary trade union co-ordinating bodies and individual unions that focused exclusively on shop-floor issues, COSATU had a highly politicised agenda from the outset. It insisted that its affiliates link up with community struggles. In fact, most of the civic leaders of the 1980s emerged from COSATU, and in many cases played dual roles in community and trade union structures (see Marais 1998).

However, in 1990, when the ANC was unbanned, it pressurised COSATU into becoming less political and more industry-oriented. The ANC wanted COSATU, with a membership of more than 3 million – about 50 per cent of the workforce – to fill a niche in its own organisational plan rather than formulate an independent agenda.

This policy appeared to have succeeded when, prior to the 1994 elections, COSATU agreed to subject itself to the ANC line and allow its leaders to stand as candidates on an ANC ticket rather than as independents. As a result, 20 of the federation's top and brightest leaders went to parliament. Some of them – Alec Erwin, Sydney Mufamadi, and Shepherd Mdladlana, among others – are still cabinet ministers. They are among the most enthusiastic implementers of neo-liberal policies.

However, COSATU has retained an independent streak that insists publicly on GEAR's contradictions. Every year, the federation's economic desk produces a 'People's budget' in anticipation of the national budget released by the minister of finance. The criticism finds a ready mass following among certain affiliates of the federation which have always shown a radical potential, such as those in the municipal, metal, clothing and textile, and mining sectors. Moreover, since 1994 a new kind of leadership has emerged in COSATU that has come to fill the void left by the leaders lost to electoral politics. These new activists have not been forged in the struggle against the apartheid state, but rather in the struggles that have ensued after its fall – over privatisation, the restructuring of government, and the trimming of the public sector. These are the trade union leaders who are clashing with the ANC.

The second strand of a 'new politics' emerges from community struggles. The civic movement emerged in the early 1980s in townships adjoining the country's major cities over the apartheid state's failure to deliver basic services such as housing, electricity, and water, as well as the undemocratic nature of imposed local authorities. The centre of this kind of politics was the South African National Civic Organisation (SANCO). Specifically, SANCO had emerged out of the rent boycotts and demands for better services around Johannesburg, and had spread to Cape Town, Durban, Port Elizabeth (were its strongest affiliate, PEBCO, was based), and other cities and towns.

After 1990, however, as in the case of COSATU, SANCO's position was challenged by the newly ascendant ANC. In this instance, the ANC wanted not just to sideline the organisation but to disband it entirely. SANCO's leadership responded with confusion, and a lack of clear ideological strategy. Many of the leaders ended up in government, as public representatives or key senior civil servants, or even in business (SANCO's founder set up an investment company that later went bust). After 1999, however, some members of the organisation (which had been dispersed but not dissolved), who in many cases had been serving as local councillors representing the ANC, began to question the effects of the government's policies on poor communities. The manifestation of GEAR at the local level, in the form of increased payments for essential services, and ensuing cut-offs, resulted in many SANCO councillors resigning. This led them to re-establish their links with local community organisations.

The 'new civics' have reappropriated the slogans, strategies of direct action, and organisational models (loose structures) of the fight against apartheid in the late 1980s. However, they also express a growing rejection of the policies adopted by the ANC, and are much less likely to be represented by leaders from the historic liberation movements or from trade union organisations.

In a place such as Soweto near Johannesburg (the largest township in South Africa), a councillor who had criticised the restructuring of services in the Johannesburg metro area (Trevor Ngwane; profiled in the documentary film 'The two Trevors go to Washington') formed the Soweto Electricity Crisis Committee (SECC) to fight ESKOM – in many cases illegally reactivating electrical services that had been disconnected as a result of non-payment since early 1999. In July 2000 Mandela's biographer, Fatima Meer, joined angry, poor residents organised as the Chatsworth Concerned Citizens' Group outside Durban in KwaZulu-Natal on the barricades in a cross-racial, cross-class struggle against the ANC-run Durban City Council intent on housing evictions, water cut-offs, and forced removals to faraway neighbourhoods. Meer told journalists: 'These are poor people, indigent people, impoverished people, people who don't have food on their plates – and now you're going to take away the roof over their heads. Where do you expect these people to go? You are just compounding their indigence. And then you move in with your dogs and your guns. If this is not fascist brutality, what is?' (quoted in Bond 2000).

The ANC's attitude towards these new movements has been hostile, when not overtly repressive. ANC leaders, including Mbeki, have labelled them 'adventurist' and 'counterrevolutionary', regarding them as threats to the party's hold on civil society. Most of the ANC activists who chose to run as 'independents' in the 2000 local government elections in order to represent new civics have been expelled from the party.

The third strand of a movement that articulates the struggles of the poor in a post-apartheid context has emerged from the universities. It has its origin in the privatisation of universities and campus services. Finding inspiration from struggles against privatisation of campuses in the United States and Western Europe, many progressive academics have found renewed energy to return to activism and link up with student groups. In August 2000, for example, some academics joined students in facing up to the administration of the University of the Witwatersrand, the country's premier university, then run by vice-chancellor Colin Bundy, who had been a leading left ideologue during the struggle against apartheid.

Finally, there is the church. Despite their social conservatism, the mainstream churches were key players in the anti-apartheid struggle. The role of Desmond Tutu, who won a Nobel prize for peace in 1984, and Dennis Hurley, who was commended by the Pope for his work against apartheid, are probably the best examples of this kind of theology. During an appearance on the American television programme 'Newshour with Jim Lehrer' in October 1999, Tutu was asked: 'You're deeply concerned about the problem of poverty in South Africa today; in fact, you recently said if the gap between the rich and the poor was not closed, we could kiss reconciliation goodbye. Is South Africa's transition really as vulnerable as that?' Tutu's response was:

> Well, it's not just an unreasonable idea that comes from Archbishop Desmond Tutu; it was one of the major recommendations of our five-volume report of the TRC [the Truth and Reconciliation Commission], that reconciliation means that those who have been on the underside of history must see that there is a qualitative difference between repression and freedom. And for them, freedom translates into having a supply of clean water; having electricity on tap; being able to live in a decent home, and have a good job; to be able to send your children to school, and to have accessible health care. I mean, what's the point of having made this transition if the quality of life of these people is not enhanced and improved? If not, the vote is useless (Tutu 1999).

As the politics and economics of the new South African transition has shaped a new brand of unionist, so the transition has bred a new kind of archbishop. Tutu's successor as Anglican Bishop of Cape Town, Winston Ndungane (a contemporary of Mbeki's in boarding school), has become the patron saint of the fights for cheaper AIDS drugs, the scrapping of interational debt incurred by the apartheid regime (still taking up a sizeable chunk of the ANC government's annual budget), and reparations for victims of apartheid. Ndungane has come to personify criticism of the state for its failure to deliver to the poor.

These groups have formed a loose, somewhat disparate coalition, which has already been tested in protests during the WTO's southern Africa meeting in Durban in 2001, and the World Conference on Racism in late August and early September 2001 in the same city.

As a movement, its most explicit expression is the Anti-Privatisation Forum, a loose coalition of civics, trade unions, university-based activists, anti-globalisation and anti-debt campaigners, and 'new civics'. Founded in Johannesburg, the forum has gathered together many of the 'new civics', and is expanding its connections with struggles and organisations in different regions. The organisation has already gained the support of trade unions, such as the municipal workers' organisation (SAMWU), in the front line of the struggle against the privatisation of municipal services. SAMWU's 'anti-privatisation campaign' – recognising the limitations of mere workplace-based actions – explicitly notes the importance of an alliance with community organisations. The union has provided the base for COSATU's successful national two-day anti-privatisation strike, and a series of local protests countrywide against the privatisation of transport services and electricity. At the time, COSATU intended calling for a people's summit on economic restructuring to hammer out an economic strategy to take South Africa out of the current economic crisis, manifest in a rapidly depreciating currency, low growth and investments, massive job losses, and widening inequality and poverty. The programme adopted in the people's summit will then serve as a platform to engage capital in an economic CODESA (the negotiating forum that set the basis for the transition to democracy in 1994) and an accord with government and business' (kaNkosi 2001).

Will these groups present a substantial electoral challenge to the ANC, and particularly to Mbeki's rule? This is not clear at this stage, but electionism is not the overriding goal. This is despite the fact that a number of independent candidates who stood in the last municipal elections in November 2000 were closely tied to and supported by elements within the trade union, civic, and anti-debt movement. They appear not to be against the ANC government *per se* – many of their supporters are ANC supporters, by and large. After all, the ANC, which won 67 per cent of the vote in the 1999 elections, rose to power on the basis of massive working-class support and a virtually unchallenged supremacy on the political left – a result of its 80-year history of opposition to state racism. The party was able to mobilise a broad array of class forces around themes of national liberation, non-racialism, and social equality. For the black working class, this meant not only access to political and civil rights, but also to the social goods essential for the full enjoyment of citizenship in a democratic state. Under the impulse of working-class struggles, 'freedom' came to mean 'that the people of our country can not only vote for a representative of their choice,' as Murphy Morobe of the UDF said in 1985, but also have 'some direct control over where and how they live, eat, sleep, work, how they get to work, how they and their children are educated, what the content of that education is' (Barchiesi 2001: 20).

All these new social movements want is for the ANC to return to its traditional commitments. They appear to take their lead from Mandela himself, who once said: 'Workers should take on the government if they feel that it is not pursuing their interests, to ensure it is brought back in line' (quoted in Barchiesi 2001: 21) One suggestion is to get back to the social demands of the RDP, the ANC's platform in the 1994 elections. Under the priority of 'meeting basic needs' and modernising infrastructures and human resources, the RDP promised a growth path leading to general land reform, employment creation programmes, an inclusive welfare system, and limits to the power of financial corporations.

This is where, finally, the argument comes to a head. We have taken seriously the extent to which Mbeki says he *wants* to change the world. But his analysis is wanting, the rhetoric invariably confuses listeners, the strategy is unidimensional, and the tactics are often ineffective. Mbeki is shaped by his history and destiny in the ANC – yet (the great paradox of this is that), because he is the ultimate pragmatist, compelled by circumstance and training to search for a bureaucratic solution to a political challenge, he has lost touch with the ANC's progressive historical aspirations. More suited, perhaps, to the responsibilities of bureaucratic management than leadership, Mbeki's craven wish to participate in a redeeming moment of history for Africa may remain unrequited. Central to this problem is the question of whom Mbeki most comfortably allies himself with. The social forces represented in the Treatment Action Campaign, among other examples considered above, are emblematic of this challenge. They evoke enormous potential for real solidarity, *for changing the balance of forces*, a more profound undertaking for which Mbeki would appear to have neither the aptitude, desire, or vision.

Notes

1. The RDP formed the basis of the ANC's platform for the 1994 elections. This policy blueprint was drawn up in consultation with the ANC's alliance partners, the SACP and COSATU, as well as the civic movement SANCO. Among its pledges were to build one million houses by 1999, redistribute 30 per cent of the land to blacks who had been forcefully dispossessed of their land under apartheid, provide clean water, sanitation, and electricity to all people, and create jobs through a massive public works programme.
2. On 12 July 2000, soon after Germany had beaten South Africa in the race for the 2006 soccer World Cup by a single vote, Mbeki told the ANC's national general council in Port Elizabeth: 'As the ANC, we therefore understand very well what is meant by what one writer has described as the "globalisation of apartheid".'
3. See, for example, Waldmeir (1997), especially chapter 4.
4. It is to the ANC's credit that it managed internal tensions and leadership struggles so well that it only publicly expelled members twice while the movement was in exile. However, this suppression of dissent also had tragic consequences. For example, a number of leading ANC members have been implicated in murder and torture in ANC camps in Angola. Even a prominent intellectual such as Pallo Jordan did not escape the Stalinist culture imposed in exile; he was detained by the ANC's security apparatus, Mbokodo, for criticising the security system. In 1991, shortly after his election as ANC president, Mandela appointed the Motsuenyane Commission to investigate alleged abuses committed in the camps, and Jordan as a commissioner. The commission reported, *inter alia*, that detention centres such as the notorious Quadro in Angola had 'developed a widespread reputation as a hell-hole where persons were sent to rot' (Motsuenyane 1993, quoted in Marais 1998: 63).
5. As we have argued in Jacobs et al (2001).
6. The summary of the state of delivery in these four areas is based on notes made by Patrick Bond for an article for Z-Net Commentary, February 2002.

References

Bernstein, A. 1999. Time for an economic miracle. *Business Day*. 24 August. http://www.cde.org.za/pub_cde-research-aug%201999.htm.

———. Undated. More of the same is not good enough. Press release. Johannesburg: Centre for Development and Enterprise.

Bond, P. 2000. Thinking globally, filming locally. *Mail & Guardian*, 7–13 July.

———. 2001. Pretoria's perspective on globalisation. *Politikon*, 28 (1). 1 May. 81–94.

Cronin, JP. 2001. Speech in the national assembly, 13 March. In Republic of South Africa, Debates of the National Assembly [Hansard], 3rd session, 2nd parliament, 6–16 March 2001, volume 3, column 1079.

COSATU. 2001. ANC allegations aimed at deflecting attention from real issues. *Cosatu Weekly News*, 19 October. http://www.cosatu.org.za/news/weekly/20011019.html.

Davis, G. 1998. Shaping of governance: the deputy president. Unpublished research report.

Hertz, N. 2001. *The silent takeover: global capitalism and the death of democracy*. London: Heinemann.

Jacobs, S, Calland R, and Power, G. 2001. *Real politics: the wicked issues*. Cape Town: IDASA.

Jacobs, S. 1999. The news media and the South African election. In A Reynolds (ed), *Elections '99: South Africa – the campaigns, results, and future prospects*. Cape Town and London: David Philip and James Currey.

kaNkosi, S. 2001. COSATU bid to heal rift. *Sunday Times*. 25 November.

Marais, H. 1998. *South Africa, the limits to change: the political economy of transition*. Cape Town and London: University of Cape Town Press and Zed Books.

Mbeki, T. 1998. Statement of deputy president Thabo Mbeki at the opening of the debate in the national assembly on 'reconciliation and nation-building', 24 May, Cape Town. http://www.anc.org.za/ancdocs/history/mbeki/1998/sp980529.html.

———. 2000. Keynote address to the National General Council. Port Elizabeth, 12 July. http://www.anc.org.za/ancdocs/history/mbeki/2000/tm0712.html.

———. 2001. Tell no lies, claim no easy victories. ANC *Today: Online Voice of the African National Congress*, 1 (31), 24–30 August. http://www.anc.org.za/ancindex.html.

Motsuenyane Commission on Treatment of ANC Prisoners. 1993. Executive summary, iii. Quoted in H Marais. 1998. *South Africa, the limits to change: the political economy of transition*. Cape Town and London: University of Cape Town Press and Zed Books.

Steenveld, L and Strelitz, L. 1998. The 1995 World Cup and the politics of nation-building in South Africa. *Media, Culture and Society*, 20. 609–29.

Tutu, D. 1999. Interview by Ray Suarez on The Newshour with Jim Lehrer, Public Broadcasting Service, 6 October. Transcript on PBS Online. http://www.pbs.org/newshour/bb/africa/july-dec99/tutu_10-6.html.

Waldmeir, P. 1997. *Anatomy of a miracle*. London: Penguin Books.

Select bibliography

Thabo Mbeki's speeches and writings since the ANC's unbanning in February 1990 have been adequately recorded, and are freely available. When the ANC launched its website in the mid-1990s, it dedicated a special section entitled 'The Mbeki Page' to public speeches by Mbeki, who had by then been elected as the organisation's national chair, and as deputy president of South Africa. Moreover, shortly before Mbeki's inauguration as president, an 'editorial committee' of some of his closest advisers and confidantes collected some of his speeches and writings in a volume entitled *Africa: the time has come* (1998).

However, what stands out is that 'The Mbeki Page' and this volume contain only two of Mbeki's speeches or writings prior to 1990: one a statement made in 1964 before a delegation of the United Nations Special Committee on Apartheid, and the other a speech made in Canada in 1978 entitled 'The historical injustice', and published in the ANC party journal *Sechaba* in March 1979.

It seems as if the editors of *Africa: the time has come* anticipated some criticism on this score, because they provided a ready response. In the foreword, they wrote:

> Until the birth of the new government in 1994, Thabo Mbeki served a considerable amount of time as a speech-writer. Almost all the speeches and documents he prepared were therefore published under the names of the leaders and organs of the ANC which presented them publicly.

From the late 1970s onwards Mbeki wrote speeches for Oliver Tambo, some of whose writings and public speeches prior to 1990 have appeared in *Preparing for power: Oliver Tambo speaks* (London: Heineman Educational, 1987), a collection edited by his wife Adelaide, and with a foreword by Nelson Mandela.

Other reasons could be cited for publishing or listing so few of Mbeki's pre-1990 writings. The first is that Mbeki did not write much while serving as an ANC representative in various African countries in the early 1970s. The second involves the context of exile and banned politics. African liberation movements encouraged collective authorship of documents, and the ANC was no different on this score. (Mbeki wrote a number of articles in the party journals *Sechaba* and *Mayibuye* that were published under other people's names.) Thirdly, fear of reprisals and identification by security agents meant that activists often wrote under pseudonyms.

However, in the course of our research, we found that Mbeki had in fact published a number of speeches and articles, and had made a number of public appearances that had been documented on film, in transcripts of radio programmes, and in newspaper reports and newsletters.

Thus the 'official' silence on Mbeki's pre-1990 work seems curious, reinforcing perceptions that Mbeki and his advisers are not too keen to draw attention to his thinking in earlier years. In this select bibliography, we have set out to redress this imbalance. It concentrates, therefore, on providing references to speeches, writings, media interviews, and documentary film appearances by Mbeki prior to 1990, while in exile in the United Kingdom, Nigeria, and Zambia.

We searched a number of databases and consulted a number of individuals familiar with the ANC's bibliography and history. The Centre for African Studies at the University of Cape Town proved to be particularly helpful. Graham Goddard, video archivist at the Mayibuye Centre of the University of the Western Cape, was particularly useful in pointing us to documentary film references to Mbeki. Peter Limb of Michigan State University was also helpful in pointing to a number of sources.

We have organised these references into two sections: primary sources prior to 1990, and secondary sources not necessarily published before 1990, but all containing material relating to Mbeki prior to 1990.

Lastly, we provide references to useful analyses with a bearing on the issues surrounding the ANC and Mbeki, and addressed in this volume.

PRIMARY SOURCES SINCE 1990

African National Congress [online]. The Mbeki Page. http://www.anc.org.za/ancdocs/history/mbeki.

Mbeki, T. 1998. *Africa: the time has come*. Cape Town and Johannesburg: Tafelberg and Mafube.

PRIMARY SOURCES PRIOR TO 1990

Speeches and contributions to books, journals, and newspapers

Mbeki, T. 1964. Statement before a delegation of the UN Special Committee on Apartheid, London, 13 April.

———. 1967. Youth in the struggle. *Sechaba*, 1 (3), March. 89.

———. 1978. Domestic and foreign policies of a new South Africa. *Review of African Political Economy*, 11, January. 6–16.

———. 1979. The historical injustice. *Sechaba*, March. 11–22.

———. 1983. Reforming apartheid doesn't end slavery. *New York Times*, 18 July.

———. 1984. ANC is indestructible. Interview by Julie Frederikse. *Africa News*, 16 July. 5–6. [Discusses the Nkomati Accord and the ANC's relations with the UDF.]

———. 1984. The Fatton thesis: a rejoinder. *Canadian Journal of African Studies*, 18. 609–12. [Mbeki was then chair of the ANC's youth and students section.]

———. 1984/5. Testimony by Oliver Tambo and Thabo Mbeki to the House of

Commons Foreign Affairs Committee. In S Johns and RH Davis Jr (eds). 1991. *Mandela, Tambo, and the African National Congress: the struggle against apartheid, 1948–90.* New York: Oxford University Press.

———. 1985. Opinion editorial. *New York Times*, 13 August.

———. 1985. The struggle inside South Africa. *Africa Report*, 30 (1), January/February. 59–60.

———. 1988. Class, race, and the future of socialism. In W Cobbett and R Cohen (eds). *Popular struggles in South Africa.* James Currey and Africa World Press. 210–28. Also published in *New Left Review*, 160, November/December 1986, 3–22. [Mbeki focuses on the ANC, its 1980s revival and ideology, and the views of Govan Mbeki, Joe Slovo, and Francis Meli.]

———. 1989. A climate for negotiations? *Africa Report*, 34, November/December. 27–9. [Speeches by Mbeki and Willie Esterhuyse to the Five Freedoms Forum Conference entitled 'South Africa at a turning point', Johannesburg, August 1990. Mbeki outlines proposals for peaceful change, and stresses the urgency of agreeing on a new constitution.]

———. 1989. Leading ANC figure and new head of ANC's department of international affairs. Interview with John Ryan. *Cape Argus*, 23 May.

———. 1989. Solving regional conflict through negotiations: does it work? *Die Suid-Afrikaan.* 24 December. 26–7.

———. 1989. The campaign for sanctions. Extracts from a speech to the Southern Africa Coalition, London, October.

———. 1989. The Harare document and the international community. Extracts from an address to anti-apartheid activists in Switzerland. September.

———. 1990. Disarming talk. Interview with Phillip van Niekerk. *Leadership SA*, 9 (2), March. 24–7. [Mbeki, then head of the ANC's international department, gives his views on the possibility of negotiating a new political dispensation, majority rule, nationalisation, the Pan-Africanist Congress (PAC), and the possibility of the extreme right wing derailing negotiations.]

———. 1990. Problems before us: the steps forward. *Sechaba*, 24 (11), November. 4–7. [Edited version of presentation by Mbeki to a meeting of the African-American Institute.]

———. 1989. Speech to Australia and Pacific Regional Conference Against Apartheid for a Democratic South Africa, Sydney, 15–17 September. 7.

Film and radio

Mbeki, T. 1979. Statement of NEC on June 16th observances, transcript of broadcast on Radio Freedom, *Mayibuye*, 7, July. 3–4.

———. 1986. Interview during *Apartheid – a television history.* London: Granada TV. Produced by B Lapping. [Part 4 covers 1980–85, and includes interviews with Mbeki, Mac Maharaj, Cyril Ramaphosa, Zinzi Mandela, and Albie Sachs.]

———. 1986. Interview during *Song of the spear: the role of culture in the struggle for freedom in South Africa.* 16 mm/video. Director: B Feinberg. 57 minutes. London: IDAF, in co-operation with the ANC. [Interviews with Mbeki, Barbara Masekela, and Jonas Gwanga.]

———. 1986. Interview on Radio Freedom. BBC Monitoring Service, August.

———. 1987. Interview during *Before dawn*. Produced by AABN/ANC, 60 minutes, PROD 4–12, Mayibuye Centre, UWC, December. [Mbeki speaks on the cultural boycott and the meaning of the slogan 'kill the witches'.]

———. 1987. Speech during *Any child is my child*. Directed by B Feinberg, produced by IDAF, 20 minutes, PROD 5–10, Mayibuye Centre, University of the Western Cape.

———. 1988. Interview during *Battle for South Africa*. Directed by Bill Moyers, produced by CBS, 45 minutes, Tape B1, Mayibuye Centre, UWC. [Mbeki speaks on the ubiquitous nature of the ANC; the significance of carrying arms, and the escalation of the struggle.]

———. 1988. Interview during *Certain unknown persons*. Produced by VNS. Duration: 45 minutes. [Mbeki speaks on attacks against ANC bases and supporters in frontline states.]

———. 1990. Panelist on *Zabalaza & Mandela*, 3 July 1990. Produced by IDAF/Arekopaneng, 20 minutes, PROD 39–15, Mayibuye Centre, University of the Western Cape.

———. 1996. Interview during *The Spear of the Nation: the story of the African National Congress*. Director: D Tereschuk, 55 minutes, produced by Thames BBC. [Mbeki speaks on early ANC protests, relations with the Communist Party of South Africa, the ANC Youth League, the Freedom Charter, and exile. The film uses archival tapes and interviews with Mbeki, Oliver Tambo, Joe Slovo, Ruth Mompati, Chris Hani, Pallo Jordan, M Shopa, Henry Msimang, Kenneth Kaunda, and others.]

SECONDARY SOURCES PRIOR TO 1990

Adam, H. 1973. The rise of black consciousness in South Africa. *Race*, 15 (2), October. 149–65.

ANC *Struggle Update*. 1988. A broad coalition of anti-apartheid forces. Harare. 4th quarter. 6–10, 12–14.

Barrell, H. 1990. *MK: the ANC's armed struggle*. Johannesburg: Penguin Books.

———. 1991. The turn to the masses: the African National Congress's strategic review of 1978–79. *Journal of Southern African Studies*, 18 (1), March.

Brewer, J. 1986. Black protest in South Africa's crisis: a comment on Legassick. *African Affairs*, 85, April, 283–94.

Bundy, C. 1987. History, revolution and South Africa. *Transformation*, 4.

———. 1989. Around which corner? Revolutionary theory and contemporary South Africa. *Transformation*, 8.

———. 1991. Marxism in South Africa: context, themes, and challenges. *Transformation*, 16.

Callinicos, A. 1986. Marxism and revolution in South Africa. *International Socialism* 2 (31), 3–66.

Charney, C. 1986. Thinking revolution: the new South African intelligentsia. *Monthly Review* 38, December. 10–19.

Dabies, R, O'Meara, D, and Dlamini, S. 1985. *The struggle for South Africa: a reference guide to movements, organisations and institutions*. London: Zed Books.

Davidson, B, Slovo, J, and Wilkinson, B. 1977. *Southern Africa: the new politics of revolution*. Harmondsworth: Penguin.

Davis, D and Fine, R. 1985. Political strategies and the state: some historical observations. *Journal of Southern African Studies*, 12 (1), October. 25–48.

Ellis, S and Sechaba, T. 1992. *Comrades against apartheid: the ANC and the South African Communist Party in exile*. London and Bloomington: James Currey and Indiana University Press.

Frederickson, GM. 1995. Black liberation: comparative history of black ideologies in the United States and South Africa. New York and Oxford: Oxford University Press.

Friedman, S. 1987. The struggle within the struggle: South African resistance strategies. *Transformation*, 3.

Gastrow, S. 1990. Who's who in South African politics, 1985–93. 4th edition. Hans Zell: London.

Gelb, S. 1987. Making sense of the crisis. *Transformation*, 5.

Gerhart, G. 1978. Black power in South Africa: the evolution of an ideology. Los Angeles: University of California Press.

Halisi, CRD. 1999. *Black political thought in the making of South African democracy*. Bloomington and Indianapolis: Indiana University Press.

Hanlon, J. 1986. *Apartheid's second front: South Africa's war against its neighbours*. Middlesex: Penguin.

Lodge, T. 1983. *Black politics in South Africa since 1945*. Harlow, Longman.

———. 1987. The African National Congress after the Kabwe Conference. In G Moss and I Obery (eds), *South African Review 4*. Johannesburg: Ravan Press.

———. 1989. People's War or negotiation? African National Congress strategies in the 1980s. *South African Review 5*. Johannesburg: Ravan Press.

Lodge T and Nasson, B. 1991. *All, here and now: black politics in South Africa in the 1980s*. Cape Town: David Philip.

Louw, C. 1989. *Journey to the ANC: reports on a visit to Windhoek, Harare, and Lusaka (Op reis na die ANC: verslae oor 'n besoek aan Windhoek, Harare, en Lusaka)*. Cape Town: Voorbrand.

McKinley, D. 1999. *The ANC and the liberation struggle*. London: Pluto Press.

Mzala. 1981. Has the time come for arming the masses? *African Communist*, 102 (third quarter).

Mzala. 1987. Towards people's war and insurrection. *Sechaba*, April.

———. 1990. Is South Africa in a revolutionary situation? *Journal of Southern African Studies*, 16 (3). September.

Nolutshungu, SC. 1982. *Changing South Africa: political considerations*. New York: Africana.

Nyawusa. 1985. New Marxist tendencies and the battle of ideas in South Africa. *African Communist*, 103, fourth quarter.

Walshe, P. 1973. *Black nationalism in South Africa: a short history*. Johannesburg: Ravan Press.

COMMENTS AND ANALYSES

Adam, H, Slabbert, F Van Zyl, and Moodley, K. 1997. *Comrades in business: post-liberation politics in South Africa*. Cape Town: Tafelberg.

Adams, S. 1997. What's Left? The Communist Party after apartheid. *Review of African Political Economy*, 72. 237–48.
Bond, P. 2000. *Elite transition: from apartheid to neo-liberalism.* Pluto Press: London.
Callinicos, A. 1992. *South Africa between apartheid and capitalism.* London: Bookmarks.
———. 1996. South Africa after apartheid. *International Socialism*, 70, Spring 1996. 3–46.
Department of finance. 1996. *Growth, employment and redistribution: a macroeconomic strategy.* Pretoria.
Desai, A. 1999. *South Africa: still revolting.* Durban: Natal Newspapers.
Fredrickson, GM. 1990. The making of Mandela. *New York Review of Books.* 37 (14). 27 September.
Halisi, CRD. 1999. *Black political thought in the making of South African democracy.* Bloomington and Indianapolis: Indiana University Press.
Jacobs, S. 1999. The imperial presidency. *Siyaya*, Summer. 4–9.
Jacobs, S, Power, G, and Calland, R. 2001. *Real politics: the wicked issues.* Cape Town: IDASA/British Council.
James, W and Levy, M. 1988. *Pulse: passages in democracy-building – assessing South Africa's transition.* Cape Town: IDASA.
Johns, S and Davis, RH Jr (eds). 1991. *Mandela, Tambo, and the African National Congress: the struggle against apartheid, 1948–90.* New York: Oxford University Press.
Lodge, T. 1983. *Black politics in South Africa since 1945.* Johannesburg: Ravan Press.
———. 1999. *South African politics since 1994.* Cape Town: David Philip.
Maloka, E. African Renaissance Reactionary. *African Communist*, 147, 3rd quarter. 37–43.
Mamdani, M. 1996. *Citizen and subject: contemporary Africa and the legacy of late colonialism.* Princeton: Princeton University Press.
Mandela, N. 1994. *Long walk to freedom.* Johannesburg: Macdonald Purnell.
Maphai, V. 1994. *South Africa: the challenge of change.* Harare: SAPES Books.
Marais, H. 1998. *South Africa: limits to change – the political economy of transition.* Cape Town and London: University of Cape Town Press and Zed Books.
McKinley, D. 1999. *The ANC and the liberation struggle.* London: Pluto Press.
Michie, J and Padayachee, V (eds). 1997. *The political economy of South Africa's transition: policy perspectives in the late 1990s.* London: The Dryden Press. 229.
Murray, M. 1994. *The revolution deferred.* London: Verso.
———. 1999. *Myth and memory in the new South Africa.* London: Verso.
Naidoo, G. 1991. *Reform and revolution: South Africa in the nineties.* Dakar and Johannesburg: CODESRIA and Skotaville.
Neocosmos, M. 1998. From peoples' politics to state politics: aspects of national liberation in South Africa. In A Olukoshi (ed), *The politics of opposition in contemporary Africa* Uppsala: Nordic Africa Institute.
Nzimande, B and Cronin, J. 1997. We need transformation, not a balancing act. *African Communist*, 146, 1st quarter.
Rich, PB (ed). 1994. *The dynamics of change in southern Africa.* New York: St Martin's Press.

Saul, J. 1993. *Recolonisation and resistance in Southern Africa.* Trenton: Africa World Press.

Shubin, V. 1999. *ANC. A view from Moscow.* University of the Western Cape: Mayibuye Books.

Sparks, A. 1994. *Tomorrow is another country: the inside story of South Africa's negotiated revolution.* Cape Town: Struik.

Waldmeir, P. 1997. *Anatomy of a miracle: the end of apartheid and the birth of the new South Africa.* New York: Viking.

Wallerstein, I. 1996. The ANC and South Africa: the past and future of liberation movements in the world system. Address to the South African Sociological Association, Durban, 7 July.

Index

Adelzadeh, Asghar   37–8, 88
affirmative action   35, 42, 94, 204
African Communist   20, 175–6
African Development Bank   66
African National Congress   1–22, 28–39
  democracy   250
  economic policy   36–49, 83–101, 251–2, 261–2
  ideology and policy   106–19, 257–74
  leadership   105–6, 110
  non-racialism   248, 250
  party development   265
  power of government   153–4
  ruling party   146, 169, 180, 187
  SACP relations   163–75
  socialism   258
  state–society relations   221–39
  trade union alliance   179–98, 269
  tribal democracy   250–4
  Youth League   7, 10, 248
African Renaissance   5, 14, 19, 43, 56, 62, 114–16, 121–35, 139–42, 156, 168–70, 173–4, 257, 263
African Union (AU)   140–1, 169
Africanism   128–31, 133, 223, 248–50, 266
Afrikaner Weerstandsbeweging (AWB)   29
Afrikaners   9, 13, 34–5
agriculture   130
  labour   89

AIDS   *see* HIV/AIDS
Algeria   62, 88
Amin, Samir   93
Amoako, KY   139
Anglo-American Corporation   41, 59, 63
Angola   66, 88, 169
Anti-Apartheid Movement   108, 123, 221, 223, 231–2, 264, 271
Anti-Ballistic Missile Treaty   141
Anti-Privatisation Forum   272
anti-retrovirals   2, 3, 70–1, 262–3
apartheid   3, 7, 8, 28, 30, 44, 62, 75, 118, 123–4, 131, 133–4, 145, 203–4, 258, 260, 271, 272
  global   55, 57, 59, 62, 64, 78, 130, 260
Argentina   56, 66
arms deals   1–2, 71, 169, 257, 263
Asmal, Kader   12
authoritarianism   16, 225, 258
Azanian People's Organisation (AZAPO)   211

banks, bonds for blacks   204–5
bantustans   6, 17, 29
Barchefsky, Charlene   70
Barrell, Howard   16, 49, 233
Bernstein, Ann   34, 40, 261
Biko, Steve   75, 129
Bisho   31

285

black/s
  business   97, 204, 206–16
  consciousness   129
  elite   48, 209, 211, 213
  empowerment   43, 75, 114, 212
  executives   117
Black Economic Empowerment (BEE)   116–17, 169, 206–17
Black Economic Empowerment Commission (BEECom)   212–15
Black Journalists Forum   12
Black Management Forum   96, 212
Black Renaissance   129
Black Sash   234
Blair, Tony   40, 142, 146, 154, 158, 259, 260
Boipatong massacre   31
Botha, PW   9, 106, 108, 252–3
  Rubicon speech   108
Botswana   7, 8, 183
bourgeoisie, black   16, 42–3, 96–8, 114, 116–18, 164, 168–9, 189, 198, 207, 210–11, 215, 251, 259, 266
Bouteflika, Abdelaziz   139, 267
Bredell community   268
Breslin, Edward   235
Bretton Woods institutions   59, 67–8, 77–8
Bullen, Alison   114–15
Bundy, Colin   271
Burundi   128
bureaucracy   273–4
business   201–16, 252–3, 261–2, 267, 269
  black   206–16
Bush, George   252
Buthelezi, Mangosuthu   6, 10, 11–12, 28–30, 32–3, 155

capital flow   99–100
capitalism   27–8, 34–5, 39, 43–5, 48, 93–7, 105, 109, 112, 115, 169, 173–4, 246–8, 251–3, 260–1, 266
  black   42, 96–7
  global   222, 229, 259, 267

Castells, Manuel   94
Centre for Development and Enterprise (CDE)   34, 40, 261
Chatsworth Concerned Residents Association   271
Chikane, Frank   148, 155
cholera   74, 268
church   271
Ciskei   31
Civil Society Initiative (CSI)   237–8
class relationships   251, 266
Clinton, Bill   62, 69, 71, 156, 237, 260
Coetsee, Kobie   9
colonialism   63, 75, 118–19, 128, 140, 198, 203
Commonwealth Heads of Government Meeting (CHOGM)   169
communication technology   259
communism   165, 169, 173–4
Compact for African Recovery   139
Conference on Security, Stability, Development and Co-operation in Africa (CSSDCA)   139
Congo, Democratic Republic of (DRC)   128
Congress Movement   173
Congress of South African Trade Unions (COSATU)   11, 12, 31, 37, 46–7, 72–3, 88–90, 110, 112–14, 157–8, 163–75, 184–91, 201–3, 211, 268–70, 272
Conservative Party   29
constitution   30, 254
constitution, 1993   146–7
constitutional court   3, 258
Constellation of Southern African States   123
consultants   235
Consultative Business Movement   253
Convention for a Democratic South Africa (CODESA)   33, 258
  economics   259, 273
Co-ordination and Implementation Unit (CIU)   149
corruption   2, 32
COSATU   see Congress of South African Trade Unions

crime   32, 47, 118, 233
Cronin, Jeremy   31, 93, 110, 166, 259
currency depreciation   56, 60, 272
customs, tribal   246

De Beers   59
debt, foreign   56, 64–7, 139
  cancellation   64–5, 272
  relief   65, 77
defence   125
Defiance Campaign   249
De Klerk, FW   9, 11, 13, 28, 30, 35, 145, 147
Delport, Tertius   110
democracy   5, 28, 45, 63, 95, 98, 109, 124–5, 131, 171–2, 184–5, 221–31, 253–4, 257
  liberal   258
  social   258
  tribal   21, 131, 243–54
Democratic Alliance (DA)   32, 211–12
Democratic Party (DP)   32, 147
deputy president's office   147–9, 155–6
deregulation   259
Deutsche Bank   60
development, sustainable   54
development programmes   204, 233–5
Dexter, Phillip   203
Didata   60
Ditlhake, Abie   203

economic development   35–48, 226, 259, 261, 265, *see also* Growth, Employment and Redistribution
Economist, The   41–2, 154, 157–8
education   116–17, 130, 272
Egypt   88, 169
elections   29, 31–2, 47–8, 77, 114, 169, 253, 271, 273
  municipal   173
electricity supply   267–8, 271–2
Electricity Supply Commission (ESKOM)   268, 271
employment   201
empowerment   74–5, 204, 215, 228–9, *see also* black, empowerment

Erwin, Alec   37, 54, 70, 73, 77, 91–2, 165, 212, 269
European Union   56, 61–3, 69
exchange controls   38, 41, 59–60, 87, 90, 96–7, 111, 126, 168, 201
exchange rates   60, 88, 90
exiles   7, 9, 10, 107–8, 169, 182–4, 261, 264
exports   54, 60, 87, 99, 122–3, 226

Fanon, Franz   41, 75
Federation of Unions of South Africa (FEDUSA)   203
Feinstein, Andrew   2
finance, development   67
Finance and Fiscal Commission (FFC)   153, 159
Financial Mail   91, 127
Financial Times   63, 69
Fischer, Bram   7
foreign direct investment (FDI)   66, 88, 96, 116
foreign investment   39, 40, 60, 66, 86–8, 96, 115, 202, 262, 267
foreign policy   125, 156
Foundation for Global Dialogue (FGD)   126
Fraser-Moleketi, Geraldine   157, 165
free market economy   33–4, 35, 37, 45, 63, 93, 126, 252
free trade   61, 99, 259, 267
freedom   272–3
Freedom Charter   35, 173, 186, 251
Freedom Front   29, 109
Freund, B   42, 197
fuel industry   214

Gaddafi, Muammar   141
Galbraith, James K   90
GCIS   *see* Government Communications and Information Service
GEAR   *see* Growth, Employment and Redistribution
Gencor/Billiton   60
General Agreement on Tariffs and Trade (GATT)   56

Gerwel, Jakes   145–6, 148
Gevisser, Mark   10
Giddens, Anthony   142
globalisation   15, 45, 53–78, 84–5, 87, 91–7, 100, 118, 126, 130, 133, 142, 172, 259, 261, 267
globalism   133
Godongwana, Enoch   195
Gomomo, John   195
Gore, Al   70–1, 156
government, local   109–10, 159, 270
Government Communications and Information Service (GCIS)   148–9, 156, 202
Government Employees Pension Fund   213
Government of National Unity (GNU)   109, 146–7
Gramsci, Antonio   173–4
Group of Eight (G-8)   61–3, 65, 141, 267
Growth, Employment and Redistribution (GEAR)   15, 34, 36, 37, 40, 44, 46, 60, 86–91, 98, 111, 112–17, 133, 165, 170, 187, 188–9, 192, 197, 210, 226, 236–7, 260, 265, 267, 269–70
gross domestic product (GDP)   87, 267

Hamill, James   8, 9
Hani, Chris   6, 10, 110
Harmel, Michael   7
health   47, 263, 268, 272
Health Department   3
Heath, Judge Willem   2
Heard, Tony   156
Highly Indebted Poor Countries (HIPC)   56, 65–6
HIV/AIDS   2–4, 12, 15, 16, 17, 48, 61, 70–1, 76, 105, 157, 205, 257, 260, 262–3, 272
homelands   123, *see also* bantustans
housing   235, 267–8, 271–2
Howarth, David   32
human relations   130
human rights   30, 63, 125, 203, 257
Human Rights Commission (HRC)   258
Hurley, Dennis   271

imperialism   169
imports   60
   tariffs   73
Independent Electoral Commission   11
Industrial Development Corporation (IDC)   122
inequality   206, 215, 237, 266
inflation rate   60, 87
information technology   203
infrastructure   66–8
Inkatha Freedom Party (IFP)   10, 11, 29–30, 32, 109, 146
Institute for Democracy in South Africa (IDASA)   17
interest rates   42, 61, 68
International Criminal Court   141
International Finance Corporation   69
International Monetary Fund (IMF)   34, 38, 54, 62, 63, 67–9, 73, 76, 92, 95, 111, 188
international relations   125, 134, 167
Investec Bank   60
investments   58, 86–8, 111, 115, 213, 233, 272
   domestic   202, 205, 262
   South African in Africa   127

job creation   92, 109, 146, 166, 172, 233, 267, 273
Johannesburg Stock Exchange (JSE)   42, 61, 85, 96, 169, 204, 207
Jordan, Pallo   148, 155, 215
Jubilee Africa   77
Jubilee South   65

Kanbur, Ravi   61
Kasrils, Ronnie   165
Kaunda, Kenneth   6, 7, 10
Kenya   128, 198
Keynes, John Maynard   77–8
Keynesianism   36, 260
Koehler, Horst   62–3

labour
   capital relations   93

laws   73, 94, 201, 210, 233
market   96, 99
movement   261, *see also* trade unions
power   97
wage   246
Labour Party   184
Labour Relations Act (LRA), 1995   187, 191
land reform   172–3, 205, 267–8, 273
landmine clearance   141
languages   130
Landsberg, Chris   33–4
law and order   232, *see also* crime
Lekota, Patrick   155
Lembede, Anton   248–50
Leninism   222, 231
Leon, Tony   147, 212
Lesotho   132, 183
Levy, Norman   150
liberalism   248
liberation movement   31, 169, 173, 180–5, 196–8, 201, 229, 231, 249, 253, 265, 269
Libya   141
Liebenberg, Chris   148
living standards   61, 67, 97, 267, 272
local government   *see* government, local
Lodge, Tom   5
Lusaka   183
Luthuli, Albert   248

Madisha, Willie   202, 210
Macro Economic Research Group (MERG)   36
macroeconomics   14–15, 18, 265, *see also* Growth, Employment and Redistribution
Mafolo, Titus   156
Magdoff, H   27–8
Mail & Guardian   12, 16, 59, 87
Makana, Sipho   6
Malaysia   94
Mamdani, Mahmood   32–3, 75
Mandela, Nelson   4, 6, 7, 9, 10–11, 13, 15, 28, 34, 35, 41, 44–5, 71, 83–6, 91, 99–100, 106, 110, 113, 124, 125, 133, 145–7, 182, 188, 191, 193, 197, 231, 237, 243–54, 261, 266, 273
Mandela, Winnie   10, 166
Manuel, Trevor   37, 54, 67–8, 77, 92, 112, 159, 202, 212
Manzini, Mavivi   155
Mankahlana, Parks   156–7
Maphai, Vincent   133, 150
market economy   216, 222, *see also* free market economy
markets, global   140–1
Marxism   7, 251
Masland, Tom   3
mass action   232–3, *see also* strikes
Mass Democratic Movement (MDM)   37, 182, 184, 186
Mavimbela, Vusi   126–7, 148, 265
Mazwai, Thami   210
Mbeki, Govan   6, 182
Mbeki, Moeletsi   6, 127
Mbeki, Thabo
  African Renaissance   19, 43, 114, 121–35, 168–70
  autocracy   46, 264–5
  background   5–14
  bureaucracy   264, 266, 274
  business concerns   201–16
  diplomacy, quiet   4, 203, 205
  economics   34, 40–9, 86–7, 89–91, 96–7, 99–100, 259, 261–2, 267
  foreign policy   156, 260, 263
  ideology   1–14, 105–19, 257–74
  logic   193–7
  negotiating for change   107–10
  NEPAD   53–79, 139–42
  personality   8, 12, 105–7, 110, 118, 142
  politics   19, 40–9, 163–75, 258, 260–3
  president   17–18, 145–59, 257–8, 261, 266
  speeches   277–8
  state–society relations   221–39
Mbekism   119
Mboweni, Tito   36, 60

Mdladlana, Membathisi 195
Mdladlana, Shepherd 269
MDM see Mass Democratic Movement
media 156–7, 167–8, 264
Medicines Act, 1997 70–1, 76, 262
Meer, Fatima 271
Meyer, Roelf 237–8
middle class see bourgeoisie, black
militants 110–11
Millennium Africa Recovery Plan (MAP) 62, 139
Mineral-Energy Complex (MEC) 41
MK see Umkhonto weSizwe
Mkapa, Benjamin 63
Mokaba, Peter 10, 170–1
Mopani Memorandum of Undertaking, 1993 206
Moseneke, Dikgang 209
mother-tongue education 130
Motlana, Nthato 209, 211
Motlanthe, Kgalema 68–9, 155, 166
Mozambique 44, 169
Mufamadi, Sydney 11, 157, 159, 165, 269
Mugabe, Robert 4, 6, 15, 105, 203, 205, 257
Multiparty Negotiating Process (MPNP) 258
multiracialism 258
Mvula Trust 235

Naidoo, Jay 148, 185, 191
National African Federated Chamber of Commerce (NAFCOC) 212–13
National Alliance Summit 167
National Economic Development and Labour Council (NEDLAC) 47, 113, 203
National Empowerment Fund 117
National Framework Agreement 165
National Intelligence Agency (NIA) 195
National Labour and Economic Development Institute (NALEDI) 158
National Party (NP) 30, 32, 106–8, 146–7, 253, 261

National Union of Metalworkers of South Africa (NUMSA) 194
National Youth Commission 156
nationalisation 85, 216, 251–2
nationalism, African 16, 53, 114, 118–19
Ndebele, Njabulo 129
Ndukwana, Sotho 209
Ndungane, Winston 6–7, 272
negotiations for change 107–9, 253, 258–9
Nel, Philip 96
neo-colonialism 164
neo-liberalism 28, 32, 34–5, 37–9, 40, 48, 63–5, 77, 84–5, 107, 111, 119, 131, 142, 222, 259–60
Neocosmos, M 223, 224–5
Netshitenze, Joel 149, 202
nevirapene 3
New Africa Investments Ltd (NAIL) 208
New African Initiative (NAI) 63, 139
New Partnership for Africa's Development (NEPAD) 3–4, 53–79, 116, 139–42, 169, 257, 267
Ngoasheng, Moss 148–9, 208, 209
Ngonyama, Smuts 155
Ngwane, Trevor 270–1
Nhlanha, Joe 166
Nigeria 8, 62, 65, 66, 77, 88
Nkrumah, Kwame 75
Nkuhlu, Wiseman 203
Nolutshungu, Sam 7
Non-Aligned Movement (NAM) 54, 57, 169
non-governmental organisations (NGOs) 117, 234–5
Normative Economic Model (NEM) 35, 39, 112
Nqakula, Charles 157
Nyerere, Julius 10, 75, 131
Nzimande, Blade 93, 155, 157, 172
Nzo, Alfred 182

Obasanjo, Olusegun 62–3, 139, 267
off-shore listing 59–60, 97, 204

oil 66, 127
Old Mutual 59–60
Olympic Games, 2004 132
Omar, Dullah 73
OMEGA Plan 139
Oppenheimer, Jonathan 63
Organisation of African Unity (OAU) 54, 63, 139, 140

Pahad, Aziz 9
Pahad, Essop 11, 12, 148–9, 151, 156–7, 165
Pan-African nationalism 114
Pan-Africanist Congress (PAC) 9, 115
peacekeeping 125, 140
People's Budget 269–70
Performance and Innovation Unit (PIU) 158
Phosa, Mathews 2, 42, 105, 208
Pieterse, Gavin 212
Pillay, Pundy 158
Plot, The 2, 13, 257
Policy Co-ordination and Advisory Services (PCAS) 151–3, 158–9
'port' 61
poverty 3, 15, 17, 33, 43, 45, 64–5, 77, 87, 158, 203–4, 206, 215, 233, 237, 244, 252, 258, 262, 271, 273
Presidential Review Commission 150
presidency in South Africa 145–58
privatisation 40, 63, 66–7, 72–3, 77, 90, 96–7, 99, 111, 115, 117, 126, 154, 165, 167–8, 187, 201, 204, 209, 252, 259, 267, 268–71
productivity 204
Property Rating Bill 159
Public-Private Partnership Unit (PPPU) 159
public service reform 267

racism 16, 32, 35, 43, 57, 96, 114, 116, 156, 173, 207, 211, 251, 258, 261, 273
Radebe, Jeff 73, 157, 165
Ramaphosa, Cyril 2, 10–11, 13, 105, 110, 155, 211, 212

Ramos, Maria 87, 159, 208
rand
  depreciation 56, 60, 272
  financial 56, 59, 60
reconciliation 254, 258, 271
Reconstruction and Development Programme (RDP) 37, 69, 86–7, 109, 112–13, 148, 159, 186–8, 191–2, 208, 226, 236, 260, 273
removals, forced 271
Renaissance, African see African Renaissance
Reserve Bank 60, 112
Rhodes, Cecil John 124
Rivonia Trial 7, 8, 244–5, 249, 252
Robben Island 7, 183, 209, 244, 264
Ruanda 128
rule of law 140, 257
ruling class, black 116, 118–19

SACP see South African Communist Party
sanctions 109
Sandler, Jonty 209
Scorpions 153
Senegal 139
September, Connie 195
services, municipal 267, 270, 272
Sexwale, Tokyo 2, 42, 105, 110, 208, 209
'sherry' 61
Shilowa, Mbhazima 11, 157, 195
Sisulu, Walter 182
Sisulu, Zwelakhe 12, 209
slavery 63, 75
Slovo, Joe 31, 110
Smith, Adam 14, 57
Smuts, Jan 122–3
social security 236–7
Social Exclusion Unit (SEU) 158
socialism 40, 43, 44, 49, 99, 170–5, 251–2, 258, 266
Society of Young Africans (SOYA) 7
Somalia 128
Soros, George 203

South African National Defence Force 235
South African Breweries 60
South African Broadcasting Corporation (SABC) 12
South African Chamber of Business (SACOB) 202
South African Communist Party (SACP) 6–10, 19, 31, 46–7, 72–3, 93, 114, 157, 163–75, 186, 193, 201, 262, 264
South African Congress of Trade Unions (SACTU) 184–5
South African Democratic Teachers' Union (SADTU) 46–7
South African Foundation 34
South African Human Rights Commission (SAHRC) 156
South African Indian Congress 250
South African Municipal Workers' Union (SAMWU) 272
South African National Civics Organisation (SANCO) 167, 270
South African National Intelligence Service (NIS) 9
South African Non-Governmental Organisation Coalition (SANGOCO) 203
Southern African Development Community (SADC) 54, 169
Soviet Union 7–8, 44, 108, 168, 171
state–society relations 221–39
Stiglitz, Joseph 61, 204
stock market 39, 42
Strategic Arms Procurement Package 2
Strauss, Conrad 127
strikes 31, 166–7, 190, 194–5, 232, 243, 249, 269, 272
Substance Control Amendment Act 105
Summers, Lawrence 61
Suttner, Raymond 31, 110
Swaziland 8, 128, 183

Tambo, Oliver 6–10, 107–8, 182, 258, 264
Tanzania 63, 77, 131, 169
taxes 68, 172, 201, 204–5
technology 89
Telkom 60
textiles 61
Thatcher, Margaret 8, 118, 154
Thatcherism 40, 44, 46
'third way' 100, 142, 154, 201, 238, 258
third world 169, 172
townships 268
trade, international 54, 56, 70, 127
trade unions 154, 173–4, 179–98, 201, 213, 221, 228, 233, 262, 269–70, *see also* Congress of South African Trade Unions
tradition 246
transformation 118, 133, 204, 216, 232, 259, 261
  social 228, 236, 259
transition 106
Transitional Executive Council (TEC) 68–9
transnational corporations (TNC) 92
Treatment Action Campaign 70–1, 274
tribalism 243–51
Truth and Reconciliation Commission (TRC) 30, 45–6, 205, 210, 272
Tshwete, Steve 2, 156
Tsoukalas, K 93–4, 97–8, 100
Tutu, Desmond 271–2

Umkhonto weSizwe (MK) 6, 7, 173, 249
unemployment 17, 47, 60–1, 89, 114, 158, 172, 174, 215, 272
United Democratic Front (UDF) 10, 186, 211, 231–2
United Nations 62, 125, 260, 263
United Nations Conference on Trade and Development (UNCTAD) 54, 70
United Nations Development Programme (UNDP) 128
United States of America 56, 61, 67, 262
unity, African 140–1
universities, unrest 271
University of the Witwatersrand 271

Value-Added Tax 68
Vavi, Zwelinzima 157, 203, 211
Viljoen, Constand 29, 109
violence 232

Wade, Abdoulaye 63, 139
wage, social 99, 111–12, 246
wages 69, 87, 97, 114
Wallerstein, Immanuel 94
Washington Consensus 67, 86–7
water supply 73–4, 235–6, 267–8, 271, 272
welfare
  organisations 237
  system 273
Wolfensohn, James 62–3
women, status 131, 156, 244
workers 154, 165, 251
working class 111, 116, 170, 171, 174, 197, 238, 273

World Bank 34, 38, 54, 61, 62, 63, 65–8, 73–4, 76–8, 92, 95, 111, 188
World Commission on Dams 54
World Conference Against Racism (WCAR) 63, 167, 190, 268–9, 272
World Economic Forum (WEF) 63, 252, 267
World Trade Organisation (WTO) 61, 70, 76, 78, 92, 111, 130, 141, 272

xenophobia 60

Yengeni, Tony 2

Zambia 7, 8, 77, 169, 183
Zimbabwe 4, 77, 88, 105, 132, 201, 203, 205, 257, 268
Zulus 29
Zuma, Jacob 9, 11, 155–6, 166